Romantic Lieder and the Search for Lost Paradise

The archetypal myth of lost paradise, found in both civilized and primitive cultures throughout history, was central to Enlightenment and Romantic thought, influencing philosophical, literary, artistic, and musical works. This book explores manifestations of the lost paradise myth in Lieder by Franz Schubert, Johannes Brahms, Hugo Wolf, and other nineteenth-century composers, with emphasis on works conveying nostalgia for classical antiquity, childhood, and folk song. Through a series of autonomous yet interrelated studies, Marjorie Hirsch examines the myth's influence on the origins and development of the Romantic Lied. The book thus takes a thematic approach to the study of Romantic Lieder, with introductory sections supplying historical context for analyses of individual songs or small groups of songs expressing nostalgia for lost paradise in various guises.

MARJORIE W. HIRSCH is Associate Professor in the Music Department at Williams College in Williamstown, Massachusetts. She is the author of *Schubert's Dramatic Lieder* (Cambridge, 1993), and her work on the Lied has appeared in books and journals including the *Journal of Musicology* and the *Journal for Musicological Research*.

Romantic Lieder and the Search for Lost Paradise

MARJORIE W. HIRSCH

CAMBRIDGE UNIVERSITY PRESS

CAMBRIDGE UNIVERSITY PRESS
Cambridge, New York, Melbourne, Madrid, Cape Town, Singapore, São Paulo

Cambridge University Press
The Edinburgh Building, Cambridge CB2 8RU, UK

Published in the United States of America by Cambridge University Press, New York

www.cambridge.org
Information on this title: www.cambridge.org/9780521845335

© Marjorie W. Hirsch 2007

This publication is in copyright. Subject to statutory exception
and to the provisions of relevant collective licensing agreements,
no reproduction of any part may take place without
the written permission of Cambridge University Press.

First published 2007

Printed in the United Kingdom at the University Press, Cambridge

A catalogue record for this publication is available from the British Library

ISBN 978-0-521-84533-5 hardback

Cambridge University Press has no responsibility for the persistence or accuracy of URLs for external or third-party internet websites referred to in this publication, and does not guarantee that any content on such websites is, or will remain, accurate or appropriate.

To my family

All peoples with a history have a paradise, a state of innocence, a golden age. Indeed, each individual human being has his paradise, his golden age that he recalls with more or less enthusiasm, depending upon how poetic his nature is.

Friedrich Schiller

Contents

List of figures   [*page* viii]
List of tables   [ix]
List of examples   [x]
Acknowledgments   [xii]

Introduction: Seeking lost paradise   [1]

PART I THE LOST WORLD OF ANTIQUITY   [25]

1 Schubert's Greek revival   [33]

2 Goethe, Wolf, and the lure of immortality   [63]

PART II THE LOST WORLD OF CHILDHOOD   [101]

3 Sleep and death in Schubert's lullabies   [111]

4 Brahms's spiral journey back home   [140]

PART III THE LOST WORLD OF FOLK SONG   [173]

5 Schubert's songs-within-songs   [182]

6 On wings of song from Reichardt to Mahler   [214]

Notes   [246]
References   [286]
Index   [303]

Figures

1 Karl Friedrich Schinkel, *The Blossoming of Ancient Greece* (1836), oil on canvas, 94 × 235 cm (copy by August Wilhelm Julius Ahlborn, after original lost in 1945), Nationalgalerie, Staatliche Museen zu Berlin, Berlin, Germany. Photo credit: Bildarchiv Preussischer Kulturbesitz / Art Resource, NY   [*page* 20]

2 Karl Friedrich Schinkel, *Medieval City on a River* (1815), oil on canvas, 90 × 140 cm, Nationalgalerie, Staatliche Museen zu Berlin, Berlin, Germany. Photo credit: Bildarchiv Preussischer Kulturbesitz / Art Resource, NY   [21]

3 The Colossi of Memnon, engraving, *Description de L'Égypte* (1809), vol. 2, pl. 20 (Statue on right is "Vocal Memnon"). From *Monuments of Egypt*, vol. 1, edited by Charles Gillispie and Michel Dewachter, 1987. Reprinted by permission of Princeton Architectural Press. All rights reserved   [43]

4 Nicolas Poussin, *Et in Arcadia ego* (1636–37), oil on canvas, 185 × 121 cm, Musée du Louvre, Paris, France. Photo credit: Erich Lessing / Art Resource, NY   [81]

5 Joshua Reynolds, *Age of Innocence* (1778), oil on canvas, 76.2 × 63.5 cm, Tate Gallery, London, Great Britain. Photo credit: Tate Gallery, London / Art Resource, NY   [103]

6 *Liedersammlung für Kinder und Kinderfreunde am Clavier: Frühlingslieder* (Vienna: Ignaz Alberti, 1791), title page. By permission of Colby College Special Collections, Waterville, Maine   [143]

7 *Des knaben Wunderhorn*, vol. 2, ed. Achim von Arnim and Clemens Brentano (Heidelberg: Mohr und Zimmer, 1808), frontispiece Courtesy of the University of Southern California, on behalf of USC Libraries   [174]

Tables

1.1 Schubert's songs of antiquity   [*page* 35]
2.1 German songs of antiquity composed after 1830   [64]
3.1 Schubert's *Wiegenlieder*   [118]
4.1 Lieder expressing nostalgia for childhood   [147]

Examples

0.1 Schubert, "Die Götter Griechenlands," 2nd version, D. 677b, mm. 1–4 [*page* 2]
0.2 Schumann, "Aus alten Märchen winkt es," Op. 48, no. 15, mm. 1–12 [2]
1.1a Schubert, "Memnon," D. 541, mm. 6–14 [49]
1.1b Schubert, "Memnon," D. 541, mm. 50–57 [52]
1.2a Schubert, "Die Götter Griechenlands," 1st version, D. 677a, mm. 48–53 [54]
1.2b Schubert, "Die Götter Griechenlands," 2nd version, D. 677b, mm. 50–52 [54]
2.1a Wolf, "Anakreons Grab" [83]
2.1b Wolf, "Anakreons Grab," vocal rhythms [86]
2.2a Schubert, "Grenzen der Menschheit," D. 716, mm. 1–6 [93]
2.2b Schubert, "Grenzen der Menschheit," D. 716, mm. 33–36 [93]
2.3a Wolf, "Grenzen der Menschheit," mm. 1–10 [94]
2.3b Wolf, "Grenzen der Menschheit," mm. 118–26 [96]
3.1 Schubert, "Wiegenlied," D. 498, mm. 1–4 [124]
3.2 Schubert, "Wiegenlied," D. 867, mm. 5–8 [125]
3.3 Schubert, "Schlaflied," D. 527, mm. 8–12 [128]
3.4 Schubert, "Der Knabe in der Wiege," D. 579, mm. 5–8 [131]
3.5 Schubert, "Wiegenlied," D. 304, mm. 9–11 [133]
3.6a Schubert, "Vor meiner Wiege," D. 927, mm. 5–8 [135]
3.6b Schubert, "Vor meiner Wiege," D. 927, mm. 27–30 [135]
3.7 Schubert, "Des Baches Wiegenlied," D. 795, no. 20, mm. 4–6 [137]
4.1a Brahms, "Heimweh I," Op. 63, no. 7, mm. 1–9 [160]
4.1b Brahms, "Heimweh I," Op. 63, no. 7, mm. 34–39 [160]
4.2a Brahms, "Heimweh II," Op. 63, no. 8, mm. 4–8 [163]
4.2b Brahms, "Heimweh II," Op. 63, no. 8, mm. 39–47 [165]
4.3a Brahms, "Heimweh III," Op. 63, no. 9, mm. 1–6 [166]
4.3b Brahms, "Heimweh III," Op. 63, no. 9, mm. 45–52 [168]
5.1 Schubert, "Der Sänger," D. 149, 2nd version, mm. 51–66 [185]
5.2 Schubert, "Szene aus Faust," D. 126, 2nd version, mm. 31–45 [187]

5.3a   Schubert, "Lied des Orpheus," D. 474, 2nd version, mm. 1–19 [190]
5.3b   Schubert, "Lied des Orpheus," D. 474, 2nd version, mm. 31–36 [191]
5.3c   Schubert, "Lied des Orpheus," D. 474, 2nd version, mm. 74–84 [192]
5.3d   Schubert, "Lied des Orpheus," D. 474, 2nd version, mm. 94–109 [193]
5.4   Schubert, "Pause," D. 795, no. 12, mm. 9–26   [194]
5.5a   Schubert, "Im Frühling," D. 882, mm. 1–10   [198]
5.5b   Schubert, "Im Frühling," D. 882, mm. 33–36   [199]
5.5c   Schubert, "Im Frühling," D. 882, mm. 48–50   [200]
5.6   Schubert, "Vor meiner Wiege," D. 927, mm. 55–70   [202]
5.7   "Der Jäger in dem grünen Wald" (traditional)   [207]
5.8a   Reichardt, "Heidenröslein"   [210]
5.8b   Werner, "Heidenröslein"   [210]
6.1   Schumann, "Mondnacht," Op. 39, no. 5, mm. 1–13   [215]
6.2   Reichardt, "Schweizervolkslied" from *Lieb und Treue*   [218]
6.3   Schubert, "Der Knabe," D. 692, mm. 6–9   [222]
6.4a   Schumann, "Die Stille," Op. 39, no. 4, mm. 1–4   [224]
6.4b   Schumann, "Die Stille," Op. 39, no. 4, mm. 17–24   [225]
6.5   Beethoven, "Sehnsucht," Op. 83, no. 2, mm. 10–16   [228]
6.6   Schubert, "Sehnsucht," D. 123, mm. 10–13   [229]
6.7a   Schubert, "Sehnsucht," D. 636, mm. 25–28   [231]
6.7b   Schubert, "Sehnsucht," D. 636, mm. 85–93   [232]
6.8   Schubert, "Sehnsucht," D. 516, mm. 33–42   [234]
6.9   Schumann, "Sehnsucht," Op. 51, no. 1, mm. 33–39   [237]
6.10   Schumann, "Flügel! Flügel!," Op. 37, no. 8, mm. 80–104   [240]
6.11   Brahms, "Auf dem Schiffe," Op. 97, no. 2, mm. 44–63   [241]
6.12   Mahler, "Ging heut' Morgen übers Feld," *Lieder eines fahrenden Gesellen*, no. 2, mm. 103–27   [244]

Acknowledgments

I offer heartfelt thanks to the many people who assisted me with this project. I benefited enormously from the suggestions of scholars who read the manuscript (in entirety, or particular chapters in article form), including Professors Susan Youens, Rufus Hallmark, Daniel Beller-McKenna, Margaret Notley, David Gramit, Scott Burnham, Jane Brown, Floyd Grave, Deborah Kauffman, Tony Sheppard, Jennifer Bloxam, the Williams College Oakley Center Fellows from 2004–05, and several anonymous readers. Their comments and corrections led to innumerable improvements. I am also extremely grateful to Jamie O'Leary, Williams 2004, for providing able research assistance in the project's early stages, to Professor Alan White for generously reviewing and refining my translations, to Guillermo Brachetta for expeditiously producing computer files of the many music examples, and to the Williams College library staff for helping track down various books, scores, recordings, and visual images. My husband Alan Hirsch and daughter Sarah Hirsch offered invaluable editing suggestions on every chapter, for which I am deeply appreciative. Penny Souster, Vicki Cooper, Becky Jones, Rosina Di Marzo, and Susan Beer at Cambridge University Press have provided enthusiastic support and excellent editorial assistance throughout the project. Finally, I would like to thank my parents, parents-in-law, siblings, husband, and three children – Sarah, Joni, and Eric – for their love, encouragement, and cheerful patience during the last half dozen years as I worked on this book. I could not have written it without them.

Introduction: Seeking lost paradise

Fair world, where are you? Return again,
Sweet springtime of nature!
Alas, only in the magic land of song
Does your fabled memory live on.[1]
      Friedrich Schiller

Oh, that land of joy,
In dreams I see it often,
But, come morning sun,
It's gone like foam.[2]
    Heinrich Heine

To a casual listener, Franz Schubert's "Die Götter Griechenlands," D. 677, and Robert Schumann's "Aus alten Märchen winkt es," Op. 48, no. 15, could hardly sound less alike. From their first notes, the two songs stake out positions at opposite ends of the Lied's expressive spectrum. "Die Götter Griechenlands," to which Schubert affixed the suggestive heading *Langsam mit heiliger Sehnsucht*, limps ahead with music conveying intense yet hopeless yearning. Anapestic rhythms that settle heavily into the downbeat and abundant chord doublings saddle the music with weightiness. A sustained 8/6 chord over the dominant supporting the opening line "Fair world, where are you?" imparts instability. The hushed dynamics and minor tonality reinforce the somber mood. "Aus alten Märchen winkt es," by contrast, bursts out of the starting gate with high-spirited playfulness. Marked *Lebendig*, the song races by. Root position tonic chords provide firm harmonic footing while forte dynamics and the major tonality enhance the air of exuberance (Examples 0.1 and 0.2).

 Given their striking contrasts, it may come as a surprise that the two songs have the same subject. Both evoke a form of paradise – for Schubert, the "fair world" of classical antiquity, for Schumann, the "magic land" of fairy tales. Both have protagonists who self-consciously lament its loss. As if experiencing anew mankind's expulsion from Eden, they contemplate the idyllic realm from beyond its closed gates, and express a fervent if futile desire to return. Both works too convey the welcome recognition that song

Example 0.1 Schubert, "Die Götter Griechenlands," 2nd version, D. 677b, mm. 1–4

Example 0.2 Schumann, "Aus alten Märchen winkt es," Op. 48, no. 15, mm. 1–12

retains traces of that realm. How do Lieder so different in demeanor communicate this common theme? On the most basic level, each work, through the interaction of poetry and music, conjures two worlds: the protagonist's dreary reality and the dreamlike paradise for which he yearns. Schubert's and Schumann's compositional strategies differ, but their intent – to express the dialectical tension between these disparate worlds – is similar.

"Die Götter Griechenlands" draws most obviously on modal contrasts, minor for the protagonist's present plight, major for his idealized conception of antiquity. Shifts between parallel keys signal changes of focus from one world to the other. As the A minor tonality of the opening measures gives way to A major, the expression of loss ("Fair world, where are you?") yields to an evocation of the distant ideal ("Return again, / Sweet springtime of nature!"). Inversely, the lines "Alas, only in the magic land of song / Does your fabled memory live on" sound first in F# major, then immediately afterwards in F# minor, suggesting different perspectives on their meaning. The brighter major tonality evokes the magic of song; the parallel minor reemphasizes antiquity's grievous absence.

"Aus alten Märchen winkt es," which unfolds entirely in the major mode, differentiates fantasy and reality primarily through rhythmic contrasts. While the first six stanzas, describing the wondrous fairy tale world of imagination, proceed at a quick pace, the seventh introduces augmented rhythms that in effect slow the tempo by half. The climactic word "ach!" beginning the seventh stanza (repeated for emphasis over four measures of dominant seventh harmony) prompts a musical scene change. The sprightly quarter and eighth notes disappear, and the opening music returns, now dressed in long note values and performed *mit innigster Empfindung* – a musical transformation that underscores the altered poetic perspective. Focus shifts from the fantastic, seemingly boundless realm of imagination (the poetic imagery becomes increasingly bizarre during the first six stanzas) to the speaker's drab reality, destroying the joyous illusion. The song's ending encourages reevaluation of its beginning. Beneath the gaiety lurks gravity.

The blatant differences between these two songs exemplify the rich variety of Romantic Lieder while the subtler similarities suggest the powerful influence of certain archetypal themes on that repertoire. Among the most prominent is the myth of lost paradise underpinning "Die Götter Griechenlands," "Aus alten Märchen winkt es," and innumerable other Romantic Lieder. This theme resonates with particular intensity and frequency in the songs of Schubert, but also finds expression in those of nearly every other nineteenth-century Lied composer.

The wealth of art songs conveying longing for paradise stems partly from the theme's profound impact on the Weimar Classicists Friedrich Schiller and Johann Wolfgang von Goethe, and several generations of Romantic poets, whose verse attracted Lied composers from the late eighteenth century through the late nineteenth. Nostalgia for a lost Golden Age was indeed central to Romanticism in many disciplines, from literature to music, art, philosophy, history, politics, and religion.[3] The Lied proved a particularly compelling medium. Art songs can communicate nostalgia in countless ways. Through the enchantments of poetry and music, they may also seem to preserve parts of the paradise whose loss they lament, offering the prospect of restored bliss, or at least a certain solace. "Die Götter Griechenlands," "Aus alten Märchen winkt es," and related Lieder might be viewed as antidotes to the very condition that gives rise to their expression of hopeless yearning.

The paradox invites deeper reflection on the intriguing relationship between Romantic Lieder and the myth of lost paradise. How did the myth find expression in the words and music of art song? How might that expression have influenced the genre's origin and subsequent development? It is no coincidence that the Lied began to gain favor among poets, composers, performers, and audiences during the later eighteenth century, a time when heightened self-consciousness, central to the myth, became a dominant feature of philosophy and aesthetics. The intensification of self scrutiny in nineteenth-century German Romantic poetry (emblematized in the figure of the *Doppelgänger*) and the continued use of Enlightenment and Romantic era poems as song texts throughout the nineteenth century made the Lied tradition's ties to the paradise myth both protracted and complex.

While music scholars have alluded to the lost paradise myth in studies of the Lied,[4] it has not represented the focus of any book. The present inquiry is intended to help fill this gap. By no means does it purport to be a comprehensive overview of Romantic *Sehnsucht* in nineteenth-century art song. The vast size of the Lied repertoire and myriad manifestations of such longing make such a goal impractical. This book does, however, aim to reveal the intimate connection between Romantic quests for lost paradise and the Lied tradition. Through a series of autonomous yet interrelated chapters, I hope to substantiate two related claims: first, that the archetypal paradise myth, with its constituent stages of unity, division, and potential reunification, finds expression thematically, stylistically, and structurally in art songs from throughout the nineteenth century, and second, that nostalgia for lost paradise in its various Enlightenment and Romantic incarnations played a crucial role in the emergence and evolution of the genre, i.e., Lieder geared towards planned performance rather than spontaneous expression. The art song might be said to arise from the infusion of self-consciousness into the natural activity of singing, from the Lied protagonist's yearning to reenter the gates of a metaphorical Eden. (In this regard, the protagonist often seems a thinly disguised surrogate for the poet and/or composer, each a representative of humanity in its fallen state.) Exploring both the diversity and commonalities of various nostalgic quests illuminates the beautiful, emotional world of Romantic Lieder, a repertory whose aesthetic riches offer intimations of paradise regained.

Lost paradise: a universal myth

To the western world, the most familiar and influential versions of the lost paradise myth involve the Greek Golden Age and Hebraic Garden of Eden. In Greece, the myth first surfaces in the works of Hesiod and Homer, recorded in writing during the eighth century BC. (The Greek form of the word "paradise" did not actually come into existence until four centuries later.)[5] Hesiod looked back with nostalgia to what he identified as the Golden Age, or first Age of Man, long preceding his own degenerate time. As described in *Works and Days* (as well as *Theogony*), during the blissful period before Zeus ruled the heavens, men lived essentially like gods:

In the beginning, the immortals
who have their homes on Olympos
created the golden generation of mortal people.
These lived in Kronos' time, when he
was the king in heaven.
They lived as if they were gods,
their hearts free from all sorrow,
by themselves, and without hard work or pain;
no miserable
old age came their way; their hands, their feet,
did not alter.
They took their pleasure in festivals,
and lived without troubles.
When they died, it was as if they fell asleep.
All goods
were theirs. The fruitful grainland
yielded its harvest to them
of its own accord; this was great and abundant,
while they at their pleasure
quietly looked after their works,
in the midst of good things
(prosperous in flocks, on friendly terms with
        the blessed immortals).[6]

Following the Golden Age were the Silver and Bronze Ages. During these times, Hesiod asserts, humans became increasingly corrupt, violent, and selfish – traits that led the gods to punish them with miserable lives and painful deaths. In the succeeding Heroic Age, people again exhibited godlike characteristics. They maintained close relationships with the deities and, upon dying, were permitted to travel to the Isles of the Blessed, or Elysian Fields. But this period too came to an end, with humankind, in Hesiod's own time, returning to a miserable state and individuals suffering cruel fates at the whim of the gods.

In Hesiod's view, the Golden Age lay in the irretrievable past. Other Greeks, including Homer, Pindar, Apollodorus, and Plato, also spoke of a Golden Age of man, but did not agree that it was entirely lost. Homer, for example, noted the paradisiacal existence of the Phaeacians and Ethiopians, and Pindar that of the Hyperboreans. These tribes, however, were thought to inhabit distant and inaccessible regions of the earth; the blissfulness they enjoyed was, to the Greeks, only an alluring fantasy.[7] For the most part, Greek writers looked back nostalgically to an idyllic past and did not entertain hopes of regaining it.

The Hebraic story of the Garden of Eden also associates paradise with a time of origins and first people. Before their transgression, as related in the Old Testament (Genesis 2, 3), Adam and Eve are without want or care, enjoying the beauty and abundance of God's creation in unconscious naturalness and innocence. They have no need to work and no death to fear, only a stern warning to obey.

And the LORD God took the man, and put him into the garden of Eden to dress it and to keep it. And the LORD God commanded the man, saying, Of every tree of the garden thou mayest freely eat: But of the tree of the knowledge of good and evil, thou shalt not eat of it: for in the day that thou eatest thereof thou shalt surely die.[8]

Upon succumbing to the serpent and tasting the forbidden fruit, Adam and Eve ensure their expulsion from blissful existence. They are driven out of the garden, away from the tree of life (whose fruit would grant them godlike immortality), to experience shame, toil, misery, and death, as will all of their descendents. Naiveté gives way to knowledge, unity to division. Humanity's new self-consciousness is founded upon the recognition of difference, opposition, and separation.

As with Hesiod's Golden Age, the Old Testament attributes the loss of paradise to defects in the human character. A willingness to flout God's will by disregarding his single prohibition leads to the expulsion from Eden. But unlike Hesiod's Golden Age, the Biblical conception of paradise is not confined to a time of origins. In the Jewish, Christian, and Islamic traditions that drew inspiration from the story of Eden, paradise also came to be associated with the future. Another Golden Age, even better than the first, was thought yet to come, as described in the New Testament's Book of Revelation.

Many world cultures, both civilized and primitive, embrace paradise myths. The Chinese Taoist Age of Perfect Virtue and the Australian Aborigines' Dreamtime, for example, display striking similarities to the Greek Golden Age and Hebraic Garden of Eden. Comparable myths have arisen on every continent and continue to play an important role in Christianity, Judaism, Buddhism, Hinduism, and Islam. This is not the place for a detailed description of paradise myths from across the globe, a project that has been ably undertaken by other scholars.[9] For our purposes, it will suffice to review some central elements of this universal myth, which captivated writers and artists of the late eighteenth and nineteenth centuries.[10]

Virtually all paradise myths describe an Age of Innocence – the first in a series of world ages – when people lived amidst a miraculous landscape featuring sacred rivers, magical trees, and mountains that reach to the heavens. In many accounts, the first humans themselves possess wondrous powers. Their skin glows; they can fly; they speak a single language, enabling all people to understand and trust one another; they understand the language of the beasts and thus can live peacefully with the animal kingdom. Typically, the first humans are of pristine moral character, exhibiting goodness, naturalness, and spontaneity. They are also blessed with immortality, thus shielded from the tensions of existence within historical time. Perhaps most significant, during the Age of Innocence, the first humans enjoy an intimate relation with the divine. Earth and heaven are in close proximity (connected by mountains, trees, ladders, ropes, and rainbows), allowing easy passage between them and granting humans direct access to the gods. Humans are perpetually in the presence of divinity and live in harmony with the divine will.

The Age of Innocence comes to an end because of a tragic event: a calamitous change in human character, leading to humanity's estrangement from both heaven and nature.[11] (Even paradise myths from ancient or primitive cultures recognize the occurrence of a Fall, a drastic alteration in the nature of human existence. For example, although later generations would look back with nostalgia to the paradise of classical antiquity, ancient Greeks such as Hesiod, regarding their own time as degenerate, associated the Golden Age with a yet earlier period.) The effects are numerous and profound. The blissfulness of the Age of Innocence disappears, along with many of the first humans' miraculous powers.

With disobedience, attachment, and forgetting come the loss of contact with the sacred Source; death and the necessity for reproduction; and limitations of various kinds, such as the loss of luminosity and the abilities to fly and to communicate with the animals. Human beings must now labor to obtain what they need to survive, must invent technologies to compensate for the diminution of their various natural abilities, and must wander through life unaware of their real nature, purpose, and collective past.[12]

Most disastrous, the gods withdraw from the human sphere. In their fallen state, humans experience a devastating estrangement from divinity.

Loss of paradise is inevitably followed by yearning for its restoration. Humans long to be reunited with the divine essence with which they had once enjoyed transcendent wholeness. They pine for the annulment of time, an escape from death, the recovery of innocent bliss. Intense nostalgia is thus a central component of the universal lost paradise myth. Man's yearning might be directed wholly toward the past, or also the imagined future when the gates to paradise, whether on Earth or in heaven, might once more be unlocked. Either way, in most versions of the myth, the "present" time of narration belongs to the tragic period after the Fall.

Romantic retellings of the lost paradise myth

Surprisingly few Romantic art songs mention either Greek or Hebraic conceptions of paradise. One is Schubert's "Elysium," D. 584, a Schiller setting resembling an extended solo cantata. The work does not portray Hesiod's Golden Age but rather what the ancient Greeks viewed as a similarly idyllic state of existence – the final resting place of the blessed dead, characterized by infinite beauty, joy, tranquility, springtime, and love: "Elysian life / Is eternal bliss, eternal lightness." Biblical Eden, in turn, plays an important role in Hugo Wolf's "Fußreise" (Mörike Lieder no. 10). In expressing the exhilaration aroused by an early morning hike through the woods, the song alludes to the sensual delights of man's primal paradise: "My dear old Adam feels / Autumn- and spring-fever too, / God-heartened, / Never-foolishly wasted / First-delight-of-paradise." Schumann's "Warte, warte, wilde Schiffmann" (Heine *Liederkreis*, Op. 24, no. 6) employs the Biblical myth in quite a different way. Here the story of Eve's transgression in Eden helps convey the speaker's bitterness at the seemingly inevitable misery inflicted upon him by the girl he loves: "Remember the ancient story / Of the serpent in Paradise, / Who, by wicked gift of an apple, / Cast our forebear into woe? // All ill has come with the apple! / Eve brought with it death, / Eris – the flames of Troy, / you – both, flames and death." Apart from such scattered references, however, Greek and Hebraic notions of paradise have little direct involvement in the Romantic Lied repertoire.

Their influence is nevertheless both powerful and palpable. Although late eighteenth- and nineteenth-century poets generally avoided Biblical imagery, they were intrigued by the myth of lost paradise related in the Holy Scriptures, and their largely secular reformulations of it served as the textual basis for innumerable Romantic Lieder. The Enlightenment and Romantic generations glimpsed the lost idyllic world in many places: in the cultures of classical antiquity and the Middle Ages, in children, women, and country folk, in nature and exotic lands, in dream visions, myths, and fairy tales, in ballads and folk song, even in death. These diverse manifestations of paradise, exemplifying naturalness, simplicity, spontaneity, the German character, and other cherished ideals, inspired intense yearning, as attested by countless works of literature, art, and music, including Romantic Lieder.

Romanticism was not, of course, confined to secular subjects; overt expressions of Christianity and religious spiritual striving figure prominently in many nineteenth-century artworks, from Novalis's (Friedrich von Hardenberg) six poetic *Hymnen an die Nacht* to the paintings of the German Nazarenes to Anton Bruckner's choral masses to Richard Wagner's music drama *Parsifal*. Within the Lied repertoire, notable examples include Ludwig van Beethoven's *Gellert Lieder*, Op. 48, nos. 1–6; Schubert's "Die junge Nonne," D. 828, and "Ellens Gesang III" (Ave Maria), D. 839; Peter Cornelius's *Weihnachtslieder*, Op. 8, nos. 1–6; Wolf's ten *Geistliche Lieder* from the *Spanisches Liederbuch*, and Antonin Dvorak's *Biblical Songs*, Op. 99. Yet many Romantics (including some of these composers) felt alienated from conventional Christianity with its notion of original sin and code of self-denial, which ran counter to their desire for self-fulfillment.[13] Although Novalis, Friedrich Schlegel, Joseph von Eichendorff, and other Romantics embraced Catholicism, and the Christian Middle Ages captivated the imagination of German writers and artists throughout the nineteenth century, in numerous Romantic artworks the expression of longing for a lost idyllic world – as in Schubert's "Der Wanderer" (D. 489, 493; "Where are you, my beloved land? / Sought, dreamt of, yet never known!") and "Kennst du das Land" (D. 321; "There, o there / I desire to go with you, my beloved!") – may be understood to represent a displaced theology. As the three main parts of this book suggest, Romantic *Sehnsucht* for a lost Golden Age had strong roots in the secular culture of the Enlightenment.

Germans – who ever since the disastrous Thirty Years War (1618–48) had suffered from an inferiority complex vis-à-vis the politically, economically, and culturally dominant French – were particularly susceptible to feelings of nostalgia for "a better world."[14] Numerous German philosophical tracts, literary works, and aesthetic essays from the late eighteenth and early nineteenth centuries are founded upon the belief that both modern man and cultured society had lost their integrity, or natural wholeness, resulting in a plethora of perplexing dualities – freedom and necessity, reason and desire, artifice and naturalness. One of the first writers to critique the modern world in terms that evoke the Biblical story of Eden was Schiller. In both his aesthetic and creative writings, he not only diagnosed the ills of his age but also proposed a means for recovery, thus extending the mythical parallel from paradise lost to paradise regained, or exile to redemption. Although grounded in Enlightenment modes of thought, his works provided a strong impetus for the fledgling Romantic movements in Germany and England (the latter especially through his impact on Samuel Taylor Coleridge), and shed light on nineteenth-century formulations of the lost paradise myth. A brief review of some of Schiller's most influential aesthetic ideas serves as a springboard for exploring how the myth shaped Romanticism and more specifically Romantic Lieder.

Writing during the 1790s, a time of cultural and political turmoil, Schiller called attention to the fragmented nature of both individuals and society as a whole – a crisis he attributed largely to the over-specialization of human knowledge and activity. In the sixth letter of *On the Aesthetic Education of Man* (1794–95; *Über die ästhetische Erziehung des Menschen*), he decries modern man's inability to develop the full range of his faculties and the sorrowful implications for contemporary culture: "One has to go the rounds from one individual to another in order to be able to piece together a complete image of the species."[15] For all the Enlightenment's vaunted claims of progress, it had become increasingly difficult to perceive the whole of man's existence, whether of individuals or society.

In various respects, Schiller's critique of the modern world echoes those of earlier writers such as Johann Joachim Winckelmann, Jean Jacques Rousseau, and Johann Gottfried Herder, but he develops his ideas in an original manner. In his famous essay *On Naïve and Sentimental Poetry* (1795; *Über naïve und sentimentalische Dichtung*), Schiller, displaying a penchant for Kantian dualities, identifies two ways of looking at the world, exemplified by two types of poet: "The poet . . . either *is* nature or he will *seek* it. The former makes for the naïve poet, the latter for the sentimental poet."[16] Although Schiller's argument is clouded by inconsistencies, shifting terminology, and a general looseness of structure, it is not difficult to discern the fundamental distinction he has in mind between the "naïve" and the "sentimental," or their relation to the myth of lost paradise.

In Schiller's view, the natural state of plants, minerals, animals, and landscapes, the natural humanity of children, country folk, and the antique world, and the natural essence of certain poetry past and present all arouse tender love and melancholic longing because of their fundamental naïveté.[17] Their un-coerced existence follows immutable laws of necessity. Consequently, these manifestations of naturalness are eternally at one with themselves, without the possibility of becoming something else. Naïve poets like the ancient writers Homer and Aeschylus but also Shakespeare and even the modern writer Goethe embody nature and therefore express it directly and instinctively from their own experience. Their naïveté "refers to the ability to accept the presence of the image without nostalgia, to take possession of the past without insecurity; it refers to a style in which pathos attaches only to the object itself, never to the relation of self to object."[18] Because the naïve poet is in harmony with both his world and himself, he does not inject his thoughts or emotions into his works, but rather articulates his subjects for their own sakes. Indeed, his presence in the work is virtually undetectable.

Sentimental poets, by contrast, including Schiller himself and such figures as Virgil and Ariosto, have lost connection with nature through their heightened self-consciousness. "Nature has disappeared from our humanity," Schiller writes, "and we reencounter it in its genuineness only outside of humanity in the inanimate world... Our childhood is the only unmutilated nature that we still encounter in the cultivated part of humanity."[19] In his works, the sentimental poet portrays nature as a distant ideal. Its various embodiments arouse intense nostalgia:

They *are* what we *were*; they are what we *should become* once more. We were nature like them, and our culture should lead us along the path of reason and freedom back to nature. Thus they depict at once our lost childhood, something that remains ever dearest to us, and for this reason they fill us with a certain melancholy. Because at the same time they portray our supreme perfection in an ideal sense, they transport us into a state of sublime emotion.[20]

The sentimental state – broadly characteristic of the modern world, although neither limited to nor fully descriptive of it (as evidenced by Schiller's conceptions of Ariosto and Goethe, respectively) – implies both separation from and yearning for another more natural state of existence. "Our feeling for nature is like the sick person's feeling for health," Schiller writes.[21] Recognizing divisions between himself and the external world as well as within himself, the sentimental poet presents his chosen subjects through the prism of his consciousness. He engages the world only indirectly, his thoughts and emotions inevitably intervening.

> We never receive the object [*Gegenstand*], but only what the reflective understanding of the poet makes of the object. Even when the poet himself is this object, when he wants to show us his feelings, we do not experience his situation immediately and firsthand, but rather as that situation is reflected in his mind, in other words, what he, observing himself, has thought about it.[22]

To the sentimental poet, the external world pales in comparison with the ideal world that exists within his mind; the imperfections of the external world are painfully apparent to him. His attitude toward this situation may vary, resulting in three fundamentally different types of poetry: *satire* (if he expresses anger at the world's defects), *elegy* (if he mourns the loss of naturalness and unity), and *idyll* (if he joyously anticipates their restoration). Despite their differences, these attitudes are united in an important respect: in each case, the sentimental poet recognizes his separation from an ideal that exists solely within the faculties of memory and imagination.

The rift between the naïve and the sentimental in Schiller's conception, as literary critic and opera scholar Herbert Lindenberger writes, "suggests a state of crisis, a fall from innocence . . . quietly echoing that earlier fall which stands behind the whole Judeo-Christian tradition."[23] Like Adam and Eve, modern man (for Schiller associates the sentimental state primarily with his own troubled times) has become increasingly self-conscious and aware of distinctions, causing him to experience alienation and angst. The corruptions of society and over-refinement of modern culture have destroyed the naturalness, innocence, and spiritual harmony he once enjoyed.

Although the loss of the primordial paradise arouses melancholy in the sentimental poet, it does not, Schiller emphasizes, represent a catastrophe. On the contrary, it is a Fortunate Fall, or viewed differently, a leap of progress, which directs humanity toward a different, and greater, state of harmony.

> For the human being who has at one time deviated from the simplicity of nature and has been perilously handed over to his own reason for guidance, it is infinitely important to see the legislation of nature in a pure exemplar once again, and in this faithful mirror to be able once again to purify himself of the corruptions introduced by art.[24]

Paradise "does not take place only prior to the beginning of culture. Rather it is also what the culture aims for as its final goal."[25] Crucially, Schiller cautions the sentimental poet against desiring re-admittance to Eden, even though that world of naturalness arouses his nostalgic yearning, because the original and final paradises are not equivalent; the poet must look ahead, not behind. "Do not let it occur to you any longer to want to *change places* with nature. Instead, take nature up into yourself and strive to wed its unlimited advantages to your own endless prerogatives, and from the marriage of both strive to give birth to something divine."[26] The final stage of Schiller's tripartite schema signifies a higher order unity than the first. The sentimental poet must seek to experience a *second* naïveté: a transcendent synthesis of the original naïveté and human knowledge. Synthesizing these two ways of looking at the world – the naïve and the sentimental – provides the means to reintegrate the self and ultimately society. Modern man must learn how to feel again, to experience beauty, which leads to freedom.

In Schiller's view, the marriage of oppositions can be approached through the faculty of imagination, which finds expression in art. Only by freely choosing to adopt the laws of necessity, a mediating posture that Schiller associates with the play or aesthetic impulse (*Spieltrieb*), can the sentimental poet (and, more generally, modern man) progress toward his transcendent goal. The aesthetic impulse holds the key to overcoming the fragmentation of life.

We are free and what they [exemplars of the naïve] are is necessary; we alter, they remain one. Yet only if both are combined with one another – only if the will freely adheres to the law of necessity and reason maintains its rule in the face of every change in the imagination, only then does the divine or the ideal emerge. Hence in *them* we forever see what eludes us, something we must struggle for and can hope to approach in an endless progress, even though we never attain it.[27]

The ideal remains forever beyond reach, but the sentimental poet must always strive for it, taking comfort, perhaps, in the recognition that his efforts are superior to those of the naïve poet, whose aims are limited. Schiller does not want to forfeit cultural sophistication, although it has contributed to the fragmentation of modern society: "It was civilization itself that inflicted this wound upon modern man."[28] Rather, he hopes to subsume it in a broader vision.

The aesthetic theories presented in *On the Aesthetic Education of Man* and *On Naïve and Sentimental Poetry* were grounded in historical reality. Shocked by the French Reign of Terror, which so swiftly made a mockery of the Enlightenment ideals of liberty, equality, and fraternity for which the Revolution was fought, and dismayed by modern society's seeming loss of the ability to feel, Schiller viewed art as possessing healing powers which offered hope during an age when enlightenment had capitulated to carnage.[29] Through creativity, feeling could be regenerated and humanity restored to a condition of wholeness. In the wake of political catastrophe, art could assume the role of religion. As literary critic Geoffrey Hartman writes, with the dawning of Romanticism, "the traditional scheme of Eden, fall, and redemption merges with the new triad of nature, self-consciousness, imagination."[30]

Schiller's concept of the sentimental quest for transcendent reunification, or paradise regained, echoes throughout nineteenth-century German philosophy, literature, and art – loudest in the first half of the century during the height of Romanticism, but still audible in the post-Romantic age that followed. His aesthetic theories, based on the distinction between two types of poetry, roughly parallel and indeed directly influenced those of Friedrich Schlegel, who first formulated the concept of "romantic poetry" during the 1790s, and his brother August Wilhelm Schlegel, who elaborated on it in his renowned Berlin and Vienna lectures of 1802 and 1808. (Schiller's distinction between naïve and sentimental poetry is not identical to Friedrich Schlegel's distinction between classical and romantic poetry. To Schiller, for example, Shakespeare was a naïve poet, while Schlegel regarded him as a romantic poet.) The Schlegels, together with the writers Novalis and Ludwig Tieck, the philosopher Friedrich Schelling, and the theologian Friedrich Schleiermacher, kindled the Romantic movement in the university town of Jena, and soon Romanticism also burned brightly in the cities of Berlin, Heidelberg, Dresden, and Vienna. Other scholars have explored Schiller's connection to the Jena Romantics,[31] and the influence that his aesthetic theories exerted more broadly on German Romanticism lies beyond the scope of this study. Here we will merely note that a Schiller-like yearning for synthesis, for the reconciliation of oppositions (ego and non-ego, mind and nature, conscious and unconscious, freedom and necessity), became a central component of Romanticism in its various outlets. German Romantics, trapped in a spiritual malaise they attributed to the rise of rationalism and dominance of analytical thought, insisted "on an art that rises from the plenitude of consciousness to absorb progressively the most sophisticated as well as the naivest experience."[32]

The lost paradise myth that underlies Schiller's aesthetic schema provides the foundation for many nineteenth-century Romantic (and late eighteenth-century proto-Romantic) works. The main structural components of the myth are readily recognizable: an original state of unselfconsciousness, rupture brought about by human knowledge, profound alienation from nature and divinity, intense yearning for what has been lost, and anticipation of a transcendent return through the faculty of imagination. Singly or together, overt or obscured, these components emerge in a panorama of nineteenth-century works, from the philosophical writings of Johann Gottlieb Fichte, Schelling, and Georg Wilhelm Friedrich Hegel to the novels and romances of Friedrich Hölderlin, Novalis, and Jean Paul (Richter); the tales of

E. T. A. Hoffmann, Heinrich von Kleist, and Jacob and Wilhelm Grimm; the poems of Goethe, Wilhelm Müller, Eichendorff, and Heine; the paintings of Philipp Otto Runge and Caspar David Friedrich; and the instrumental and vocal compositions of Schubert, Schumann, Wagner, Johannes Brahms, Gustav Mahler, Wolf, and Richard Strauss. Teleological progression resulting from the attempt to synthesize opposing states – a spiral-like movement involving return as well as advancement – became a hallmark of both German Idealist philosophy and Romantic art. The lost paradise myth indeed represents a cornerstone of nineteeth-century German culture; a survey of its influence would require volumes.

As noted, in most versions of the lost paradise myth, the present time of narration takes place after the Fall. For Romantics, self-consciousness represents a kind of "death-life," an intermediary state that holds the poetic protagonist in solitary confinement. Hartman explains,

> One of the themes which best expresses this perilous nature of consciousness, and which has haunted literature since the Romantic period, is that of the Solitary, or Wandering Jew. He may appear as Cain, Ahasuerus, Ancient Mariner, and even Faust . . . These solitaries are separated from life in the midst of life, yet cannot die. They are doomed to live a middle or purgatorial existence which is neither life nor death, and as their knowledge increases so does their solitude. It is consciousness, ultimately, which alienates them from life and imposes the burden of a self which religion or death or a return to the state of nature might dissolve. Yet their heroism, or else their doom, is not to obtain a release from self.[33]

This solitary wanderer, having left behind a more natural existence and yearning to return, evokes the figure of the Romantic poet.

> Both are story-tellers who resubmit themselves to temporality and are compelled to repeat their experience in the purgatorial form of words . . . The Solitary may also be said to create his own, peculiarly Romantic genre of poetry. In "Tintern Abbey," or "X Revisited," the poet looks back at a transcended stage and comes to grips with the fact of self-alienation. The retrospective movement may be visionary, as often in Hölderlin, or antiquarian, as in Scott, or deeply oblique, as in the lyrical ballad and monologue. In every case, however, there is some confrontation of person with shadow or self with self. The intense lyricism of the Romantics may well be related to this confrontation. For the Romantic "I" emerges nostalgically when certainty and simplicity of self are lost.[34]

As Hartman suggests, Romantic nostalgia often takes the form of a protagonist's pilgrimage or life journey reflecting a desire for transformation. The *Wanderlied* and *Bildungsroman* clearly lend themselves to the expression of such longing, but many other genres, from the fairy tale to the music drama, may serve a similar function; quests for renewed wholeness are ubiquitous in German Romantic art. Like Schiller's sentimental poet, most Romantics did not seek to return to a place of origin, or state of natural unconsciousness, but rather to progress circuitously, through consciousness, to a transcendent, synthesizing culmination. As the narrator of Kleist's story "The Puppet Theater" (1807) discovers, one has to "eat again of the Tree of Knowledge to fall back into the state of innocence."[35] Guiding the way toward this ultimate goal was the principal function of the "new mythology" so ardently sought by Friedrich Schlegel, Schelling, and others. Romantics did not discount the evil and suffering to be encountered along the way; they recognized that the path to a higher level integration of self and society would be arduous. But they remained committed to pursuing their transcendent ideal.

Over the course of the nineteenth century, Romantic optimism gradually weakened while nostalgic longing intensified. In 1800, Schlegel could speak with uncontained excitement about the "progressive universal poetry" of Romanticism, which held out hope for the transformation of both individuals and society. If politics would not solve the world's problems – as the French Reign of Terror had so appallingly borne out – art might. After the Congress of Vienna, however, during what has come to be known as the *Biedermeier* era (*c.* 1815–48), many German writers and artists began to project a sense of *Weltschmerz*, or melancholy world weariness. The French Revolution had failed, the Napoleonic wars had exacted a heavy toll, and the Restoration had imposed harsh new restrictions on both political and artistic expression. Although life under Prince Clemens von Metternich had again assumed a degree of stability, a pronounced strain of pessimism, often conveyed through the disruptive, distancing effects of irony, infuses many works of this late phase of Romanticism. Disturbed by the tenor of their times, members of the *Biedermeier* generation looked back longingly to the remote, idealized cultures of Greek antiquity, the Christian Middle Ages, the Italian Renaissance, Shakespearean England, and even, more recently, to the comparatively enlightened reign of Joseph II during the 1780s. Of course, nostalgic attitudes had also characterized eighteenth-century thought, as the brief introductions to the three main parts of this book describe. But whereas most Enlightenment thinkers believed in the possibility of human progress – the correction of the modern world's defects through rational and utilitarian processes – the *Biedermeier* generation held little hope for a return to any Golden Age, at least not during their earthly existence.

As the nineteenth century progressed, new strains of nostalgic yearning compounded the old. The failure of the 1848 revolutions, the ill effects of industrialization and urbanization (including child labor, overcrowding, pollution, disease, poverty, and crime), and the increasing specialization of human knowledge and activity made paradise seem ever further removed from present reality. In the late nineteenth century, classical antiquity, the Middle Ages, and other such long-cherished ideals continued to inspire longing, but with new emphases and approaches. Now even the early nineteenth century aroused nostalgia. As Lied scholar Susan Youens writes, "Schubert's Vienna seemed a Biedermeier Paradise Lost to the anxious inhabitants of a latter-day culture on the way to disintegration."[36] During the post-Romantic era of *Realpolitik* and scientific positivism, Romantic longing for transcendence gave way to a general attitude of resignation and accommodation. Rather than view art as the primary vehicle for the transformation of self and society, many instead saw it as a means of refuge from the harsh realities of the modern world – a perspective that all too easily led to nostalgic excesses and sickly sentimentality. For many late- and post-Romantics, death seemed the only true avenue of release.

The lost paradise myth in Romantic Lieder

Different facets of the lost paradise myth find expression in Romantic Lieder. Some songs focus principally on a paradisiacal world (whether past or future) in one or more guises, with minimal or no reference to any sense of loss. In these works, paradise is often associated with the glories of nature (e.g., Beethoven, "Mailied," Op. 52, no. 4; Brahms, "Feldeinsamkeit," Op. 86, no. 2; Strauss, *Vier letzte Lieder* no. 2: "Frühling"); the joyful innocence of both nature and youth (Schubert, "Das Lied im Grünen," D. 917); or the blissfulness of love (Schubert, "Das Rosenband," D. 280, "Des Fischers Liebesglück," D. 933; R. Schumann, "Widmung," Op. 25, no. 1; C. Schumann, "Liebst du um Schönheit," Op. 12, no. 4; Brahms, "Wie bist du meine Königen," Op. 32, no. 9; Strauss, "Wie sollten wir geheim sie halten," Op. 19, no. 4). Sometimes paradise assumes another form, such as an existence seemingly outside time and worldly reality (Mahler, "Ich bin der Welt abhanden gekommen"). Yet even if there is no explicit mention of loss, the poem or music generally hints at paradise's evanescence.

Other songs dwell on a metaphorical exile from paradise; the protagonist mourns the loss of a previous "happy time" and expresses lonely isolation, or *Einsamkeit*. The Lied repertoire includes countless examples (e.g., Zelter, "Erster Verlust"; Schubert, "Nur wer die Sehnsucht kennt" D. 877, no. 4, "Frühlingstraum," D. 911, no. 11, "Einsamkeit," D. 911, no. 12,

"Vor meiner Wiege," D. 927, "Der Atlas," D. 957, no. 8; Schumann, "Schöne Wiege meiner Leiden," Op. 24, no. 5; Cornelius, "Trauer und Trost, no. 1: 'Trauer'"; Mahler, "Um Mitternacht"; Wolf, "Nachtzauber," "Heimweh," "Sonne der Schlummerlosen"). Frequently *Einsamkeit* combines with *Sehnsucht* to convey nostalgic longing for a lost idyllic world (Beethoven, "Abendlied unterm gestirnten Himmel"; Schubert, "Kennst du das Land," D. 321, "Der Leidende," D. 432, "Vollendung," D. 989; Brahms, "Heimweh" Lieder, Op. 63, nos. 7–9; Wolf, "Im Frühling"; Mahler, *Das Lied von der Erde* no. 6: "Der Abschied"). As suggested, this longing often takes the form of a journey with both physical and spiritual dimensions (Schubert, "Wandrers Nachtlied I," D. 224; "Der Wanderer," D.489, 493; "Wandrers Nachtlied II," D. 768; "Der Pilgrim," D. 794; *Die schöne Müllerin*, D. 795; *Winterreise*, D. 911; "Der Kreuzzug," D. 932).

The Romantic Lied repertoire also embraces songs that suggest different mythical outcomes. At one extreme are expressions of unalloyed optimism – works that insinuate, or even directly enact, the possibility of transcendent homecoming, or paradise regained. Within Schubert's oeuvre, for example, a positive denouement is conveyed by the settings of "Verklärung," D. 59, "Ganymed," D. 544, "Nachtstück," D. 672, "Die junge Nonne," D. 828, and "Totengräbers Heimweh," D. 842. In each of these works, a transformation occurs; a longing is stilled. We hear this in the music as well as the words. At the other extreme are songs of hopeless despair, works that, in one way or another, imply the impossibility of escaping self-conscious alienation and the pangs of longing, e.g., "Der Pilgrim," D. 794, "Das Wirtshaus," D. 911, no. 21, "Der Lindenbaum," D. 911, no. 5, "Der Atlas," D. 957, no. 8. The metaphorical journey has led nowhere and the protagonist experiences no comfort or consolation. Between these extremes is a broad range of attitudes, conveyed textually and musically in endless ways. Exploring the rich diversity is one of the principal aims of this study.

Organization and approach

The book is divided into three parts, each focusing on a particular manifestation of lost paradise encountered in Romantic Lieder: Greek antiquity, childhood, and folk song. Romantic *Sehnsucht* is, of course, not limited to these three ideals. One could also, for example, explore its expression in relation to love, the natural landscape, Christianity, and medieval lore. I have confined my discussion to three topics largely for reasons of practicality. Even focusing on antiquity, childhood, and folk song may seem overly ambitious, for each by itself could easily support a full-length study. The intersections among them are illuminating, however, making their joint investigation valuable.

It may seem surprising that the first part of the book is devoted to songs involving Greek antiquity rather than the Middle Ages, which, as numerous commentators have noted, Romantics turned to with newfound enthusiasm, championing its societal cohesion and the close relations they believed had then existed between man, nature, and God.[37] For many Romantic writers and artists, the medieval era, which fed German national pride, was the Golden Age that most fired the imagination. I have several reasons for beginning the book with an investigation of nostalgia for Greek antiquity. First, eighteenth-century philhellenism had a strong impact on both the emergence and evolution of nineteenth-century art song through the poetic texts of Goethe and Schiller, as well as later devotees of ancient Greece, such as Johann Mayrhofer. Schubert's numerous songs of antiquity demonstrate the powerful influence that the mythological Classical period operas of Christoph Willibald Gluck and Wolfgang Amadeus Mozart exerted on the early development of the Romantic Lied. Moreover, although the Middle Ages eclipsed Greek antiquity in the minds of many Romantics, antiquity remained a subject of intense interest to Germans throughout the nineteenth century. This dual fascination is expressed visually in paintings by Prussian architect and painter Karl Friedrich Schinkel. *The Blossoming of Ancient Greece*, painted in 1824–25, presents an idealized vision of ancient Athens, whose aesthetic beauty and functional design could serve as a model, Shinkel thought, for a reconstructed Berlin (Figure 1). *Medieval City on a River*, painted in 1815, depicts a similarly idealized vision of a spectacular Gothic cathedral, framed by the arc of a symbolic rainbow, uniting earth and heaven much like the Christian faith drawing hordes of worshippers to the cathedral doors (Figure 2). Like the Middle Ages, classical antiquity supported the rise of German nationalism, and it played an important if limited role in the late Romantic Lieder of Wolf, again with ties to opera. In any event, the lure of medieval culture receives attention in the third part of the book, which focuses on folk song as an object of Romantic yearning.

Antiquity, childhood, and folk song form a cohesive trio in that each, according to Enlightenment and Romantic writers, exemplifies the naturalness that eludes modern man. While closely related in this and other respects, they also differ significantly, forming a logical sequence for discussion. As an idealized societal past, antiquity represents a paradise far removed from the plight of the modern, self-conscious individual. For most eighteenth- and nineteenth-century Germans, the culture of the ancient Greeks survived as a distant abstraction. Childhood, an idealized personal past, brings the

Figure 1 Karl Friedrich Schinkel, *The Blossoming of Ancient Greece* (1824–25). Copy by August Wilhelm Julius Ahlborn (1836) (original lost in 1945).

Figure 2 Karl Friedrich Schinkel, *Medieval City on a River* (1815).

object of longing closer to home. The nostalgic adult remembers but feels disengaged from the blissfulness of his youth. Folk song in turn, although originating in the past, carries over into the present as a musico-poetic paradise lying just beyond the grasp of the art song protagonist (and by extension, the poet and composer). Unable to sing with the spontaneity of the *Volk*, the protagonist finds himself estranged from his own expressive discourse – a division within the self that, in extreme cases, engenders almost unbearable feelings of angst and alienation.

Each of the three main parts of the book comprises two chapters. The first chapter of each part concentrates on works by Schubert, who explored the art song's expressive potential both earlier and in greater depth than did any other Romantic composer. The second focuses primarily on works by his successors, nearly all of whom drew inspiration from his example. "There is no song of Schubert's from which one cannot learn something," Brahms once remarked.[38] As the nineteenth-century art song became increasingly complex in almost every musical dimension (harmony, melody, texture, form, rhythm, declamation, etc.), ever further removed from the ideal of *Volkstümlichkeit* which supplied the impetus for the genre, the early Romantic songs of Schubert came to be recognized as the "Golden Age" of

Lied composition. Most mid and late nineteenth-century song composers regarded Schubert's works with reverence; whether direct or oblique, his influence can be felt throughout the Romantic Lied repertory. Brahms, for example, who thought that contemporary song composition was headed on the wrong course, sought to adopt a more folk-like manner,[39] which characterizes many of Schubert's strophic Lieder. In Wolf's oeuvre, Schubert's influence is less apparent in the musical language than in the selection of song texts. Wolf avoided poems that, in his judgment, Schubert (and others) had set well, but composed new settings for those he believed had been misinterpreted; both options, one endorsing, the other criticizing, involve interaction with Schubert's legacy. Tellingly, neither Brahms nor Wolf tried to emulate Schubert's Lieder directly. Like earlier Romantics, they engaged with the past in order to forge new approaches to Lied composition.

The second chapter of each part thus provides a glimpse at how later nineteenth-century composers both drew upon and transformed subject material that Schubert had previously employed. Wary of extrapolating from a few examples, I would nevertheless suggest that the later nineteenth-century songs discussed in chapters 2, 4, and 6 reflect the deflation of Romantic ideals broadly characteristic of their time. Like earlier Romantic works, they convey yearning for lost paradise, but generally do so with greater pessimism and resignation. (As will be discussed in chapters 1, 3, and 5, Schubert's nostalgic songs from the 1820s bear a similar relation to his songs from the 1810s.)

Before we proceed, some brief remarks about methodology are in order. Rather than survey the lost paradise theme in different subsets of Romantic Lieder, each chapter focuses on a small number of representative songs in which the theme resonates with particular poignancy and beauty. This approach has several advantages. First, it allows room for an in-depth study of songs in conjunction with the Enlightenment and Romantic ideas that helped bring them into existence and in relation to which they convey meaning. A contextual approach to interpretation, moving fluidly among the poetic and musical components of a song and their various biographical, historical, and cultural contingencies, is well suited to enhancing aesthetic understanding and appreciation. Studies that devote only limited attention to individual songs resist this kind of hermeneutic exploration.

Second, the decision to focus on relatively few songs has enabled me to proceed inductively, from the individual work to the larger phenomenon of the archetypal lost paradise myth. This approach is most faithful to the manner in which the songs came into being. Poets and composers generally draw inspiration from within their immediate sphere of knowledge, beliefs, and experiences, not trans-historical abstractions. Aesthetic interpretation is admittedly a different kind of activity from aesthetic creation, but it too is grounded in historical reality and particularity and may succeed best when it begins with such recognition.

Finally, the approach taken in this book places emphasis on enhancing appreciation of individual works of art – songs whose beauty and power have long lured listeners. As suggested at the outset, the Lied, a potent vehicle for the expression of nostalgia, offers a glimpse of paradise regained through its own aesthetic riches. The synthesizing capacity of Schiller's *Spieltrieb*, or aesthetic impulse, finds historical realization in the Romantic art song, a genre whose first masterpieces date from just two decades after *On Naïve and Sentimental Poetry*. The play of imagination in both the creation and apprehension of Romantic Lieder seems to unlock the gates to a lost Golden Age.

PART I

The lost world of antiquity

Veneration of classical antiquity is more commonly associated with the Renaissance and Enlightenment than German Romanticism, many of whose adherents – Novalis, Wilhelm Heinrich Wackenroder, Tieck, Kleist, Achim von Arnim, Clemens Brentano, the Grimm brothers, Johann Ludwig Uhland, Adelbert von Chamisso, and Wagner, among others – showed a predilection for the medieval world of chivalry, minstrelsy, and Christianity. Yet throughout the late eighteenth and nineteenth centuries, ancient Greece and Rome, then still regarded as the cradle of western civilization, retained a firm hold on the European imagination and continued to inspire new art works, including Romantic Lieder.

Contemporary political and social conditions played an important role in sustaining European interest in the classical lands. In the early decades of the nineteenth century, the Greek populace, suffering under Turkish rule, won sympathy from all segments of European society. Its struggle for independence came to symbolize the very idea of freedom, which lay at the heart of Romantic thought, and helped energize other nationalist movements. From the eruption of hostilities in 1821 until the signing of the Treaty of Constantinople in 1832, the Greek War of Independence prompted an outpouring of support for the revolutionaries and heightened interest in Greek culture, both modern and ancient. Especially galvanizing was the 1824 death in Missolonghi of the Romantic writer Lord George Gordon Byron, whose poem "Childe Harold's Pilgrimage" of 1812 had opened Europeans' eyes to the valor and suffering of modern-day Greeks. Byron had traveled to Greece to join the fight for freedom, and his untimely passing turned philehellenism into "a romantic crusade."[1] Italians too chafed under foreign domination. Subject to French and then Austrian governance, the various Italian-speaking duchies, republics, and kingdoms spent much of the nineteenth century seeking unification under Italian rule, a goal for the most part accomplished by 1871. The *Risorgimento*, like the unspoiled beauty of the Italian countryside, kindled the Romantic imagination.

Germans, as suggested by the writings of Herder, Goethe, Schiller, Wilhelm von Humboldt, Hölderlin, Hegel, and the young Friedrich Schlegel, felt a special kinship to, as well as longing for, antiquity. Indeed, when German Romanticism and, more specifically, the Romantic Lied tradition, took root, the culture of Greek antiquity was widely perceived as the embodiment of an ideal, a "more perfect antecedent" of the modern German world.[2] To those who witnessed the failure of the French Revolution, suffered the restrictions of the Restoration, or confronted the ills of an increasingly urban, industrialized society, antiquity beckoned like a lost paradise, a world of simplicity, naturalness, freedom, and unity that eluded modern man – and Germans in particular.

Stimulated by archaeological discoveries at Paestum (1730), Herculaneum (1738), and Pompeii (1748), German philhellenism had grown rapidly after the middle of the eighteenth century, particularly in response to the writings of Winckelmann. Obsessed with Greek art, Winckelmann settled in Rome in 1755 to study it near its source, and there embarked on an aesthetic program that would help to raise public consciousness of the unsurpassed achievements of Greek civilization. In his *Reflections on the Imitation of Greek Works in Painting and Sculpture* (1755; *Gedanken über die Nachahmung der griechischen Werke in der Malerei und Bildhauerkunst*) and *History of Ancient Art* (1764; *Geschichte der Kunst des Alterthums*), he claimed that ancient Greek art exemplified "noble simplicity and tranquil grandeur" (*eine edle Einfalt und eine stille Grösse*) and urged modern artists to create works in the spirit of Greek culture: "The only way for us to become great or, if this be possible, inimitable, is to imitate the ancients."[3] During the seventeenth century, the study of Greek, considered inferior to Latin, had been undertaken primarily to enable reading of the New Testament. In the eighteenth century, however, thanks largely to Winckelmann's influence, it came to serve a broader purpose: enhancing understanding of Homer, Plato, Sophocles, and other ancient authors, and, more generally, Greek aesthetics and public life.

Although the statuesque serenity that Winckelmann saw as the fundamental quality of Greek art was not hailed with equal vigor by succeeding generations, his sense of wonder and awe at the beauty of classical culture soon became deeply rooted in the German imagination. Winckelmann's passion, together with later writers' study of classical languages and encounters with ancient art (e.g., copies of statues such as the Apollo Belvedere and Laocoön in Mannheim's Hall of Antiquities, as well as original works in Italy and Greece), nourished a growing fascination with antiquity. They also fostered a view of ancient Greece as a highpoint in human history. Herder,

Goethe, Schiller, and Hölderlin celebrate the ancient Greeks for their physical beauty, vigor, athleticism, joy, youth, naturalness, and nobility of soul. Greece's cult of aesthetics and freedom, its sunny, temperate climate, and its vivid and symbolic myths of gods and heroes are similarly lauded. To Schiller, as historian George S. Williamson writes, "Greece was a land of fables, where humans intermingled freely with gods and life was enriched by an endless series of festivals."[4] During this polytheistic age when gods resembled humans in image and behavior, humans in turn were godlike, at least more so than in modern times, Schiller asserted.[5]

Writers differed on various points – whether ancient Greek culture was characterized by a greater degree of noble restraint or sensuous abandon (what came to be known as its "Apollonian" and "Dionysian" qualities); how one might reconcile various dualities (ancient and modern, pagan and Christian, southern and northern); if it was possible, or even desirable, to restore Greek culture through imitation. Moreover, individual writers espoused different views on antiquity over their careers, as evidenced, for example, by comparison of Goethe's *Sturm und Drang* works with those of his later Classical years.

A number of sources explore the nature and development of German philhellenism.[6] Here it will suffice to note that, whatever their differences, writers from Winckelmann on tended to look back to ancient Greece with one eye focused on the state of their own culture. Greek civilization, of abiding interest in its own right, was frequently enlisted to support polemics against the modern world, or at least reassessments of its validity.

For many observers, the modern world failed to measure up. Winckelmann, for one, recoiled from Christianity's sharp distinction between the human and the divine.[7] Herder, although inclined to historicist thinking, far preferred the noble nudity of Greek statues to the elaborate dress in which modern figures customarily appeared.[8] Schiller contrasted the modern world's complexity, artificiality, and self-consciousness with the ancient world's simple naturalness:

Recall the beauty of nature surrounding the ancient *Greeks*. Consider how confidently this people was able, under its serendipitous sky, to live with nature in the wild; consider how very much nearer to the simplicity of nature lay its manner of thinking, its way of feeling, its mores, and what a faithful copy of this is provided by the works of its poets.[9]

Hölderlin too proclaimed the superiority of the ancient world and mourned its disappearance:

Blessed Greece! Home of all the immortals,
Is it true, then, what we heard in our youth?
Hall of feasting! Its floor is the ocean! Its tables the mountains!
Built truly from of old for one purpose only!
But where are the thrones and the temples, and where are the beakers of nectar,
Where, to pleasure the gods, is the joy of song?
Where, where do they glisten, those words that strike from a distance?
Delphi sleeps – none hears the echo of fate . . .
Ah friend! We come too late. The gods may yet live,
But far over our heads, high above us, in another world.[10]

Veneration of ancient Greece and critiques of contemporary culture combined to produce feelings of intense longing. As August Wilhelm Schlegel noted, "The poetry of the ancients was the poetry of enjoyment, and ours is that of desire: the former has its foundation in the scene which is present, while the latter hovers betwixt recollection and hope."[11] Herder's attraction to Greek myths; Goethe's and Wilhelm Heinse's travels to southern climes; Schiller's tributes to Greek naturalism and polytheism; J. M. Gesner's, Christian Gottlob Heyne's, and Humboldt's efforts to introduce the study of Greek art, language, and literature into German educational curricula; Johann Heinrich Voss's translation of Homer; Friedrich August Wolf's pioneering work in classical scholarship – each may be understood as an expression of yearning for an ancient culture that, like a beacon of light, could help to set the modern world on a correct course. Crucially, the transformation was intended for the cultural, not political, arena. Historian Jeremy McInerney explains, "Aesthetic romanticism led the Philhellenes to set Classical Greece up as a spiritual model, but they never proposed abolishing the institutions of the German states in favour of Athenian-style democracy."[12]

Although Schelling's and Friedrich Schlegel's simultaneous call in the spring of 1800 for a "new mythology" suitable for the modern age led to an explosion of interest in Germanic lore, prompting scholars and amateurs alike to search for medieval legends, fairy tales, and folk songs, classical mythology continued to attract attention.[13] Schlegel's conception of the "new mythology" did not in fact exclude the Greek myths, but rather placed them alongside other wellsprings of mythic material, both Germanic and non-Germanic (e.g., the works of Dante, Shakespeare, and Goethe, the Norse epic *Edda*, and Oriental literary traditions):

For this is the beginning of all poetry, to cancel the progression and laws of rationally thinking reason, and to transplant us once again into the beautiful confusion of imagination, into the original chaos of human nature, for which I know as yet no more beautiful symbol than the motley throng of the ancient gods.

Why won't you arise and revive those splendid forms of great antiquity? Try for once to see the old mythology, steeped in Spinoza and in those views which present-day physics must excite in every thinking person, and everything will appear to you in new splendor and vitality.

But to accelerate the genesis of the new mythology, the other mythologies must also be reawakened according to the measure of their profundity, their beauty, and their form. If only the treasures of the Orient were as accessible to us as those of Antiquity.[14]

The myths of ancient Greece, brought alive again in a "more beautiful, a greater way," would help modern man to understand himself and his place in the universe, and thereby usher in a new state of paradise:

And thus let us, by light and life, hesitate no longer, but accelerate, each according to his own mind, that great development to which we were called. Be worthy of the greatness of the age and the fog will vanish from your eyes; and there will be light before you . . . It seems to me that he who could understand the age – that is, those great principles of general rejuvenation and of eternal revolution – would be able to succeed in grasping the poles of mankind, to recognize and to know the activity of the first men as well as the nature of the Golden Age which is to come. Then the empty chatter would stop and man would become conscious of what he is: he would understand the earth and the sun.[15]

To Schlegel, revisiting antique myths represented an important means of revitalizing contemporary culture. Other mythical material, whether drawn from medieval romances, Oriental tales, Shakespeare plays, or fairy tales, could also serve this purpose; Schlegel, who famously described romantic literature as a "progressive universal poetry,"[16] was nothing if not inclusive in his understanding of how the Romantic imperative was to be accomplished.[17] But despite Romanticism's attraction to non-classical sources and embrace of qualities antithetical to classical art – the idiosyncratic, mysterious, supernatural, grotesque, irrational, ironic, infinite, sublime and so on – Greek antiquity exerted a strong influence on Romantic thought and its various social and artistic manifestations. Even during the late-Romantic (*Biedermeier*) era, classical mythology retained its appeal.[18]

Enthusiasm for classical antiquity during the early 1800s took a variety of forms: government-sanctioned and private excavations of antique sites, the collecting (or plundering) of ancient artifacts, sight-seeing trips south of the Alps, the formation of philhellenic societies in England, France, and Germany, and the creation of literary, art, and musical works based on antique subjects. As the century progressed, philhellenism became firmly entrenched in German educational and cultural institutions. In the early 1800s, through the efforts of philologists such as Wolf and Humboldt, neo-humanist ideals were introduced into the Prussian *Gymnasien* and universities, resulting in a broad overhaul of pedagogical methods and the concomitant rise of *Altertumswissenschaft*, the "science" of classical scholarship aimed at recovering the spirit of the Greeks through precise historical interpretation of texts.[19] As historian Suzanne Marchand writes, "Thanks especially to Winckelmann, Goethe, and Schiller, the study of the Greeks had taken on the quality of a redemptive return to mankind's origins; thanks to Wolf and Humboldt, this vision had become an official academic and bureaucratic creed."[20] Extensive research conducted in a broad range of academic disciplines (including such new fields as epigraphy – the study of ancient inscriptions, and papyrology) vastly increased knowledge about many aspects of the ancient world: its language, literature, art, architecture, philosophy, religion, politics, economics, ethnicity, and history. Huge scholarly projects, involving the combined efforts of many researchers, were undertaken with increasing frequency. State-funded German institutions of art and archaeology also evinced the powerful influence of classical ideals, as well as a proclivity for scientific precision and specialized knowledge.[21] By the later nineteenth century, philhellenism had become an activity for the academically-minded, with aesthetics playing a secondary role.

Schiller and Schlegel, among others, believed that engaging with antiquity could assist modern man in the essential and the never-ending process of self-cultivation, or *Bildung*, which aspired toward the formation of the complete human individual. From a broader perspective, it could help heal modern society, transforming its fragmented essence into a single glorious whole. According to Wolf and Humboldt (who was strongly influenced by Schiller), the study of the Greek language and culture would play a critical role in helping Germans rebuild Prussian society and foster national integration. (Unlike England and France, which had enjoyed political unity for centuries, Germany remained divided into over 300 separate states until the mid 1860s. It also embraced two religions – Catholicism and Protestantism.) Although German national consciousness had begun to emerge as early as the Renaissance and Reformation, and had intensified during the French cultural hegemony of the seventeenth and eighteenth centuries, Prussia's humiliating defeat at the Battle of Jena in 1806 supplied a strong new impetus. As Humboldt proclaimed in 1807 (contemporaneous with Fichte's stirring *Addresses to the German Nation*, intended to reinvigorate his despondent compatriots),

> In the Greeks we have before us a nation in whose fortunate hands everything, which, according to our deepest feelings, sustains the noblest and richest aspects of human existence, matured to the utmost perfection ... To know them is for us not just pleasant, advantageous and indispensable; only in them do we find the ideal of that which we ourselves should like to be and to produce.[22]

Thus throughout Romanticism's infatuation with the Middle Ages, and continuing long after the Greek War of Independence (which in any event Metternich's repressive policies had prevented Germans from openly supporting),[23] philhellenism remained a crucial aspect of German culture.[24] Although its character changed, it continued to play an important role in the rise of German nationalism.

If fewer nineteenth- than eighteenth-century German writers focused on classical antiquity, they expressed their thoughts with no less passion. They did, however, convey greater pessimism. The classical works of the Austrian dramatist Franz Grillparzer, for example, project deep resignation. In both *Sappho* (1818) and the trilogy *Das goldene Vlies* (1821), Grillparzer stresses the futility of striving for transcendence, portraying the tragedy that inevitably results from efforts to unite the godlike and the human, the civilized and the barbarian.

The writings of Friedrich Nietzsche, revealing the strong influence of Arthur Schopenhauer's pessimistic philosophy, draw attention to the dark and irrational side of ancient Greek culture. In so doing, Nietzsche's works echo those of Hölderlin, who produced nearly all of his lyric verse before 1806 (when his shaky mental condition deteriorated to the point of insanity). Veering away from Goethe's post-*Sturm und Drang* conception of ancient Greek literature as calm, balanced, and dispassionate, Hölderlin had instead emphasized its turbulent, unbalanced, and emotional qualities; Dionysus, the Greek god of wild ecstasy and drunken orgies, he insisted, was far more representative of Hellenic culture than Apollo, the god of light, art, and beauty. Nietzsche, in *The Birth of Tragedy Out of the Spirit of Music* (1872; *Die Geburt der Tragödie aus dem Geiste der Musik*), espouses a similar view, arising from his conviction that the essence of Greek art lies in its tension between Apollonian and Dionysian forces. The latter, he claims, which had essentially lain dormant from the time of the pre-Socratics until the advent of contemporary German music (namely Wagner), had made Greek tragedy possible, and the cultivation of Dionysian artistic energies holds the key to a rebirth of European culture. Nietzsche asserts that the ancient Greeks experienced the pain and terror of existence, but created great art through brute willpower, by harnessing the Dionysian. Modern German culture, he urges, should follow suit, taking Greek tragedy as its model.

Concurrent with the increased pessimism of later nineteenth-century writings on Greece was a heightened emphasis on the martial aspects of Hellenic culture. Militaristic Sparta replaced democratic Athens as the embodiment of ancient Greece in the minds of many Germans. Historian David Gress explains,

Unlike the scholarship of Britain, the German interest in Greece was to discover the causes of Greek political decline to prevent a similar fate from overtaking Germany. In particular, historians explored the reasons for the Greek failure to organize nationally against foreign enemies. This focus often led to a contempt for the Athenian democracy, since ancient Greek writers themselves, notably Plato, had suggested that democracy was a hindrance to effective governance in war and therefore to victory. The lessons drawn were obvious: national cohesion, martial vigor, athletic training, and indoctrination of youth, or keep your powder dry and never trust the French.[25]

By the turn of the twentieth century, the German cult of Greece, and Sparta in particular, had assumed a character that presaged the aggressive, militaristic regime of the National Socialists. The long-standing belief that Germans were essentially modern-day Greeks led extremists to the view that the German nation, like its Hellenic predecessor, was uniquely called upon to save the world – an attitude that paved the way for Adolf Hitler's racist policies.[26]

Romantic Lieder with classical subjects, it should be evident, represent artistic emblems of an extended philhellenic movement that arose in Germany during the Enlightenment and continued, with significant modifications, throughout the nineteenth century. "Ganymed" (Schubert, 1817; Wolf, 1889), "An Aphrodite: Ode der Sappho" (Loewe, 1836), "An eine Aolshärfe" (Brahms, 1858; Wolf, 1888), "Cupido, loser Knabe" (Franz, 1864), "Gesang der Apollopriesterin" (Strauss, 1896–7) – these and other classical Lieder underscore antiquity's continuing, if changing, allure throughout the Romantic and post-Romantic eras. The fact that Lied composers often set poetic texts from before their own time helped perpetuate the cult of Greece long after the emergence of German philhellenism in "Winckelmann's century," as Goethe put it. In their own way, nineteenth-century Germans were just as absorbed by the ancient world as their eighteenth-century forebears, as the *Antikenlieder* of Schubert and Wolf, the focus of the following two chapters, illustrate.

1 | Schubert's Greek revival

Schubert first met the famous Vienna court opera singer Johann Michael Vogl in March 1817 at the home of his friend Franz von Schober. The 48-year-old baritone, although past his prime as a stage performer, remained an imposing figure, and Schubert, nearly thirty years younger and little known, revered him. Schober and other members of Schubert's circle had long tried to arrange such a meeting. As Josef von Spaun relates,

> Schubert, who always had to sing his own songs, ... frequently expressed a great desire to find a singer for his songs, and his old wish to get to know the Court opera singer, Vogl, grew stronger and stronger. It was now decided in our little circle that Vogl must be won over for the Schubert songs. The task was a hard one, as Vogl was very difficult to approach ... [Schober] told Vogl, with glowing enthusiasm, about Schubert's beautiful compositions and invited him to try them out. Vogl replied that he was fed to the teeth with music, that he had been brought up on music and was far more concerned to get free of it than to get to know any new music. He had heard about young geniuses hundreds of times and had always been disappointed, and this was certain to be the case with Schubert too. He wanted to be left in peace and wished to hear nothing more about it. – This refusal upset us all deeply, all except Schubert, who said he had expected just such an answer and found it perfectly understandable. Meanwhile Vogl was approached repeatedly by Schober, and by others as well, and finally he promised to come to Schober's one evening to see what it was all about, as he put it.[1]

Schubert, idolizing Vogl for his riveting performances in mythological operas like Gluck's *Iphigénie en Tauride* and Luigi Cherubini's *Medea*, brought several songs for the singer to peruse. Among them were two on classical themes – settings of Goethe's "Ganymed" and Mayrhofer's "Memnon."[2] Knowing that the highly cultivated singer possessed a keen interest in ancient Greece and Rome but little enthusiasm for Lieder, Schubert chose to introduce himself with works that bridged the disparate worlds of classical opera and romantic art song.[3] Lieder with antique subjects, he may have reasoned, could capture Vogl's attention.

The singer was entranced. Over the next decade, as his operatic career wound to a close, Vogl built a new reputation as the first great interpreter of Schubert's Lieder, with the composer as his frequent accompanist. Eduard von Bauernfeld, a member of Schubert's circle, speculates that Schubert composed many of his *Antikenlieder* (among other songs) with Vogl specifically in mind: "'Memnon,' 'Philoktet,' 'Der zürnenden Diana,' the 'Wanderer,' 'Ganymed,' 'An Schwager Kronos,' the 'Müllerlieder' and so forth were little musical masterpieces and might have been created for Vogl's style and manner of performances."[4] Certainly the songs of antiquity, a staple of the two artists' performing repertoire, served as a strong bond between them and played a critical role in establishing Schubert's fame.[5]

Schubert and classical antiquity

Over his career, Schubert composed roughly thirty-five songs (several in two versions) with subjects drawn from classical mythology or that otherwise allude to antiquity (Table 1.1).[6] Most of these works date from the mid-1810s – with an especially strong concentration in 1817 – but they also appeared sporadically in the 1820s right up to Schubert's final year. The majority (sixteen) are settings of poetic texts by Mayrhofer, with whom Schubert shared living quarters from late 1818 through 1820. Following are songs with texts by Schiller (eight) and Goethe (five), the two leading representatives of Weimar Classicism. Schubert also set one "classical" text each by six other writers of past and present: Pietro Metastasio, Johann Georg Jacobi, Georg Friedrich von Gerstenberg, Theodor Körner, Heine, and Franz Bruchmann.

Classical subjects are relatively uncommon in the songs of Schubert's immediate predecessors. While Lied composers from the mid-eighteenth century often set rococo verse depicting shepherds and shepherdesses cavorting amidst idyllic Arcadian landscapes (see, for example, Friedrich Wilhelm Marpurg's three-volume collection *Berlinische Oden und Lieder*; 1756, 1759, 1763), composers active during the late eighteenth and early nineteenth centuries gravitated toward newly-written poems employing conventional topics of folk song and medieval balladry, e.g., times of day, the seasons, love, nature, country life, *Heimat*, wandering, hunting, soldiering, death, heroism, family relationships, religion, and mystery.[7] As a penchant for the playful (*scherzhaft*) yielded to a preference for the sentimental (*empfindsam*), classical subjects and imagery became increasingly scarce. There are, to be sure, some late eighteenth- and early nineteenth-century Lieder with antique associations, most notably Johann Friedrich Reichardt's settings of classical poems by Goethe (Reichardt's dramatic settings, or "declamations," of Goethe's large classical hymns "Ganymed" and "Prometheus" may have

Table 1.1 Schubert's songs of antiquity

D	Title	Text	Composed
166	Amphiaraos	Körner	1 Mar. 1815
246	Die Bürgschaft	Schiller	Aug. 1815
312	Hektors Abschied	Schiller	
	version a		19 Oct. 1815
	version b		c.1815
323	Klage der Ceres	Schiller	9 Nov. 1815–June 1816
360	Lied eines Schiffers an die Dioskuren	Mayrhofer	1816
369	An Schwager Kronos	Goethe	1816
391	Die vier Weltalter	Schiller	Mar. 1816
396	Gruppe aus dem Tartarus (1) (frag.)	Schiller	Mar. 1816
450	Fragment aus dem Aeschylus	Mayrhofer	June 1816
474	Lied des Orpheus	Jacobi	
	version a		Sept. 1816
	version b		1816
510	Vedi quanto adoro	Metastasio	Dec. 1816
526	Fahrt zum Hades	Mayrhofer	Jan. 1817
540	Philoktet	Mayrhofer	Mar. 1817
541	Memnon	Mayrhofer	Mar. 1817
542	Antigone und Oedip	Mayrhofer	Mar. 1817
544	Ganymed	Goethe	Mar. 1817
548	Orest auf Tauris	Mayrhofer	Mar. 1817
554	Uraniens Flucht	Mayrhofer	Apr. 1817
573	Iphigenia	Mayrhofer	Jul. 1817
583	Gruppe aus dem Tartarus (2)	Schiller	Sept. 1817
584	Elysium	Schiller	Sept. 1817
585	Atys	Mayrhofer	Sept. 1817
674	Prometheus	Goethe	Oct. 1819
677	Die Götter Griechenlands	Schiller	
	version a		Nov. 1819
	version b		?
699	Der entsühnte Orest	Mayrhofer	Sept. 1820
700	Freiwilliges Versinken	Mayrhofer	Sept. 1820
707	Der zürnenden Diana	Mayrhofer	Dec. 1820
	version a		
	version b		
716	Grenzen der Menschheit	Goethe	Mar. 1821
737	An die Leyer	Bruchmann	?1822 or 1823
753	Aus 'Heliopolis' (I)	Mayrhofer	Apr. 1822
754	Aus 'Heliopolis' (II)	Mayrhofer	Apr. 1822
764	Der Musensohn	Goethe	
	version a		Dec. 1822
	version b		c.1822
801	Dithyrambe	Schiller	by June 1826
805	Der Sieg	Mayrhofer	Mar. 1824
890	Hippolits Lied	Gerstenberg	July 1826
957/8	Der Atlas	Heine	1828

inspired Schubert's own settings of these texts), and Loewe's four settings of texts by the ancient Greek poet Anacreon.[8] Other examples can also be found, e.g., Johann Rudolph Zumsteeg's "Daphne am Bach" (1783; text by Friedrich Leopold Graf zu Stolberg-Stolberg, for which Schubert composed a setting in 1816) and Friedrich Wilhelm Rust's "Elysium" (1796; text by Friedrich von Matthisson).[9] But borrowing elements from Greek mythology does not necessarily signify an attempt to conjure the ancient world; a classical *mise-en-scène* or allusion may be "peripheral, even decorative" rather than central to the song's meaning (as with the frequent references to Cupid in rococo poetry).[10] On the whole, Schubert's powerful attraction to classical themes distinguishes him from earlier Lied composers.

Beyond providing the chance to improve upon pre-existing settings, a number of factors likely motivated Schubert's *Antikenlieder*. As suggested, at the beginning of their relationship, Schubert may have written such works in hopes of enticing Vogl to perform his Lieder. This would help explain the great number of songs with classical themes written in 1817, the year they met. (One of them, "Orest auf Tauris," composed in the month of their first meeting, enabled Vogl to assume the role of Orestes, which had won him acclaim in performances of Gluck's *Iphigénie en Tauride* at the Vienna Hofoper.)

Schubert may have wanted to explore techniques of dramatic music – recitative, arioso and aria styles, dialogue exchanges, progressive tonal schemes, through-composition, etc. – and thereby demonstrate his potential as a composer for the stage, especially of operatic works with classical subjects. By March 1817, he had already attempted one such opera, *Die Bürgschaft*, D. 435, and he would soon begin another, *Adrast*, D. 137. Perhaps Schubert intended to prove himself a worthy successor to Gluck and Mozart, who composed mythological operas during what he apparently perceived as the genre's Golden Age; according to Spaun, after hearing Gluck's works, "again and again [Schubert] used to ask sadly whether the happy time of such delights had vanished from us for ever."[11] (Schubert followed Gluck in depicting not only Orestes but also Iphigenia and Orpheus.) Ironically, composing dramatic songs with subjects drawn from ancient times may have helped satisfy a longing to return to the later eighteenth century. In borrowing operatic compositional techniques, Schubert may also have hoped to elevate the status of the Lied, a genre that Franz Joseph Haydn, Mozart, and even Beethoven had held in relatively low regard.

Schubert's interest in composing songs of antiquity surely owed much to his educational background and friendships. As a student at the Vienna *Stadtkonvikt*, and later as a teacher-in-training at the *Normal Hauptschule*, he pursued an extensive course of study in Latin.[12] In 1812, he also began studies in Greek, receiving high grades. In the reactionary political climate that prevailed in Austria during the years of his upbringing, modern languages and literatures (German, French, Italian, English) were rarely taught. The standard Latin-based curriculum, on the other hand, provided a solid foundation in the classics, and the time Schubert spent grappling with grammar exercises and the works of Greek and Roman authors may have inspired him to bring antique subjects to life through his music.

The close friendships that Schubert developed during and after his years at the Stadtkonvikt provided a perhaps more direct impetus for his *Antikenlieder*. In the mid-1810s, Schubert's Linz circle of friends, strongly influenced by the writings of Herder, Goethe, and Schiller, embarked on an ambitious program of self-improvement and education.[13] Striving to ascertain the good, the true, and the beautiful, the idealistic youths dedicated themselves to the study of great men and ideas from previous ages, a project that involved extensive reading in Greek and Latin literature and the history of antiquity. The classical past, they felt, offered valuable lessons for the present. The "heroic and patriotic lives of Greek youths [could] provide inspiration for their own conduct, threatened as they were (in May 1813) by the Napoleonic wars," writes Schubert scholar David Gramit.[14] Schubert's friends not only aimed to improve themselves but also sought to influence others. In their various writings – poetry, drama, essays, and the short-lived yearbook *Beyträge für Jünglinge* – they exhorted their compatriots to cultivate virtue by imitating the ancients. They refashioned the Greek myths in accordance with modern concerns and perspectives, including those of Romanticism.[15] The circle's reverence for antiquity, supported by the classical training its members had received in the conservative Austrian school system and intensified by their zealous program of self-betterment, likely influenced Schubert, encouraging him to explore its potential within his own chosen medium.

Underlying these various factors – professional, musical, educational, and social – was a fundamental conviction that the antique world represented a standard by which the modern world could measure and define itself. Vogl's portrayal of Greek heroes, Schubert's borrowing of mythological subjects and classical operatic styles and early training in Latin and Greek, and the circle's ambitious reading program in ancient literatures all point to the paradisiacal aura surrounding classical antiquity for eighteenth- and nineteenth-century Germans.

Members of Schubert's Biedermeier generation generally agreed with earlier German philhellenists that, in comparison to antiquity, the modern world was deeply flawed. They were pessimistic, however, about the likelihood of experiencing a new Golden Age, or state of transcendent wholeness, during their earthly existence. Biedermeier Vienna, subject to the strict censorship and harsh repression of Metternich's regime, seemed far removed from Periclean Athens. The failure of the French revolution to improve modern society, compounded by the humiliation inflicted on Germans by Napoleon and the French occupying forces, had drained Romantic optimism. If anything, nostalgia for antiquity during the Restoration was more intense than during the revolutionary and pre-revolutionary years. Witnessing the struggle of modern-day Greeks to escape from Ottoman rule, Schubert's generation looked back to the freedom, beauty, and vibrancy of ancient Greek culture with deep longing, as Anton Ottenwalt, a member of Schubert's circle, conveys in his poem "Griechenland":

Bright, holy land, cradle of the Graces,
High temple of art, mother of more noble humanity
And the higher wisdom
Of Plato and Socrates!

Alas, where are you? The temple and the hall lie fallen
In ruins! Crude barbarians
Rule over the land of freedom;
The vestiges of beauty never move them![16]

Perhaps then, in addition to the factors noted above, Schubert was led to compose *Antikenlieder* by a desire, shared by many of his contemporaries, to escape the ills of the modern world. If he could not actually experience paradise regained, but was instead fated, like Mignon, to yearn for "the land where the lemon trees bloom," he might at least mitigate the harshness of present reality by imagining an idealized world and conveying that vision through art. The Lied, with its subtle interactions of text and music, was well suited to representing fallen humanity and the purified state to which it aspired.

From a broad perspective, all of Schubert's *Antikenlieder*, on account of their classical subjects, may be regarded as engaging a lost paradise myth. Outwardly, they seem a diverse lot, reflected in the many genre terms commonly used to describe them, e.g., dramatic ballad, *scena*, cantata, aria, arioso, and *tableau vivant*, as well as looser designations like "fragment from an unwritten opera seria" and "sublimation of a students' song." The songs feature through-composed as well as rounded and strophic forms,[17] declamatory as well as lyrical styles,[18] operatic as well as Liedlike gestures,[19] progressive as well as unified tonal schemes.[20] They range from two to nearly twenty pages in length. Their subject matter is also varied. Certain songs dwell on the harshness of fate: "Gruppe aus dem Tartarus," "Fragment aus dem Aeschylus," "Philoktet," "Fahrt zum Hades," "Grenzen der Menschheit," and "Der Atlas." Others portray the protagonist's heroic acceptance of fate: "Amphiaraos," "Hektors Abschied," "Antigone und Oedip," "Lied eines Schiffers an die Dioskuren," "Der zürnenden Diana," "Freiwilliges Versinken," and "Prometheus." (The latter songs, offering a model for imitation, fit the educational aims of Schubert's circle.) "Elysium" and "Der Sieg," by contrast, conjure images of a blissful after-life. Despite these manifold differences, Schubert's *Antikenlieder* form a cohesive group, especially when considered in light of more traditional Lieder. All look back to antiquity, and most also borrow compositional traits of classical opera, which Schubert revered. The double return – to antique subjects and eighteenth-century opera – calls attention to the nostalgic spirit infusing this important Lied subgenre.

A number of Schubert's *Antikenlieder* also express longing in a more immediate sense, and are therefore especially relevant to this study, e.g., "Antigone und Oedip," "Ganymed," "Memnon," "Iphigenia," "Atys," "Der entsühnte Orest," "Aus Heliopolis I," "Der Sieg," "Dithyrambe," "Der Atlas," and "Die Götter Griechenlands." While the mythical subject matter varies, in each work the protagonist yearns to alleviate present suffering through return to a distant world. Oedipus, facing his doom, thinks back longingly on "happy days, in the halls of my great fathers, / Amid the songs of heroes and the peal of horns" when he drank the "golden light" of the sun god Helios. Ganymed longs for, and feels drawn into, the embrace of the "all-loving Father." Memnon, slain in battle, yearns to reunite with his mother, the goddess of dawn. Iphigenia, Atys, and Orestes have been separated from their native lands and pine for home. In "Aus Heliopolis I," the protagonist craves the city of the sun, i.e., the realm of art. The protagonist of "Der Sieg" imagines enjoying the "fruits of Paradise" after a self-inflicted death. In "Dithyrambe," the poet seeks immortality in the company of the gods by drinking heavenly nectar. Atlas sought endless happiness, and now suffers its absolute loss. "Die Götter Griechenlands" most explicitly invokes the lost paradise myth, encapsulating the protagonist's unrelieved yearning in a single question: "Fair world, where are you?"

Two songs – "Memnon" and "Die Götter Griechenlands" – exemplify Schubert's evocation of the lost paradise myth through allusions to antiquity. The first, although widely praised, has received little scholarly attention. The powerful symbolism of the Memnon myth and the artistry of

Schubert's music are ripe for analysis. The relationship between text and music intriguingly suggests that poet and composer held different perspectives on the myth of lost paradise. "Die Götter Griechenlands," existing in two versions, has been the subject of several published analyses (due in part to Schubert's reuse of its music in his *String Quartet in A Minor*, D. 804). Comparison with "Memnon" enhances understanding of "Die Götter Griechenlands" and sheds light on oft-criticized changes Schubert made to the first version.

These songs offer unusually clear yet contrasting manifestations of the lost paradise myth. "Memnon" is a comparatively positive rendering. Although the poetic text alone conveys little optimism, the structural, stylistic, and tonal qualities of Schubert's musical setting suggest the possibility of a temporary return to paradise, understood as a reunion of the human and the divine. "Die Götter Griechenlands" intimates that man's alienation from paradise is permanent and his longing without end; the modern world cannot recapture the idyllic past – a notion conveyed by both text and music. (Of course, other songs could also form useful comparisons. For example, like "Memnon," "Ganymed" suggests the restoration of paradise by depicting the uniting of man and god. "Ganymed" is indeed a more straightforward example in that both Goethe's text [1774] and Schubert's music clearly illustrate the Phrygian youth's apotheosis. "Der Atlas" reveals a fundamental similarity to "Der Götter Griechenlands" in its depiction of the Titan's expulsion from Olympus for having dared to wage war against Zeus. Both Heine's text [1823–4] and Schubert's music [1827–8] convey the permanence of Atlas's rupture with divinity.)

"Memnon" and "Die Götter Griechenlands" also invite study because of their extraordinarily rich interpretive potential. The poetic texts of both songs involve mythologies that captivated eighteenth- and nineteenth-century philosophers, writers, and artists, linking the songs to myriad expressions of Romantic thought. Not only are the texts deeply resonant with meaning, the musical settings display considerable variety and complexity. To convey the protagonists' state of alienation, Schubert draws upon many kinds of musical contrast: vocal–instrumental, operatic–Liedlike, declamatory–lyrical, minor–major, chromatic–diatonic, low register–high register, unstable–stable, irregular–regular. While the two songs share some of the same compositional strategies in addressing the myth, their differences are more striking. Schubert adopted new approaches in tandem with new views on paradise lost.

Finally, when considered in chronological order, the two songs point to a significant trend in Schubert's composition of *Antikenlieder*, with important implications for the broader corpus of his Lieder. "Memnon," the earlier work, presents an identifiable protagonist drawn from Greek mythology. Schubert steps into the past, into the body of a familiar figure from classical antiquity. In this respect, the song is characteristic of many of Schubert's early *Antikenlieder*. "Die Götter Griechenlands," by contrast, portrays a nameless protagonist, as do most of his *Antikenlieder* from the 1820s. We infer that this protagonist inhabits the modern world but learn nothing more about his identity. His object of longing (antiquity) also seems further away than Memnon's (the goddess of dawn, with whom Memnon reunites periodically). The anonymity of the protagonist and the song's greater pessimism foreshadow the darkness of many Schubert Lieder from the 1820s.

Schubert's interest in *Antikenlieder* was a passing phase, most intense during the later 1810s. Although in his last years Schubert occasionally turned to classical subjects, for the most part he directed his attention elsewhere.[21] Yet the nostalgic quality of the *Antikenlieder* continued to play an important role in Schubert's late Lieder, finding expression in many songs with nonclassical themes. Wilhelm Müller, whose passionate support of the modern Greek struggle for independence earned him the appellation "Griechen-Müller" (and who taught both Latin and Greek), wrote numerous poems that exemplify the nostalgic spirit if not always the ancient imagery of philhellenism. "To my Greeks I remain true, if everything vacillates," he wrote in a letter of 1822.[22] His cycle *Die Winterreise*, to which Schubert turned in 1827, evokes the lost paradise myth by expressing the anonymous wanderer's feelings of alienation, longing, and despair. Unsurprisingly, in setting Müller's texts, Schubert drew on compositional strategies from "Memnon," "Die Götter Griechenlands," and other *Antikenlieder*. The same holds true for his settings of verse by other Biedermeier poets, such as Matthäus von Collin, Johann Ladislaus Pyrker, Karl Gottfried von Leitner, Johann Gabriel Seidl, and Heine. Schubert's continued attraction to the lost paradise myth had, of course, a deeply personal dimension. Stricken with syphilis and confronting an early death, he remained tantalized by the vision of an ideal world beyond the reach of reality.

"Memnon," D. 541

Schubert composed "Memnon" in March 1817 to words by his friend Mayrhofer. The song focuses on the mythological Ethiopian king slain by Achilles in the Trojan War. Although Homer barely mentions Memnon, other sources relate his story.[23] Quintus of Smyrna, a fourth-century AD poet, describes in detail the clash between the two warriors. Memnon, a towering figure, is eager to fight. On the battlefield, he slaughters innumerable Greeks, including the valiant Antilochus, son of Nestor. In angry retaliation, Achilles charges at him, and the two slash away at each other, each unyielding since, as Quintus tells, "Zeus's mind was filled with love for them both, and he put vigor into both and made them untiring and larger, not at all like men, but like gods."[24] After a seemingly endless struggle, Achilles hurls the fatal spear, and Memnon falls.

The martial aspects of Memnon's story find no place in either Mayrhofer's poem or Schubert's setting. In this early nineteenth-century rendering, Memnon is not a warrior but a sufferer – an icon of the modern, alienated artist. This conception derives from another facet of the Memnon myth, one that came to overshadow his battlefield heroics. According to the Greeks, after Memnon fell, his mother Eos, the goddess of dawn, pleaded with Zeus to revive her dead son. Moved by her misery, Zeus decided to let Memnon return to life for one brief moment each day. At the first warming rays of morning, Memnon would respond to his mother's arrival with a sorrowful wail. He would then languish, silent and immobile, until the following dawn.

Memnon's singular fate achieved new prominence in late antiquity because of a strange phenomenon: a cracked Egyptian statue. The statue is one of two adjacent colossal figures of the Pharaoh Amenophis III (mid-second millennium BC) at the city of Thebes (Figure 3). Damaged by an earthquake in 27 BC, the 60-foot high, 1000-ton statue contained fissures which, as temperatures warmed at daybreak, allegedly produced an eerie wailing sound. The mysterious noise evoked Memnon's fate and led the Greeks to associate the Egyptian statue with the fallen warrior.[25] Despite, or perhaps because of, claims that the sounds actually resulted from mechanical trickery, the statue became a popular tourist site.[26] Hundreds of ancient visitors, including poets, generals, and emperors, chiseled inscriptions in Latin and Greek on the statue's feet and legs claiming that they had heard the mystical tones.

Although the statue ceased to emit any sounds after being repaired by Emperor Septimius Severus in 199 AD, it retained its fame and association with Memnon long afterwards. Numerous eighteenth- and nineteenth-century travelogues record the awe their authors experienced in confronting "Vocal Memnon" (as the statue came to be known) on journeys down the Nile. Vivant Denon, a French artist, writer, collector, and diplomat who accompanied Napoleon on his expedition to Egypt in 1798, was one of many to describe the striking appearance of the colossal statues (which he also portrayed in an important series of drawings):

Figure 3 The Colossi of Memnon. *Description de L'Égypte* (1809), vol. 2, pl. 20. Statue on right is "Vocal Memnon."

I then went to the two colossi, supposed to be those of Memnon, and took an accurate drawing of their actual state of preservation. These two pieces of art, which are without grace, expression, or action, have nothing which seduces the judgment; but their proportions are faultless, and this simplicity of attitude, and want of decided expression, has something of majesty and seriousness, which cannot fail to strike the beholder. If the limbs of these figures had been distorted in order to express some violent passion, the harmony of their outline would have been lost, and they would be less conspicuous at the distance at which they begin to strike the eye, and produce their effect on the mind of the spectator, for they may be distinguished as far as four leagues off. To pronounce upon the character of these statues, it is necessary to have seen them at several intervals, and to have long reflected on them; and after this it often happens, that what is at first considered as the work of the infancy of art, becomes assigned to its maturer age. If the group of the Laocoon, which speaks to the soul as well as to the eyes, were executed in a proportion of sixty feet, it would lose all its beauty, and would not present so striking a mass of workmanship as this; in short, if these statues were more agreeable, they would be less beautiful, as they would then cease to be (what they now are) eminently *monumental*, a character which should belong peculiarly to that outdoor sculpture, which is intended to harmonize with architecture, a style of sculpture which the Egyptians have carried to the highest pitch of perfection.[27]

Some travelers of romantic inclination strained to "hear" the ancient sounds, while others, more scientifically bent, tried to determine their source. Allusions to the statue and its otherworldly "music" are scattered throughout poetry and aesthetic writings from the eighteenth century and after, including works by Herder, Novalis, Jean Paul, Gotthard Ludwig Kosegarten, Ernst August Klingemann, Brentano, and Hegel, as well as numerous French, British, Hungarian, and American writers.[28] Interestingly, two Viennese reviews of Schubert's "Memnon" from 1822 explicitly link the song to the statue:

'Memnon,' considered as a poem, is a masterly delineation of a noble mind wrapped up in itself and afflicted by profound grief, into whose agitated soul falls a soothing ray of dawning hope from another world... The introduction to 'Memnon' conjures up the magic sounds of the famous Egyptian statue.[29]

...

Dramatic songs, worked chiefly in recitative, are 'Memnon' and 'Oedipus and Antigone' [sic]. The former strikingly weaves the sounding of Memnon's statue into the accompaniment, giving tone and shape to the whole. The original character of the tune should also be noticed: it represents, as a departure from the usual sentimental manner, something like the antique way of feeling by seriousness and a quieter tone of complaint, and with the more reason because it is Memnon who laments.[30]

The reviewers' casual references to the noise-making Egyptian statue suggest that the Memnon myth was common knowledge in Schubert's native city.

Mayrhofer and Schubert were likely drawn to the myth of "Vocal Memnon" for somewhat different reasons. The myth not only suited Mayrhofer's classical leanings but also symbolized his personal plight. Like Goethe, Schiller, and Hölderlin, all of whom strongly influenced him, Mayrhofer championed the aesthetic ideals of antiquity.[31] In his poetry, he gravitated toward classical themes and often chose to speak through the voices of mythological figures, particularly in climactic moments when they were stoically accepting fate or eagerly anticipating apotheosis.[32] Memnon, enduring eternal suffering while yearning for release, proved an exemplary subject.

"Memnon"
Den Tag hindurch nur einmal mag ich sprechen,
Gewohnt zu schweigen immer und zu trauern:
Wenn durch die nachtgebor'nen Nebelmauern
Aurorens Purpurstrahlen liebend brechend.

Für Menschenohren sind es Harmonien.
Weil ich die Klage selbst melodisch künde
Und durch der Dichtung Glut das Rauhe rünapproved,
Vermuten sie in mir ein selig Blühen.

In mir, nach dem des Todes Arme langen,
In dessen tiefstem Herzen Schlangen wühlen;
Genährt von meinen schmerzlichen Gefühlen
Fast wütend durch ein ungestillt Verlangen:

Mit dir, des Morgens Göttin, mich zu einen,
Und weit von diesem nichtigen Getriebe,
Aus Sphären edler Freiheit, aus Sphären reiner Liebe,
Ein stiller, bleicher Stern herab zu scheinen.

. . .

      "Memnon"
Once only in the whole day may I speak,
used always to be silent and to mourn:
then, when through the night-born walls of mist
break lovingly Aurora's purple rays.

To human ears my speech is harmony.
Because my plaint I proclaim melodically,
tempering its roughness with the glow of poetry,
they suppose in me a happy blossoming.

In me, for whom Death's arms are reaching out,
deep in whose heart serpents gnaw;
me, who am nourished by my agonies,
near crazed with unappeased desire

to unite myself with you, Goddess of Morn,
and from this futile commotion far removed,
from spheres of noble freedom and pure love,
shine down, a pale and silent star.[33]

   Drawing on Greek mythology represented more than an abstract commitment to classical aesthetic principles. It clearly supported the aims of Schubert's Linz coterie of friends (including Mayrhofer), who sought to instill in modern youth the virtues of ancient heroes. With politically subversive subjects, writing under the cover of Greek mythology may have helped the intensely patriotic Mayrhofer escape the watchful eyes of the

Viennese censor (ironically so, for he became one himself).[34] But with the Memnon myth, Mayrhofer was likely motivated by a profoundly personal connection: the gargantuan statue stood as a heroic representation of the artist, and his sorrowful wail as a potent symbol of modern poetry.[35]

It is easy to see Mayrhofer himself in the figure of that artist. In another one of his poems, a mocking condemnation of the Viennese public's shallow taste in poetry, Mayrhofer himself seems to acknowledge as much: "What is honest Johann thinking / in wanting to be Orestes or Memnon?" an interlocuter asks.[36] The fact that the Egyptian Colossus sits in a state of ruin – over time the statue has lost its face – makes the comparison with the emotionally shattered poet all the more compelling.

Memnon's twilight zone between life and death paralleled Mayrhofer's own tortured existence. Trapped in a state of self-hatred and chronic depression – likely stemming from both his nature and his odious employment as a censor – Mayrhofer found life insufferable, and twice sought to end it, the second time successfully. Bauernfeld, a member of Schubert's circle who wrote an extended verse portrait of Mayrhofer sometime after his suicide in 1836, describes the poet's reclusive behavior in terms that evoke Memnon's stony solitude, as suggested by the following excerpts:

He was sickly and peevish,
fled the merry circle's dealings,
occupied himself only with studies;
. . .
His countenance was serious, stony [*steinern*],
He never smiled or joked.
. . .
He spoke little – what he said
Was weighty . . .
. . .
Only music could at times release
Him from his mute stiffness [*der stumpfen Starrheit*],
And his whole being was transfigured
When he heard the songs of his Schubert.[37]

At one social gathering, according to Bauernfeld, Mayrhofer, the "poet-mummy [*die Dichter-Mumie*] in the corner," suddenly sprang to life, rhapsodizing on freedom and nationhood: "Yes, I say to you prophetically: / Bad times will come, / and men of darkness will / battle against light and truth. // But in the end / the new beautiful era will come, / the spirit, freedom, and the new / teachings of equality will triumph!" Bauernfeld insists, however, that such an outburst occurred only once. "Usually he sat there mute and dull, / like the stone on a grave" [*Wie auf einem Grab das Stein-Mal*].

In forsaking fellowship for solitude, Mayrhofer assumed the quintessential posture of the modern artist, alienated from society and drawn to the imagination. But poetic inspiration did not come easily. As Youens notes, "Only in privileged poetic moments could he leave earth and roam among the immortals on Mount Olympus."[38] In the opening lines of "Memnon," Mayrhofer seems to allude to his own painful condition: "Once only in the whole day may I speak, / used always to be silent and to mourn." His silence, like Memnon's, gave way to artistic expression sporadically. For Memnon, only the first warming rays of dawn could alleviate the misery of a solitary, silent existence, suspended between the living and the dead. For Mayrhofer, only poetic inspiration could ease the pain of an existence suspended between mundane activity and self-obliteration.

If Memnon, anxiously longing for release "from this futile commotion," symbolizes the alienated poet, his intermittent wail represents the poet's voice. Those who hear Memnon's cry perceive it as art: "To human ears my speech is harmony." Memnon too views himself as an artist: "my plaint I proclaim melodically, / tempering its roughness with the glow of poetry."

Mayrhofer was not alone in associating Memnon's wail with poetic speech. Novalis, paraphrasing the Dutch philosopher Frans Hemsterhuis, writes, "The spirit of poetry is the morning light, which makes the statue of Memnon sound."[39] To Novalis, poetic genius and divine inspiration are virtually indistinguishable: "Genius and divine inspiration work in the same way – they often appear mixed."[40] The goddess of dawn, whose arrival Romantics commonly understood to herald the beginning of not just a new day but a new era, caresses the lifeless statue, inspires its cries, and transforms them into poetry. Memnon's wailing might thus be taken to signal the dawn of a new poetic age.[41] This interpretation of the Memnon myth has far-reaching significance. The mythological meeting of Memnon and his immortal mother may be understood as a "mute scene of *reading*, in which the mind (represented by the 'solar eyes of dawn') adverts to, and thereby sees and hears something intelligible in, the senseless and disfigured stone of the statue."[42]

Memnon's "art" fools men into believing it the product of happiness. Although this consequence of an anguished existence might seem wholly positive, it is not. The misunderstanding that leads others to imagine Memnon as joyful compounds the tragedy of his fate; his sense of isolation intensifies. In a never-ending cycle, the poet's alienation leads to artistic creation, whose reception results in even greater alienation. In a certain respect,

Mayrhofer's poem recalls Novalis's *Hymnen an die Nacht*, whose poetic speakers also yearn to escape the anguish of the present. Unlike Novalis's speakers, however, Memnon does not yearn for death. He longs not for the black of night but for the light of day: "to unite myself with you, Goddess of Morn," he cries. In Mayrhofer's poetic vocabulary, the realm of the sun, which radiates light and warmth, is the realm of art – an allegorical relation developed in his *Heliopolis* cycle.[43] Memnon's yearning to reunite with the goddess of dawn symbolizes not only the alienated poet's desire to escape the painful present but also his longing for the "divine" gift of artistic inspiration.

Mayrhofer's pessimism, which ultimately led him to hurl himself out an upper-story window, kept him from believing that his cherished goal was attainable. While high Romantic writers like Friedrich Schlegel optimistically pursued their ideals, Mayrhofer and other Biedermeier-era poets harbored few illusions. To this post-revolutionary generation, regaining lost unity with the external world, or within the self, no longer seemed possible. Permanently merging with the divine, as in Ganymede's apotheosis, could barely be imagined. The myth of "Vocal Memnon," who yearns for reunion with Eos and finds relief only in periodic outbursts, captured the plight of both Mayrhofer and his late-Romantic generation.

Biographical and musical evidence suggests that Schubert was drawn to the Memnon myth for different reasons than Mayrhofer's. Memnon's fate is unlikely to have resonated as personally with the composer as with the poet. It was not until 1822 when he contracted syphilis that Schubert became deeply despondent. In March 1817, when he wrote "Memnon," he had little cause for complaint. Temporarily liberated from teaching duties at his father's school, and gaining confidence in his abilities, he could expect to enjoy both composing and the company of his friends for years to come.

Schubert composed his setting of "Memnon" at least partially as an expression of friendship. He often set poems by his friends, and he chose Mayrhofer texts more frequently than those of any poet except Goethe. In this instance, he may have written the song as a gesture of sympathy for his friend's suffering. Although Schubert's letters indicate Mayrhofer was a hypochondriac (which, if true, would likely have strained their relation as housemates), in 1817 the friendship remained close.[44] (The two men were to part ways several years later.)

Schubert may also have had more self-serving reasons for setting "Memnon." As noted, he may have hoped to entice Vogl to perform his songs,[45] to explore techniques of dramatic music, to show his operatic potential, to

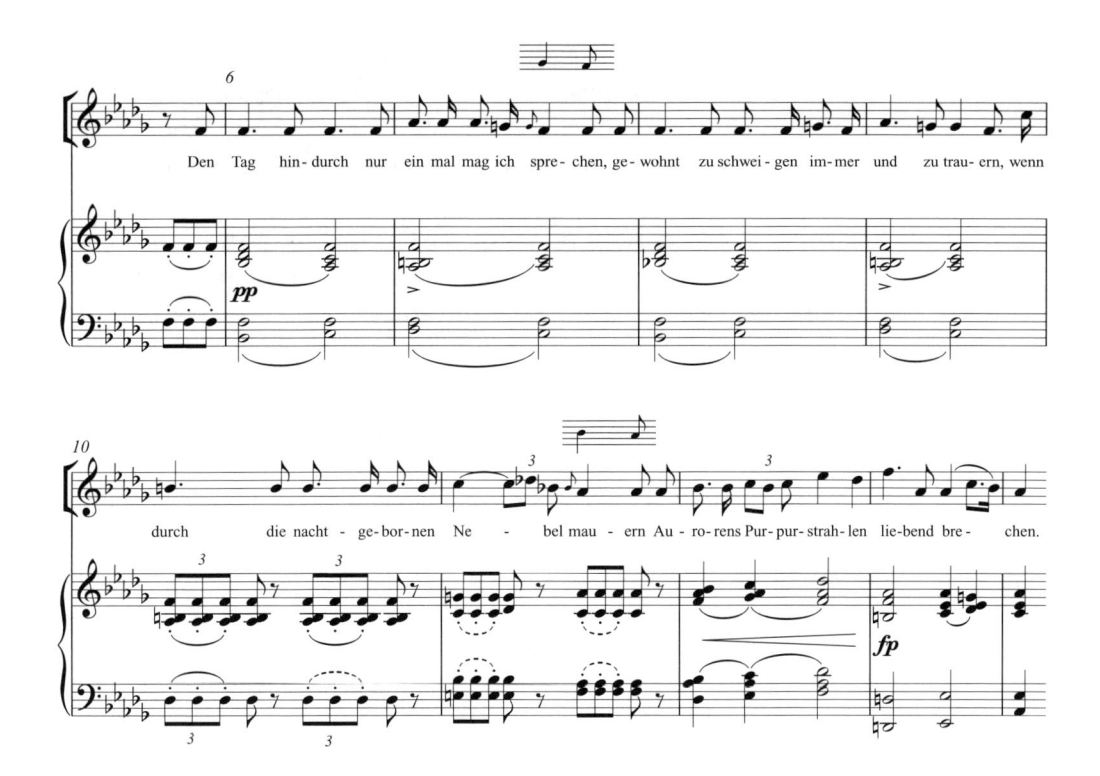

Example 1.1a Schubert, "Memnon," D. 541, mm. 6–14

emulate (or compete with) Gluck and Mozart, and to elevate the Lied. In addition, he may have recognized the specific relevance of the song's mythical content – the fallen hero's longing to reunite with his divine mother, thereby escaping present misery and regaining lost happiness – to what so many eighteenth- and nineteenth-century German writers and artists perceived as the alienated condition of modern man.

Beyond borrowing from Greek myth (which in turn borrows from Egyptian statuary), Schubert draws on operatic compositional procedures to dramatize Mayrhofer's formulation of the antique myth. This is evident in the vocal line's fluid mixture of declamatory and lyrical passages. Lines 1–2, for example, are monotonic and speech-like, while lines 3–4, with a wider melodic range and decorative triplet rhythms, are more songlike (Example 1.1a). The fusion of styles recalls the flexible vocal writing in the large scene-complexes of Gluck's reform operas.

Schubert's reverence for Gluck's works is well documented. According to Spaun, a performance of Gluck's *Iphigénie en Tauride* "shook [Schubert] to the depths of his being. The impression made by that evening was for him a never-to-be-forgotten one; its outcome was the keenest study of all Gluck's scores which, for years, quite enraptured Schubert."[46] Spaun claimed that Schubert could play all of Gluck's operas "almost from memory,"[47] and Anton Holzapfel noted that Schubert "went through the whole of Gluck"[48] and often played portions of these works to his friends. Given his intimate knowledge of this music, it is unsurprising that, in a song with an antique subject, Schubert would adopt a flexible arioso style reminiscent of Gluck's mythological operas – works he allegedly felt belonged to a happy time that had vanished.

What is surprising, perhaps, is the particular operatic *topos* to which Schubert alludes: the oracle. Various aspects of lines 1–2 evoke conventional operatic means of representing voices from another world.[49] Both the abrupt tonal shift and the sudden change in accompaniment texture at the start of the vocal line call attention to the otherworldly sound source. The voice repeats a single pitch in a quasi-psalmodic manner, with the overall melodic range confined to a minor 3rd and the tessitura comparatively low. The vocal declamation is syllabic, the mode minor, the dynamics quiet, the tempo slow. The homophonic piano accompaniment, all in half notes, evokes a brass or wind choir. A recurring coloristic augmented 6th chord infuses the solemn atmosphere with mystery.

Many of these stylistic elements appear in the famous oracle scenes of Gluck and Mozart operas, e.g., *Telemaco, Alceste, Idomeneo*, and *Don Giovanni*. The compositional conventions for presenting otherworldly voices had begun to develop as early as the sixteenth century and can be traced through the operatic works of Claudio Monteverdi, Alessando Scarlatti, George Frideric Handel, Jean-Baptiste Lully, Jean-Philippe Rameau, Gluck, Mozart, and Gioachino Rossini, as well as through certain songs by Schubert (e.g. "Der Tod und das Mädchen").[50] The numinous voice might be that of a god, like Apollo in *Alceste*, or a representative of the Underworld, like the Commendatore in *Don Giovanni*. Either way, the voice typically emanates from the mouth of an immense statue in a temple or other sacred space. Often the statue glows when it speaks, signaling its divinity, and its oracular pronouncement is brief.

Similarities between these operatic oracles and the colossal statue of "Vocal Memnon" illuminate the opening lines of Schubert's setting. Like traditional oracular voices, Memnon pronounces about fate. An important difference, of course, is that it is *his* fate. Mayrhofer casts the ancient myth as a monologue, with the oracular voice, drawn forth by divinity (or genius), that of the self-conscious, suffering artist. Accordingly, Schubert takes the oracular topos out of its usual operatic context and introduces it into a solo genre, the Lied. The traditionally public pronouncement becomes a prompt for soliloquy.[51]

As the oracular pronouncement morphs into self-reflection and fantasy, the vocal style changes, reflecting the transformation of Memnon spurred by the arrival of his heavenly mother. In mm. 6–9, the psalmodic style suggests that Memnon's voice sounds from another world. Like the monotonic music of Death in "Der Tod und das Mädchen," the vocal line's repeated pitches seem to emanate from an inanimate being incapable of the lyricism of the living; the line rises slightly, only to fall back to its initial pitch. In mm. 10–14, however, the melodic range expands to a major 6th, and the line assumes a more conventional arch shape. Two decorative triplet patterns, echoing the repeated triplet rhythms in the accompaniment (and in the piano introduction), enhance the lyrical effect. As the harmony moves away from the key of B-flat minor (vi) toward a full cadence in A-flat major (V), the melody becomes more active and Liedlike, climaxing on a high F at the word "liebend." Eos's loving embrace brings her son – and his music – back to life. The lyrical, songlike quality is maintained in mm. 17–29 through vocal sequences and arpeggios, triplet rhythms, an undulating melodic line, phrase repetition, and extended harmonic stability in F major.

Memnon's transformation results from the arrival of dawn, first heard in the gently pulsating music of the D-flat major piano introduction. As in "Der Tod und das Mädchen" (also composed in 1817), the introduction serves a dramatic role, suggesting an unidentified presence to which the vocal persona responds. In "Der Tod und das Mädchen," the funereal tones of the introduction (later revealed to be Death's music) incite the maiden's frightened reaction; before long she succumbs to his advances, and his pavane rhythms. A similar pattern occurs in "Memnon," although the introductory music differs markedly in mood. The introduction ends with a sharp disjunction, but then seems to influence the material that follows. Aspects of the introduction – appoggiaturas, triplet rhythms, and major mode – increasingly surface in Memnon's music. When the introductory D-flat major music returns as an interlude in the key of A-flat (mm. 14–16), the sun seems to have flooded the sky; Memnon waxes lyrical as he reflects on the illusion of his happiness.

The truth erupts in the third stanza. Once again, the vocal line becomes declamatory, with repeated pitches and constricted melodic movement, now over a tremolo accompaniment (cf. mm. 6–9 and 31–33). This music has less the feel of an operatic oracle, however, than an *accompagnato* – a style suggesting agitation, not otherworldliness. Unlike the first stanza, which conveys emotional uplift through an ascending vocal line, the third stanza

Example 1.1b Schubert, "Memnon," D. 541, mm. 50–57

captures Memnon's anguish with a plunge into the song's deepest vocal register at the phrase "deep in whose heart serpents gnaw" (mm. 33–35). Whereas the first stanza moves upward and outward in focus, the third stanza moves downward and inward.

In a seeming reflection of heroic resistance to death and despair, the vocal line leaps up an astounding major 13th to a high F (m. 35), the climactic pitch of the first stanza. The "colossal" effort pays off, at least to the extent that the last line of stanza three (which, as Lawrence Kramer notes, concludes with the same descending fourth as "Herzen Schlangen wühlen" but an octave higher) never sinks back into the deep vocal register.[52] The F minor tonality, a darkening of the F major tonality in stanza two, indicates that the illusion of happiness has been stripped away.

As Memnon expresses his desire to reunite with Eos, the harmony returns to D-flat major, the key associated with the goddess from the song's introduction. The music remains in that key throughout the fourth stanza and postlude. This, together with the triplet rhythms in the accompaniment and vocal part (also linked to Eos), suggests that Memnon to some extent achieves the unity he seeks. In Mayrhofer's poem, his desire remains a fantasy; in Schubert's setting, the fantasy is realized in music that exudes both lyricism and simplicity (Example 1.1b). Interestingly, no disjunction separates the end of the fourth stanza and the piano postlude, an altered version of the introduction. The continuous chords in triplet rhythms carry over into the postlude, connecting Memnon's final stanza and the music of Eos. The song ends not with a sense of continued yearning but with completion.

In sum, Schubert dramatizes the myth of lost paradise, as formulated by Mayrhofer, with contrasting vocal styles in a tonally closed, through-composed structure. As the operatic finally merges with the Lied-like, Memnon seems to approach the object of his longing: restored happiness. Was this intended as a subtle hint to Vogl? A gesture of encouragement to Mayrhofer? A statement about Schubert's own compositional inclinations? Whatever his motives, the masterful setting of "Memnon" suggests that in 1817, Schubert, unlike the melancholy poet, could imagine a return to paradise. The joining of classical opera and romantic art song, reflecting the reunion of Memnon and Eos, as well as the budding relationship between Vogl and Schubert, gave rise to a Lied that offers intimations of transcendence.

"Die Götter Griechenlands," D. 677

"Die Götter Griechenlands," a Schiller setting composed two years after "Memnon," presents a more pessimistic perspective on the lost paradise myth. Both versions of the song (the second resulting from several small but significant changes to the first) leave the listener feeling unsettled.[53] Neither version concludes with a strong tonic resolution. In the first version (D. 677a), the piano accompaniment ends not on a root position tonic chord but rather on an 8/6 sonority over the dominant (Example 1.2a). The tonic pitch (A) sounds only in the vocal part on the weak second beat of the penultimate measure. In the second version (D. 677b), the accompaniment does close with a root position tonic harmony – a modification that has

Example 1.2a Schubert, "Die Götter Griechenlands," 1st version, D. 677a, mm. 48–53

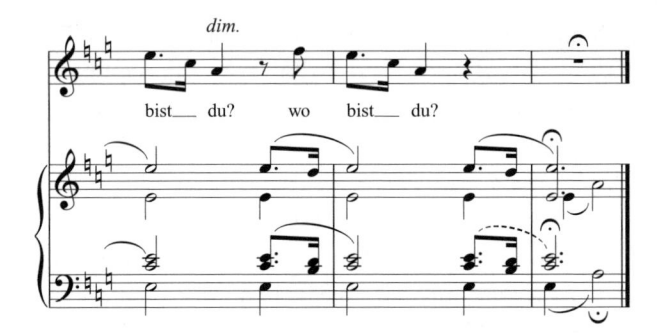

Example 1.2b Schubert, "Die Götter Griechenlands," 2nd version, D. 677b, mm. 50–52

elicited criticism from various writers[54] – but here too the resolution is relegated to a weak beat and is immediately preceded by the 8/6 sonority rather than a dominant 7th (Example 1.2b). Thus in the conclusions to both versions, Schubert avoids a strong authentic cadence. While the vocal line in "Memnon" eventually descends to the tonic over a clear V-I progression (echoed several times in the postlude), the vocal line in "Die Götter Griechenlands" reaches the tonic with little or no sense of harmonic resolution. The vocal protagonist's repeated question ("Fair world, where are you?"), set to a falling melodic line over the unstable 8/6 chord, is shown to be more rhetorical than real. No answer is expected, and certainly none is provided.

By the end of "Memnon," the statue achieves at least temporary reunion with the goddess of dawn, conveyed musically through his adoption of the introduction's triplet rhythms and D-flat major tonality, as well as his music's increased lyricism. The anonymous protagonist of "Die Götter Griechenlands," however, remains in the same position at the song's conclusion as at its opening – yearning for the beautiful lost world. Numerous aspects of the final measures – the unanswered question, sustained 8/6 harmony, lack of a clear authentic cadence, minor mode, and diminuendo from pianissimo to silence – together create an impression of open-endedness and continued melancholic longing.

Curiously, the song (both versions) also conveys overall balance and unity; the return of the opening poetic lines and musical material in the latter part of the setting results in a rounded A B A' form. This quasi-symmetrical structure produces a strikingly different effect than the throughcomposed layout of "Memnon." (In "Memnon," the postlude revives material from the introduction, but the vocal part does not include any strophic repetitions or variations.) One might expect that, because of its continuously new music, throughcomposition would be better able to express endless yearning than a rounded form. Yet, as the settings of "Memnon" and "Die Götter Griechenlands" reveal, in certain cases the opposite may hold true. A succession of new musical sections can suggest the protagonist's transformation, while a return to the opening musical material may indicate a static state, resistant to change.[55] In "Die Götter Griechenlands," the rounded form does not detract from the endless longing suggested by the song's open-endedness. Instead, it supports the pessimistic tenor of the poetic message: escaping the barren modern world and returning to the idyllic past is impossible.

The combination of open-endedness and roundedness in both versions of "Die Götter Griechenlands" raises the intriguing and controversial question of whether the song can legitimately be considered a "fragment." On Schubert's autograph manuscript, the song is headed "Strophe von Schiller / Schöne Welt wo bist du?" But when published in 1848 in volume 42 of the *Nachlass*, it appeared with the title "Fragment aus dem Gedichte: Die Götter Griechenlands." The change originated with the publisher Anton Diabelli, not Schubert. On those grounds alone, one might be tempted to abandon the newer heading, which remains one of the song's familiar titles. Moreover, various writers have deemed the term "Fragment" misleading, if not entirely false.[56] Others, howeer, have claimed the term has merit.[57] The disagreement sheds light on the song's combination of open-endedness and roundedness, as well as the oft-criticized changes that Schubert made to the first version.

The song is certainly a "fragment" as the setting of a single stanza extracted from a long poem. This does not imply that Schubert ever planned to set more or all of the stanzas, a scenario for which no documentary evidence exists. As several writers have noted, the stanza he selected encapsulates the poem's central message and can easily stand alone; Schubert did not need to set the other stanzas. Thus while the text of Schubert's "Die Götter Griechenlands" might justifiably be viewed as a fragment of Schiller's poem, the song is not incomplete – although, paradoxically, incompleteness understood in a somewhat different way (i.e., open-endedness) is one of its most salient qualities. This observation holds true most obviously for the first version of the song, but also for the second.

The song's open-endedness (conveyed by the unanswered question and missing or weak harmonic resolution of the final measures) more significantly qualifies it as a fragment. Like the Romantic literary fragments of Novalis and Friedrich Schlegel, "Die Götter Griechenlands" crosses the boundaries of conventional expression to offer a glimpse of the infinite. The fragmentary quality created by the inconclusive ending hints at the existence of a greater, un-fragmented, and inexpressible reality. As Gramit writes, "Schiller's poem is anything but open-ended, but Schubert's single strophe, modified to end with its opening question, reaches beyond Schiller's expression of noble sadness to imply continuous searching but irreversible loss."[58] Like a Romantic fragment, Schubert's setting stands as a symbol of something immeasurably greater, which defies definition. It attempts to express the inexpressible, necessarily falling short of achieving its goal.

Gramit suggests that by extracting and modifying the single stanza, Schubert not only radically compresses the essence of Schiller's poem but also subtly alters its meaning. The change in emphasis becomes apparent through a comparison of Schiller's stanza with Schubert's song text.

SCHILLER "Die Götter Griechenlands"
    Schöne Welt, wo bist du? Kehre wieder,
    Holdes Blüthenalter der Natur!
    Ach, nur in dem Feenland der Lieder
    Lebt noch deine fabelhafte Spur.
    Ausgestorben trauert das Gefilde,
    Keine Gottheit zeigt sich meinem Blick,
    Ach! Von jenem lebenwarmen Bilde
    Blieb der Schatten nur zurück.

SCHUBERT "Die Götter Griechenlands"
    Schöne Welt, wo bist du?
    Kehre wieder, holdes Blüthenalter der Natur,
    kehre wieder, holdes Blüthenalter der Natur!

Ach, nur in dem Feenland der Lieder
lebt noch deine fabelhafte Spur,
ach, nur in dem Feenland der Lieder
lebt noch deine fabelhafte Spur.
Ausgestorben trauert das Gefilde,
keine Gottheit zeigt sich meinem Blick
Ach! Von jenem lebenwarmen Bilde
blieb der Schatten nur zurück,
blieb der Schatten nur zurück.
Schöne Welt, wo bist du?
Kehre wieder, holdes Blüthenalter der Natur,
kehre wieder, holdes Blüthenalter der Natur!
Schöne Welt, wo bist du?
wo bist du?
. . .

SCHILLER "The Gods of Greece"
    Fair world, where are you? Return again,
    Sweet springtime of nature!
    Alas, only in the magic land of song
    Does your fabled memory live on.
    The deserted fields mourn,
    No god reveals himself to me;
    Of that warm, living image
    Only a shadow has remained.

SCHUBERT "The Gods of Greece"
    Fair world, where are you?
    Return again, sweet springtime of nature!
    Return again, sweet springtime of nature!
    Alas, only in the magic land of song
    Does your fabled memory live on.
    Alas, only in the magic land of song
    Does your fabled memory live on.
    The deserted fields mourn,
    No god reveals himself to me;
    Of that warm, living image
    Only a shadow has remained,
    Only a shadow has remained.
    Fair world, where are you?
    Return again, sweet springtime of nature!
    Return again, sweet springtime of nature!
    Fair world, where are you?
    Where are you?

Through abundant line repetitions, Schubert creates a far greater sense of urgency than Schiller's original stanza. The protagonist seems more desperate, more alienated. By bringing back the first two lines at the end, and then paring these down to the first line alone, and then a fragment of the first line, Schubert casts a spotlight on what he perceives to be the poem's core: a simple three-word expression of calamitous loss.

The 16-stanza poem "Die Götter Griechenlands" from which Schubert drew his song text is itself a revised version (one might say a "fragment") of an earlier 25-stanza poem bearing the same title. Schubert in effect creates a third version with ties to each of the first two but its own distinct character.

The first version of the poem, a relatively early work that Schiller wrote in 1788 in Weimar while under the influence of Goethe, Herder, and Christoph Martin Wieland, sharply contrasts the ancient Greek world and the modern world. The first eighteen stanzas focus on the idealized age of antiquity, a time of love, joy, art, beauty, and virtue, when the gods ruled and men were without cares. A wealth of mythological references helps convey the age's vibrant life. The remaining seven stanzas (the first of which ultimately became Schubert's song text) redirect attention to the stultifying conditions of the present. In modern times, thanks to the emergence of Christian monotheism and Enlightenment rationalism, the ancient gods have been banished, and nature demythologized. Through the influence of Newtonian physics, the universe has come to seem purely mechanical, "like the dead stroke of a pendulum-clock." Images of deadness abound, e.g., "Of that warm, living image / Only a shadow has remained." In the Greek world, truth and beauty were united; now they are separated. Confronted by his solitary existence within a fragmented world, modern man finds comfort only in his ability to imagine an improvement.[59] But the poem offers no suggestion that the world will enter a new Golden Age; the poetic speaker mourns a permanent loss.

The first version of "Die Götter Griechenlands" met with harsh criticism for its anti-Christian qualities. Several years later, Schiller produced a second version (written 1793, published 1800) that softens the poetic message and reflects his maturing philosophy of art. Reduced to sixteen stanzas (with offensive and superfluous stanzas removed, and two new ones added), the second version conveys a markedly less pessimistic outlook. Whereas the first version suggests that the modern world possesses no advantages over antiquity, or indeed *any* redeeming qualities, the second version is more positive. The new final stanza presents a compromise. Schiller scholar Lesley Sharpe explains, "The gods have withdrawn from the world but their perfection is preserved through art and so their immortality is assured. Even the pain of loss can thus be transmuted through art into something beautiful and permanent."[60] The new last lines of the poem – "What lives on undying in song / Must perish in life" – thus provide some comfort.

The revised poem, with its focus on beauty and art, not polytheism, soon came to be viewed as a classic expression of modern man's perception of the Greek ideal. As Sharpe writes, "its rejection of the dry-as-dust rationalism of some Enlightenment thought made it almost a revolutionary document. Certainly it helped to shape the consciousness of the Romantic generation, of Hölderlin and Novalis, as well as of Hegel."[61] To this group, we may add Schubert.

It is not surprising that Schubert chose to set the twelfth stanza (originally the nineteenth) from Schiller's poem. In both versions, the stanza appears at a critical juncture – the moment when focus shifts from the past to the modern world. This stanza is also more lyrical and emotionally expressive than the others, which abound in mythological imagery and philosophical ideas. Schiller himself envisioned musical settings of several of the poem's stanzas.[62] Given its critical structural position, elegiac tone, and reference to the "magic land of song," the twelfth stanza was surely one of them.

While Schubert drew his song text from the second version of the poem (evident from the second version's wording, e.g., "der Schatten" instead of the original "das Gerippe"), in certain respects it seems more closely aligned with the first version. Although the song text does not convey the first version's anti-Christian sentiment, it does share its pessimism. The last stanza of the second version, with its tribute to art, offers some comfort. Schubert's song text, however, expresses sadness and resignation, emphasized by line repetition and the gradual paring down of the poem to its core unanswered question. As Reinhold Hammerstein points out, even the protagonist's assertion that the beautiful world lives on in song conveys a sense of anguish: "*Alas*, only in the magic land of song / Does your fabled memory live on" (emphasis added)[63]

Schubert's text, then, as Schubert scholar John Reed writes, is "[n]ot so much an ode to the glory of Greece as a lament for that lost paradise of the Romantic imagination."[64] The fact that neither the poetic speaker nor "die Götter" are identified in text or title (in contrast to Memnon and Eos) suggests that the idealized Greek world has become an abstraction. Unlike "Memnon," "Die Götter Griechenlands" does not recreate a particular antique myth. The theme of searching for lost paradise emerges not from ties between mythological characters but from the relationship of the modern protagonist to antiquity itself. Consequently, the protagonist seems further removed from his object of longing. It is not the actual Greek world for which he yearns, but rather what, by the early nineteenth century, it had come to symbolize: an ideal state of simplicity, naturalness, and unity.[65]

In striving to convey endless longing for a lost paradise, Schubert's song text embodies the essence of the Romantic fragment. The single strophe – diminutive yet profoundly meaningful – reduces itself to its core, then fades into silence. There is no definitive end but instead a suggestion that the process of reduction continues indefinitely, beyond the human mind's apprehension or comprehension.

Schubert's musical setting expresses the fragmentary nature of the text in multiple ways. Harmony plays a particularly important role on both local and structural levels. Consider the 8/6 harmony over the dominant heard at the beginning, in the middle, and at the end of the song (passages that, according to Nicholas Temperly, reveal the influence of the trio from Beethoven's *Symphony No. 7*) (Example 0.1).[66] Implying a tonic 6/4 but missing the tonic pitch, the chord hovers in an ambiguous harmonic realm.[67] The chord's voicing obscures its tonal function. Schubert sounds the note E in three voices of the accompaniment, giving the chord a dominant quality, but the 8/6 sonority does not resolve conventionally to a dominant 7/5.[68] In the first version of the song, the 8/6 sonority eventually absorbs the tonic pitch (in the voice) and proceeds directly to the tonic major. The effect is not so much of dominant to tonic as of tonic minor to tonic major. At the end of the song, no such modal shift occurs; the 8/6 sonority reasserts itself and fades into silence. In the second version, the 8/6 chord does move to a root position tonic minor harmony, but the "resolution," if one can call it that, occurs only on the weak second beat and without a preceding dominant 7th. Thus in both versions of the song, the 8/6 sonority has an empty, ambiguous quality.[69] The absence of the tonic pitch suggests fragmentation, emptiness, and loss.[70]

A more familiar harmonic means by which Schubert conveys the text's fragmentary quality involves modal contrasts. As in songs such as "Gute Nacht" and "Frühlingstraum" from *Winterreise*, D. 911 (nos. 1 and 11, respectively), the minor mode helps evoke the harsh reality of the present – here a godless state.[71] The major mode, on the other hand, conjures a lost world of youth, nature, fantasy, and divinity. In m. 4, the harmony shifts from A minor to A major to signal the hint of hopefulness in the protagonist's plea "Return again" (a hopefulness that is subtly undermined by the substitution of F-sharp minor for A major sonority at "wieder" during the line repetition – cf. mm. 6 and 10 – and ultimately by the return to A minor). The unexpected move to F-sharp major (instead of the subdominant) at m. 15 lends the reference to song a magical aura;[72] the shift from F-sharp major to F-sharp minor when the lines are repeated beginning at m. 19, however, suggests art's inadequacy as a substitute for the lost beautiful world. The move to C major at the line "No god reveals himself to me" helps conjure that distant world in which the gods reigned; the return to A minor ushers in the present world in which only shadows of the divine remain.[73] Through frequent changes between parallel and relative keys, Schubert creates a kaleidoscopic reality, marked by abrupt shifts between fantasy and disillusionment.

The fragmentary nature of the text – and, by extension, of the protagonist's modern world – is also conveyed by Schubert's general avoidance of root position V-I progressions in the tonic key, which would lend stability to the setting as a whole. Such progressions occur only at the phrase "Return again, sweet springtime of nature!"[74] As noted, both versions of the song lack a strong final authentic cadence.

Other techniques too play a role. In continually returning to the fifth scale degree, the wavering neighbor-note motive (E–D–E) of the opening seems to symbolize the protagonist's unappeasable quest. The voice descends to the tonic in measure 4, suggesting that the protagonist expects no answer, but the accompaniment remains on E, as if to remind us that a question, even if rhetorical, hangs in the air. The repetition of motivic fragments suggests a disjointed world,[75] as do contrasts between vocal styles – e.g., declamatory for the question, songlike for the protagonist's plea.[76]

Given the many ways that Schubert's setting conveys fragmentation, of what significance is its rounded A B A' form? What led him to choose this more traditional song form over throughcomposition? Instead of counteracting those aspects of the setting that suggest fragmentariness, the rounded form supports them. Unlike Memnon, the protagonist of "Die Götter Griechenlands" undergoes no transformation, even temporarily. He may envision the idyllic past, but he does not re-experience its bliss. Indeed, nothing really changes during the course of the song; there is no dramatic action. The return to the bleak opening material confirms the permanence of the protagonist's loss.[77]

That opening material serves an entirely different function than the introductory music of "Memnon." Instead of symbolizing the desired "other," the first four measures of "Die Götter Griechenlands" conjure the suffering self, transfixed by Romantic *Sehnsucht*. Unlike "Memnon," the Schiller setting has no piano introduction. The voice participates in the opening measures, strengthening their association with the mournful protagonist. The return of the opening material at the end of the song confirms the hopelessness of his quest; the blissful past ultimately yields to the brutal present. Schubert's altering of the song's final measure (as well as the two earlier corresponding measures) by "resolving" the 8/6 sonority to a root position tonic harmony supports the pessimism implied by the rounded form (and implicit in the voice's descent to the tonic). The change, far from weakening the sense of yearning, reveals its endlessness. The protagonist is trapped in his A minor world with no way of escape.

2 | Goethe, Wolf, and the lure of immortality

The idealized conception of antiquity espoused by Winckelmann and Goethe persisted well into the nineteenth century, providing a firm foundation for institutionalized philhellenism. Over time, however, burgeoning knowledge about ancient Greek history and culture, changing political and social conditions in modern-day Europe, and the revolutionary aesthetics and ideas of figures such as Wagner and Nietzsche gave rise to new perspectives on antiquity which, in the latter part of the century, vied with, and in some contexts supplanted, the traditional conception. The German obsession with Greek antiquity did not weaken with the passing decades. Antiquity's increased remoteness actually seemed to intensify nostalgic longing for its recovery. The powerful expressivity of certain mid and late nineteenth-century *Antikenlieder* suggests that yearning for ancient Greece from the vantage point of the post-Romantic era was often compounded by a strong if ambivalent attraction to preceding periods of philhellenism and their aesthetic creations.

Although interest in antiquity remained robust throughout the nineteenth century, it must be admitted that no composer after Schubert produced nearly as many classical songs as he did (Table 2.1). There are several likely reasons. Some nineteenth-century composers, such as Felix Mendelssohn, Schumann, and Mahler, were primarily drawn to Romantic topics derived from medieval legend, balladry, and folk song. Moreover, the eighteenth-century compositional idioms of mythological operas by Gluck and Mozart, which served as models for Schubert's *Antikenlieder*, rarely inspired imitations from later Romantics, who had grown used to the expressivity of a more chromatic and dissonant harmonic language.

Perhaps most significantly, as philhellenism metamorphosed from the private passion of individuals to the public face of institutions, aesthetics yielded to academics as the primary arena for enagement with the ancient world. The relative dearth of *Antikenlieder* composed after 1830 mirrors that of contemporaneous poems on classical subjects; while scholarship involving the ancient world flourished in German universities and museums, poets largely inclined towards other topics.[1] There are some notable exceptions. Hölderlin, the nineteenth-century German writer perhaps most devoted

Table 2.1 German songs of antiquity composed after 1830

Composer	Title	Text	Composed
Berg, Alban	Grenzen der Menschheit	Goethe	1902
Brahms, Johannes	An eine Äolsharfe (Op. 19/5)	Mörike	1858–9
	Die Kränze (Op. 46/1)#	Daumer	c.1864
	Die Mainacht (Op. 43/2)*	Hölty	1866
	Die Schale der Vergessenheit (Op. 46/3)*	Hölty	1868
	Sapphische Ode (Op. 94/4)*	Schmidt	1884
Franz, Robert	Cupido, loser Knabe (Op. 33/4)	Goethe	1864 pub
Kinkel, Johanna Mathieux	Sehnsucht nach Griechenland (Op. 6/1)	Geibel	1837
Loewe, Carl	[Auf sich selbst ("Es sagen mir")#	Anacreon	1815?]
	[An die Leier#	Anacreon	1815?]
	[Auf sich selbst ("Weil ich steblich")#	Anacreon	1815?]
	An die Grille (Op. 9, ix, 5)#	Anacreon	1835
	An Aphrodite: Ode der Sappho (Op. 9, ix, 4)#	Sappho	1836
	An die Muse: Hymn an die Kalliope#	Dionysius	1842
	Ganymed (Op. 81/5; 4vv)	Goethe	1836–7
Mendelssohn, Fanny	Die Mainacht (Op. 9/6)*	Hölty	1838
Pfitzner, Hans	Venus Mater (Op. 11/4)	Dehmel	1901
Strauss, Richard	Gesang der Apollopriesterin for soprano and orchestra	Bodmann	1896–7
	Frühlingsfeier	Heine	1903–6
Wolf, Hugo	An eine Äolsharfe	Mörike	1888
	Anakreons Grab*	Goethe	1888
	Prometheus	Goethe	1889
	Grenzen der Menschheit	Goethe	1889
	Ganymed	Goethe	1889
	Genialisch Treiben	Goethe	1889

* – employs Greek poetic meters and/or verse forms
\# – translated from the Greek original

to the Hellenic world, authored many poems that draw inspiration from antique culture. Virtually none of them, however, were set to music during the nineteenth century.[2] Not only did the structural and syntactical complexities of Hölderlin's rhapsodic verse prove resistant to songs settings, but his poetic gift went largely unrecognized until the twentieth century.[3] Müller wrote over fifty poetic "Griechenlieder" during the years 1821–26, attesting to his support of the Greek independence movement and fascination with Greek culture, but composers sidestepped them (unsurprisingly, given their elongated lines and non-stanzaic structures).[4] As noted, Mayrhofer expressed enthusiasm for Greek antiquity, but only Schubert set his poems, both classical and non-classical.[5] While a fair number of nineteenth-century writers – Justinus Kerner, Uhland, Grillparzer, Heine, Eduard Mörike, Nietzsche, Hans Schmidt, Richard Dehmel, and Emanuel, Freiherr von Bodmann, among others – occasionally wrote poems with classical subjects, forms, or meters,[6] only a handful of these attracted the attention of Lied composers.

On occasion, composers turned to modern translations of ancient verse, various collections of which were published during the nineteenth century. Mörike produced an anthology of Greek and Latin poetry entitled *Classische Blumenlese* (1840). Similarly, Georg Friedrich Daumer compiled the collection *Polydora, ein weltpoetisches Liederbuch* (1855), the first and most extensive section of which, *Antike Musen: Hellas*, contains translations of 135 ancient Greek poems intended to familiarize the German public "with... this lost paradise of aesthetic-humanistic culture."[7] As with newly written poems on classical subjects, however, translations of ancient verse inspired comparatively few Lied settings. Brahms used Daumer's translated poem "Hier ob dem Eingang seid befestiget" for his song "Die Kränze," Op. 46, no. 1, while Loewe employed translations by Carl von Blankensee for "An Aphrodite" (text by Sappho) and "An die Grille" (text by Anacreon). Thus most *Antikenlieder* composed after 1830 have texts by eighteenth-century poets, particularly Goethe and Ludwig Heinrich Christoph Hölty.

The changing nature of philhellenism during the nineteenth century is evident in both the comparatively small number of poems on classical subjects from that period and the nature of the poems that nineteenth-century composers chose to set. Beginning in the late eighteenth century, philological investigations that ultimately helped establish the field of *Altertumswissenschaft* sparked interest in ancient verse forms and meters, leading various poets to attempt modern German imitations.[8] These poems inspired several nineteenth-century song settings. Brahms, although unschooled as a youth in Latin and Greek as well as ancient literature, was intrigued by the metrical/rhythmic challenges posed by such literary experiments, as revealed by three of his solo Lieder – "Die Mainacht," "Die Schale der Vergessenheit," and "Sapphische Ode" – whose texts employ classical meters.[9] "Die Schale der Vergessenheit" and his setting "An eine Äolsharfe" involve motives and imagery from Greek mythology and literature. "Die Kränze," as noted, derives from an ancient Greek poem. Fanny Mendelssohn also composed a setting of "Die Mainacht," while Wolf produced one of "An eine Äolsharfe" (which he introduced with the same Horatian epigraph that had prefaced Mörike's poem, thus emphasizing its ties to antiquity). The text of Wolf's "Anakreons Grab," in addition to using the death of an ancient Greek poet as its principal subject, is written in the form of a classical epigram. Loewe's half-dozen settings of verses by Anacreon, Sappho, and Dionysius, two of which include the original Greek in addition to the German translation,[10] convey a similar desire to engage with the ancient world through scholarship as much as through imagination.

Beyond revealing an attraction to classical forms and meters, *Antikenlieder* from the later nineteenth century reveal the influence of pessimistic philosophies that had gained prominence in German intellectual circles. Strauss's two large-scale works "Gesang der Apollopriesterin" and "Frühlingsfeier," for example, evoke Nietzsche's conceptions of the Apollonian and Dionysian as described in *The Birth of Tragedy*.[11] (Nietzsche's dual conceptions are indebted to Schopenhauer's contrast between representation and will. Although not sharing the earlier philosopher's attitude of pessimistic resignation, Nietzsche was deeply influenced by Schopenhauer, as suggested by Nietzsche's reissuing of the book in 1886 with the revised titled *The Birth of Tragedy, Or: Hellenism and Pessimism* (*Die Geburt der Tragödie, Oder: Griechentum und Pessimismus.*) The first song, composed for soprano and orchestra, as Lied scholar Peter Russell writes, "is set in a classical temple above a serene and idyllic pastoral landscape, and is a measured, richly harmonized paean sung by a priestess in homage to the divinity she serves, Apollo the sun god."[12] Strauss's music conveys noble serenity through its distinct brass, wind, and string sonorities, textural and rhythmic clarity, and strongly tonal harmonic language. The second song, by contrast, originally composed for voice and piano but later orchestrated, "depicts bare-breasted maenads storming wildly through the night woods with their torches in search of the dead Adonis, 'weeping and laughing and sobbing and screaming,' their cries climaxing each stanza."[13] The savagery of the scene is captured by surging rhythms, intense chromaticism and dissonance, and extended, wailing high notes in the vocal line.

Philosophical pessimism also influenced the *Antikenlieder* of Hugo Wolf, the late nineteenth-century song composer on whom the ancient classical world exerted the strongest pull, two of whose works form the focus of this chapter. Although Wolf composed only six songs directly linked to ancient Greek culture, they include some of his most powerful and emotionally charged works, affirming the continuing importance of antiquity for late Romantic Lieder. In this small but significant subset of his Lied oeuvre, Wolf grapples with competing notions of the ancient Greek world.[14] The songs engage the classical conception of Winckelmann and the mature Goethe, emphasizing balance, calm, and noble restraint, which had prevailed through much of the nineteenth century. They also evoke the more modern conception of Nietzsche, emphasizing unbridled passion, orgiastic frenzy, and heroic resistance. Wolf's *Antikenlieder* explore tensions between these opposing views, and examine their implications for the development of the modern Lied.

Music drama, song, and the rebirth of ancient Greek tragedy

Despite the very different historical and music-historical contexts of their works, Wolf and Schubert were attracted to *Antikenlieder* for similar reasons. Like Schubert, Wolf yearned to write opera, although he completed just one: the Spanish comic opera *Der Corregidor* (1896). As we have seen, the desire to compose music for the stage likely helped inspire Schubert's classical songs, which in various respects look back to the mythological operas of Gluck and Mozart, works he revered. Wolf, although a member of what conservative Viennese critic Eduard Hanslick termed the "Musical Secession" (which also included Mahler and Strauss), shared Schubert's enthusiasm for Gluck and Mozart. In reviewing an 1884 performance of Gluck's *Iphigénie en Tauride* by the Vienna Court Opera, he wrote:

Let Gluck, Mozart and Wagner be our holy trinity, first consolidated from three to one in Beethoven. It is them we have to thank for life's sublimest pleasure. Profoundest pain and loveliest rejoicing, the tortures of Prometheus and the euphoria of Nirvana, every human impulse is embraced for us in the music of these masters. It is through utter involvement in this music that we first become aware of our better selves. Their melodies are genii guiding us over the dull lethargy of everyday existence to a world such as we have imagined, perhaps, only in the blessed dreams of childhood.[15]

For Wolf, as for Schubert, the operas of Gluck and Mozart assumed a paradisiacal aura inspiring longing (and, in Wolf's case, also animosity for many modern operas). But while Wolf welcomed performances of their music (after the Vienna Court Opera's 1885 presentation of Gluck's *Alceste*, he noted with disgust that it had been a full seventy-five years since the work had last been staged there),[16] he was not inclined to adopt eighteenth-century operatic styles. It is the third figure in Wolf's "holy trinity" of esteemed opera composers who most strongly influenced (both positively and negatively) his mature Lieder. Enamored with Nietzsche's claim that "what can be done well today, what can be masterly, is only what is small,"[17] Wolf sought, with some ambivalence, to become the "Wagner of the Lied," an effort that, ironically, led audiences also to perceive him as the "new Schubert."[18] Beginning with the Mörike songbook of 1888, he introduced hallmarks of Wagner's music – extreme chromaticism, prose-like melodies, complex contrapuntal textures, etc. – within the compressed framework of the Lied, showing both indebtedness to and independence from the operatic composer he had worshiped for more than a decade.

In *The Birth of Tragedy*, Nietzsche (like Wagner) had associated Wagner's music dramas with the restoration of Greek classical tragedy.[19] Although Wagner drew the subjects of *Tannhäuser, Tristan und Isolde, Der Meistersinger von Nürnberg, Der Ring des Nibelungen,* and *Parsifal* from medieval romance and German folk tradition, for Nietzsche (then a young classical philologist and a great admirer of Wagner) the works embodied Dionysian energies and heralded artistic renewal in the modern age.

Let no one try to blight our faith in a yet-impending rebirth of Hellenic antiquity; for this alone gives us hope for a renovation and purification of the German spirit *through the fire magic of music.* What else could we name that might awaken any comforting expectations for the future in the midst of the desolation and exhaustion of contemporary culture? In vain we look for a single vigorously developed root, for a spot of fertile and healthy soil: everywhere there is dust and sand; everything has become rigid and languishes . . . But how suddenly the desert of our exhausted culture, just described in such gloomy terms, is changed when it is touched by the Dionysian magic! . . . Confused, our eyes look after what has disappeared; for what they see has been raised as from a depression into golden light, so full and green, so amply alive, immeasurable and full of yearning [emphasis added].[20]

Many of Wolf's mature Lieder, created within Wagner's magnetic field, might be viewed as attempts to capture in miniature Nietzsche's notion of ancient Greek tragedy. (Orchestral and choral versions of solo songs with piano accompaniment enabled Wolf and others to simulate the grandiose effects of opera, enhancing the Lied's prestige and attracting a wider audience.)[21] More practically, the Lied served as an alternative to opera while Wolf cast about for a libretto to his liking before settling years later on the text (by Rosa Mayreder, after Pedro Antonio de Alarcon's novel *El Sombrero de tres Pico*) for *Der Corregidor*.

If the desire to infuse his songs with musical and dramatic traits of Wagner's music dramas helped inspire Wolf's mature Lieder, so too did the verses of poets from the past. As indicated by his numerous Heine, Mörike, Eichendorff, and Goethe settings, Wolf was strongly attracted to poetry from the late eighteenth and early nineteenth centuries. Indeed, as a devotee of Wagner and "Music of the Future," he met with criticism for being insufficiently supportive of poets from his own time.[22] Wolf scholar Amanda Glauert rightly asserts that "Wolf's artistic identity should not be seen as exchangeable with that of the poets he set"; he could "maintain a critical distance" from them.²³ But literature of the past exerted an undeniable influence on the development of his mature compositional style. In his late Romantic Lieder, Wolf breathed new life into poems that many of his contemporaries saw as outmoded – monuments of German culture perhaps, but anachronisms nonetheless.

Wolf's *Antikenlieder* owe their existence especially to the poetry of Goethe, which he began setting in a virtual frenzy during the fall of 1888. (All but one of the fifty-one settings in his Goethe songbook date from between 27 October 1888 and 12 February 1889, supporting Hanslick's claim that "Hugo Wolf does not compose mere poems but one might say whole poets."²⁴) A century old and looking back to a culture that flourished several millennia earlier, Goethe's classical poems, Wolf discovered, could be reanimated in the post-Wagnerian era through song. Yet the songs betray the influence of later nineteenth-century modes of thought; Wolf maintained a "critical distance" from Goethe's conception of Greek antiquity. In these works, the composer scrutinizes eighteenth-century notions of the Hellenistic world, exploring their relevance to his own art and existence.

Wolf's absorption with Goethe's poetry might be linked to his reaction to the appearance of Nietzsche's *The Case of Wagner, A Musician's Problem* (May–August 1888; *Der Fall Wagner, Ein Musikanten-Problem*), which offered a radically different perspective on Wagner from that of *The Birth of Tragedy*. In a startling reversal, Nietzsche now wrote, "Is Wagner a human being at all? Isn't he rather a sickness? He makes sick whatever he touches – *he has made music sick*."²⁵ Wagner's music dramas are here presented as the epitome of modern culture yet also the height of decadence, and those who revere Wagner as deeply misguided. "One pays heavily for being one of Wagner's disciples," Nietzsche states over and over in his postscript to the book; "Wagner is bad for youths."²⁶ According to Wolf's friend Friedrich Eckstein, *The Case of Wagner* sent Wolf into a mental tailspin.²⁷

In attacking the idea of redemption through art, Nietzsche mocks Wagner for trying to "save" Goethe through his music:

> One knows Goethe's fate in moraline-sour, old-maidish Germany. He always seemed offensive to Germans; he had honest admirers only among Jewesses . . . What did they hold against Goethe? The "mount of Venus"; and that he had written *Venetian Epigrams*. Klopstock already felt called upon to deliver a moral sermon to him; there was a time when Herder liked to use the word "Priapus" whenever he spoke of Goethe. Even *Wilhelm Meister* was considered merely a symptom of decline, 'going to the dogs' as far as morals go . . . Above all, however, the higher virgins were indignant: all the petty courts, every kind of "Wartburg" in Germany crossed themselves against Goethe, against the 'unclean spirit' in Goethe.

This is the story Wagner put into music. He *redeems* Goethe, that goes without saying; but in such a way that at the same time he himself sides shrewdly with the higher virgin. Goethe is saved: a prayer saves him, a higher virgin *lures him to perfection*.

What Goethe might have thought of Wagner? – Goethe once asked himself what danger threatened all romantics: the fatality of romanticism. His answer was: 'suffocating of the rumination of moral and religious absurdities.' In brief: *Parsifal*.[28]

In Nietzsche's view, Wagner's "opera is the opera of redemption,"[29] and thus Wagner wishes to redeem the great German poet who contented himself with the earthly rather than the divine, the finite rather than the infinite. Through Wagner's intervention, Goethe could be turned into a proper Romantic – to Nietzsche, an absurdity. Given the temporal proximity of the publication of *Der Fall Wagners* and Wolf's immersion in Goethe's verse, as well as the mental turmoil into which Nietzsche's new book reportedly threw the composer, Nietzsche's critique of Wagner may have spurred Wolf to wrestle with Goethe's poetry and aesthetic ideals.

As suggested, Wolf's classical Lieder parallel Schubert's in various ways. The two composers set several of the same Goethe texts: "Ganymed," "Prometheus," and "Grenzen der Menschheit." Both composers created *Antikenlieder* in the shadow of opera, which informed many of their compositional decisions. Both too explored different perspectives on antiquity with which eighteenth- and nineteenth-century operas had been associated. Underlying these similarities is the theme of lost paradise.

In Schubert's early Romantic *Antikenlieder*, "paradise" connotes a broad variety of idealized states. The sought-after ideal might be identified with home, artistic inspiration, union with divinity, nature, unselfconsciousness, or antiquity itself. Wolf's late Romantic *Antikenlieder*, inflected by the attitudes and aesthetics of six additional decades, broach the theme somewhat differently. In his songs "Anakreons Grab" and "Grenzen der Menschheit," for example, Wolf turns to antiquity to express yearning for endless existence. Both songs explore the essence of mortality, or certainty of death. How does (and should) man respond to his exclusion from the paradise of immortality, sole province of the gods? What is the meaning of death? What are its implications for artistic creation, imitation, and tradition? "Anakreons Grab" tackles these questions through a complex dialectic between past and present infusing both text and music. Goethe ponders the fate of an ancient Greek poet and the long-lived literary tradition his works inspired, while Wolf explores the relevance of eighteenth-century attitudes towards antiquity and the musical heritage of his modern Lieder. "Grenzen der Menschheit" exemplifies a greater degree of abstraction (recalling the relation of "Die Götter Griechenlands" to "Memnon") and turbulence (evoking Dionysian energies); here focus lies on man's relation to divinity. Both songs depict man grappling with mortality. But whereas "Anakreons Grab" projects calm acceptance of the human condition, "Grenzen der Menschheit" projects continuous if futile resistance.

"Anakreons Grab"

"Anakreons Grab" is both enticing and puzzling. The song – the twenty-ninth of Wolf's fifty-one published Goethe Lieder – has long been a recital favorite.[30] In December 1888, just one month after its composition, a performance of this and eight other Wolf Lieder met with great enthusiasm.[31] According to biographer Frank Walker, "The success of Wolf's songs with the audience was immediate and remarkable," even overshadowing the Beethoven works played that evening.[32] By 1895, Wolf regarded "Anakreons Grab" as "unavoidable" in the programming of his works,[33] and it has remained entrenched in the vocal repertory.

What accounts for the song's popularity? Christopher Hatch suggests that "Anakreons Grab" is "easily understood and enjoyed,"[34] presumably offering performers and listeners respite from the technical and aural challenges of other Wolf Lieder. In explaining the song's accessibility, Hatch points to Wolf's use of familiar musical tropes – *siciliano* rhythms suggestive of pastoral scenes and melancholy emotions, melodic gestures associated with lullabies and other sleep music, horn calls conveying "distance, absence, and regret," and other borrowings from composers such as Beethoven and Schubert. On the whole, "Anakreons Grab" sounds more songlike than declamatory and less like an excerpt from a Wagnerian music drama than do many of Wolf's Lieder.[35] Indeed, much of "Anakreons Grab" sounds like it predates Wagner's musical revolution.

While the song seems fairly accessible compared to other Wolf Lieder, it has nevertheless caused confusion. In two letters to his friend (and mistress) Melanie Köchert, Wolf mentions a rehearsal and performance of his orchestrated version of the song in which both the audience and the performers failed to grasp its meaning:[36]

Tonight is the concert. Margits Gesang went very badly at yesterday's rehearsal. Frl. Corver sang uncertainly and also recited very badly. The piece will fall short. Anakreon's Grab won't have any effect either. But Ochs concerned himself too little with the orchestra. The attacks are sloppy and the detail is blurred. I'm very dissatisfied. Not to mention the tenor, who screams out the tender song to the audience like a bullfighter . . . I was so depressed at yesterday's rehearsal of Margits Gesang and Anakreon that I wanted to leave Berlin on the spot.[37]

. . .

But I owe you a report on the actual concert. So here goes, Margits Gesang and Anakreons Grab got practically no applause. Performances of both pieces were extremely flawed in terms of the orchestra and soloists . . . Anakreons Grab was simply hurried through, especially by the singer who couldn't wait for it to be over.[38]

Wolf summarized the debacle to another friend, Emil Kauffmann: "Margit and Anakreons Grab were simply not understood, either by the conductor, by the singers, or by the audience. They were, so to speak, rejected."[39] How could a work that has enjoyed such long-lasting popularity prove so impenetrable and distasteful?

Wolf's comments suggest that the performance was flawed, and the orchestration may also have been to blame. Moreover, according to Walker, "To go through most of the symptoms of an epileptic fit was, in fact, Wolf's normal reaction to the first imperfect performances of any one of his works."[40] But the music itself may be primarily responsible. Various aspects of the song are undeniably strange, particularly the intensified chromaticism, contrapuntal writing, and metrical irregularity of the middle section. That section appears to be written in a different, and later, compositional style than the outer sections; the work as a whole seems a conglomeration of pre- and post-Wagnerian musical idioms. Evidence from Wolf's sketches reveals the difficulties he experienced in composing the song, especially mastering the poetic and rhythmic complexities of lines 3–4 in Goethe's quasi-free verse poem.[41] Wolf's struggles to complete the setting and the music's stylistic inconsistency cast doubt on the notion that the work is easily understood. "Anakreons Grab" has deeper meanings and historical resonances than might first appear.

Max Kalbeck, a strong Brahms supporter disinclined to find much of value in Wolf's music, criticized this and several other songs as "childish, tinkling, barren stuff," noting in particular their "oddly banal melodies and ludicrous harmonic convulsions."[42] In lambasting the disparate qualities of "Anakreons Grab," Kalbeck unwittingly calls attention to the fundamental duality through which meaning emerges. Far from representing a compositional failure, the combination of banal and bizarre, familiar and strange, suggests the dialectic between past and present infusing text and music and giving rise to the song's elegiac expression. "Anakreons Grab," as Hatch notes, involves what Charles Rosen calls a "double time scale, the representation of the past through the immediate sensation of the present."[43] The vocal protagonist's reflections on the fate of the ancient Greek poet Anacreon, whose overgrown grave he has ostensibly just stumbled upon, lead to a meditation on death and immortality. Confronting signs of an idyllic past in the environs of the present prompts the protagonist to envision the future. The same can be said of both poet and composer; in creating "Anakreons Grab," Goethe and Wolf each look back on the past as a means of grappling with their human and artistic destinies.

Composed in Weimar in 1785, Goethe's epigram engages the past on multiple levels. On the surface, it casts a backward glance at Anacreon of Teos (*c.* 572–490 BC), renowned for his lighthearted lyric verse celebrating beauty, love, song, and wine. But the poem also more subtly reflects upon Anacreon's ancient and modern literary imitators, including Goethe himself in his younger years. The retrospective stance of the poem thus has both historical and personal dimensions; Goethe seems to have written it as a means of reevaluating the Anacreontic tradition to which he had once contributed. At the same time, "Anakreons Grab" represents a recasting of several ancient epigrams included in the massive poetry collection known as the *Greek Anthology*, which captivated Goethe's Weimar circle in the early 1780s and inspired his first efforts to write in ancient poetic forms. Viewed in this light, the poem might signify a broader reconsideration of the legacy of Greek antiquity.

Active in the cities of Thrace, Samos, and Athens, Anacreon composed songs for the entertainment of the ruling tyrants and their courtiers. Both during and after his lifetime, his poetry acquired a reputation as frivolous, witty, and decadent, reflecting the glittering court settings in which he worked. The image of Anacreon as carefree hedonist actually owes less to his own poetry than to the *Anacreontea*, a collection of sixty poems imitating his style from the late Hellenistic/Roman to Byzantine periods (first century BC to sixth century AD).[44] Although these later poetic imitations employ similar themes, motifs, forms, and meters, they avoid the sophistication and occasional seriousness of the original verse. As Classics scholar Patricia Rosenmeyer writes,

The poems are basically variations on a theme, namely *la dolce vita*, the simple pleasures of life. All complications and potential problems are eliminated from the anacreontic sphere: money and power are rejected, death is merely a non-threatening reminder to enjoy what is left of life, and old age never interferes with the erotic urge. Love itself is easy and available; there is no jealousy or distress involved, but rather a gentle and pervasive sense of well-being, an eros that is more sensual than sexual. The anacreontic atmosphere is thus created by combining the best of the erotic and the symposiastic worlds – it celebrates wine, beauty, friendship, and love.[45]

An important difference between Anacreon and his imitators, especially relevant to Wolf's setting of "Anakreons Grab," emerges in the treatment of death as a poetic subject. Anacreon's own poems reveal that, for all his joviality, he feared the passage of time and inevitability of death:

No. 395
My temples are already grey and my head is white; graceful youth is no more with me, my teeth are old, and no long span of sweet life remains now. And so I often weep in fear of Tartarus: for the recess of Hades is grim, and the road down to it grievous; and it is certain that he who goes down does not come up again.[46]

In a number of the *Anacreontea* poems, however, the poet appears far more concerned with pleasure than perishing. For example:

No. 7
The ladies say, 'Anacreon, you are old. Take a mirror and look: your hair is no longer there, and your brow is bare.' But I do not know whether my hair is still there or has gone; I do know that the closer Fate is, the more fitting it is for the old man to enjoy his fun and games.[47]

No. 38
Let us be merry and drink wine and sing of Bacchus, the inventor of the choral dance, the lover of all songs, leading the same life as the Loves, the darling of Cythere; thanks to him Drunkenness was brought forth, the Grace was born, Pain takes a rest and Trouble goes to sleep. So the drink is mixed and tender boys are bringing it, and grief has fled, mingling with the wind-fed storm: let us take our drink, then, and let our worries go: what is the good of hurting yourself with cares? How can we know the future? Man's life is unclear. I want to be drunk and dance, to perfume myself and have fun (with the handsome youths and) with beautiful women too. Those who wish can bother with worries. Let us be merry and drink wine and sing of Bacchus.[48]

No. 40
Since I was created a mortal to journey on the path of life, I can tell the years that I have gone past, but do not know the years I have to run. Let me go, worries: let there be no dealings between you and me. Before death catches up with me, I shall play, I shall laugh and I shall dance with lovely Lyaeus.[49]

Written by multiple authors over many centuries, the *Anacreontea* poems were collected during antiquity and transmitted together under Anacreon's name in an appendix to the tenth-century codex of the Palatine Anthology.[50] Rediscovered at a library in Louvain in the mid-sixteenth century, the manuscript was hailed as containing an unknown set of lyric poems by Anacreon.[51] Although some scholars suspected that the poems were inauthentic, their publication in Paris in 1554 met with enthusiasm in literary circles and provided a strong impetus to the emerging Anacreontic movement in sixteenth-century French poetry. This movement (also known as French rococo classicism), which blossomed over the next two hundred years, directly influenced a group of German writers active in the mid eighteenth century. Like the French poets who inspired them (and whom they often translated and referenced in their poetry), the German Anacreontics, including Salomon Gessner, Johann Ludwig Wilhelm Gleim, Johann Nikolaus Götz, Friedrich von Hagedorn, Jacobi, Karl Wilhelm Ramler, Johann Peter Uz, Justus Friedrich Wilhelm Zacharia, clung to the sentimentalized conception of Anacreon set forth in the *Anacreontea*. According to Goethe scholar Humphrey Trevelyan,

> [T]he Anacreontic of the 1740's and 1750's did nothing to help the deeper understanding of Greek poetry. It made popular an utterly false picture of Greek life, according to which the Greeks spent their days, and especially their nights, reclining flower-wreathed around the convivial board, in endless flirtation with easy-kissing girls. This view of the Greeks ... made of them the idealisation of rococo manners.[52]

Not until the mid nineteenth century did improvements in comparative philology allow scholars to recognize that the *Anacreontea* poems were written not by Anacreon but by later imitators. Thus the image of Anacreon as carefree hedonist retained its hold on the public imagination during Goethe's own youthful involvement with Anacreontic poetry.

Goethe composed about a dozen poems in the manner of the German Anacreontics.[53] Written in Leipzig in the later 1760s, they are witty, light, playful verses employing elements of Greek mythology for ornament more than substance. Before long, Goethe's attraction to Anacreontic poetry received a new stimulus. In the early 1770s, having finally mastered the Greek language, Goethe embarked on reading ancient authors such as Homer, Plato, and Xenophon in the original. During the fall of 1771 and winter of 1772, he turned to the Greek poets, including what he thought to be Anacreon (actually the *Anacreontea*).[54]

Within a few months, however, Goethe's interest shifted to Pindar, whose poetry "opened his eyes to the fact that Anacreon and Theocritus, the two gods of rococo classicism, were only 'sidestreams' of the true Castalian flow of Greek poetry."[55] This deeper engagement with Greek verse, coupled with his recent meeting with Herder, who reviled false modern poetic imitations, triggered a dramatic transformation in Goethe's conception of antiquity. Whereas previously he had echoed the rococo Hellenism of Götz, Jacobi, and other Anacreontics, now his understanding of the Greeks developed into something far grander. During his *Sturm und Drang* years of the 1770s, Goethe became consumed with how to master the daemonic forces that gripped him and had similarly gripped the ancients. Obsessed with antique artworks as exemplars of such mastery, and with the ancient Greeks as models of human greatness, right conduct, direct feeling, and truth to nature, he now rejected the prettified Anacreontic notion of antiquity. The publication of Wieland's *Alcestis* and *Letters on the Alcestis* in early 1773 brought matters to a head. Goethe attacked Wieland's sentimentalized classicism with his farcical play *Götter, Helden und Wieland* (Oct. 1773, pub. March 1774). Although Goethe remained on friendly terms with various members of the German rococo, his own days of writing light-hearted Anacreontic verse were over.

Goethe's early involvement with and subsequent rejection of the Anacreontic tradition are critical to an understanding of "Anakreons Grab." In this post-*Sturm und Drang* work, Goethe broaches the subject of Anacreon but without any hint of his former scorn; by 1785, when he composed the poem, he had come to terms with the rococo style that captivated him in his youth. The poetic speaker's contemplation of Anacreon's grave seems at once a reflection on the ancient poet and a reconsideration of the modern literary imitators that he inspired. Through the words of the poetic speaker, Goethe bids a gentle farewell to the Anacreontic tradition and his own early contributions.

"Anakreons Grab" may have represented Goethe's adieu to the Anacreontic tradition, but it did not signify a repudiation of classical antiquity. Composed shortly before his surreptitious flight to Italy in 1786, the poem might be understood to express longing for an idyllic past in the temperate lands to the south. The immediate inspiration for this poem was, in fact, Goethe's engagement with ancient verse – epigrams from the *Greek Anthology* in new German translations by Johann Christoph Tobler and Herder.[56]

The *Greek Anthology*, a collection of 4000 ancient epigrams dating from the seventh century BC to the sixth century AD, provided a useful counter-image of ancient Greece to that which prevailed during Goethe's *Sturm und Drang* years. With their urbanity, refinement, and thoughtfulness of expression, the ancient epigrams, as Trevelyan writes, helped

> ban the ghost of Electra whose cries for blood and vengeance still disturbed [Goethe's] good relations with the Greek genius. They helped him to forget the truth that he had once realised so clearly, that Greek greatness was founded on strength, and to regard delicacy of thought and outline as an essential quality of Greek formal perfection. Even the once despised Anacreontics were now held in honour and thought worthy of translation.[57]

Goethe was stimulated to translate Anacreon's poem "An die Cicade" (1781) and, more significantly, used the ancient epigrams as models for his own verse – his first attempts to imitate the form and meter (as opposed to the mythological content or broad aesthetic ideals) of ancient poetry.[58]

Although Goethe had encountered antique epigrams in his youth and read Lessing's essay, "Zerstreute Anmerkungen über das Epigramm" (1771),[59] Herder's determination to introduce the *Greek Anthology* to eighteenth-century readers had the strongest impact on him.[60] In the fall of 1780, Herder gave German translations of thirty ancient epigrams to his friends in Weimar, and Goethe may have seen them at this time. The following summer, Goethe made his first attempt to write imitations and adaptations of the ancient verse.[61] When Tobler sent Goethe further translations from the *Greek Anthology* in March 1782, Goethe was again inspired to compose epigrams in elegiac meter. In the early summer of 1782, he wrote ten epigrams. Although Goethe then turned to other projects, Herder continued to work assiduously on translations of the *Anthology* poems. In November 1784, he gave Goethe a copy of his manuscript, published the following year under the title *Blumen, aus der Griechischen Anthologie gesammlet*. Goethe responded with enthusiasm.[62] Herder's translations, along with his essay "Anmerkungen über die Anthologie der Griechen," inspired Goethe in 1784–85 to compose a dozen additional epigrams – including "Anakreons Grab."

Unlike Herder, Goethe did not devote his efforts to translating epigrams from the *Greek Anthology* (there is no evidence that he worked with the *Anthology* poems in the original language) but rather used the German translations as a springboard for his own verse. Some of his epigrams build upon Herder's translations; others are free variations on antique themes or occasional poems in the form of Greek epigrams with no other ties to antiquity.[63] While he often selected subjects that would have appealed to ancient Greek writers, his epigrams have a modern feel.[64] Goethe in fact intended his epigrams to be used as gravestone inscriptions in Weimar parks, and delayed publishing them until 1789.[65]

"Anakreons Grab" bears a particularly close connection to poems from the *Greek Anthology*, including those translated and published by Herder. Among the "Sepulchral Epigrams" in the complete, un-translated *Anthology* are thirteen on the subject of Anacreon's grave by authors including Simonides (?) (fifth-sixth centuries BC), Antipater of Sidon (second century BC), Dioscorides (third century BC), and Julianus, Prefect of Egypt (fifth century AD), as well as one or more anonymous writers. Three of the thirteen epigrams appear (although not sequentially) under the title "Anakreons Grab" in Herder's *Blumen, aus der Griechischen Anthologie gesammlet*.[66]

"Anakreons Grab"
Um dich müsse mit vollen Beeren der frischeste Ephen
   grünen! Es müssen um dich schönere Blumen erziehn
Diese Purpurwiesen! Es strömen Ströme von Milch dir:
   Ströme von süßen Wein dufte die Erde dir zu,
Daß noch deine Asche, daß deine Gebeine sich laben,
   O Anakreon, wenn Asche der Todten genießt.
Antipater of Sidon

[Let the four-clustered ivy, Anacreon, flourish around thee, and the tender flowers of the purple meadows, and let fountains of white milk bubble up, and sweet-smelling wine gush from the earth, so that thy ashes and bones may have joy, if indeed any delight toucheth the dead.][67]

"Anakreons Grab"
Mutter des allerquickenden Weins, jungfräulicher Weinstock
   und der Rebe, die sich kräuselnd in Ranken erhebt,
Winde dich, zart Gewächs, rings um Anakreons Grabmal
   reich an Trauben, und klimm' oben zur Säule hinan,
Daß der trunkene Sänger des Weins auch unten die lange
   Nacht sich kürze mit nie-schweigendem Cittergesang
Von der Liebe Bathylls, daß der zur Erde gesunkne
   Greis zum Haupte sich noch glänzende Trauben erseh
Und mit dem labenden Thau sich netzte, der von der Lipp' ihm
   einst so holden Geruch süsser Gesänge verlieh.
Simonides (?)

[O vine who soothest all, nurse of wine, mother of the grape, thou who dost put forth thy web of curling tendrils, flourish green in the fine soil and climb up the pillar of the grave of Teian Anacron; that he, the reveller heavy with wine, playing all through the night on his lad-loving lyre, may even as he lies low in earth have the glorious ripe clusters hanging from the branches over his head, and that he may be ever steeped in the dew that scented the old man's tender lips so sweetly.][68]

"Anakreons Grab"
Dessen innerstes Herz von Smerdias Liebe geschmelzt war,
   Du einst König und Freund jeder geselligen Lust,
Musengeliebter Anakreon, der um seinen Bathyllus
   oft mit dem fröhlichen Wein sehnende Thränen gemischt;
Quellen müssen Dir noch im Todtenreiche von süssem
   Nektar strömen und Dir bringen der Seligen Trank.

Veilchen müssen Dich dort und Zephyrliebende Blumen
    kränzen, ein Myrthenkranz, sprießend im zartesten Thau;
Daß du auch bei Proserpinen noch im trunkenen Tanze
    Fröhlich die liebende Hand um die Euripyle schlingst.
Dioscorides

[O Anacreon, delight of the Muses, lord of all revels of the night, thou who wast melted to the marrow of thy bones for Thracian Smerdies, O thou who often bending o'er the cup didst shed warm tears for Bathyllus, may founts of wine bubble up for thee unbidden, and streams of ambrosial nectar from the gods; unbidden may the gardens bring thee violets, the flowers that love the evening, and myrtles grow for thee nourished by tender dew, so that even in the house of Demeter thou mayest dance delicately in thy cups, holding golden Eurypyle in thy arms.][69]

Given Goethe's enthusiastic reaction to receiving Herder's *Blumen* manuscript, as well as various similarities between his own "Anakreons Grab" and these three ancient epigrams, it is reasonable to assume that he read them and employed them as models.[70] Neither a translation nor a paraphrase, his poem is instead a recasting of the ancient material.

        "Anakreons Grab"
Wo die Rose hier blüht, wo Reben und Lorbeer sich schlingen,
    Wo das Turtelchen lockt, wo sich das Grillchen ergetzt,
Welch ein Grab ist hier, das alle Götter mit Leben
    Schön bepflanzt und geziert? Es ist Anakreons Ruh.
Frühling, Sommer und Herbst genoß der glückliche Dichter;
    Vor dem Winter hat ihn endlich der Hügel geschützt.
Goethe

        "Anacreon's Grave"
Here, where the rose blooms, where vine round laurel twines,
    Where the turtle dove calls, where cricket doth delight,
What grave is here, that it with life all gods
    Should plant and ornament with beauty? Here rests Anacreon.
Spring, summer, autumn that happy poet has enjoyed;
    From winter, at the last, has this mound protected him.

As in the ancient epigrams, Goethe's poetic speaker stands before Anacreon's grave and contemplates the ancient poet's demise. Here too flowers and vines entwine the tomb, the thriving vegetation implying continuity. In Goethe's poem, as in the ancient epigrams, death appears far less harsh than the actual Anacreon had feared.

But differences also emerge. In each of the three ancient epigrams, the poetic speaker calls for Anacreon's grave to be enveloped by emblems of the hedonistic existence the poet had once enjoyed, and may continue to enjoy in death. In Goethe's poem, however, the grave is already enveloped when the speaker comes upon it, and the emblems suggest not hedonism but a kind of rococo delicacy. Although Goethe follows the ancient writers in alluding to Anacreon's propensity for drunkenness through the image of vines (*Reben*) winding around the grave, he does so with subtlety, avoiding any direct mention of wine, Bacchus, or revelry. He ennobles Anacreon by also symbolically encircling his grave with a wreath of poetic laurels (*Lorbeer*), suggesting the ancient poet's venerability. By introducing *Rose* and the diminutives *Turtelchen* and *Grillchen*, Goethe infuses the scene with tenderness. His mention of the passing seasons – without precedent in the three ancient epigrams but common in rococo poetry – imparts wistfulness.

Goethe's poem also diverges from the ancient epigrams in focus. The ancient poems direct attention to Anacreon and express the hope that, even in death, he will continue to enjoy that which he enjoyed in life. Details about those activities (e.g., his lyre-playing, drunken revelry, and attraction to boys) produce a clear picture of his earthly existence. In Goethe's poem, on the other hand, Anacreon remains a shadowy figure. Little information about him is supplied, and even his name remains unmentioned through two-thirds of the poem. Goethe grants far more attention to the natural setting of Anacreon's gravesite, beginning four introductory phrases with "wo." Suspense mounts as the speaker takes in his verdant surroundings and wonders, "Whose grave lies here?"

As Hatch notes, the image recalls Nicolas Poussin's famous painting "Et in Arcadia ego" (1636–37), in which four young Arcadians – three shepherds and a maiden – quietly contemplate a sepulchral monument within an idyllic landscape (Figure 4). The painting's title appears as an inscription on the tomb. According to art historian Erwin Panofsky,

> The Arcadians are not so much warned of an implacable future as they are immersed in mellow meditation on a beautiful past. They seem to think less of themselves than of the human being buried in the tomb – a human being that once enjoyed the pleasures which they now enjoy, and whose monument 'bids them remember their end' only in so far as it evokes the memory of one who had been what they are.[71]

In contrast to previous paintings of youth encountering its inevitable end (including an earlier "Et in Arcadia ego" painting by Poussin), the picture does not show a terrifying confrontation with death but rather calm consideration of life's finitude.[72]

Figure 4 Nicolas Poussin, *Et in Arcadia ego* (1636–37).

Goethe was likely familiar with the inscription "Et in Arcadia ego" (if not also Poussin's painting) when he composed "Anakreons Grab," for it had become a favored expression among eighteenth-century German writers, including Jacobi, Wieland, Herder, and Schiller.[73] (Goethe himself used the phrase "Auch ich in Arkadien!" as the motto for both volumes of his *Italienischen Reise*, published in 1816 and 1817.) Understood as elegiac rather than threatening, the inscription evokes the sentiment of Goethe's poem. In contemplating Anacreon's grave, the speaker reflects upon the ancient poet's demise and, indirectly, his own. In what sense might Anacreon or any poet experience immortality?

Whereas the ancient epigrams call for Anacreon's grave to be surrounded with emblems of his life, Goethe's poem asserts that the gods have already done so. Regardless whether "alle Götter" alludes to antique theology, a more modern form of pantheism, or perhaps the many literary imitators who surrounded Anacreon's memory with new 'poetic' life, their adornment of the grave does not mark the conclusion to the poem. Goethe goes a step further, indicating in the last two lines that Anacreon's grave offers not continued enjoyment but eternal protection. The passing seasons conjure passing phases of life, but also vicissitudes in the reception of Anacreontic poetry. In stressing the grave's protective function, Goethe seems to distance himself from the harsh attitude toward rococo Hellenism that characterized his *Sturm und Drang* years; death shields Anacreon from his detractors, including the Goethe of the 1770s.

Ultimately, Goethe's elegiac farewell to Anacreon suggests recognition that the fate of the grave's occupant will one day be his own. Even as he says goodbye, his comforting message forms a bond between them.

Wolf's musical setting of Goethe's poem adds new levels of retrospection and self-assessment. Composed on 4 November 1888 just one week after Wolf immersed himself in Goethe's poetry, the work pays homage to the Weimar bard and his idealization of antiquity as much as to Anacreon.[74] But homage does not imply acceptance. Wolf had long been anamored with the writings of Nietzsche, who asserted that the essence of Greek art lies in its tension between Apollonian and Dionysian forces, between calm and turbulence, dispassion and emotional frenzy. In setting "Anakreons Grab," Wolf maintained a "critical distance" from Goethe and the Apollonian classicism of his epigram. The song thus helped initiate a period of intense reflection on how Goethe's poems could remain viable as Lied texts in the late nineteenth century. For Wolf as for Goethe, contemplating the fate, or posthumous influence, of an artistic forbear shed light on his own artistry.

What drew Wolf to this poem – the first of his Goethe songs whose text does not derive from the novel *Wilhelm Meisters Lehrjahre*?[75] He may well have been attracted by the poem's retrospective stance, and the opportunity it afforded him to explore in music the dialectic between past and present – a dialectic which implicates not only Wolf's relationship to Goethe and Anacreon but also his ties to previous composers. Although Wolf was not prompted to compose "Anakreons Grab" by any prior setting (none exists), he did, as Hatch has discussed, draw upon compositional tropes and practices from the eighteenth and early nineteenth centuries (i.e., the Age of Goethe). What Hatch and others have not addressed is the music's conflation of these archaic style traits with those of the late nineteenth century. By joining pre- and post-Wagnerian musical idioms, Wolf may have sought to trace the roots of his own compositional style and to fathom its future. Nietzsche's conception of ancient Greek tragedy – great works of art created through the harnessing of Dionysian energies (which for a time is how Nietzsche also viewed Wagner's music dramas) – may have helped to motivate the unusual stylistic duality of Wolf's setting. As noted, Wolf began introducing Wagnerian musical traits into the Lied in the late 1880s.

The stylistic duality becomes evident as the musical structure unfolds. Wolf employs a ternary form (A B A') to set Goethe's six-line poem, with each of the three sections corresponding to one distich, or pair of lines (Example 2.1a). The varied repetition of the first section's music (mm. 1–6)

Example 2.1a Wolf, "Anakreons Grab"

Example 2.1a *(cont.)*

in the third section (mm. 13–18) parallels the textual relation between the first and third distichs. Both distichs present four related images (lines 1–2: rose, vines and laurels, turtledove, and cricket; lines 5–6: spring, summer, fall, and winter). The first distich, however, comprising four dependent clauses, emphasizes place, while the third distich, with two independent clauses, emphasizes time. Both place and time represent means by which the vocal protagonist strives to understand the significance of the grave and the fate of its occupant, and both convey a sense of comfort and peacefulness. Although the rococo imagery of lines 1–2 and 5–6 each arise from the contemplation of death, it calls for musical expression that is neither disruptive nor threatening.

Wolf sets these two sections in an archaic manner, as if turning back the clock to the early years of Lieder composition. In both sections, the texture is homophonic, with the piano clearly subordinate to the voice. (Wolf rewrites the vocal line for the third section, but the accompaniment and the relationship between voice and accompaniment remain the same as in the first section.) Aside from occasional passing chromatic tones (significant on a motivic level), the harmonies are diatonic and, as Hatch discusses, in various ways recall the early nineteenth-century harmonic practices of Schubert and Beethoven.[76] Both sections remain within the sphere of D major (although the third section begins in G major, an oddity to be discussed shortly); the first vocal strophe moves from the tonic to a half cadence on the dominant, while the third vocal strophe opens and closes in the tonic. The first section and, to a lesser extent, the third section also project an archaic tone through metrical regularity. Wolf sets the classical hexameters of lines 1–2 to four measures of music. Each of the four clauses (half of the hexameter line) maps onto a one-measure phrase, with each poetic foot forming a rhythmic module of either three or six eighth-note beats (Example 2.1b). Lines 5–6 also extend through four measures, although the music, following the poetic syntax, divides into two two-measure phrases, rather than four one-measure phrases. (Rhythmic extensions across the bar line in the vocal part obscure the accompaniment's further subdivisions).

By contrast, the middle section of the song (mm. 7–12) draws upon a markedly different, and later, compositional style suggesting the influence of Wagner. Homophony gives way to an effusion of contrapuntal writing, a striking musical illustration of the interlacing vines and laurels that adorn the grave. Harmonies arise primarily from the interplay of melodic lines, rather than functional progressions. The harmonic language is also far more chromatic than previously – a consequence of Wolf's complex interweaving of chromatic motives first heard in a more conventional harmonic context

Key:

Dotted vertical lines indicate subdivisions based on natural rhythmic accents.

Solid lines indicate notated measure lines.

Numbers indicate # of eighth-note beats in each natural grouping.

Example 2.1b Wolf, "Anakreons Grab," vocal rhythms

in the piano introduction. The manipulation of rising and falling half step motives (sometimes heard singly, other times consecutively or simultaneously) serves a variety of functions. It creates affective mode switches (as at the word "Grab"), produces a rich harmonic palette (mirroring the profusion of vibrant natural life surrounding the grave), and conveys complexity and confusion (suggesting the protagonist's attempt to pass through that vibrant life, as well as perhaps to "see" through it – literally, to read the tomb's inscription, or figuratively, to grasp the human condition). Chromaticism also heightens the emotional intensity of the protagonist's question. Suspense mounts as the accumulation of half step motives finally coalesces into an augmented sixth chord at m.11, leading to the resolution in G major at the long-delayed revelation of the tomb occupant's identity.

The dense contrapuntal texture of both voice and piano disrupts the previous metrical regularity. Syncopated vocal rhythms (involving several greatly extended note values) produce a continuous flow of music suggestive of Wagner's "endless melody." (Although the middle section begins with a four-measure phrase, the lack of any clear subdivision or of a subsequent four-measure phrase to balance it destroys any sense of metrical regularity.) The unpredictable placement of rests within each measure and jagged melodic contour of the middle section indicate that Wolf has temporarily forsaken the more traditionally songlike character of the Lied's first section.

The tonality of the middle section also indicates a late nineteenth-century compositional style, although, ironically, in a manner that simultaneously points to the past. While the section begins in D major (and D octaves in the bass initially serve as tonal anchors beneath the chromatic upper voices), the contrapuntal texture fairly quickly undermines the tonal stability; from the middle of m. 8 until the middle of m.10, the harmonic direction remains uncertain. When the music lands unexpectedly on a first inversion C minor chord in m.10, and then cadences even more surprisingly in G major at the words "Anakreons Ruh" in m.12, the effect is disorienting. Instead of following convention by moving to the key of the dominant in the middle of the work, Wolf heads in the opposite direction and cadences in the subdominant – a strategy that threatens the stability of the original tonic (by casting it as V of IV).

In weakening the song's tonal foundation, the unconventional cadence in the subdominant (preceded by heavy emphasis on *its* minor subdominant) resembles other progressive strategies of late nineteenth-century music, e.g., non-tonic beginnings and endings, simultaneous soundings of different keys, modal writing, and mode mixture. Yet moving in the flat direction around the circle of fifths (from D to G) also evokes the act of retrospection. Landing in G major precisely when the poem exposes the antique nature of its subject helps the listener hear Rosen's previously mentioned "double time scale."

The late-Romantic quality of the middle section seems to retain some influence over the more traditional-sounding music that follows. The third section, like the middle one, includes several ties across the bar line, lengthening the phrases. Moreover, the third section, like the middle one, has a fairly disjunctive vocal melody, including leaps of a third, fourth, tritone, fifth, and sixth (the first section includes only those of a third and fourth). The third section also begins in the seemingly "wrong" key of G major – a holdover from the subdominant cadence at "Anakreons Ruh." (The music slips into the "right" key by m. 15).

If the first section of the song conveys Apollonian serenity, and the middle section Dionysian restlessness, the third section suggests a fusion of the two. Here, one might say, the Dionysian energies are harnessed, loosely paralleling Nietzsche's notion of ancient Greek tragedy. The carry-over of qualities from the middle section into the third section helps portray life's voyage (symbolized by Anacreon's "seasons") as complex and unpredictable, while also beautiful and enjoyable.

The piano postlude extends an elegiac farewell to the past. As Hatch notes, the horn fifths in m. 18 are an early Romantic musical symbol for "distance, absence, and regret." Chromatic descents in the soprano and tenor lines, tolling quarter notes in the alto (marked "verklingend"), and the tonic pedal in the bass evoke the inexorable arrival and immutability of death. The circling motion in the piano right hand suggests vines winding tightly around the grave, perhaps now closing it from view. Yet the image of death conveyed by these final measures is more gentle than harsh. Although the chromatic B-flat in m. 20 creates a momentary darkening of harmony, the prevailing major mode, sturdy tonic foundation, hushed dynamics, and compound duple meter with continuous triplet rhythms create the feel of a lullaby. What the vocal protagonist encounters amidst the vibrant natural setting is Anakreon's *Ruh*. Death's arrival is not to be feared, this song suggests, because the past is not gone. Anacreon, his ancient and modern imitators, Goethe, Schubert, Beethoven, and Wagner – all of these departed, "sleeping" figures enjoy continued existence in the realm of art.

Youens has attributed the stylistic shift that occurs in the middle section of "Anakreons Grab" to Wolf's effort to master the more complex prosody (e.g., varying poetic feet and enjambment) of lines 3–4; in her discussion of the song sketch, she details his struggle to find a suitable setting for these lines, which eventually led him to recompose nearly the whole passage.[77] As we have seen, there is a complementary explanation. The stylistic contrasts of the song might reflect the dialectic between past and present that infuses the text. Just as Goethe engages the literary past, including his own involvement, so Wolf reflects upon *his* artistic heritage – the poetry, philhellenic ideals, and musical idioms that contributed to the development of his late Romantic Lieder. Each artist salutes the aesthetic traditions that gave rise to his work and gently lays them to rest.

"Grenzen der Menschheit"

Goethe's poem "Grenzen der Menschheit" had already found a place in the Lied repertory when Wolf composed his setting on 9 January 1889; Schubert set it to music (D. 716) in the spring of 1821, a time when he too was immersed in Goethe's poetry.[78] Wolf knew Schubert's Lieder intimately.

The implied criticism suggested by his decision to compose a new setting of "Grenzen der Menschheit" invites a comparison of the two works, which provides insight into Wolf's interpretation of the text.[79]

"Grenzen der Menschheit"
Wenn der uralte
Heilige Vater
Mit gelassener Hand
Aus rollenden Wolken
Segnende Blitze
Über die Erde sät,
Küss' ich den letzten
Saum seines Kleides,
Kindliche Schauer
Treu in der Brust.

Denn mit Göttern
Soll sich nicht messen
Irgendein Mensch.
Hebt er sich aufwärts
Und berührt
Mit dem Scheitel die Sterne,
Nirgends haften dann
Die unsichern Sohlen,
Und mit ihm spielen
Wolken und Winde.

Steht er mit festen
Markigen Knochen
Auf der wohlgegründeten
Dauernden Erde,
Reicht er nicht auf,
Nur mit der Eiche
Oder der Reben
Sich zu vergleichen.

Was unterscheidet
Götter von Menschen?
Daß viele Wellen
Vor jenen wandeln,
Ein ewiger Strom:
Uns hebt die Welle,

Verschlingt die Welle,
Und wir versinken.

Ein kleiner Ring
Begrenzt unser Leben,
Une viele Geschlechter
Reihen sich dauernd
An ihres Daseins
Unendliche Kette.

. . .

   "Man's Limitations"
When the age-old
Holy Father,
With a calm hand,
Scatters beneficent thunderbolts
Over the earth
From the rolling clouds,
I kiss the extreme hem
Of his garment,
With childlike awe
Deep in my heart.

For no mortal
Shall measure himself
Against the gods.
If he reaches upwards
And touches the stars
With his head,
Then his unsure feet
Have no hold,
And clouds and winds
Sport with him.

If he stands firm
With vigorous limbs
On the solid
Enduring earth,
He cannot even reach up
To compare himself
With the oak-tree
Or the vine.

What distinguishes
Gods from Men?
Before them many waves
Roll onwards,
An eternal river;
But the wave lifts us up,
The wave swallows us,
And we sink.

A narrow ring
Bounds our life,
And generations
Forever succeed one another
In the infinite chain
Of their existence.[80]

    Written in 1781 or shortly before, Goethe's philosophical poem bears a less explicit connection to classical antiquity than does "Anakreons Grab," or for that matter the great hymns "Prometheus" and "Ganymed," with which it appeared in Goethe's *Schriften* of 1789. Neither the title nor the body of the poem identifies historical or mythological figures by name. But Goethe's absorption with the works of Pindar and Homer around the time he composed "Grenzen der Menschheit," along with his decision to group it with "Prometheus" and "Ganymed" (as well as "Das Göttliche") in its first publication, encourages an association with classical antiquity.[81] Various aspects of the poem lend support. While the opening image of the ancient Holy Father, "whose lightning comes from his hands and marks the individual deeply," might refer to the god of the Old Testament, it also evokes Zeus, the Greek god who hurled thunderbolts.[82] Moreover, the poem's conception of divinity expands to include multiple gods, as if embracing all of Mount Olympus. Man's relationship to the gods of antiquity serves as Goethe's means of staging a philosophical inquiry into the limitations of human existence.

    As the Schubert comparison helps reveal, Wolf's "Grenzen der Menschheit" portrays man as foiled in his efforts to emulate the gods, yet resistant to his fate. Whereas Schubert's setting suggests that man willingly accepts his limitations, Wolf's involves greater tension. His late nineteenth-century setting suggests that although man inevitably faces death, he continues to yearn for immortality. The fact that humanity achieves a kind of timelessness through the unending chain of generations offers only minimal consolation.

Schubert's and Wolf's settings resemble one another in various respects. On a broad level, both are powerful works that seek to convey philosophical ideas and, not surprisingly, display little *Volkstümlichkeit*. Both involve audacious harmonic strategies that weaken the tonal foundation. The opening of each song (both the piano introduction and the first vocal stanza) includes pronounced plagal gestures that suggest the religious dimension of the poetic subject. Each work also includes a major mode cadence at the end of the fourth stanza – surprising in that it coincides with an assertion of man's doom ("But the wave lifts us up, / The wave swallows us, / And we sink"). In addition, Schubert's and Wolf's settings both return to a variation of the opening musical strophe during the last of the five poetic stanzas. (The stanzas are unequal in length, consisting of ten, ten, eight, eight, and six lines, respectively.)

These musical similarities may reflect congruencies in the two composers' poetic interpretations. They could also, of course, indicate Wolf's approval, and consequent retainment, of certain aspects of Schubert's setting. In any event, Wolf and Schubert plainly perceived that a poem exploring complex philosophical issues demanded very different musical treatment than poems with more conventional Lied subjects. Both recognized the rich symbolic potential of excursions into distant tonal regions, mode switches, and structural returns. The significance of the shared features, however, can best be grasped in the context of the songs' more pronounced differences.[83]

The most discernable difference involves the focus of each song. From its first measures, Schubert's setting evokes divine grandeur and power (Example 2.2a). Full chords (with multiple doublings) in the bass register succeed one another in extended note values. The stately tempo, plagal progressions, and extreme dynamic contrasts help forge an association between the introductory music and the omnipotent "age-old, Holy Father" of the first stanza. (In prolonging the dominant harmony, the piano introduction propels itself toward this image of the divine, which coincides with the tonic arrival.) The association of the first thirty-two measures (especially their ubiquitous drawn-out rhythms) with divinity is strengthened by Schubert's switch to new musical material (built from a pattern of half and quarter notes) as the poetic focus shifts to humanity – specifically, the protagonist's declaration of his reverence and awe before the godhead (Example 2.2b). Revealingly, most of Schubert's setting consists of material derived from the majestic opening music. Its rhythm patterns dominate the accompaniment, even for sections of the poem that focus on man, rather than the gods (e.g., mm. 60–7, 87–104). Divine omnipotence is thus never far from mind; it represents the focus of the song. Rather than accentuate man's desire to

Example 2.2a Schubert, "Grenzen der Menschheit," D. 716, mm. 1–6

Example 2.2b Schubert, "Grenzen der Menschheit," D. 716, mm. 33–36

transcend the limitations of his existence, the musical setting emphasizes his willing submission. (The straining of both the piano and voice beyond their natural capabilities suggests the challenge of depicting the divine, not an attempt to represent human striving.[84] The recurring opening rhythm pattern maintains focus on the gods.) Tellingly, the tonic key (E major) is established during an assertion of man's humility.

Wolf's setting, by contrast, underscores man's vain effort to emulate the gods, rather than divine omnipotence and man's willing acceptance of his limitations. The relationship between mortal and immortal beings brims with tension. Whereas in Schubert's setting the majestic rhythms of the introduction persist through much of the song, conveying thematic unity (supported by the song's tonal unity), Wolf's setting involves greater contrasts between sections. The mood of the music changes as the poetic focus shifts from one dimension of the human experience to another, culminating not in humble submission but rather in inescapable doom.

The tension-ridden dialectic finds musical expression in each section of the song. In the piano introduction, Wolf evokes a conception of the

Example 2.3a Wolf, "Grenzen der Menschheit," mm. 1–10

divine that differs significantly from that of Schubert's setting. While Schubert's introduction projects majesty and power, Wolf's opening – a subdued chord progression in steady half-note rhythms with a hint of text-painting in the thunderous bass tremolos – projects timelessness, or existence without change (Example 2.3a). Continuing into the first strophe with its image of the "age-old, Holy Father," the pattern underscores the link between divinity and immortality. Eternal existence (not omnipotence), this music insinuates, is what distinguishes the gods from humankind. In Wolf's setting, unlike Schubert's, no rhythmic, textural, or harmonic disjunction separates lines 1–6 (focusing on the ancient divinity) from lines 7–10 (focusing on the human speaker). The shift to new musical material in m. 33 of Schubert's setting accentuates the separation of gods from men and helps convey man's humble submission. The lack of a corresponding shift in Wolf's setting suggests both that the "limits" of human existence are not clearly demarcated and that man refuses to abase himself. Several flirtations with the minor mode (mm. 21, 23) cast doubt on the vocal protagonist's declaration of reverence for the ancient god. His cadence in C-sharp major, or #III, at the end of the first stanza also bespeaks a certain audacity.

In the second stanza, man's attempt to measure himself against the gods and the consequences of such vanity are illustrated through the shape of the vocal line, which includes several large ascending leaps followed by inevitable descents (e.g., mm. 28–35). The precariousness of man's position as his head brushes the stars (mm. 36–43) is conveyed through metrical conflicts between the voice (in common time) and accompaniment (in an irregular 3 + 3 + 2 pattern). A succession of augmented 5th harmonies suggests the insecurity of his footing.[85]

The third stanza, describing man's similarly vain attempt to emulate the gods while standing firmly on Earth, presents sharply contrasting music.

Beneath a monotonic vocal line (implying steadfastness, but also evoking numinous voices in opera), the accompaniment unfurls a repeating two-measure pattern with heavy bass octaves delineating the D minor tonality. The effort to convey man's sturdiness, however, seems excessive, and the illusion is soon dispelled. The vocal line starts to waver, expanding to encompass several large dissonant leaps (e.g., mm. 63–64 at "He cannot even reach up"). The repeating accompaniment pattern also breaks from its mold, leading towards a succession of unstable downbeat diminished 7th chords (mm. 63–66). At the end of the stanza, the music rings with irony. The extended (i.e., exaggerated) tonicization of C major at "To compare himself / With the oak-tree" seems to taunt man with nature's incomparably greater magnitude and strength.

The fourth stanza, like the second, conveys the insecurity of human existence through reaching vocal lines, conflicting metrical patterns (now with the $3 + 3 + 2$ pattern in rhythmic diminution, creating a wavelike effect), and dissonant harmonies (augmented triads and 7th chords). The unexpected D major cadence in mm. 92–93, coming immediately after the tumultuous wavelike music, perhaps suggests a positive perspective on human fate: in succumbing to death ("we sink"), man escapes life's turbulence. Such an interpretation, however, seems more applicable to the corresponding major mode cadence in Schubert's setting, which, as suggested, projects man's humble submission to the will of the gods. Given the tensions of Wolf's song, the major mode cadence might actually impart a cynical message: the gods are not impervious to man's destruction (as Goethe's poem itself might indicate) but take some pleasure in it.

In the fifth stanza, the human seems to merge with the divine through a succession of augmented triads in slow steady rhythms (first whole notes evoking small "rings" of human life, then half notes recalling the musical representation of eternity from the song's opening). A similar impression is created by the lengthy piano postlude, which sandwiches moments of harmonic and dynamic tension (evoking individual lives, or even generations) between sturdy pillars of D major harmony. Uniting musical elements conveying human striving and divine immutability suggests that humanity does achieve a kind of immortality, although only through the unending chain of generations; the individual human life remains circumscribed.

The tensions of the song are never fully resolved, as becomes clear in the postlude. After establishing a regular pattern of alternating consonant and dissonant harmonies (mm. 112–18), Wolf disrupts it. In the last nine measures of the song, dissonant harmonies rise to the fore, as if breaking through boundaries that have hitherto restrained them (mm. 118–19

Example 2.3b Wolf, "Grenzen der Menschheit," mm. 118–26

include three successive dissonant chords and mm. 120–23 include five) (Example 2.3b). Dissonance is ultimately brought back under control – not, however, through the anticipated resolution to D major or a return to the original key of A minor, but with an unexpected cadence in D minor. The song's progressive tonality (supported by the sounding of the fifth scale degree at the end of the vocal part and in the top line of the last accompaniment chord) leaves a final impression of open-endedness, as if to suggest that human striving to emulate the gods will continue indefinitely.

Beyond focusing on different elements, Schubert's and Wolf's settings also display different musical structures, and here too a comparison helps illuminate Wolf's interpretation. Schubert composes new music for each stanza except the last, which he gives a condensed version of the first stanza's music, producing the overall form A B C D A'. His setting thus concludes with music possessing the half- and quarter-note rhythmic pattern and E major tonality associated with man's humble reverence of the gods. Although touches of the minor tonic and subdominant harmonies in mm. 153 and 158 cast a slight shadow on the ending, a peaceful mood prevails. The vocal protagonist's final posture seems to be one of calm acquiescence.

Wolf, on the other hand, forges musical connections between both the second and fourth stanzas, and the first and fifth stanzas, resulting in the form A B C B' A', to which he appends the postlude. The varied return of the B music serves several purposes. It highlights the close relation of the lines "For no mortal / Shall measure himself / Against the gods" (beginning stanza two) and "What distinguishes / Gods from Men?" (beginning stanza four) – a relation obscured by Schubert's music. The statement (sounding somewhat like a warning) and the question (sounding somewhat like a challenge) both present the central issue of the poem, although from different angles. Bringing back aspects of the B music also enables Wolf to expose parallels between the latter parts of the second and fourth stanzas. The precariousness of man's existence – whether in striving to reach godlike heights or to remain afloat on the waves of fate – is conveyed through extended passages of harmonic instability and metrical confusion. The varied return of the A music (with the fusion of augmented 5th harmonies and drawn-out rhythms) evokes the fifth stanza's image of human generations achieving a kind of immortality by joining together to form an unending chain.[86] (A series of ascending and descending leaps of tenths and octaves in the vocal line also shifts focus from the individual mortal to whole generations of men.)

In concluding with a lengthy piano postlude, Wolf gives music the final say on man's relation to divinity. The postlude represents a response to, or elaboration on, Goethe's poem, which ends without specifying the speaker's attitude toward the "Grenzen der Menschheit." How does the speaker regard the endless chain of human generations? Does this path to "immortality" compensate for the annihilation of individual souls? The tolling chords of the postlude seem to proclaim death's inevitability even as the dissonant harmonies suggest man's continuing resistance, his refusal to accept the limitations imposed on his existence. In shifting abruptly to the minor mode in its final measures (and thus recalling the last measure of the fifth stanza), the postlude concludes in a darkened tone. Replacing the sense of calm acceptance conveyed by Schubert's setting is an implication of tragedy.

A final point of comparison between Schubert's and Wolf's settings of "Grenzen der Menschheit" involves their relation to other Lieder. As noted, Schubert composed his setting while deeply engaged with Goethe's poetry. He did not, however, group this song with any others. It does not belong to a song cycle or even a particular opus of songs. Although Goethe had grouped the poem with "Ganymed" and "Prometheus" in the *Schriften* of 1789, Schubert did not compose his settings of the three texts at the same time: "Ganymed," D. 544, dates from March 1817, "Prometheus," D. 674, from October 1819, and "Grenzen der Menschheit" from March 1821. Of the three songs, only "Ganymed" was published during Schubert's lifetime.[87] There is also no documentary evidence that the songs were performed together at Schubertiades or other concerts.[88] Thus, although its ties to classical antiquity may lead listeners to associate "Grenzen der Menschheit" with the two mythological monologues or other *Antikenlieder*, Schubert seems to have conceived his setting as a solitary Lied.[89]

Wolf, by contrast, composed and published his setting of "Grenzen der Menschheit" in close proximity with those of "Prometheus" and "Ganymed." He wrote all three settings in just over a week – "Prometheus" on the 2nd of January 1889, "Grenzen der Menschheit" on the 9th, and "Ganymed" on the 11th.[90] For their publication, he placed the three settings together (in the order "Prometheus," "Ganymed," and "Grenzen der Menschheit.") at the end of his Goethe songbook, balancing the three Harper songs (from *Wilhelm Meisters Lehrjahre*) that appear at the beginning.[91] It thus seems clear that Wolf intended "Grenzen der Menschheit" to be considered in conjunction with, and perhaps as a response to, these other works.

Various writers have assumed as much. Eric Sams writes, "This final song of the Goethe volume explores the ways of the universe, the nature of gods and men. Within this mighty music the conflicting moods of the two previous songs – emulation of godhead in *Prometheus*, surrender to divinity in *Ganymed* – are absorbed and reconciled."[92] Walker too suggests that the songs form a cohesive trilogy: "The poems illustrate three aspects of man's relationship to divinity."[93] "Prometheus," he explains, portrays a rebel. The gods are "impotent in the face of Prometheus's courage and independence."[94] "Ganymed" represents a stark contrast: "Here all is radiance and sweetness; after the heroic poetry of Prometheus's defiance, the composer was able no less wonderfully to find tones to express Ganymede's acceptance and adoration."[95] "Grenzen der Menschheit," in turn, "passes far beyond either love or revolt. Man recognizes his own littleness, in space and eternity, and has no more room in his heart for anything except awe and submission."[96] Walker suggests that "Grenzen der Menschheit" derives meaning from its relation to the other two songs, but he does not elaborate.

Lawrence Kramer offers more penetrating insights into relations among the songs:

"Prometheus" is a corrective song that, most unusually, stages the failure of the piano to dominate the voice. (Wolf rightly felt that his orchestral arrangement went wrong because it undid that failure.) Prometheus brutally mocks and defies the paternal god, who storms noisily on the keyboard in a series of vain attempts to intimidate his accuser into silence and obedience. "Ganymed" reverses the situation, erotically yielding to and even seducing the "all-loving Father" in an ambience of diffuse bliss. "Grenzen der Menschheit" closes the volume by sublimating Prometheus's defiance and Ganymede's erotic submission into an attitude of sacred awe. The linear progression of the harper trilogy is thus counteracted and replaced by a dialectical spiral.[97]

The notion that "Grenzen der Menschheit" represents the product of a dialectical conflict between opposing conceptions of man's relation to divinity (one defiant, the other yielding) is compelling. Not only does it comport with the sequence of the three songs in the Goethe songbook, but, as we have seen, Wolf's setting of "Grenzen der Menschheit" itself foregrounds dialectical relations. It makes sense that Wolf would publish the song in a way that would amplify those relations.

But the claim that "Grenzen der Menschheit" sublimates "Prometheus's defiance and Ganymede's erotic submission into an attitude of sacred awe" is contestable. "Sacred awe" may represent some kind of compromise or resolution between defiance and submission, but the point calls for clarification. As the preceding analysis has shown, Wolf's musical setting does not duplicate the central message of Goethe's text. Whereas the poem emphasizes man's humble submission to his inevitable fate (an attitude reflected in Schubert's setting), Wolf's music emphasizes man's continuing resistance. "Sacred awe" does not capture the tension of the setting. Youens, in discussing the song's postlude, writes, "One finds in this postlude an example of a Lied composer engaged in confrontation with his chosen text, wrestling with it, not just agreeing but arguing with its premises as only the best song composers can do."[98] Indeed, the song suggests a dispute between composer and poet (to be sure, a one-sided dispute: the music responds to the words, not vice versa). As Youens writes, "Wolf knew from *Faust* and many other works by Goethe that this poet found grandeur in human striving, against whatever odds, and the composer incorporates this understanding into a poem which seems to state the opposite: that we are significant only as links in a biological chain. 'No,' Wolf insists, and writes music to prove it."[99]

With some adjustment, Kramer's image of the dialectical spiral serves as a useful means of conveying relations among the three final songs of Wolf's Goethe volume. Like Ganymede, the protagonist of "Grenzen der Menschheit" (and every human) succumbs to the gods, but, unlike Ganymede, he does not do so willingly. Although facing inevitable annihilation, he continues to resist, i.e., to strive for immortality. In this sense he resembles the proud and defiant Prometheus, who scorns the gods' vaunted superiority. Prometheus, however, succeeds in overpowering divinity. As Kramer remarks, Jupiter "storms noisily on the keyboard in a series of vain attempts to intimidate his accuser into silence and obedience"; at the end of the song, Prometheus remains unvanquished. The same cannot be said for the protagonist of "Grenzen der Menschheit" – an individual human who finally succumbs to the force of the D minor cadence. Yet the song as a whole conveys the distinct impression that humanity's resistance to the immutable laws of the universe carries on unabated.

PART II

The lost world of childhood

To Enlightenment and Romantic thinkers, classical antiquity represented an idealized societal past, the "childhood" of modern culture. Actual childhood signified an idealized personal past, the state of natural purity characterizing the start of a human life. Parallels between these two temporal periods are numerous. Both antiquity and childhood evoke the "naïve" in Schiller's estimation,[1] exemplifying cultural as well as chronological primitivism.[2] As ideal states associated with a past time of beginnings, both became linked with notions of lost paradise, and perception of the gulf separating them from the modern world of adults (whether of society or individuals) inspired nostalgic yearning. Antiquity and childhood were both "discovered" during the middle of the eighteenth century and glorified long into the nineteenth.[3] Both too were fundamentally re-conceptualized in the later nineteenth and early twentieth centuries. The study of idealized childhood and its artistic representations, of central importance to Romanticism, thus covers some of the same ground as idealized antiquity. But childhood had its own allure, involving issues of selfhood, domesticity, gender, and religion. This lost Golden Age was, literally and figuratively, closer to home.

Since the publication in 1960 of Phillipe Ariès' seminal study *L'Enfant et la vie familiale sous l'ancien régime*, scholars have debated when the modern notion of childhood developed. Ariès claims that, until the eighteenth century, children were widely viewed as miniature adults and often treated harshly, distantly, and with little affection.[4] As evidenced by adult-like portrayals of children in art, childhood in the pre-modern period did not signify a phase of life separate from adulthood. Linda Pollock, in *Forgotten Children: Parent–Child Relations from 1500 to 1900*, counters that the history of childhood is characterized more by continuity than radical change.[5] Parents throughout history, she asserts, have shown close emotional ties to their children and been intimately involved in raising them. The modern conception of childhood thus has strong ties to the past. In recent years, writers have attempted to reconcile these competing claims.[6] The present study, side-stepping the dispute, focuses on a phenomenon no one denies: the gradual emergence of childhood as a cherished ideal.

First signs of idealized childhood appeared in the seventeenth century. Scholars have attributed the development to various factors, including a growing awareness that the traditional agrarian world (associated with the child) was starting to disappear, and the rise of middle class domesticity.[7] Whatever its causes, its significance was profound. Not only did childhood receive new attention, but its essence was reconceived. Previously, in accordance with the Calvinist and Puritan doctrine of original sin, children were perceived as "vessels of error and ignorance that must be cleansed and filled with knowledge through the authority of parents, preceptors, and priests."[8] But the seventeenth-century metaphysical poets Henry Vaughan and Thomas Traherne, drawing on personal ecstatic memories as well as Platonized Christian beliefs, placed emphasis not on original sin but its opposite.[9] Childhood, as depicted in their verse, is a time of innocence and divine grace – equivalent to both the Golden Age of humanity and the blissfulness of the blessed soul. Adults, who enjoy free will, can fall out of grace, but children are innocent. John Earle, in his *Microcosmographie* of 1628, conveys this idea through several deft metaphors: "[The Child] is the best copy of *Adam* before he tasted of Eve or the apple... He is nature's fresh picture newly drawn in oil, which time, and much handling, dims and defaces. His Soul is yet a white paper unscribbled with observations of the world, wherewith, at length, it becomes a blurred notebook. He is purely happy, because he knows no evil, nor hath made means by sin to be acquainted with misery."[10] Striving to regain childlike purity through memory of one's early experiences enables the sinful adult to find divinity. As Vaughan writes, childhood is "an age of mysteries! Which he / Must live twice, that would God's face see."[11]

Propagation of the new positive view of childhood was spurred by Rousseau's educational treatise *Émile* of 1762, the first extended literary work to focus on the subject. Rejecting the still prevalent notion of children as little adults, Rousseau instead insisted on their uniqueness. Childhood, he thought, marked a separate phase of human existence, with its own traits and needs: "Childhood has ways of seeing, thinking, and feeling to itself; nothing can be more foolish than to substitute our ways for them."[12] Instead of regarding children as inherently sinful, Rousseau, like the seventeenth-century metaphysical poets and various early eighteenth-century writers, emphasized their essential purity. He celebrated children's closeness to nature – which allied them with other embodiments of primitivism, from the Noble Savage to Woman and the Folk – as well as their limitless potential. He also argued that they must be carefully shielded

Figure 5 Joshua Reynolds, *Age of Innocence* (1778).

from the corrupting influences, and especially the educational methods, of modern society: "Everything is good as it comes from the hands of the Author of Nature; but everything degenerates in the hands of man."[13] In so doing, he coupled the burgeoning eighteenth-century cult of sensibility with the concept of childhood, the period in life when humans experienced the greatest degree of naturalness.[14] The eighteenth- and early nineteenth-century British portraitists who drew inspiration from Rousseau, including Sir Joshua Reynolds, Thomas Gainsborough, and Sir Thomas Lawrence, supported this view of childhood by routinely depicting children in outdoor settings, enveloped by animals, flowers, sunshine, and other embodiments of nature (Figure 5).[15]

While Rousseau emphasized children's natural innocence, he also dwelled on their weakness, helplessness, and ignorance – conditions he felt could be ameliorated through appropriate education, i.e., a pedagogy aimed at cultivating feeling and imagination rather than reason (as John Locke and others had advocated). Such an education would allow children to develop their mental and physical capabilities in far more natural and enjoyable ways than customary in modern society; they would be spared tedious learning exercises as well as the rod. The utopian, child-centered education that the fictional boy Émile receives as he passes from infancy to adulthood (with Rousseau acting as his sole tutor in the secluded countryside setting) avoids the unnatural restraints typically placed on eighteenth-century children. Émile is allowed, even urged, to dress comfortably, move about freely, and exercise his mind and body through activity rather than abstract thought or reading.

Instead of allowing him to stagnate in the polluted air of his chamber, let him be taken out daily into the open meadow. There let him run and frolic and fall down a hundred times a day; so much the better, for by this means he will learn the sooner to pick himself up. The blessings of liberty are worth many wounds. My pupil will often have bruises; but in return he will always be in good spirits.[16]

Despite the attention he gave to childhood's special character and needs, Rousseau did not encourage children's play entirely for its own sake, and he did not attempt to prolong childhood. Nor did he encourage adults to become once again like children. Rather, his goal was to facilitate children's maturation, to guide them step-by-step toward a wholesome existence within modern adult society. The Romantic concept of ideal childhood that his treatise did so much to inspire developed from Enlightenment pedagogy and perspectives.

With the emergence of Romanticism in the 1790s, reverential attitudes toward childhood intensified.[17] For many Romantic and even post-Romantic writers,[18] children's innate goodness, naturalness, simplicity, imaginative freedom, and joy make them worthy of adoration. Their weaknesses are not faults but virtues, and no attempt should be made to eradicate these qualities through rationalist educational methods or punishment. As Schiller writes, "In the child are exhibited the *potential* and the *calling*, in us their fulfillment, and the latter always remains infinitely behind that potential and that calling. The child is thus for us a realization of the ideal, not, of course, the fulfilled ideal, but the projected one."[19]

Drawing inspiration from Rousseau's belief in original innocence (and supporting the principles, if not all the particulars, of his pedagogy), many Romantics perceived in children a holiness suggesting proximity to God. Brentano, in the poem "Ermunterung zur Kinderliebe und zum Kindersinne," associates the divine nature of children with that of the Christ child:

> Oh how holy is a child!
> According to the Word of God's Son,
> All children are angels
> Waking before the Father's throne.
> Oh how holy is a child!
> He who has ever once sensed this
> Is joined with children through the Christ child!
>
> What mystery is a child?
> God has also been a child;
> Because we are God's children,
> A Child came to redeem us.
> What mystery is a child?
> He who has ever once sensed this
> Is joined with children through the Christ child!

In Mörike's "Stimme des Kindes," the serene image of a sleeping child conjures a vision of heavenly bliss:

> A sleeping child! Oh hush! In this visage
> You could resurrect paradise;
> He laughs sweetly while the angelic hosts listen,
> Around his mouth flits heavenly delight.

A similar poem, Eichendorff's "Gottes Segen," depicts the slumbering child enjoying the special protection of God's angelic guard:

> The child rests from play;
> The cool of the night
> Rustles at the window,
> While God's angels
> Faithfully keep watch.
>
> At the little bed they stand quietly,
> The morning barely yet begins to dawn,
> They kiss him before they go;
> The little child laughs as he dreams.

The high child mortality rate during the nineteenth century ensured that images of dead children figured prominently in Romantic poetry. Those who grieved the loss of children could find comfort in the notion that death had led them back to God's holy realm, as Uhland conveys in his brief poem "Auf den Tod eines Kindes":

> You came, you went with a faint trace,
> A fleeting guest on Earth;
> From where? To where? We only know:
> From God's Hand to God's Hand.

In Eichendorff's "Auf meines Kindes Tod," the deceased child speaks from beyond the grave to reassure his parents that he is now in paradise, in the presence of the Holy Virgin and Child:

> Father and Mother, why are you weeping about me?
> I am in a much more beautiful garden
> That is so big and wide and wonderful;
> Many flowers of pure gold are there,
> And beautiful children with wings fly
> All around, above and below, and sing. –
> I know them well from the springtime,
> As they went far over mountains and valleys
> And many called me there from the blue heavens
> When I slept below in the garden. –
> And between the flowers and the apparitions
> Stands the most beautiful of all women,
> A glowing Child at her breast. –
> I can not speak nor even cry,
> But ever and always sing and again then look,
> Quieted by a greater, more blessed joy.

Belief in the divine essence of children is also central to English Romantic poetry. In William Blake's *Songs of Innocence*, the child's imagination and natural sympathy for all created things enables man to recognize traces of divinity in himself; God and the universe "are not separate from Man, but humanized and contained in his Vision."[20] Although William Wordsworth actually regarded the new-born child as a *tabula rasa* to be impressed upon by Nature rather than as a vessel of virtue, his famous "Ode: Intimations of Immortality from Recollections of Early Childhood" – a *locus classicus* for nineteenth-century literature on the subject – exalts childhood as humanity's ever-receding link to a transcendent realm:

> Our birth is but a sleep and a forgetting:
> The Soul that rises with us, our life's Star,
>   Hath had elsewhere its setting,
>   And cometh from afar:
>   Not in entire forgetfulness,

>   And not in utter nakedness,
> But trailing clouds of glory do we come
>   From God, who is our home:
> Heaven lies about us in our infancy!
> Shades of the prison-house begin to close
>   Upon the growing Boy,
> But He beholds the light, and whence it flows,
>   He sees it in his joy;
> The Youth, who daily farther from the east
>   Must travel, still is Nature's Priest,
>   And by the vision splendid
>   Is on his way attended;
> At length the Man perceives it die away,
> And fade into the light of common day.

Childhood, to Wordsworth, is the "seed-time of the soul," a period of spontaneity, enthusiasm in nature, and unbounded creativity. Coleridge likewise celebrates the intuitive, imaginative quality of the soul, which he perceives in the figure of the child. Only through the organic, uninterrupted development of self-consciousness can the child's wonder, joy, and spontaneity be carried into mature adulthood.

For the Romantics, as Schopenhauer writes in *The World as Will and Representation*, "Childhood [is] the time of innocence and happiness, the paradise of life, the lost Eden, to which we look back longingly throughout the course of our lives."[21] Adults can learn more from children's naturalness and purity than children can ever learn from adults' knowledge and experience – a common theme in nineteenth-century literature (expressed in the famous introductory lines to Wordsworth's "Intimations Ode": "The Child is Father of the Man / and I could wish my days to be / Bound each to each by natural piety"). The idealized Romantic child held out hope for mankind. Only by returning to childhood could adults begin to satisfy their spiritual longings; the recovery of childlike qualities would lead them "home," i.e., to a state of transcendent wholeness. Children (like other manifestations of the naïve), Schiller writes, "are what we were; they are what we should become once more,"[22] a statement echoed in Romantic writings of many national traditions.

The notion that recovering childlike traits is essential to spiritual renewal has strong biblical support. In Matthew 18:3, when Christ's disciples ask who is the greatest in the kingdom of heaven, he places a child in their midst and responds, "Verily I say unto you, Except ye be converted, and become as little children, ye shall not enter into the kingdom of heaven." Christ's love of children, conveyed in this episode and elsewhere in the New Testament, intimates that adults must return to childhood's paradise in order to regain a state of blessedness.[23]

Romantic evocations of ideal childhood were usually accompanied by expressions of nostalgia. "The child, not suspecting my anxious eavesdropping, / Has blessed my heart with gloomy sounds, / More than the trees rustling in the quiet woods; / A deeper homesickness has overcome me," admits the poetic speaker of Mörike's "Stimme des Kindes." Many other late eighteenth- and nineteenth-century German poems convey similar sentiments, e.g., "O Heaven, if only I were still a child!" (Friedrich Wilhelm Gotter); "Wasn't I also once a child?" (Eichendorff); "Oh I wish I knew the way back, / The lovely path to the land of childhood!" (Klaus Groth); "How blessed was the time of child's play / When trouble had not yet nightly surrounded me" (Novalis); "Child's play is over, / And everything passes by – / Money and world and time / And belief and love and fidelity" (Heine); "From the time of my youth, from the time of my youth / Sounds ever a song for me; / Oh how can it be so far away, oh how can it be so far away, / What once was mine!" (Friedrich Rückert); "So once again, again and again, / Sing yourself back into your youth! / These children's songs / aim only to renew your youthful bliss" (August Heinrich Hoffmann von Fallersleben).[24]

As Enlightenment perspectives yielded to Romanticism, the relationship of childhood to adulthood thus underwent a significant reversal. Eighteenth-century philosophers and poets, whether oriented toward the cultivation of reason or of feeling, typically focused on how to turn children into upstanding adult citizens. Their nineteenth-century successors, on the other hand, dwelled on how adults could become once again like children.

The Romantic vision of childhood bore little resemblance to the actual living conditions of nineteenth-century children, especially those of the lower classes, who often faced lives of toil and hardship. Middle- and upper-class children, safely ensconced within their comfortable homes under the watchful eyes of parents and nannies, might enjoy some of the pleasures associated with the Romantic child (although they surely experienced various emotions – jealousy, anger, fear, grief, etc. – never connected with the prototype). But in Victorian England as well as Europe, the children of the factories, the mines, the chimneys, and the streets had little chance to partake in childhood joys. Although their lives drew attention, inspiring efforts at social reform,[25] they were hardly the objects of Romantic yearning. As the nineteenth century progressed, tensions between idealized notions of childhood and social realities became ever harder for artists and audiences to ignore. Such conflicts figure prominently in the novels of Charles Dickens and fairytales of Hans Christian Anderson.

While representations of the Romantic child continued to appear in art and literature until the end of the century, the concept suffered increasing strain. Excessive sentimentality weakened the aesthetic quality of many works. Often childhood served not just as a "repository of good feelings and happy memories which could help the adult to live through the stickier patches of later life," but as a refuge, a fantasy-like means of escape from the problems and pressures of reality.[26] (James M. Barrie's character Peter Pan, the boy who refuses to grow up, is one obvious example.) The expression of nostalgia for childhood, substituting for religion, came to assume an obsessive quality. Literary scholar Peter Coveney notes, "At the turn of the century, the child needed emancipation, not only . . . from the Puritan family, but from the careless and very widely accepted falsification of the myth of its 'innocent' nature. Both 'original sin' and 'original innocence' in their general acceptance had become impediments to an objective assessment of the nature of the child, and the significance to be attached to his education and experience.[27]

As the new century began, Sigmund Freud's pioneering work in psychoanalysis wrought a cataclysmic change in the general conception of childhood. In his "Essay on Infantile Sexuality" of 1905, Freud claims that children come into the world geared toward sexual activity. Far from the asexual "Romantic child," the actual child is subject to libidinal urges that, while perhaps buried deep in the subconscious, are very real and whose early gratification is critical to its development. Restricting too soon the child's natural sexual impulses (whether directed toward the self or a parent of opposite gender) results in a plethora of adult neuroses, such as anger, guilt, or fear.

Some see in Freud's theory of infantile sexuality a return to the concept of original sin, i.e., signs of sexuality in early infancy are like seeds of corruption. But the concepts of innocence and sin have no place in his works; he was repelled by the traditional Christian belief that children's nature is inherently corrupt and evil. Indeed, in one important respect, Freud found himself in agreement with those whose positive views led to the emergence of the Romantic child. Coveney notes, "For all his destruction of the idea of childhood's innocence, Freud's ideas were in fact in fundamental sympathy with the original romantic assertion of childhood's importance, and its vulnerability to social victimization. He discussed . . . the acute damage that could be inflicted on the child's innocent sexuality through the mindless prohibitions of parents, teachers, and priests."[28] Despite this shared recognition that adults bear deep responsibilities to both individuals and society in the tasks of child-rearing and education, Freud's ideas fundamentally altered perceptions of childhood. As the early twentieth century wrestled with the implications of his ground-breaking theories of infantile sexuality, the long-lasting Romantic concept of childhood, which had already grown fragile, shattered under societal and scientific pressures it could no longer withstand.

If, as Wordsworth suggested, "heaven lies about us in our infancy" but "shades of the prison-house begin to close upon the growing Boy," the cradle song would seem to offer the optimal opportunity to idealize childhood through words and music. The next chapter discusses the repertoire of early nineteenth-century lullabies, with particular attention to those of Schubert, which range from the folk-like to the artful. In evoking images of peacefully sleeping children, the *Wiegenlied* held promise of paradisiacal death. A sense of adult (usually male) yearning for the blissfulness of both infancy and death infuses many of Schubert's art song lullabies. The subsequent chapter briefly describes how the idealization of childhood found expression in Lieder other than lullabies, then examines the nostalgia for childhood in one of Brahms's most moving and highly regarded "minicycles" of songs. Here again we encounter the sounds of lullaby music, with their transcendent implications, but as if from a distance, i.e., through the ever-deepening recesses of memory.

3 | Sleep and death in Schubert's lullabies

The Biedermeier generation prized domesticity, as Friedrich Sengle describes in his magisterial study of the period.[1] With the expansion of the middle classes in the late eighteenth and early nineteenth centuries, ever more families acquired the financial means to enable mothers to stay home with their children. By remaining at home, rather than working in the family business or public sphere, a woman signaled her husband's success in providing for his family, and thus women of sufficient wealth usually did not pursue careers in the outside world.[2] As the case of Fanny Mendelssohn attests, while confinement to the home could prove frustrating to those with talent or ambition, Biedermeier era women generally embraced their domestic roles. Men too, despite, or perhaps because of, their more public lives, placed great value on the home. The restrictions of Metternich's regime, the strain of supporting their families in times of economic hardship, and other difficulties led many men to seek relief after hours within the domestic sphere, where they could enjoy the affection, respect, and privileges due the *paterfamilias*.

The home was a sanctuary, a "heaven on earth,"[3] whose routines and activities were cherished. Music-making played an especially important role.[4] Amidst the comfort and privacy of their rooms, family and friends entertained one another with performances of Lieder, operatic arias, piano works, and chamber music. Eligible young men and women engaged in musical courtship. Children sang while they played, and mothers crooned to their infants. This last example – the lullaby – merits close attention, for it epitomizes the intimacy of Biedermeier music-making.[5] It also illuminates the relation between art song and the Romantic idealization of childhood. Sung by one to an audience of one within the enclosed space of the nursery, the lullaby's repeating melodic strains radiated love, tranquility, and protection.[6] These qualities played a crucial role in the genre's aesthetic transformation by Schubert and others. As poets and composers (especially male) sought refuge from life's sorrows in the comforting sounds of cradle music, the traditional folk genre gave birth to a more artistically sophisticated type of Lied that confronted the troubling issue of human mortality.

Lullabies and the transformation of genre

Wiegenlieder figure prominently in the folk song repertory,[7] and Biedermeier era mothers, like women throughout history, drew heavily on oral tradition in singing their babies to sleep. But the broad appeal of *Volkstümlichkeit* during the late eighteenth and early nineteenth centuries also led to the composition of many new lullabies in a folk-like style, as demonstrated by a flood of *Wiegenlieder* on the song market. C. F. J. Girschner, in a short article about lullabies and spinning songs for the *Berliner Allgemeine musikalische Zeitung* (1828),[8] notes their recent proliferation: "In almost every newly appearing volume of Lieder one finds a lullaby or spinning song; this shows that both genres must have a special attraction for composers."

Yet Girschner remarks with consternation that a transformation had taken place. Almost none of these newly composed settings, he complains, are true representatives of their genres.

> Only very few of such songs, however, are true lullabies or spinning songs. Most, in the designs of both poet and composer, are entirely misguided. Consider the aim of such songs: they should be sung at the cradle or spinning wheel, and thus be folk songs. Can this happen, however, when neither the text nor the music have the character of folk song?

Girschner laments that modern lullaby texts are often not fit for the nursery: "Most *Wiegenlieder* texts namely contain images that are highly incomprehensible to the child and unthinkable in its performance circle." Like spinning song texts, he insinuates, lullaby texts should reflect the lowly station of their intended listeners with no higher aspiration; they must remain popular in character. The newly composed musical settings also meet with criticism for straying beyond the domain of folk lullabies:

> The first melody that the child should take in is indeed that of the lullaby; can one expect this, however, if strange, even harsh modulations occur in the melody, or if the pianoforte accompaniment should contain a kind of tone-painting as, for example, the rocking itself? If difficult rhythms appear in the Lied? Certainly not.

Disturbed by such textual and musical oddities, Girschner urges a return to the qualities of traditional folk song: accessible lyrics, simple melodies, and negligible accompaniments. As an appropriate model, he holds up Carl Maria von Weber's lullaby "Eia popeia schlief lieber als du."[9]

Other writers, however, recognized a distinction between two kinds of lullaby – one for children and the other for adults – without criticizing the more artful qualities of the latter. In a brief article entitled "Über Wiegenlieder" appearing in the journal *Caecilia* (1825), for example, Johann Stephan Schütze writes:

All lullabies that are actually sung before children fall asleep generally present only familiar phenomena that lie within the circle of their perception, especially animals, like sheep, lambs, geese, ducks and so forth, with which children happily sympathize and whose images, newly presented in a song, thereby lead to comfort, dreams, and thus sleep. These songs of natural necessity proceed from the Folk, although one cannot identify their origins. Later on, art lullabies were also written, but they in no way aspired towards those, but diverged entirely from them and went down a completely different path. Lullabies appeared everywhere, and still appear today, year by year, in large numbers, yet they are not written for children but for adults who keep watch over the sleeping children and occasionally in so doing edify themselves. Such songs are now picked out on pianos, without any one of them actually serving to sing children to sleep.[10]

The proliferation of *Wiegenlieder* during the early nineteenth century resulted from a variety of factors. In seeking potential Lied texts, composers encountered lullaby lyrics in the volumes of nearly every contemporary poet.[11] Folk lullaby texts, such as those in *Des knaben Wunderhorn*, also beckoned. The abundance of such lyrics led naturally to a profusion of musical settings. Additional stimulus came from the expanding female market for songs and other small-scale musical works (as well as novels, poetry, ladies' magazines, etc.), the rise in domestic music-making and music education, and the burgeoning enthusiasm for literary and musical folk traditions.[12]

In some cases, a political motive underlay the composition and publication of *Wiegenlieder*: the desire to counter an emerging women's movement in Germany with images of mothers who nurse and sing to their own children.[13] Reichardt's *Wiegenlieder für gute deutsche Mütter* (*Lullabies for Good German Mothers*), a collection of twenty lullabies published in Leipzig in 1798, had such an aim.[14] Reflecting the influence of Rousseau's *Émile* with its program for healthy child-rearing, Reichardt begins his preface by asserting that "good German mothers themselves quiet and tend to their children and gladly themselves sing them to sleep."[15] This image of loving motherly care contrasts sharply (and humorously) with that of the wet nurse: "With hasty jolting movements and a loud, shrill voice, a stupid, irrational nurse can try to daze a restless child and force it to sleep."[16] By singing and rocking her own child to sleep, a mother could ensure not only its peaceful slumber but also its future well being; the health and happiness of a German citizen lay in her hands.[17] German nationalist sentiment, both during and after the

Napoleonic era, was closely tied to musical manifestations of what many considered natural and healthful maternal conduct; nursing one's children came to be seen as a patriotic duty.[18]

The oddities that irked Girschner also had several causes. As the Lied gained prominence as a genre in the late eighteenth and early nineteenth centuries, composers began to experiment with such elements as harmony and rhythm to enhance the musical illustration of poetic imagery – a technique familiar from vocal genres such as oratorio and cantata. Text-painting, which involves the conscious manipulation of aesthetic components, was often perceived to undermine the spontaneity and naturalness of *Volkstümlichkeit*, widely seen as essential to lullabies. It also ran counter to still prevalent notions of *Affektenlehre*, the attempt to capture a poem's primary mood or *Hauptaffekt*, rather than textual details, in a single repeated musical strophe.[19] But even its opponents could not deny that text-painting reflected a desire to forge a close bond between words and music. If the means to that end were the subject of dispute in contemporary discussions on Lieder composition, the end itself was nevertheless widely lauded. By the 1820s, the technique had become a necessity in the Lied composer's tool box.

More significant than text-painting (indeed giving rise to it) are the lullaby's multiple potential functions. The genre's principal aim, of course, is to assist children in falling asleep. At the same time, a lullaby can serve as a means to appeal to higher powers (to seek protection or ward off harmful influences), express emotions, or just pass time.[20] Lullabies vary widely in content and tone, as well as attitude toward the child (for whom the singer may or may not wish to have responsibility).[21] As Emily Gerstner-Hirzel discusses, they may pacify, exhort, promise, express affection, bore, threaten, lament, dramatize, mock, slander, gossip, or tell stories.[22] Lullabies can thus provide entertainment – for the singer, and for anyone else who may be listening.[23] (The child himself might be too restless, drowsy, or young to grasp the meaning of the words.) To achieve any of these secondary functions while simultaneously putting a child to sleep (whether the task is literal or metaphorical), the poet and composer may introduce nuances, complexities, or unconventional elements into the song. The paradox of ostensibly inducing sleep while holding the listener's attention played a crucial role in transforming the folk lullaby into an art genre, a metamorphosis that Girschner seems to have sensed but neither understood nor appreciated.

Lulling a child to sleep requires that the music sound both soothing and monotonous. In many *Volkswiegenlieder*, a two-beat pulsation, either within the measure or across two measures, and the regular alternation of tonic and dominant harmonies, implied through the unaccompanied melodic line, create a steady rocking motion, mimicking that of a cradle. (In *volkstümliche Wiegenlieder*, the tonic and dominant harmonies are sometimes realized in a simple instrumental accompaniment, but the accompaniment is usually nonessential and, with the composer's tacit approval, may be omitted.)[24] The tempo is moderate to moderately slow, and the dynamics are quiet. Major modes and diatonicism predominate, as do circumscribed melodies with recurring figures. Compound meter and triplet rhythms are common, strophic repetitions the rule. The text typically takes the form of a direct address, with the mother quietly urging her child to sleep (e.g., "Sleep, child, sleep!"), and promising him rewards (flowers, animals, food, musical instruments, gifts, visitors, future health and happiness).[25] Usually the verses, employing soothing sound combinations and formulaic expressions, present a stream of pastoral or celestial imagery – shepherds and sheep, flowers and fields, stars and sky – with no harsh or troubling thought allowed to disrupt the tranquility.[26] Often, the lullaby assumes an air of religiosity as the mother invokes the protection of God or angels and equates the baby's slumber with the holy serenity of heaven.

While the song's placidity is intended to hasten the child's sleep, the singer hopefully remains alert, at least long enough to accomplish the primary goal. In the introduction to *Wiegenlieder für gute deutsche Mütter*, Reichardt expresses an eagerness to assist mothers in this regard, presumably by supplying his lullabies with aesthetic or intellectual interest.

For that reason, in choosing these lullabies, I have thought as much of the devoted and sensible mother as of the child. The little ones crying in the rocking cradle need only a gentle, soothing melody, and a lullaby must always have that, no matter what the content of the verses. At the same time, the singer at the cradle also wants to stay awake and be pleasantly entertained. For this are many songs in the little collection, which many readers would not consider actual lullabies, yet which also therefore the singer will gladly take up.[27]

Directed toward both infant and mother, Reichardt's *Wiegenlieder* are designed to pacify as well as entertain, a double function that he acknowledges might lead some to question the works' legitimacy (foreshadowing Girschner's criticism).

The inclusion of simple accompaniments suggests that Reichardt's lullabies could be performed in different ways. The mother could sing the melodies without accompaniment in the manner of folk lullabies, freeing her hands to hold or rock her infant. Or she might choose to sing (to the child, herself, or others) while accompanying herself at the piano, or even while someone else accompanied. Alternatively, another person, such as a child learning music or playing with her dolls, might sing and/or perform the lullabies.[28] The range of possibilities underscores the blend of functionality and aestheticism that characterizes Reichardt's collection, paving the way for the *Kunstwiegenlieder* of Schubert and other composers.

Although Reichardt does not specify which aspects of the lullabies were intended for the mother's enjoyment, they apparently involved both text and music. The composer drew his poems from the works of more than a dozen writers, male and female, ensuring some diversity of form and content. As Matthew Head notes, the twenty lullabies, in which "the conceit of functionality . . . emerges not as the purpose so much as the topic (or fiction) of the songs," embrace a broad array of subjects.[29] The mother-narrator's "mind wander(s) over maternity past, present, and future, over fate, hope, and tragedy; love, health, and sickness; the inconstancy of men."[30] Moreover, the collection displays surprising musical variety. While some of Reichardt's accompaniments (e.g., nos. 1, 2, 3) are so slight as to be extraneous, others have more substance. Among the settings, one encounters *alberti* bass (nos. 4, 5, 9, 14), *murki* bass (nos. 6, 11), chordal or single line accompaniments (nos. 10, 12), delayed entrances (no. 13), parallel thirds (nos. 7, 8), parallel sixths (no. 8), chromaticism in the melody and/or accompaniment (nos. 10, 14), minor modes (nos. 10, 14, 15, 16), deceptive progressions (no. 14), diminished harmonies (no. 4), non-tonic beginnings (no. 10), horn fifths (nos. 8 and 13), large vocal leaps (no. 14), extended vocal range (no. 16), metrical changes (no. 18), and even through-composition (of a single strophe) (nos. 13, 15). Some of the songs (nos. 4 and 5) have the feel of simple classical keyboard pieces. Several with texts expressing a mother's lament (nos.10 and 14, both entitled "Wiegenlied einer unglücklichen Mutter") evoke operatic airs. Nos. 12 (a setting of Schiller's brief, quasi-philosophical verse "Das Kind in der Wiege") and 17 (a setting of Herder's "Annchen von Tharau," from the "old Prussian") are hardly recognizable as lullabies, so attenuated are their textual or musical connections to the genre. Such variety was well calculated to maintain the mother's interest.

The compositional challenge of entertaining the mother while simultaneously creating an atmosphere of soporific monotony had important implications for concert audiences. *Wiegenlieder* were by no means confined to the nursery. In the late eighteenth and nineteenth centuries, the unassuming genre also made its way into more public performance spaces, both inside and outside the home. Like Reichardt's "gute deutsche Mütter," concert audiences were presumably to be soothed and simultaneously absorbed by the lullabies they heard. Thus in art song and instrumental lullabies (especially character pieces for piano), chromatic harmonies, rhythmic intricacies, virtuosic passage work, and other compositional complexities combine with traditional lullaby traits to produce music that could suitably entertain listeners in the drawing room, salon, or recital hall.[31]

What motivated the *Wiegenlied*'s emergence from the nursery? Why did such an intimate and lowly genre associated primarily with female domesticity find a new home in the public sphere, especially given the restrictions imposed on nineteenth-century women? In Girschner's view, poets and composers had lost sight of the true purpose of lullabies; the unconventional aspects of their *Wiegenlieder* represented a mistake. With the advantage of hindsight, however, we can recognize that the genre's transformation formed part of a larger trend; the *Wiegenlied* was but one of many folk genres appropriated by composers of art music during the nineteenth century.[32] Lullabies, barcarolles, serenades, spinning songs, spring songs – these and other types of folk song were aesthetically enriched through the introduction of poetic and musical complexities. The transformation sometimes met with resistance, but led in many instances to the creation of masterworks.

To say that other genres underwent a similar transformation does not, however, explain what inspired the artistic appropriation of the *Wiegenlied*. An incidental comment by the late nineteenth-century folklorist Franz Magnus Böhme suggests that the phenomenon may be rooted in masculine needs and desires.[33] Böhme notes with disgust that lullabies such as "Schlafe, mein Prinzchen!" (long attributed to Mozart) can be heard in concert settings for all-male choirs – arrangements he considers wholly inappropriate:

> This lullaby was first taken up and appeared in the Mozart celebration year of 1887 and was then as now at times sung in concerts – where the lullaby does not belong – and indeed not merely by theatre actresses, who are presumably all cheerful when they don't have children of their own they need to rock, but also by male singing circles, thus gentlemen in black coats, white collars, and white gloves, on the podium in glittering, brightly illuminated rooms! One has heard all of that, and famous Kapellmeisters have actually arranged this piece and other lullabies for male choirs! If sleep arias and lullabies are sung in operas, or even to the Christ child in churches, they belong to the scenery and make sense; in the concert hall, performed with bouquets in hand, they are nonsensical. I cannot help on this occasion describing such behavior as unnatural, tasteless and designed to lead artists astray, and if all first and second ladies, who flirt with lullabies, and male singing society participants, who don't think anything of performing "Schlafe, mein Prinzchen" and "Eia popeia!", that makes me angry. If a serious word doesn't help, so perhaps soon it will be the custom that lullabies will not be performed in concert halls.[34]

Table 3.1 Schubert's *Wiegenlieder*

D	Title	Text	Composed
304	Wiegenlied	Körner	15 Oct. 1815
498	Wiegenlied	anon.	Nov. 1816
527	Schlaflied	Mayrhofer	Jan. 1817
579	Der Knabe in der Wiege	Ottenwalt	Sept. 1817
795/20	Des Baches Wiegenlied	Müller	1823
867	Wiegenlied	Seidl	?1826
927	Vor meiner Wiege	Leitner	Fall 1827

If performances of *Wiegenlieder* by elegantly attired, all-male choirs in glittering theaters proved distasteful to Böhme, so presumably would have lullaby settings for full orchestra, such as Ferruccio Benvenuto Busoni's *Berceuse élégiaque: Des Mannes Wiegenlied am Sarge seiner Mutter*, Op. 42 (1909; *Elegiac Lullaby: A Man's Lullaby at His Mother's Coffin*). In such large-scale and public incarnations of the genre, the traditional figure of the nursing mother is replaced by multitudes of men. Tellingly, many nineteenth-century art song lullabies also involve male rather than female vocal protagonists. As the title of Busoni's orchestral *Berceuse* intimates, when brought into the male domain, the lullaby assumed different functions and meanings from those handed down through tradition. A mother's lament for a dead child is an archaic lullaby trope; a grown son's lullaby-lament for his dead mother bespeaks something new.

The transformation of the lullaby from folk song to art song in the early decades of the nineteenth century is beautifully illustrated by Schubert's contributions to the genre (Table 3.1). His roughly half-dozen *Wiegenlieder*, ranging from folk-like to artful, help explain the lullaby's proliferation as well as the peculiarities that bothered Girschner – both arising from male appropriation of the genre. In the hands of male poets and composers, the lullaby became an important vehicle for expressing disillusionment and anxiety. To many, an infant's gentle sleep held promise of the blessed tranquility of death.

Schubert and the sleep–death nexus

Unlike Reichardt, Schubert did not direct his *Wiegenlieder* toward a female market. His lullaby settings were not all published during his lifetime, and those that did find their way into print appeared with other kinds of Lieder, rather than in a single collection.[35] "Schlaflied," for example, joins the dramatic setting "Gruppe aus dem Tartarus" in Schubert's Op. 24, while "Wiegenlied" is grouped with three other Seidl settings ("Widerspruch," "Am Fenster," and "Sehnsucht") in his Op. 105. Encouraging women to be good mothers by singing to their infants does not seem to have been a concern of Schubert's or of his predominantly male circle of friends. Although two of Schubert's lullaby texts were composed by members of that circle (Mayrhofer's "Schlummerlied" and Ottenwalt's "Der Knabe in der Wiege"), neither constitutes a mother's direct address to her child. Instead, like most of Schubert's other lullaby texts, they seem to be delivered by, and to express the concerns of, a male.

Schubert's lullabies thus do not represent an offering to women so much as a borrowing from them. The male composer and his male poets return to the nursery – a manifestation of Biedermeier domesticity – where they appropriate a traditionally female genre both to express angst and seek comfort. Not surprisingly, female Lied composers, such as Luise Reichardt, Fanny Mendelssohn, and Clara Schumann, produced few if any lullaby settings.[36] Most nineteenth-century women, even touring artists like Schumann (mother of eight), never lost connection with children and their milieu. Their ties to the nursery, both literal and figurative, remained strong. Men, on the other hand, whose lives typically played out in the public sphere, were more likely to yearn for a return to the realm of childhood – not to assume the domestic duties traditionally assigned to women, but to re-experience the blissfulness of youth.[37] They sought to reenter childhood's paradise through song.

The lullaby, as Schubert and his poets clearly recognized, possesses powerful metaphorical potential. Its gentle strains can express a desire for comfort and protection in the face of life's torments, as well as evoke a vision of what awaits after life's completion. Frequent textual allusions to death in Schubert's *Wiegenlieder* suggest that the vocal protagonists are preoccupied by adult-like fears and worries. While a sleeping child might represent the ostensible focus of the song, the true subject is often the adult speaker who yearns for comparable serenity and an escape from life's tribulations in the comforting sounds of cradle music.[38]

The sleep-death nexus, borrowed from antiquity but fitted to an image of Biedermeier domesticity, presents death as a desirable state – an idyllic existence resembling an infant's peaceful slumber. In this formulation of the lost paradise myth, death represents the object of man's intense yearning. To die is essentially to return home, to reenter the nursery, to be held snugly in the loving embrace of one's mother.

It is not surprising that Schubert gravitated toward texts associating death and sleep. Death was all too familiar to him. In the early decades of the nineteenth century, Vienna posed constant risks to the health of its citizens.[39] Overcrowding, pollution, poor sanitation, an inferior food supply, limited medical care, and poverty had turned it into a virtual hotbed of disease and death. The fresh air and green expanses of the surrounding countryside offered some respite, inspiring many Viennese, including Schubert and Beethoven, to try to preserve or improve their health by taking frequent trips beyond the city limits. But the city inevitably lured them back with its cultural enticements and employment opportunities, and thus illness remained a continual and grave threat. As musicologist Leon Botstein writes, "Death and its ceremonial rituals – requiems, funeral processions, and burials – were a visible and regular part of daily life."[40]

Nearly every family suffered the agony of child mortality (echoing through posterity in numerous poetic elegies to dead children),[41] and Schubert's was no exception. Of the fourteen children born to his mother, Elisabeth Schubert (née Vietz), nine died in infancy or young childhood – seven before Schubert's birth and two a few years later. Although Schubert did not know his dead siblings (one of whom, Franz Karl, bore his first name), their deaths likely had an effect on him, as these brutal losses must have influenced his parents' relations with their surviving children. Elisabeth herself passed away in 1812, when Schubert was fifteen years old. Although there is no documentary evidence concerning his reaction, it appears that their relation was close, and the death may well have affected him strongly. A significant family history underlies Schubert's attraction to death-related lullaby texts.[42]

Of course, Schubert's most personal confrontation with death was with his own. In the fall of 1822, when he contracted syphilis, his death was assured. The question was not "if," but "when," with important implications for "how." Would he survive long enough to enter the third and final stage of the disease, with its accompanying dementia and paralysis? Would he, in the words of Schubert scholar and pianist Graham Johnson, "have to endure the worst fate for a musician, his creative faculties benumbed and the stream of his music frozen within a diseased brain?"[43]

The dangerous living conditions in Vienna, the Schubert family's numerous tragic losses, and the composer's contraction of a fatal yet unpredictable disease ensured that the subject of death would preoccupy him to varying degrees throughout his career.[44] It makes sense that song texts linking death with an infant's peaceful slumber would attract his attention. (The image of so many deceased Schubert babies must have invested the lullaby metaphor with extra force.) Schubert's interest in sleep-death lullaby texts also reflected the influence of new, more positive attitudes toward death that had emerged in the late eighteenth century.

Changing perspectives on death

Until the eighteenth century, the medieval image of death as a fearsome skeleton with scythe and hourglass remained a powerful tool with which Christianity could threaten potential sinners. Death was widely regarded as a punishment, inspiring dread and terror. But with the turn from superstition toward more enlightened modes of thought and the reawakening of interest in classical antiquity, a different conception of death began to take hold. Lessing, in an essay entitled *How the Ancients Represented Death* (1769; *Wie die Alten den Tod gebildet*) that built on several passages in Winckelmann's *Reflections on the Imitation of Greek Works in Painting and Sculpture*, rejected the harsh medieval image of death in favor of the gentler antique one. The ancient Greeks, as Winckelmann noted, portrayed death as a beautiful allegorical figure – a young spirit (or Genius), the twin brother of sleep.[45] The arrival of death, like that of sleep, was indicated by the spirit's inverted, extinguished torch. Both Lessing and Herder, who penned an essay in response to (and with the same title as) Lessing's in 1774, were attracted to the Greek conception of death and thought it "more worthy of the 'Christianity of reason' in an enlightened age."[46] Lessing writes,

[I]t is a fact that the religion which first revealed to man that even natural death is the fruit and wages of sin necessarily magnified the terrors of death infinitely. There have been sages who thought life a punishment; but to think death a punishment could, without Revelation, occur to no person who used his reason alone.

From this point of view, then, it was presumably our religion which expelled the old serene image of death from the precincts of art! But since that same religion did not intend to reveal that dreadful truth for our despair, since it too assures us that the death of the pious can only be gentle and consoling, I do not see what should prevent our artist from abandoning the hideous skeleton and again availing themselves of that better image. Scripture itself speaks of an angel of death; and what artist ought not rather to aim at portraying an angel than a skeleton?

Only misunderstood religion can lead us away from the beautiful, and it is evidence of true religion rightly understood if in all cases it guides us back to the beautiful.[47]

Although Herder doubted that the Greeks regarded the actual process of dying as peaceful, he nevertheless accepted their beautiful allegorical image of death: "Thus our last friend is no horrifying specter, but an ender of life, the lovely youth who puts out the torch and imposes calm on the billowing sea."[48] Dying might involve pain, but death – a permanent sleep – did not. The conviction that death is ultimately good and akin to sleep found strong support in Socrates' *Apology* (which Matthias Claudius translated into German in 1790). Attempting to mollify his friends before embracing the fatal punishment imposed on him, Socrates reasons that death is either an eternal sleep undisturbed by dreams or a journey of the soul to another place.[49]

Poets responded with enthusiasm to the positive conception of death presented in Lessing's and Herder's essays. In *Dichtung und Wahrheit,* Goethe writes about its profound impact on his generation: "Most of all we were delighted by the beauty of the thought that the Ancients acknowledged death as the brother of sleep and formed both of them alike to the point of confusing them, as is proper with twin brothers. In this theme we could now really celebrate the triumph of beauty in lofty terms, and banish ugliness of every kind."[50]

In "Die Götter Griechenlands," Schiller sets the ancient image of death as a beautiful youth in opposition to the gruesome skeleton of medieval Christianity: "Before the bed of death / No ghastly spectre stood; – but from the porch / Of life, the lip – one kiss inhaled the breath, / And a mute Genius gently lower'd his torch."[51] Although Schiller, a former medical student, did not deny the painful reality of death, he rejected the skeleton as an adequate symbol for death on account of its ugliness.[52] In hailing the classical image of the beautiful spirit with inverted torch, Schiller (despite his attempt to deflect criticism for the supposedly anti-Christian tenor of the original poem by producing a second version) proved himself a strong proponent of the new spirit of paganism that swept through eighteenth-century Germany.

Novalis, responding to Schiller, rejected the ancient image of death but retained its positive quality. In the fifth of his *Hymnen an die Nacht* (1800), he suggests that the Greek image, while beautiful and serene ("A pale wan youth puts out the light to rest,– / Soft is the end, as harp-strings touched by wind,–"), fails to alleviate mankind's fear and anguish in confronting life's inevitable end; only Christian faith can do so.[53] Novalis presents his own positive conception of death in an ecstatic, rhapsodic fusion of erotic and religious imagery. In the sixth poem, entitled "Sehnsucht nach dem Tode," death is portrayed as the object of man's greatest yearning.

Down to Earth's bosom deep below
Far from where Light can reach us!
Our stresses and sharp pains of woe
Joyful departure teach us.
Within a narrow boat we come
And hasten to the heavenly home.

All hail, then, to eternal Night,
All hail, eternal sleeping,
Warmed have we been by daily light,

Withered by grief's long weeping.
Strange lands no longer joys arouse,
We want to reach our Father's House.[54]

Although Schubert's lullaby texts contain no references to the classical image of death as a beautiful spirit with an extinguished, inverted torch, the songs (like Novalis's *Hymnen*) reflect the legacy of antiquity in their positive conception of death, and more specifically in their association of youth, death, and sleep. The interrelationship of these *topi* varies, resulting in lullaby settings with very different functions, meanings, and aesthetic properties. Examining these works with special attention to the poetic speaker and the sleep–death nexus reveals the emergence of art song out of folk tradition.

From folk song to art song: Schubert's *Wiegenlieder*

"Wiegenlied," D. 498, composed in November 1816, is the only Schubert lullaby to have passed into the oral tradition, and it remains one of the most famous and beloved cradle songs. Although the text was initially attributed (in the song's first published edition of July 1829 and several early copies) to Matthias Claudius, it does not appear in his collected works.[55] The autograph manuscript of the song is lost. While Claudius certainly could have authored the poem (he wrote several other lullaby texts),[56] so could another writer. It may be fanciful to imagine that the anonymous poet was a woman, but it is worth noting that this is the only Schubert lullaby text without an identifiable male author, and the only one to suggest a mother singing to her child. (Although the speaker is not identified as the mother, that interpretation seems most convincing; no textual evidence suggests otherwise.)[57] The anonymity of its author places this poem in the company of innumerable authentic folk songs, whose words, originating in obscurity and altered over many generations by those who sang them, cannot be attributed to any single figure.

Schlafe, holder, süßer Knabe,
Leise wiegt dich deiner Mutter Hand;
Sanfte Ruhe, milde Labe
Bringt dir schwebend dieses Wiegenband.

Schlafe in dem süßen Grabe,
Noch beschützt dich deiner Mutter Arm,
Alle Wünsche, alle Habe
Faßt sie liebend, alle liebewarm.

Sleep, dear, sweet boy,
Your mother's hand rocks you softly,
This swaying cradle strap
Brings you gentle peace and tender comfort.

Sleep in the sweet grave;
Your mother's arms still protect you.
All her wishes, all her possessions
She holds lovingly, with loving warmth.

Example 3.1 Schubert, "Wiegenlied," D. 498, mm. 1–4

Schlafe in der Flaumen Schoße,	Sleep in her lap, soft as down;
Noch umtönt dich lauter Liebeston,	Pure notes of love still echo around you.
Eine Lilie, eine Rose,	A lily, a rose
Nach dem Schlafe werd' sie dir zum Lohn.	Shall be your reward after sleep.

The direct address to the child (a common trait of folk lullabies), together with the folk-like simplicity of Schubert's strophic setting, helps account for the song's absorption into the oral tradition (Example 3.1). Both words and music support the lullaby's traditional function. The text, comprising three similarly structured quatrains of alternating trochaic tetrameter and pentameter, projects the eternal warmth, comfort, and protection of maternal love. As Youens writes, the lullaby has the "profound resonance of an archetypal work, the song not of a particularized individual but of Every Mother singing to her child."[58] The musical setting, in the key of A-flat major,[59] exhibits an array of conventional lullaby traits: slow tempo, quiet dynamics, circumscribed melody, middle range, two-measure phrasing, rhythmic simplicity, alternating tonic and dominant harmonies, diatonicism, etc. While the accompaniment, with its stream of rocking eighth notes and occasional horn fifths, contributes to the gentle mood, it is not essential; the melody can easily stand alone. Schubert's lyrical expression avoids all complexity.

Even the reference to death in the second stanza has no power to disrupt the song's serenity. Youens notes that it is unclear whether the stanza alludes to the child's eventual death or implies that the child is already dead. Either way, "his mother's love, all powerful and beneficent … remains with him and protects him even after death."[60] The repeated word "still" [*noch*] ("Your mother's arms still protect you"; "Pure notes of love still echo around you") emphasizes that maternal protection will never cease. The song's structural repetitions (both textual and musical) offer further confirmation that death (the focus of stanza two) is no different from sleep (the focus of stanzas

Example 3.2 Schubert, "Wiegenlied," D. 867, mm. 5–8

one and three). The nature of death, however, is not of primary concern in this song. Rather, every word and tone seems geared toward expressing a mother's infinite love for her child.

"Wiegenlied," D. 867, a Seidl setting dating from around 1826, has the same key and tempo marking as "Wiegenlied," D. 498, and also exudes melodic charm (Example 3.2). This later lullaby, however, displays traces of artfulness and moralizing foreign to the earlier one, and, unsurprisingly, has not passed into the oral tradition. Following convention, the poetic speaker (perhaps the mother, although conceivably another figure) addresses the slumbering child, marveling at its beautiful appearance. But instead of urging the child to sleep, the speaker counsels it to guard those qualities – innocence and love – that ensure its present blissfulness, and to adopt the same peaceful pose when one day death arrives.

Wie sich der Äuglein Kindlicher Himmel,	How carelessly the eyes' childlike heaven
Schlummerbelastet, lässig verschließt! –	Closes, laden with slumber!
Schließe sie einst so, lockt dich die Erde:	Close them thus, when one day the earth calls you:
Drinnen ist Himmel, außen ist Lust!	Heaven is within you, outside is joy!
Wie dir so schlafroth glühet die Wange!	How your cheeks glow red with sleep!
Rosen aus Eden hauchten sie an:	Roses from Eden have breathed upon them;
Rosen die Wangen, Himmel die Augen,	Your cheeks are roses, your eyes are heaven,
Heiterer Morgen, himmlischer Tag!	Bright morning, heavenly day!
Wie des Gelockes goldige Wallung	How the golden waves of your locks
Kühlet der Schläfe glühenden Saum.	Cool the edge of your burning temples!
Schön ist das Goldhaar, schöner der Kranz drauf:	Your golden hair is lovely, and even lovelier the garland upon it;
Träum' du vom Lorbeer, bis er dir blüht.	Dream of the laurel until it blooms for you.

Liebliches Mündchen, Engel umweh'n dich:	Sweet little mouth, the angels hover round you;
Drinnen die Unschuld, drinnen die Lieb!;	Inside is innocence, inside is love!
Wahre sie Kindchen, wahre sie treulich:	Guard them, my child, guard them faithfully:
Lippen sind Rosen, Lippen sind Glut.	Lips are roses, lips are warmth!
Wie dir ein Engel faltet die Händchen;	As an angel folds your little hands,
Falte sie einst so, gehst du zur Ruh'!;	Fold them thus one day when you go to rest!
Schön sind die Träume, wenn man gebetet:	Dreams are beautiful when you pray,
Und das Erwachen lohnt mit dem Traum.	And your awakening rewards you no less than your dream.

Like "Wiegenlied," D. 498, the song suggests that death resembles a child's gentle sleep, but its music is both simple and nuanced. Schubert's setting evokes traditional lullabies through various means: slow rocking motion, entrancing melody, tranquil mood. Yet the composer sets Seidl's ten quatrains of dactylic dimeters with an extended musical strophe that divides into contrasting halves and features subtle melodic and harmonic variations in its subsequent occurrences (cf. mm. 10–11 and 35–36; 15–22 and 40–47). Mode switches and chromatic harmonies impart mystery and solemnity to the prevailing serenity, implying that the song evokes, but does not imitate, folk lullabies.

In other Schubert *Wiegenlieder*, the mother is silent, or assumes a non-human or symbolic form. Although the maternal image remains, the text comprises the words of another poetic speaker – one whose gender is male, or unspecified, a change with important implications for the poetic content and its musical elaboration. "Schlaflied," D. 527, for example, composed in January 1817 to a text by Mayrhofer, employs third person narration instead of the traditional direct address, and introduces unconventional musical elements into an otherwise folk-like setting. In three quatrains of iambic tetrameter (a conventional structure of folk poetry), an anonymous speaker relates a brief, present tense narrative embodying the traditional lullaby conceit. A boy, lured by the sounds and sights of nature, wanders out to the forest, river, and fields, and lies down in the cool grass, where dreams soon lull him to sleep. The maternal voice becomes audible in the "songs" (quoted or merely mentioned) of the natural world:

Es mahnt der Wald, es ruft der Strom:	The woods exhort, the river cries out:
'Du liebes Bübchen, zu uns komm!'	'Sweet boy, come to us!'
Der Knabe kommt, und staunt, und weilt,	The boy approaches, marvels and tarries,
Und ist von jedem Schmerz geheilt.	And is healed of all pain.

Aus Büschen flötet Wachtelschlag,	The quail's song echoes from the bushes,
Mit irren Farben spielt der Tag;	The day makes play with shimmering colours;
Auf Blümchen rot, auf Blümchen blau	On flowers red and blue
Erglänzt des Himmels feuchter Tau.	The moist dew of heaven glistens.
Ins frische Gras legt er sich hin:	He lies down in the cool grass
Läßt über sich die Wolken ziehn,	And lets the clouds drift above him;
An seine Mutter angeschmiegt,	Nestling close to his mother,
Hat ihn der Traumgott eingewiegt.	He is lulled to sleep by the god of dreams.

Schubert responded to Mayrhofer's allegorical tale – in which a youth's gentle sleep in the embrace of Mother Earth, or the uniting of man and nature, prefigures the serenity of death – by composing peaceful lullaby music in the pastoral key of F major. (Mayrhofer, who tried to commit suicide on several occasions, would presumably have yearned for such a comforting death.) The hypnotic swaying motion, arising from the 12/8 meter and half-measure harmonic changes, which in another context might evoke a barcarolle, here conjures the image of a rocking cradle.

As in "Wiegenlied," D. 498, the work forges an association between sleep and death, but with a different emphasis. Although there is no explicit reference, death represents the song's focus. The boy's peaceful outdoor slumber, free of all pain, suggests the state of tranquility that awaits humankind after death's arrival – a message like that of the similarly symbolic song "Der Tod und das Mädchen," composed in February 1817, a month after "Schlaflied." In associating death with sleep, both works reveal ties to antiquity. "Der Tod und das Mädchen," whose text was written by Claudius (by 1775), first portrays death as a frightening skeleton, but reveals it actually to be "Freund Hain," a gentle (if unavoidable) being who promises to rock the maiden to sleep. "Schlaflied," the text of which dates from some forty years later, replaces the medieval image of death with one that appealed strongly to Romantics: the merging of man and nature, captured in the image of a sleeping boy, nestled in the grass as if in a grave. The text's third person perspective suggests a new understanding of the maternal being providing eternal protection through her embrace. Nature, in all its abundance and variety, here replaces the archetypal human mother, whose voice is projected through the words and music of "Wiegenlied," D. 498, and other folk lullabies.

Unlike "Wiegenlied," D. 498, "Schlaflied" derives its musical charm from harmony as well as melody. Particularly notable are the rapid, chromatic chord changes in the middle of the strophe; in mm. 8–12, the harmony moves up sequentially from an F major sonority (I) to A major,

Example 3.3 Schubert, "Schlaflied," D. 527, mm. 8–12

B flat major, and C major, before a conventional cadence in the tonic (Example 3.3). This progression coincides with the last two lines of each stanza, and may well have been inspired by those of stanza three, which describe the boy's symbolic sleep ("Nestling close to his mother, / He is lulled to sleep by the god of dreams"). Out of place in folk song, the chromatic progression – which irritated one 1824 reviewer[61] – draws attention to the veiled allusion to death and imparts an artfulness to the piano accompaniment.

Much would be lost (both harmonically and rhythmically) if the melody were to be sung without that accompaniment. But it is not this progression alone that takes the song outside the realm of folk song. The vocal line also breaks with convention through its octave leaps and large range of an 11th. While exhibiting *Volkstümlichkeit*, this is not a functional *Wiegenlied* intended for "good German mothers" to sing privately in the nursery, but, like Seidl's "Wiegenlied," a stylized lullaby, meant for public performance. The art song mimics the soporific quality of the folk lullaby, but for very different ends. It both requires and rewards attentive listening.

"Der Knabe in der Wiege," D. 579, composed in September 1817 to a text by Ottenwalt, takes the perspective of a speaker (presumably male) who observes a human mother rocking her child to sleep. We do not hear her voice.

Er schläft so süß, der Mutter Blicke hangen	He sleeps so sweetly; his mother's gaze
An ihres Lieblings leisem Atemzug,	Hangs on her darling's lightest breath;
Den sie mit stillem sehnsuchtsvollem Bangen	So long and anxiously she carried him
So lange unterm Herzen trug.	With quiet longing under her heart.
Sie sieht so froh die vollen Wangen glühen	With joy she sees his round cheeks glow,
In gelbe Ringellocken halb versteckt,	Half hidden in his golden curls,
Und will das Ärmchen sanft herunter ziehen,	And gently covers up the little arm
Das sich im Schlummer ausgestreckt,	Flung outward in his sleep.
Und leis' und leiser schaukelt sie die Wiege	Ever more gently she rocks the cradle,
Und singt den kleinen Schläfer leis' in Ruh;	Softly singing the tiny baby to sleep;
Ein Lächeln spielet um die holden Züge,	A smile plays round his sweet features,
Doch bleibt das Auge friedlich zu.	But his eyes stay peacefully closed.
Erwachst du Kleiner, o so lächle wieder,	When you awake, little one, ah, smile once more,
Und schau ihr hell ins Mutterangesicht:	And look up into your mother's face:
So lauter Liebe schaut es auf dich nieder,	So you will see pure love look down on you,
Noch kennest du die Liebe nicht.	Though as yet you don't know what love is.
Bald aber lenst du sie aus ihren Blicken,	But soon you will learn about it from her eyes,
Aus ihrem Herzen, wenn es sanft bewegt	And from her heart, when it beats
Von mütterlichem volleren Entzücken	Against your tiny heart,
An deinem kleinen Herzen schlägt.	In a rapture of motherly delight.
Und lernest Sprache zu des Herzens Triebe,	And you will learn to speak at the prompting of the heart,
Zuerst mit Stammeln nur den Mutterlaut,	Stammering at first the sounds your mother makes,
Und bald noch manches süße Wort der Liebe,	And soon many another sweet word of love,
Und wirst den Deinen so vertraut.	And so gain confidence in your own words.
Und lernst den theuren Vater auch erkennen,	Also you will learn to know the loving Father,

Und eilst ihm zu von deiner Mutter Brust,	Hastening toward him from your mother's breast;
Und lernst die Dinge scheiden und benennen,	Learn to distinguish things and to name them,
Und fühlst des Denkens neue Lust.	Feel the unaccustomed delight of thought.
Und lernest beten aus der Mutter Munde	And from your mother's mouth you will learn to pray,
Nach ihres Herzens kindlich frommem Sinn,	Following the simple pious ways of her heart.
Er weiset dir in stiller Abendstunde	In the quiet evening hours, the Father will show you
Der Vater nach den Sternen hin;	The way to the stars,
Dort, wo der Vater aller Menschen wohnet,	Where dwells the Father of mankind,
Der dich, und alle seine Kinder liebt,	Who loves you and all his children,
Der alles Gute väterlich belohnet,	Who rewards all goodness like a father
Und jedem seine Freude gibt.	And bestows the gift of joy upon all.
Da wandelst du so rein und froh auf Erden,	So you will make your way on earth untainted and in good spirits,
Dein Herz so gläubig und so gut und weich!	Your heart faithful, tender and good.
So bleibe, Holder, willst du glücklich warden,	Stay thus, my sweet, if you would be happy,
Denn solcher ist das Himmelreich.	For of such is the kingdom of heaven.[62]

A subtle disjunction in Ottenwalt's lengthy poem calls attention to the fact that this song is not a lullaby so much as a meditation on a lullaby. In the first three stanzas, the poetic speaker describes the blissful domestic scene: a mother tenderly singing and rocking her infant to sleep. In the remaining seven stanzas, the speaker addresses the sleeping child directly, telling him about the world of love, language, thought, and piety he will soon come to know. The image of the doting mother leads to that of the honorable father, and eventually to the all-loving God, "the Father of mankind," who rewards human goodness with the gift of joy. The poem thus shifts discreetly from description to exhortation. While partially employing the lullaby's traditional mode of direct address, the speaker does not urge the child to sleep (indeed the mother seems to have already taken care of that) but to lead the life of a devout and moral citizen by always retaining his goodness and innocence. Although the speaker's identity is not specified, all evidence (access to the intimate scene, enthrallment by the child's looks, implicit approval of the mother's conduct, concern for the child's future well-being) points to the father. The person to whom the child will come from his mother's breast and who will show the child "the way to the stars, / Where

Example 3.4 Schubert, "Der Knabe in der Wiege," D. 579, mm. 5–8

dwells the Father of mankind," the father is a conduit between maternal and heavenly bliss.

For this lullaby "once-removed," Schubert composes a lovely musical setting that combines traditional *Wiegenlied* traits with artfulness. With its 6/8 meter, initial tonic-dominant alternations, consistent figuration, and quiet dynamics, the music has the lulling effect characteristic of the genre. The regular phrasing, rhythmic simplicity, and strophic repetitions evoke *Volkstümlichkeit* (Example 3.4). But if the song's strophic form is folk-like, its proportions and internal organization are not: the single musical strophe, encompassing two poetic stanzas (each with substantial text repetitions) spread across a ternary musical structure (A: mm. 5–32, B: mm. 33–50, A': mm. 51–65),[63] extends through a full sixty measures, with the B section introducing a new texture and tonality. The musical setting also conveys emotional nuances (especially wistfulness) in various ways: e.g., chromatic melodic alterations (cf. mm. 13–14 and 21–22), unexpected touches of minor (e.g., mm. 9, 17, 22), flat harmonies (e.g., m. 18), and phrase extensions (mm. 49–50). The tempo marking ("Etwas lebhaft") serves as further evidence that this *Wiegenlied* departs from the genre's traditional function.

These signs of artfulness, however, do not disrupt the prevailing impression of simplicity and serenity. It is possible that the song, as Schubert expected it to be performed, had less of a paternal, moralistic message than might appear from the score. The substantial length of the musical strophe suggests that he may not have intended all ten poetic stanzas – requiring five run-throughs – to be sung. (In their Deutsche Grammophon recording, Dietrich Fischer-Dieskau and Gerald Moore present only the first two stanzas. Richard Wigmore, in *Schubert: The Complete Song Texts*, includes just the first four stanzas.) Abbreviating the text alters the message of the song, diminishing the portion given over to the poetic speaker's exhortation and placing greater emphasis on the initial description of mother and child. While Schubert's setting hints at the speaker's broad, quasi-religious perspective on the intimate domestic scene he observes, the music seems calculated primarily to convey the homey blissfulness of that scene. Although the poet progresses toward an image of the "kingdom of heaven," the composer, in essence, remains in the nursery.

In "Wiegenlied," D. 304, composed in October 1815 to a text by Körner, the poetic speaker is again ostensibly an adult male who observes a child sleeping in its mother's arms, but here the domestic scene fades more rapidly, giving way to exuberant (self) reflection, resulting in a strikingly different sort of "lullaby."[64] The sight of the slumbering child leads the speaker to ruminate on the three times in life a man is cradled in love: as an infant in the arms of his mother, as a young man in the arms of his sweetheart, and as an old man in the arms of death's angel, carried to heaven.

Schlummre sanft! – Noch an dem Mutterherzen	Slumber softly! Close to your mother's heart
Fühlst du nicht des Lebens Qual und Lust;	You do not yet feel life's torment and joy;
Deine Träume kennen keine Schmerzen,	Your dreams know no sorrows,
Deine Welt ist deiner Mutter Brust.	Your world is your mother's breast.
Ach! wie süß träumt man die frühen Stunden,	Ah, how sweet are the dreams of those early hours,
Wo man von der Mutterliebe lebt;	When we live by our mother's love;
Die Erinnerung ist mir verschwunden,	My memory of them has vanished,
Ahnung bleibt es nur, die mich durchbebt.	They remain a mere impression to stir me.
Dreimal darf der Mensch so süß erwarmen,	Three times a man may experience such a sweet warmth;
Dreimal ist's dem Glücklichen erlaubt,	Three times the happy man is permitted
Daß er in der Liebe Götterarmen	To believe in the higher meaning of life,
An des Lebens höh're Deutung glaubt.	Embraced by the divine arms of love.
Liebe gibt ihm ihren ersten Segen,	Love gives him her first blessing,
Und der Säugling blüht in Freud' und Lust,	And the infant blooms in joy and happiness.
Alles lacht dem frischen Blick entgegen;	All smile at his fresh gaze;
Liebe hält ihn an der Mutterbrust.	Love holds him to his mother's breast.
Wenn sich dann der schöne Himmel trübte,	Then, when the fair heavens darken,
Und es wölkt sich nun des Jünglings Lauf:	And the youth's path becomes clouded,
Da, zum zweiten Mal, nimmt als Geliebte Ihn die Lieb' in ihre Arme auf.	Then, for the second time, love takes him As her sweetheart in her arms.

[Musical example: Schubert, "Wiegenlied," D. 304, mm. 9–11]

dei - ne Welt___ ist dei - ner Mut - ter Brust,
Ahn-ung bleibt___ es nur, die mich__ durch- bebt,

Example 3.5 Schubert, "Wiegenlied," D. 304, mm. 9–11

Doch im Sturme bricht der Blütenstengel,	But in the storm the flower's stem breaks,
Und im Sturme bricht des Menschen Herz:	And in the storm a man's heart breaks:
Da erscheint die Lieb' als Todesengel,	Then love appears as the angel of death,
Und sie trägt ihn jubelnd himmelwärts.	And bears him jubilantly up to heaven.

In this song, the philosophical overwhelms the functional. Unlike "Der Knabe in der Wiege," the musical setting bears little resemblance to a traditional lullaby (apart from the hushed dynamics, slow tempo, and strophic form). There is no rocking motion or alternating pattern of tonic and dominant harmonies. The texture is largely chordal, and Schubert occasionally injects sudden forte passages (Example 3.5). The phrasing, as Youens remarks, is surprisingly asymmetrical (particularly given the regularity of Körner's trochaic pentameters).[65] Still, the title "Wiegenlied" is not entirely misleading as Reed (who describes the song as "a hymn in praise of love") suggests.[66] The tempo marking "Langsam, ruhig" might indicate not just the "serenity of contemplation" but also the peaceful "sleep" of death, an interpretation supported by the *pavane* rhythms (half note-quarter note-quarter note) in eight of the song's nineteen measures. The image of a sleeping child prompts a "lullaby" that sounds more like a chorale, a fitting – and common – compositional approach for a song whose text climaxes with the soul's ascension to heaven.[67]

By briefly alluding to his own situation ("My memory of them has vanished, / They remain a mere impression to stir me"), the speaker reveals that his philosophical ruminations are of deep personal significance. Although the image of the sleeping child before him inspires his meditation, the speaker's focus seems to be the trajectory of his own life (Youens notes that Körner was blessed with an extraordinary family, and enjoyed a loving childhood),[68] particularly the journey of his soul at life's conclusion. Once again, the speaker implies, he will be carried in loving arms, with his human mother transformed into an angel of death.

A far more blatant infusion of subjectivity into the lullaby (or, perhaps more accurately, the infusion of lullaby music into an overtly subjective Lied) occurs in "Vor meiner Wiege," D. 927, composed in 1827–28 to a text by Leitner. Strangely, in this art song, the figure of the mother is not merely silent, but also physically absent; her lullaby and her image exist only in the speaker's memory. The child is missing too. Unlike Schubert's other lullabies, "Vor meiner Wiege" does not open with a vision of the mother-child dyad. That comforting image belongs to the remembered past and the imagined future, but not the experienced present. It is the very absence of intimate interaction between mother and child that leads the sleep–death nexus to take center stage. The poetic speaker, it soon becomes apparent, longs to be enfolded once again in his mother's protective arms, to re-experience the security and warmth of eternal maternal love as he passes into death. (He yearns, one could say, to be the infant to whom Schubert's D. 498 is sung.)

Das also, das ist der enge Schrein,	So this is the narrow chest
Da lag ich einstens als Kind darein,	Where I once lay as a baby;
Da lag ich gebrechlich, hilflos und stumm	Where I lay, frail, helpless and dumb,
Und zog nur zum Weinen die Lippen krumm.	Twisting my lips only to cry.
Ich konnte nichts fassen mit Händchen zart,	I could grip nothing with my tiny, tender hands,
Und war doch gebunden nach Schelmenart;	Yet I was bound like a rogue;
Ich hatte Füsschen und lag doch wie lahm,	I possessed little feet, and yet lay as if lame,
Bis Mutter an ihre Brust mich nahm.	Until mother took me to her breast.
Dann lachte ich saugend zu ihr empor,	Then I laughed up at her as I suckled,
Sie sang mir von Rosen und Engeln vor,	And she sang to me of roses and angels;
Sie sang und sie wiegte mich singend in Ruh,	She sang and with her singing lulled me to sleep,
Und küsste mir liebend die Augen zu.	And with a kiss lovingly closed my eyes.
Sie spannte aus Seide, gar dämmerig grün,	She spread a cool tent of dusky green silk
Ein kühliges Zelt hoch über mich hin.	Above me.
Wo find ich nur wieder solch friedlich Gemach?	Where shall I find such a peaceful chamber again?
Vielleicht, wenn das grüne Gras mein Dach!	Perhaps when the green grass is my roof!
O Mutter, lieb' Mutter, bleib' lange noch hier!	O mother, dear mother, stay here a long time yet!
Wer sänge dann tröstlich von Engeln mir?	Who else would sing to me comforting songs of angels.
Wer küsste mir liebend die Augen zu	Who else would close my eyes lovingly with a kiss
Zur langen, zur letzten und tiefesten Ruh'?	For the long, last and deepest rest?

Example 3.6a Schubert, "Vor meiner Wiege," D. 927, mm. 5–8

Example 3.6b Schubert, "Vor meiner Wiege," D. 927, mm. 27–30

In the outer sections of Schubert's ternary form (stanzas 1–2 and 5), the speaker stands alone by the side of the cradle in which he once lay as an infant; he is first embittered, then frightened, by his isolation. Schubert sets these verses in the key of B minor with a declamatory style more suggestive of speech (i.e., an internal monologue) than song (Example 3.6a). In the middle section (stanzas 3–4), however, the mother-child dyad of yore assumes a ghostly presence. As the speaker remembers his mother's long-ago lullabies ("she sang to me of roses and angels"), the music slips into a strongly contrasting section evocative of *Wiegenlieder* (Example 3.6b). Songful lyricism is conveyed through the elongated vocal line, triplet subdivisions of the beat (an un-notated shift into 12/8 meter), and B major tonality (a mode switch anticipated in the setting of the last line of stanza 2: "Until mother took me to her breast"). This lullaby music suggests various interpretations. One could regard the vocal line as an echo or memory of a lullaby that the speaker's mother used to sing (the speaker remembering the song's melody but not its words). Alternatively, the treble notes of the piano accompaniment – sometimes in counterpoint with the vocal line, sometimes doubling it – could play that role. Or one could view the lyrical B section (both vocal line and accompaniment) as only loosely related to the songs that the speaker remembers, or imagines, from his infancy. It might represent his conscious or semi-conscious aesthetic stylization of those songs, or simply a musical realization of the tenderness of maternal love. However one conceives it, the B section is set off from the surrounding musical material, and its gentle lyricism holds promise of death's serenity.

Schubert's most well-known art song lullaby is "Des Baches Wiegenlied," D. 795, no. 20, which concludes the *Die schöne Müllerin* cycle. In this serene strophic setting of Müller's text, the heart-broken miller finds release from his suffering in the watery embrace of the brook, a substitute mother who lovingly and protectively rocks him to sleep. (As Lied scholar Arnold Feil observes, this is the only song in the cycle besides "Das Wandern" to include as many as five stanzas, and it lasts longer than any of the other songs.[69] As in "Das Wandern," Schubert creates the impression that the singing could go on forever,[70] here enhancing the music's soporific quality.)

Gute Ruh', gute Ruh'!	Rest well, rest well!
Tu' die Augen zu!	Close your eyes!
Wandrer, du müder, du bist zu Haus.	Weary wanderer, this is your home.
Die Treu' ist hier,	Here is constancy,
Sollst liegen bei mir,	You shall lie with me,
Bis das Meer will trinken die Bächlein aus.	Until the sea drinks up all brooks.
Will betten dich kühl,	I shall make you a cool bed
Auf weichen Pfühl,	On a soft pillow
In dem blauen krystallenen Kämmerlien.	In this blue crystal chamber.
Heran, heran,	Come, come,
Was wiegen kann,	All you who can lull,
Woget und wieget den Knaben mir ein!	Rock and lull this boy for me!
Wenn ein Jagdhorn schallt	When a hunting-horn echoes
Aus dem grünen Wald,	From the green forest,
Will ich sausen und brausen wohl um dich her.	I shall surge and roar about you.
Blickt nicht herein,	Do not peep in,
Blauen Blümelein!	Little blue flowers!
Ihr macht meinem Schläfer die Träume so schwer.	You will give my slumberer such bad dreams.
Hinweg, hinweg	Away, away
Von dem Mühlensteg,	From the mill-path,

Example 3.7 Schubert, "Des Baches Wiegenlied," D. 795, no. 20, mm. 4–6

Böses Mägdelein, daß ihn dein Schatten nicht weckt!	Wicked girl, lest your shadow should wake him!
Wirf mir herein	Throw me
Dein Tüchlein fein,	Your fine shawl,
Daß ich die Augen ihm halte bedeckt!	That I may keep his eyes covered!
Gute Nacht, gute Nacht!	Good nicht, good night,
Bis alles wacht,	Until all awaken,
Schlaf aus deine Freude, schlaf aus dein Leid!	Sleep away your joy, sleep away your sorrow!
Der Vollmond steigt,	The full moon rises,
Der Nebel weicht,	The mist vanishes,
Und der Himmel da oben, wie ist er so weit!	And the sky above, how vast it is!

A dirge recast as a lullaby (the half notes that toll in the piano's outer voices throughout most of the strophe sound a death knell but have a comforting, hypnotic effect), "Des Baches Wiegenlied" depicts the miller's death as tranquil yet tinged with melancholy (Example 3.7). The twin concepts of death and sleep, manifested in nearly all of Schubert's *Wiegenlieder*, are here thoroughly fused. The miller – perhaps like the infant addressed in "Wiegenlied," D. 498 – has already died and, as the brook assures us, slumbers peacefully. As Youens notes, the brook suppresses any doubts about the miller's arrival "zu Haus," in part by substituting A major, the subdominant, for the expected C-sharp minor harmony in m. 11: "In the somber submediant is awareness of the tragedy that has brought this wanderer to this house, and the brook-piano will have none of it."[71] The vocal line's high E in m. 10 (on the word "bist") forms the third of the C-sharp minor sonority and thus hints that the miller's current state is cause for sorrow. In the next several measures, however, during the brook's repeated lines "Here is constancy, / You shall lie with me," the high E (sounding six times) is reinterpreted as the fifth of the A major harmony, and the melancholy dissipates. When the vocal line eventually ends, the same E is restored to its original function as the tonic root, with all tension released. There are other suggestions of emotional pain (e.g., the recurring downbeat, half diminished seventh sonority in mm. 16–18, followed by an even tenser fully diminished seventh in m. 19; the heavy chordal texture of mm. 16–19; the melodic outline of a descending augmented fourth in m. 6 and descending diminished fourth in m. 19). These too, however, ultimately give way, confirming that the miller sleeps peacefully in his watery bed and leading to an ecstatic vision of celestial reawakening.

As in "Wiegenlied," D. 498, the text of "Des Baches Wiegenlied" is a mother's direct address to her child, but here both figures must be understood metaphorically. The masculine brook ("der Bach"), like the eerie skeleton figure of death ("der Tod") in "Der Tod und das Mädchen," assumes the role of the "good mother," rocking his/her child to sleep. In "Des Baches Wiegenlied," the masculine usurpation of the lullaby, a traditionally feminine genre, thus seems complete. The male speaker (or "singer")[72] seems to take over the very body of the female (an arresting image that conveys the sense of violation that Girschner attached to the lullaby's transformation). The brook, an emblem of nature, sings through the archetypal mother's voice, embraces through her arms, and shelters through her love. He does not merely quote her song, describe her appearance, or insinuate her presence – he actually becomes her. The miller, in turn, by settling in the brook's lap, becomes the protected, loved, comforted child that the speaker of "Vor meiner Wiege" – and implicitly every other male or gender-unspecified speaker of Schubert's *Wiegenlieder* – yearns to be. In the soothing strains of the brook's lullaby and the depths of his watery grave (which together merge with the concept of "home"), he finds sanctuary.

Although part of a compositionally complex song cycle, "Des Baches Wiegenlied" is closely tied to folk tradition. If the song has not entered the oral tradition, like the somewhat similar "Wiegenlied," D. 498, this is due to the replacement of a human mother with a male brook, the narrative specificity of the text (implying the listener's familiarity with the previous songs in the cycle), the poetic address to an adult "weary wanderer" rather than a child, the expressive nuances of the vocal line, and the *obbligato* piano accompaniment. Nevertheless, in concluding its tale of the hapless miller with a strophic lullaby that, for all its artfulness, seems folk-like in relation to what has come before (only "Das Wandern" is comparable), the cycle effectively draws folk song into the cluster of interrelated concepts – antiquity, childhood, death, home, immortality, mother, nature, and sleep, among others – that to Romantics held the allure of a lost paradise. The art song lullaby, as "Des Baches Wiegenlied" compellingly shows, fused *Volkstümlichkeit* with artistry to convey man's yearning for restored spiritual health in an era of alienation.

4 | Brahms's spiral journey back home

Art song lullabies are but one musical manifestation of the Romantic nostalgia for childhood; other nineteenth-century Lieder express a similar longing. Many of these works are not well known. Listeners today are most likely to associate childhood and the yearning it inspires with sets of short piano pieces, such as Schumann's oft-performed *Kinderszenen*, Op. 15, or his *Album für die Jugend*, Op. 68.[1] One writer argues that the apotheosis of childhood during the early nineteenth century was linked to that of purely instrumental music and implies that song settings whose texts involve depictions of childhood or childlike themes are comparatively insignificant.[2] This suggestion is problematic, for the Lied repertory contains a number of works engaging the new conception of childhood that emerged in the wake of Rousseau, and these include songs of high quality. As both icons of Romantic childhood and artistic entities in their own right, nineteenth-century *Kinderlieder* deserve close consideration.[3]

Kinderlieder: songs for children and adults

Lieder on the subject of childhood fall into several broad, overlapping categories. One consists of songs sung, and sometimes also created, *by* children – that is, Lieder belonging to an oral tradition of children's music-making, or *Volks-Kinderlieder*. In German-speaking lands, the first extensive documentation of such a tradition is Arnim and Brentano's folk song collection *Des knaben Wunderhorn* of 1808, an appendix to which contains the texts to nearly 150 *Kinderlieder*.[4] Later nineteenth-century compilations of children's songs, such as Karl Simrock's *Deutsches Kinderbuch* of 1848 (including *c.* 550 *Kinderlieder*) and Böhme's *Deutsches Kinderlied und Kinderspiel* of 1897 (with 1,870 *Kinderlieder*, 630 *Kinderspiele* and 160 *Rätsel/Rätselfragen*), reflect a similar passion to preserve this special form of folk music. As with folk song generally, but perhaps to an even greater extent, the collection, publication, and enjoyment (by adults) of *Kinderlieder* was largely motivated by nostalgia. As Böhme explains in the introduction to his monumental compendium,

We have generally become much too serious; we need rejuvenation, a return to nature and naturalness. That has been often enough said, but not followed. If we can not be born anew and cannot set ourselves again playing on father's and mother's lap, this book, with its rejuvenating, childlike contents, could nevertheless serve as a fountain of youth, as refreshment and a source of magic, should we sometime want to withdraw for an hour from the bustle of the everyday world, with its cares and battles for existence, to withdraw into the dreamlike, playful, harmless, and carefree world of children. Oh, how blissful still to be a child![5]

During the late eighteenth and early nineteenth centuries, *Volks-Kinderlieder* inspired two further kinds of song, reflecting the burgeoning interest in childhood: Lieder *for* children and Lieder *about* children.[6] Both types are adult creations (words as well as music), and both give voice to adult concerns. The second type, however, differs from the first in that the songs are primarily intended for adult performers and listeners, with important implications for the poetic content and musical expression. These art songs, or *Kunst-Kinderlieder*, present childhood from the perspective of one who has left that world – often viewed as paradisiacal – behind.[7]

The composition of *Kinderlieder* was stimulated by Enlightenment ideals. In the second half of the eighteenth century, swayed by Rousseau's positive conception of childhood and revolutionary pedagogy, poets and composers produced numerous collections of secular *Kinderlieder* intended to cultivate virtue while producing joy.[8] Such songs, it was hoped, would teach children honesty, industriousness, obedience, and politeness. Christian Felix Weiße, one of the most prolific eighteenth-century authors of *Kinderlieder* poems, shared Rousseau's belief in children's naturalness and aim of helping them develop into upstanding adults. In his *Lieder für Kinder*, Weiße employed images of nature, youthful pastimes, and other scenes from childhood to teach moral lessons.[9] The numerous *Kinderlied* poems of Gottlob Wilhelm Burmann evince a similar didactic intent.[10] They differ from Weiße's, however, in drawing a sharp distinction between girls' and boys' future lives (in the domestic and public spheres, respectively) and the character traits to be nourished in each gender.

The *Kinderlied* poems of Weiße, Burmann, and other eighteenth-century writers received musical settings from many composers, including Burmann himself, Johann Adolph Scheibe, Johann Adam Hiller, Gottlob Gottwald Hunger, Reichardt, Georg Carl Claudius, Carl Spazier, and Karl Gottlieb Horstig.[11] Whereas the earlier, galant-style settings sometimes involve musical complexities (melismas, embellishments, high notes, large vocal leaps, and adventurous harmonies) beyond the easy grasp of young musicians, those from the last decades of the century generally exhibit folk-like qualities (simple declamation, limited range, small melodic intervals, and easy modulations), following the aesthetic tenets of the Berlin school composers. Indeed, the *Kinderlied* collections of Reichardt and the *Lieder im Volkston* (three volumes: 1782, 1785, 1790) of Johann Abraham Peter Schulz – many of which are suitable for children, although not so identified – demonstrate a shared commitment to simplicity and naturalness, traits widely associated with both children and the folk in the late eighteenth century.

With their folklike melodies and simple accompaniments, Reichardt's *Kinderlieder* exemplify another Enlightenment objective besides fostering morality in children: promoting artistic education. Like Horstig's *Kinder-Lieder und Melodien* of 1798, Reichardt's *Kinderlied* collections aimed to enhance children's musical receptiveness, laying the groundwork for future training.[12] Even his *Wiegenlieder für gute deutsche Mutter* could be used to teach children the rudiments of music, as Reichardt notes in the preface: "All these songs, however, can also be utilized very well in beginning keyboard and singing instruction, to which, in my judgment, generally nothing seems more suitable for children than easy, comprehensible songs whose styles are wholly appropriate to the character and structure of the verse, and for themselves have a good melody with clear harmonic accompaniment."[13]

Eighteenth-century *Kinderlieder*, especially those of Reichardt and Schulz, continued to appear in school songbooks throughout the Romantic and even post-Romantic eras. Nineteenth-century composers also produced collections of children's songs designed to instruct, amuse, and engage the imagination. Examples include Loewe's eight *Jugendlieder*, WoO; Schumann's *Lieder-Album für die Jugend*, Op. 79; Wilhelm Taubert's *Kinderlieder*, Opp. 145 and 160; Joseph Rheinberger's *Thirty Children's Songs*, Op. 152; Carl Reinecke's *Kinderlieder* (many opuses);[14] Brahms's *Volks-Kinderlieder*, WoO 31; and Engelbert Humperdinck's *Junge Lieder*, Op. 107. Some songs were newly composed, while others were arrangements of pre-existing folksongs. Besides collections of *Kinderlieder*, composers wrote numerous individual songs for children, e.g., Wolf's "Epiphanias," composed to celebrate the birthday of his mistress Melanie Köchert, and sung in costume by her three children, with Wolf at the piano, on the day of Epiphany.

The proliferation of *Kinderlieder* during the late eighteenth and nineteenth centuries reveals the rise of domestic music-making among the middle classes. Parents' desire to further their children's moral and musical education led to increased musical consumerism. As demand grew for music that could instruct as well as entertain, composers responded with Lieder that children and adults could enjoy singing and playing together. Some collections were designated for musicians both young and old. An example is the

Figure 6 *Liedersammlung für Kinder und Kinderfreunde am Clavier: Frühlingslieder* (Vienna: Ignaz Alberti, 1791), title page.

Liedersammlung für Kinder und Kinderfreunde am Clavier: Frühlingslieder (1791), a collection of thirty songs including Mozart's "Sehnsucht nach dem Frühling," K. 596; "Im Frühlingsanfang," K. 597; and "Das Kinderspiel," K. 598.[15] On the title page is an engraving depicting communal music-making of the sort the collection invites. In the lively domestic scene, a woman seated at a keyboard (likely the mother) directs and accompanies six children of different ages (and degrees of attentiveness) cheerfully playing the harp, violin, drum, flute, dulcimer, and lute (Figure 6). Of course, a dual designation, like "für Kinder und Kinderfreunde," "für Jung und Alt," or even "für Kenner und Liebhaber," was not essential to this sort of mixed-generational activity; *Kinderlieder* without such a heading could also be enjoyed by children together with their parents, teachers, or adult friends.[16]

Kinderlieder for both young and old helped pave the way for the composition of *Kunst-Kinderlieder* intended primarily for adults.[17] Reichardt's desire to entertain mothers who sing his *Wiegenlieder* helps explain various textual and musical elements that might strike listeners as out of place in a traditional lullaby. A similar preoccupation with adult sensibilities is evident in the texts of a number of Reichardt's other *Kinderlieder*, which often seem less motivated by a desire to teach moral lessons than to celebrate the joys of childhood and wondrousness of nature. In praising God through depictions of children amidst nature's bounty, these works signal a subtle yet significant change in the genre: the increasing portrayal of childhood as an object of adult yearning. Rather than dwell (as, for example, does Burmann) on the child's necessary progression toward maturity, Reichardt focuses on the special pleasures of childhood.[18] Similarly, in expressing children's love of play, Mozart's "Sehnsucht nach dem Frühlinge" and "Das Kinderspiel" depict childhood as a time of delights; although presented from the perspective of children, the songs conjure an image of childhood that accords with the paradisiacal conception that became pervasive after Rousseau.

The late eighteenth and early nineteenth centuries witnessed the gradual emergence of *Kunst-Kinderlieder*: songs in which the speaker reflects on the world of childhood with wonder, reverence, longing, and sometimes regret. Although evoking the sounds of children's songs, these works often involve textual and musical complexities uncharacteristic of Lieder for the young. Ill suited to children's music-making, such traits aided the depiction of idealized childhood in works intended for adult concert performance. Contemplating the child was ultimately a means of contemplating the self – of grappling with the troubling divisions within adult consciousness. Indeed, representations of idealized childhood, like those of idealized antiquity, often masked deep-seated angst.

Kunst-Kinderlieder include various kinds of song: stylized lullabies, laments for dead children, what might loosely be termed "odes to childhood," and songs expressing nostalgia. The lullaby presents an obvious opportunity for reflection on childhood.[19] The traditional image associated with the genre is of a mother gazing at her child while singing and rocking it to sleep – a physical and emotional intimacy that invites musing on the infant's present and future life. As noted in connection with Schubert, in *Kunst-Wiegenlieder*, modifications of the lullaby *topos* – philosophical or religious reflections inspired by the sight of both mother and child ("Der Knabe in der Wiege"), reminiscences of the speaker's own childhood ("Vor meiner Wiege") or metaphorical reinterpretations of an infant's sleep ("Des Baches Wiegenlied") – often suggest that the speaker's preoccupation is not with childhood but adulthood. The child's blissful sleep suggests an existence untouched by human misery, like Eden before the Fall. Louis Spohr's "Wiegenlied (In drei Tönen)," Op. 103, no. 4; Mendelssohn's "Bei der Wiege," Op. 47, no. 6; Schumann's "Kinderwacht," Op. 79, no. 21; Cornelius's "Wiegenlied," Op. 1, no. 3; Brahms's "Gestillte Sehnsucht," Op. 91, no. 1, and "Geistliches Wiegenlied," Op. 91, no. 2; Wolf's "Die ihr schwebet"

(*Spanisches Liederbuch: Geistliches Lieder*, no. 4); Strauss's "Meinem Kinde," Op. 37, no. 3, "Wiegenlied," Op. 41, no. 1, and "Wiegenliedchen," Op. 49, no. 3; Max Reger's "Mariä Wiegenlied," Op. 76, no. 52 – these are but a handful of the many *Kunst-Wiegenlieder* (besides Schubert's) that draw upon the Romantic vision of idealized childhood.

Like lullabies, laments typically present an adult speaker contemplating a child – whether in actuality or memory.[20] Laments too can serve different purposes: expressing sorrow or offering solace to the bereaved by emphasizing the child's new, more blissful existence in heaven (supporting the Romantic notion of children's natural divinity). *Klagelieder* are often addressed to grief-stricken parents. In Zelter's "An eine Mutter, deren Tochter als Kind Starb," Z123/9, the speaker comforts a mother mourning the loss of her daughter: "Oh mother, do not weep. / She sits now on God's shoulder; a gentle little dove, and she will fly / To your hand when one day you come." Schubert's "Todtenkranz für ein Kind," D. 275, presents a variation on the theme. Here, the speaker comforts a deceased child by contrasting the beneficence of death with the painful uncertainties of life: "You sleep in peace; we stumble, / Confused and troubled, through the turmoil of this world, / And seldom know peace." Yet the speaker's principal aim may actually be to comfort himself, since he, too, will ultimately leave life's difficulties (including the experience of grief) behind; the child's death holds promise of an eventual return to paradise. The genre reached its apogee in Mahler's five *Kindertotenlieder* (1901–4) to texts by Rückert, powerfully expressive works deemed by one writer "the most moving monument to children" in the entire Lied repertoire.[21]

While songs celebrating the joys and virtues of childhood ("odes to childhood") may resemble children's songs, they often bear traces of adult consciousness. For example, although the speaker in Claudius's "Die Kindheit" is ostensibly a child,[22] Burmann's text conveys sentiments only an adult would voice: "I am still a child, I still feel only innocence and joy, and do not know what suffering and grief are." The same holds true for several Schubert Lieder. In "Lied eines Kindes," D. 596, a fragment of twenty-four measures, the unknown poet attributes sentimental self-reflection to a child: "I feel only joy, I hear only love, I so fortunate a child at my happy games. // Over there my good father, here my dear mother, and around them us children."[23] "Der Knabe," D. 692, also presented through the voice of a child, expresses certain childlike desires (to fly like a bird, enjoy endless sweets, snuggle in a mother's lap), but both the title, which objectifies the figure of the boy, and the expression of yearning, with flight symbolizing transcendence, indicate an adult's authorship.

Some songs about the paradise of childhood are explicitly presented from the perspective of an adult. Schubert's "Die Knabenzeit," D. 400, in a tone first sentimental, then tongue-in-cheek, describes the freedom and joyfulness of young childhood, which both disappear at the start of schooling: "Soon you will be sweating, not always happily, / In the cramped classroom, / Learning fusty Latin / From a fat tome of Cicero!" In "Freude der Kinderjahre," D. 455, the adult speaker reminisces about the beauty, hope, and happiness of his youth, which continue to glow in the realm of memory. Similarly, in "Der Vater mit dem Kind," D. 906, a father feels infinite happiness (as well as melancholy tenderness) in cradling his sleeping child. Franz Liszt's "Jugendglück," S. 323/R. 615, celebrates the love that reigns when youth and joy unite. In Strauss's "Auf ein Kind," Op. 47, no. 1, the speaker escapes life's afflictions by contemplating a child's divine essence.

In various respects, songs expressing nostalgia for childhood resemble the previously mentioned kinds of *Kunst-Kinderlieder*. These too present idealized visions of childhood and involve self-reflection. But here the contrast between childhood and adulthood takes center stage, with the latter state shown to be far inferior. The adult speaker, whether observing, remembering, or simply pondering the blissfulness of youth, experiences profound loss arising from awareness of time's progression; the innocent happiness of childhood (in some songs broadly understood to include the period of young love) belongs to the irretrievable past. The Romantic Lied repertory includes numerous songs that convey awareness of childhood's idyllic essence and intense longing for its return. A sampling of nostalgic *Kunst-Kinderlieder* ranging from the late eighteenth through early twentieth centuries appears in Table 4.1. The works differ greatly in compositional style but converge on a common theme.

Although all songs that evoke idealized childhood might be said to engage the myth of lost paradise, those expressing an adult's longing to return to the blissful days of youth do so most directly and often most poignantly. Of the many composers who produced such settings, Brahms figures most prominently. His nostalgic *Kunst-Kinderlieder* established the yearning for lost childhood as a powerful topos for art song.

Brahms and the music of childhood

Like many Romantics, Brahms was drawn to the world of childhood, as evidenced by his personal relations as well as his music. Although never a father, he possessed a deep affection for children, taking delight throughout

Table 4.1 Lieder expressing nostalgia for childhood

Composer	Title	Text	Composed
Brahms	Abenddämmerung (Op. 49, no. 5)	Schack	1867
	Regenlied (Op. 59, no. 3)	Groth	1873
	Heimweh I (Op. 63, no. 7)	Groth	c. 1873
	Heimweh II (Op. 63, no. 8)	Groth	1874
	Heimweh III (Op. 63, nos. 9)	Groth	c. 1873
	Mit vierzig Jahren (Op. 94, no. 1)	Rückert	c. 1883
Loewe	Jugend und Alter (Op. 9 vol. x, no. 1)	Hoffmann von Fallersleben	1837
	Der alte Goethe (Op. 9 vol. ix, no. 2)	Förster	1835
Mendelssohn	O Jugend, o schöne Rosenzeit (Op. 57, no. 4)	Rhenish folksong	1841
Nietzsche	Aus der Jugendheit (NWV8)	Rückert	1862
Schoeck	Jugendgedenken (Op. 24b, no. 10).	Keller	1906–15
Schubert	Das Lied im Grünen (D. 917)	Reil	1827
	Vor meiner Wiege (D. 927)	Leitner	1827
Silcher	Jugendland (Op. 33, no. 3)	Zimmermann	
Spohr	Der Rosenstrauch (Op. 105, no. 2; S/T)	Ferrand	1838
Strauss	Rückleben (Op. 47, no. 3)	Uhland	1900
	Rückkehr in die Heimat (Op. 71, no. 2)	Hölderlin	1921
Wolf	Der neue Amadis (1889)	Goethe	1889
Zelter	Die Kindheit (Z120/2)	Matthisson	1796

his adult years in his friends' offspring.[24] Brahms's devotion to the Schumann children found musical expression in a set of fourteen charming *Volks-Kinderlieder* that he composed for them in 1858, two years after their father's death. On a happier occasion, Brahms composed his famous "Wiegenlied," Op. 49, no. 4 (text from *Des knaben Wunderhorn*; 1868) for his friends the Fabers at the birth of their second child.[25] Similarly, he wrote "Geistliches Wiegenlied," Op. 91, no. 2 (text by Emmanuel Geibel after Lope Felix de Vega Carpio; 1863/64) as a marriage gift for Josef Joachim and his bride, and it was soon put to practical use after the birth of their first child.

It is debatable whether any of Brahms's works should be considered pure children's music. Although "Wiegenlied," Op. 49, no. 4, has entered the oral tradition, becoming one of the world's most beloved "functional" lullabies, it was performed during Brahms's lifetime in concert settings,[26] as was "Geistliches Wiegenlied," its companion piece "Gestillte Sehnsucht," Op. 91, no. 1, for contralto, viola, and piano (Rückert; 1884), and the *Wiegenlied-Romanze* "Ruhe, Süßliebchen," Op. 33, no. 9, from the *Magelone* cycle

(Tieck, 1868). One writer asserts that even the *Volks-Kinderlieder*, settings of traditional melodies Brahms found in August von Kretzschmer and Wilhelm von Zuccalmaglio's collection *Deutsche Volkslieder mit ihren Original-Weisen* (2 vols., published 1838 and 1840), should not be considered children's music, but rather folk music.[27] This issue aside, Brahms's Op. 49, no. 4 and *Volks-Kinderlieder* are plainly more suitable for young listeners or performers than are his nostalgic *Kunst-Kinderlieder* "Abenddämmerung," Op. 49, no. 5; "Regenlied," Op. 59, no. 3; "Heimweh I–III," Op. 63, nos. 7–9; and "Mit vierzig Jahren," Op. 94, no. 1.[28] In these works, childhood's simplicity, purity, and joy are recalled but not recovered; a stretch of time and range of experiences separate the adult speaker from the youthful paradise of which he sings. The path back to childhood winds its way through memory and imagination.

As we have seen, Brahms was not the first to compose *Kinderlieder* for adults; a tradition of such works began to develop during the last two decades of the eighteenth century and continued throughout the nineteenth. But Brahms's nostalgic *Kunst-Kinderlieder* differ from those of his predecessors in the intensity of their speakers' emotional responses to the lost paradise of childhood. This intensity is particularly striking in the three "Heimweh" Lieder, which together relate a narrative of mounting pain and disillusionment in the recognition of that loss.

"Heimweh" Lieder, Op. 63, nos. 7–9

Brahms's "Heimweh" Lieder are often analyzed and performed individually,[29] with greatest attention given to the surpassingly beautiful second song, "O wüßt ich doch den Weg zurück."[30] But abundant evidence – documentary, textual, and musical – suggests that Brahms thought of them as a unit and intended their joint presentation.[31] Considering the three songs together is indispensable to their interpretation as a late nineteenth-century expression of Romantic *Heimweh*.[32]

Like Schumann's *Kinderszenen* cycle, the "Heimweh" Lieder open a vista on the world of childhood. Both sets depict its pleasures and pastimes, comforts and fantasies.[33] Both make reference to the lens of adult consciousness through which youth's domain comes into view. But whereas Schumann's vignettes focus on various aspects of *Kindheit*, with adult subjectivity conveyed chiefly in the wistful concluding piece "Der Dichter spricht," all three "Heimweh" Lieder are infused with nostalgia. Neither dispassionate reflections nor sentimental reminiscences, the songs express an adult's yearning for a simpler, more natural existence – an imagined return to the Golden Age of childhood. But the desire to re-experience childlike bliss collides with recognition of the quest's futility, leaving the protagonist in a state of melancholy.

Brahms's "Heimweh" Lieder resonate on multiple levels. The songs possess a childlike melodic charm yet tell the story of one advanced in age. They abound in images of cradles, flowers, maternal love, dreams, forests, and fields, but are fundamentally about regret, loss, despair, isolation, confusion, and fading memories. The childhood evoked recedes further and further in the haze of memory, and the dialectical relation of childhood and adulthood grows increasingly strained.

Brahms expresses the protagonist's nostalgia in various ways. One involves conjoining traits of *Volks-Kinderlieder* and *Kunst-Kinderlieder*.[34] To varying degrees, each of the three "Heimweh" Lieder conjures the contrasting worlds of childhood and adulthood by fusing the folk-like qualities of children's song with the compositional complexities of art song. The impression of temporal distance from the simplicity of childhood finds an analogue in the range of stylistic elements. As Georges Starobinski has noted, Brahms may have come to associate childhood with folk song, and adulthood with art song, while reading the works of Herder and Justus Thibaut.[35] By incorporating aspects of *Kinderlieder* into otherwise highly artful compositions, he conveys musically that the "Heimweh" songs are presented from the perspective of an adult who longs for youth. The sounds of children's music permeate the settings like ancient echoes.

The expression of nostalgia takes place not just within the songs but also among them. For this reason, treating the songs as a minicycle rather than individually is crucial.[36] The retrospective nature of the songs emerges from textual reminiscences of childhood as well as from various facets of Brahms's settings, including the recurrence and transformation of musical patterns and motifs.[37] Each successive song recalls aspects of the previous one(s), the repeated elements evoking what Walter Frisch has called "recollective memories."[38]

Apprehending the songs together also enables recognition of the quasi-narrative that unfolds from "Heimweh I" to "Heimweh III." If not the story of a single protagonist, the three song texts nevertheless seem to depict sequential stages of nostalgia, at ever-greater remove from childhood. In the first poem, the speaker, enraptured by memories of his early years, appears only moderately troubled by his current existence, about which he says little. The second poem focuses far more on painful present emotions, with memories of childhood dimmed and assuming greater symbolic import.

The last poem seems to reflect on the distant past from the vantage point of old age, when one is least able to remember childhood's pleasures and most susceptible to disorientation and angst. The ravages of time become increasingly evident as the cycle progresses.

Finally, joint consideration of the three "Heimweh" Lieder exposes the different emotional trajectories traced by text and music, a discrepancy that reveals Brahms's perspective on nostalgia. Despite the despondency of the speaker in each poem, the musical settings together convey a positive message: Death brings a state of tranquility greater than that of life's beginnings. As in his *Requiem, Alto Rhapsodie, Vier ernste Gesänge*, and various other Lieder, Brahms offers comfort to those who suffer life's afflictions and mourn the loss of happiness.[39] Daniel Beller-McKenna has shown that in the second of the *Vier ernste Gesänge*, the musical setting does not so much mirror the text as comment upon it, responding to the pessimistic tenor of the words by unveiling a more optimistic view of the human condition.[40] Something similar takes place with the "Heimweh" Lieder. The incongruity between text and music allows us to hear the composer comforting those beset by the anxieties of age.

How is this manifested? The discrepancy between textual and musical trajectories creates a spiral-like pattern – progressing yet also circling – reminiscent of the archetypal "Romantic version of emanation and return" described by M. H. Abrams in reference to literary and philosophical works.[41] With Brahms's "Heimweh" Lieder, however, the spiral-like pattern produces a more tempered effect than that exemplified by works from the early nineteenth century.[42] Although attracted to Romantic aesthetics, Brahms composed in an era more attuned to practical realities than idealistic fantasies. He draws upon a Romantic concept yet restrains and thereby redefines it. In keeping with the scaled-back artistic goals of the post-Romantic years, he offers the nostalgia-stricken adult not the promise of transcendence but the gift of consolation.

The centrality of nostalgic expression both within and among the three songs is announced in their titles. Brahms's initial indecision about the titles led to an exchange of letters with the poet Klaus Groth that provides important clues as to how Brahms conceived the works.[43] In September 1874 he wrote,

In a forthcoming volume of my songs there will appear your poems: "How cosy was that little hamlet," "O would I knew the way back," "As a boy, I saw the flowers bloom" (p. 35, 36, 37 in your High German poems). Now I would like to ask if perhaps a collective title, or a heading for each one comes to your mind?

I am unfortunately not satisfied with my composition of the pretty 2nd one! I want to reserve the possibility of setting it to music again and better, one of these days; meanwhile and till then this will have to suffice – I should like to keep the 3 together.[44]

Groth gave serious thought to the matter of titling and responded with several possibilities:

In vain have I tortured my brain for two days, trying to find suitable titles or something appropriate. If the title isn't both short and pregnant, one is always better off using the opening words. "Heimweh" and "Longing" [*Sehnsucht*] and their synonyms are too over-used, two-part headings such as "Child's Happiness, Man's Yearning" [*Kinderglück, Mannessehnen*] sound and taste too sophisticated. Were you to write "From the Paradise of Childhood" [*Aus dem Kinderparadies*] it would be fine with me; should you find something suitable for all three songs together or for each one separately on your own, go ahead and use whatever titles you like: Most important, after all, are the words underneath, and even more important for me, your music (for I am not attached to my own words).[45]

Brahms finally made up his mind. Disregarding Groth's criticism of "Heimweh," he chose that heading for all three songs, differentiating them only by number.[46]

This exchange between composer and poet is illuminating on several counts. First, while Brahms was unsure whether to unite the songs under a joint title or give each its own title, he eventually settled on a compromise. By titling the songs "Heimweh I," "Heimweh II," and "Heimweh III," he highlighted their interconnection and simultaneously underscored their sequential progression. The titles suggest that the songs must be performed in order.[47] As Imogen Fellinger has argued, Brahms "laid special emphasis on the sequence of texts within his opera and attached importance to the succession of his songs as he had determined it when ordering them for publication."[48] His statement "I should like to keep the 3 together" – despite his dissatisfaction with "O wüßt ich doch den Weg zurück" – is further evidence of a unified conception of the "Heimweh" Lieder.[49]

Groth's proposed titles and Brahms's reaction to them are also revealing. Groth favored "Aus dem Kinderparadies" over the two-part "Kinderglück, Mannessehnen," which he thought too sophisticated, as well as over "Heimweh," "Sehnsucht," and their synonyms, which he thought hackneyed.[50] "Aus dem Kinderparadies" focuses on the blissful past. Not surprisingly, Brahms rejected it, showing a different understanding of the poetic subject – an adult's increasing despondency – than did the poet.[51] The double heading "Kinderglück, Mannessehnen" places emphasis equally on childhood and adulthood. Brahms rejected this title as well, perhaps sharing

Groth's sense that it sounded too sophisticated or objecting to its overemphasis on childhood (this title would imply – inaccurately – that the songs are as much about a child as about a man). "Heimweh" and "Sehnsucht" focus on the adult's yearning; both words signal nostalgia. Despite its "overuse," and perhaps even because it evokes other musical, literary, artistic, or philosophical works, Brahms ultimately chose "Heimweh." In selecting this title, he tapped into a deep vein of Romantic philosophy and aesthetics. Consideration of how the word became linked to Romanticism enhances appreciation of the expression of nostalgia in these post-Romantic Lieder.

Heimweh, a word of Swiss origin in use since the mid sixteenth century,[52] is often translated as "yearning for home" or "homesickness." These renderings, while accurate, hardly capture the richness of the conception as it developed over time.

Initially *Heimweh* designated a medical condition that affected people (especially soldiers from areas surrounding the Swiss Alps) who were separated for lengthy periods of time from their native lands.[53] If left untreated, the condition, marked by increasing degrees of physical and mental decline, was believed to culminate in death. Returning the sufferer to his home, or promising to do so soon, allegedly resulted in a swift and certain cure.

Absorbed into Romantic writings in the late eighteenth and early nineteenth centuries, *Heimweh* took on an expanded range of meanings, extending beyond the realm of medicine to philosophy and aesthetics.[54] Isaiah Berlin conveys the centrality of *Heimweh* within Romantic thought in a characteristically colorful description:

When Novalis was asked where he thought he was tending, what his art was about, he said 'I am always going home, always to my father's house.' This was in one sense a religious remark, but he also meant that all these attempts at the exotic, the strange, the foreign, the odd, all these attempts to emerge from the empirical framework of daily life, the writing of fantastic stories with transformations and transmogrifications of a most peculiar kind, attempts at writing down stories which are symbolic or allegorical or contain all kinds of mystical and veiled references, esoteric imagery of a most peculiar kind which has preoccupied critics for years, are all attempts to go back to home to what is pulling and drawing him, the famous infinite *Sehnsucht* of the romantics, the search for the blue flower, as Novalis called it.[55]

The poetry of Brentano, Eichendorff, and Mörike, the romances of Novalis, and the philosophical writings of Schelling and Hegel, among other Romantic works, associate yearning for home with a quest for the infinite, with the desire to escape modern society's artificial, corrupted state. The word *Heimweh* thus became identified with Romantic longing for release from alienation.

To arrive "home" would be to regain a sense of transcendent wholeness. Romantics, in their extreme self-consciousness, perceived that they had lost connection with an original absolute unity. They lamented not only their separation from the outer world but also cognitive and moral divisions within the self.[56] Romantic speculative philosophy sought to overcome such divisions, reconciling oppositions through the very act of consciousness that had produced them. The desire for reconciliation was fundamentally a yearning for home. As Novalis stated, "Philosophy is actually homesickness – the urge to be everywhere at home."[57]

Novalis's phrasing echoes a formulation by Schiller, whose philosophical and aesthetic writings, as noted, provided a strong impetus for Romanticism. According to Schiller, modern man's alienation gives rise to an intense yet unrealizable desire to revert to childhood's unselfconscious state:

We then see in nonrational nature only a more fortunate sister who remained at home with her mother, while we stormed out into an alien world, arrogantly confident of our freedom. With painful urgency we long to be back where we began as soon as we experience the misery of culture and hear our mother's tender voice in the distant, foreign country of art. As long as we were mere children of nature we were happy and complete; we became free and lost both happiness and completeness.[58]

But the path from home into alien worlds and back home again is not circular. According to Schiller, "The goal toward which man strives by means of culture . . . is infinitely higher than that which he reaches by means of nature."[59] He cautions, "Do not let it occur to you any longer to want to *change places* with nature. Instead, take nature up into yourself and strive to wed its unlimited advantages to your own endless prerogatives, and from the marriage of both strive to give birth to something divine."[60]

For Schiller, as for Goethe, Coleridge, Schelling, and Hegel, seeking renewed unity with nature, i.e. returning home, holds promise of transcendence.[61] Synthesis of oppositions does not lead back to the original undifferentiated unity but to a new, higher state of existence – higher because it preserves the differences it has overcome. Distinctions are retained yet fully integrated within an organic whole. The effect is that of a spiral: circling, synthesizing, uniting, but also ascending.[62]

The spiral pattern mirrors Christianity's myth of Creation, Fall, Redemption, and Apocalypse (or, within an individual's life: birth, sin, salvation, and resurrection), and for some Romantics, the word *Heimweh* associated with that spiral pattern had strong religious connotations.[63] But the pattern also appears in secular contexts in scores of early nineteenth-century poems, novels, dramas, and philosophical or aesthetic tracts.[64] These disparate writings speak to the Romantics' nostalgia for some form of lost paradise and convey their belief in the importance of striving for (if not actually achieving) transcendent homecoming.

Although the idealism of high Romanticism withered in response to political repression, urbanization, industrialization, and failed revolutions, the movement remained influential in the latter half of the nineteenth century. Romantic hopes and fantasies, ideas and imagery, survived in genres such as the Lied, although they were rarely expressed with the exuberant optimism that characterized many works from the early 1800s. The grim realities and restrictions of the *Biedermeierzeit* and the succeeding age of realism and scientific positivism altered the tone if not the content of later compositions.[65]

As noted, Brahms's "Heimweh" Lieder exemplify a spiral-like pattern reminiscent of earlier Romantic works but more tempered in effect. The pattern and its message of consolation become apparent through analysis of Groth's nostalgic poems and Brahms's musical settings.

Groth's three poems display several broad similarities, encouraging their joint interpretation.

Heimweh I	*Homesickness I*
Wie traulich war das Fleckchen,	How cozy was that tiny village,
Wo meine Wiege ging!	Where my cradle rocked!
Kein Bäumchen war, kein Heckchen	There was no little tree, no little hedge
Das nicht voll Träume hing.	That wasn't filled with dreams.
Wo nur ein Blümchen blühte,	Whenever a flower blossomed,
Da blühten gleich sie mit,	They would at once blossom, too,
Und Alles sang und glühte	And everything sang and shone
Mir zu bei jedem Schritt.	For me with every step I took.
Ich wäre nicht gegangen,	I wouldn't have gone away,
Nicht für die ganze Welt!	Not for the whole world!
Mein Sehnen, mein Verlangen,	My yearning, my longing,
Hier ruhts in Wald und Feld.	Dwells here in forest and field.
Heimweh II	*Homesickness II*
O wüßt ich doch den Weg zurück,	Oh, if I only knew the way back,
Den lieben Weg zum Kinderland!	The lovely path to the land of childhood!
O warum sucht ich nach dem Glück	Oh, why did I seek for fortune
Und ließ der Mutter Hand?	And leave my mother's hand?

O wie mich sehnet auszuruhn,	Oh, how I long to rest thoroughly,
Von keinem Streben aufgeweckt,	Aroused by no striving,
Die müden Augen zuzutun,	To close my weary eyes,
Von Liebe sanft bedeckt!	Gently covered by love!
Und nichts zu forschen, nichts zu spähn,	And to hunt for nothing, to seek out nothing,
Und nur zu träumen leicht und lind,	And merely to dream lightly and gently,
Der Zeiten Wandel nicht zu sehn,	Not to see the passage of time,
Zum zweiten Mal ein Kind!	A child for the second time!
O zeigt mir doch den Weg zurück,	Oh, please show me the way back,
Den lieben Weg zum Kinderland!	The lovely path to the land of childhood!
Vergebens such ich nach dem Glück,	In vain I seek for fortune,
Rings um ist öder Strand!	Round about me is a barren shore.

Heimweh III — *Homesickness III*

Ich sah als Knabe Blumen blühn–	As a boy I saw flowers blossoming –
Ich weiß nicht mehr, was war es doch?	I don't know any more – what was it actually?
Ich sah die Sonne drüber glühn–	I saw the sun shine above them –
Mich dünkt, ich seh es noch.	I seem to see it still.
Es war ein Duft, es war ein Glanz,	There was a fragrance, there was a brightness,
Die Seele sog ihn durstend ein.	My soul drank it in thirstily.
Ich pflückte sie zu einem Kranz–	I picked them for a wreath –
Wo mag er blieben sein?	What could have become of it?
Ich such an jedem Blümchen nach	I look at every little flower
Um jenen Schmelz, um jenes Licht,	To rediscover that sweetness, that light,
Ich forsche jeden Sommertag,	I hunt for them every summer day,
Doch solche find ich nicht.	But I don't find any like that.
Ihr wußtet nimmer, was ich trieb?	You never knew what I was about?
Ich suchte meinen alten Kranz.	I was looking for my old wreath.
Er war so frisch, so licht, so lieb–	It was so fresh, so bright, so dear –
Es war der Jugendglanz.	It was the glow of youth.[66]

Each poem presents an adult speaker, presumably male, who reflects on his childhood. (Because Groth's verse supplies no indication of gender, the poetic speakers could conceivably be female, and women do often sing Brahms's "Heimweh" Lieder. But given that the poems date from the mid nineteenth century and that the poetic speakers have each ventured boldly beyond the domestic sphere, as suggested, for example, by the verbs *forschen* and *spähen*, it seems reasonable to assume they are male.)[67]

All three poems also portray childhood as a paradise. In "Heimweh I" and "Heimweh III," for example, images of blossoming flowers forge an association between childhood and natural beauty, and both songs depict childhood as illuminated by a mystical glow. "Heimweh I" and "Heimweh II" link childhood to peaceful sleep and evoke the comforts of home (directly in the first case, obliquely in the second).

In addition, each speaker longs to re-experience the joys of the past, a desire that can be fulfilled only by force of memory or imagination. Each expresses regret at having left the blissfulness of childhood and, to varying degrees, recognition of irretrievable loss.

Finally, all three poems involve a shift of focus in the last stanza, an abrupt disjunction that calls attention to the gulf separating the adult speaker from the past. With the force of romantic irony, the sudden alteration of perspective tears the veil of illusion.[68] In "Heimweh I," the shift involves a change of tense. Stanzas 1 and 2 are presented wholly in the past tense, with the speaker reflecting on the idyllic essence of his early years. Stanza 3 then jumps into the present tense, redirecting the focus to his current circumstance. In a circuitous manner, the exclamation "I wouldn't have gone away, / Not for the whole world!" reveals that he *did* go away but would not have done so had he understood the cost. While the childlike locution indicates that the speaker of "Heimweh I" may not yet be old, the adult sentiments conveyed by "yearning" [*Sehnen*] and "longing" [*Verlangen*] indicate that childhood lies behind.

"Heimweh II" unfolds primarily in the present tense, but here too a shift of perspective occurs near the end. The first two lines of the fourth stanza circle back to the opening lines of the poem, again expressing yearning but with greater intensity (stanza 1: "Oh, if I only knew the way back"; stanza 4: "Oh, please show me the way back"). The last two lines of the fourth stanza also look back to the beginning of the song, but now regret over past actions is replaced by bitter acknowledgment of their futility. Youthful dreams and ambitions have led to desolation (stanza 1: "Oh, why did I seek for fortune / And leave my mother's hand?"; stanza 4: "In vain I seek for fortune, / Round about me is a barren shore"). In the last two lines of the fourth stanza, the speaker's emotions plummet to a new low, marked by hopelessness, isolation, and despair. The final pronouncement, imbuing the surrounding landscape with layers of meaning, is abrupt and unexpected.

In the first three stanzas of "Heimweh III," the speaker reminisces semi-deliriously about the flowers he used to collect as a child. His memories have grown dim, and he seeks in vain to find again that which he can barely remember. The last stanza then leaps to an unspecified future time, with the speaker reflecting on his futile attempts to recapture the past as in stanzas 1 to 3. He now identifies the object of his search, stripping the floral wreath (a traditional birthday tribute) of its metaphorical cover to reveal "the glow of youth."

While the "Heimweh" texts have elements in common, they also differ significantly in imagery, structure, diction, and tone. Their reflections on lost childhood from ever greater distances create a quasi-narrative effect. The particular sequence of texts is crucial. From the first poem to the third, the mood shifts from sentimentality to wistfulness, despondency, disorientation, and finally resignation.

The text of "Heimweh I" presents the least anguished vision of the past; the speaker seems still fairly close to that Golden Age. Tellingly, he recounts aspects of his childhood with more precision than do the speakers of the following poems. The cozy little village he remembers is replete with emblems of life and natural beauty: rocking cradle, trees, hedges, and flowers. Sounds and sights alike are aglow with the bliss of youth and innocence. Abundant diminutives (*Fleckchen, Bäumchen, Heckchen, Blümchen*) conjure a fairytale world of doll-like proportions, bursting with potential. The verse structure – three quatrains of regular iambic trimeter – contributes to the atmosphere of childlike simplicity. Through its small dimensions, short line lengths (with three rather than the normative four stresses per line), and consistency of meter and rhyme (a simple alternating line pattern: abab cdcd efef), the verse structure mimics the poetic subject. The idealized memory of childhood presented in the first two stanzas radiates comfort. In the third stanza, however, the tone shifts as the speaker acknowledges having left childhood's paradise. Expressions of regret and longing replace the rosy reminiscences.

The speaker in "Heimweh II" seems further removed from childhood. While the first poem recalls specific childhood images of beauteous surroundings and youthful exuberance, the second offers few particulars about the past. The scenes and sounds of childhood have begun to fade. To be sure, traces of imagery from the first poem survive. The lovely path to the land of childhood (II, line 2) evokes the child's steps (I, line 8) that led away from that world. The speaker's yearning to rest, "gently covered by love," (II, 8), recalls the infant sleeping in a cradle (I, 2). His desire to dream, "lightly and gently" (II, 10), echoes the child's dreams, blossoming on every tree and hedge (I, 3–4). But while its textual imagery may derive from that of "Heimweh I," the second poem shifts focus away from the childhood paradise to the path ("the passage of time") that led to adulthood. Although the speaker yearns to return to the happy past, his thoughts are confined to the painful present.

With the shift in perspective from past to present, foreshadowed in the last stanza of "Heimweh I," the speaker's world seems to close in on itself. The only indication of *mise-en-scène* is the "barren shore," and that image, presented in the last line, suggests a symbolic as much as physical space (more so, in any event, than the "tiny village" or "forest and field" of "Heimweh I"). Ironically, the barren shore represents the most vivid image in "Heimweh II," although the landscape is stripped of detail.

Emotional expression intensifies in "Heimweh II." Overwhelmed by regret and weariness, the speaker yearns for release. Exclamations (four introduced by an expressive "O") and rhetorical questions help convey his passionate longing for the embrace of death. Even within the song itself, the speaker's desperation mounts, as evidenced by the transformation of "Oh, if I only knew the way back" in line 1 into the more gripping "Oh, please show me the way back" in line 13. Isolation and loneliness infuse his minimal description of the seascape.

Differences in verse structure between the texts of "Heimweh I" and "Heimweh II" suggest that time has elapsed and that childhood is now more distant. "Heimweh II" comprises four quatrains rather than three, and the first three lines of each quatrain contain four stressed syllables instead of three. Although some structural traits are retained (e.g. quatrains, iambic meter, alternating line rhyme scheme), the verse of "Heimweh II" has a weightier, more adultlike feel than that of "Heimweh I." Furthermore, the cyclical nature of the form (the fourth stanza's echoing of the first), fused with a series of increasingly intense emotions (wistfulness, regret, yearning, urgency, despair), suggests a complexity of thought and expression at odds with the simplicity of childhood.

In the third poem, childhood all but disappears in the gaps of memory. Specific images are mostly gone; only flowers and sun remain. The lovely scenes of childhood joy – the village, forest, and fields of "Heimweh I" – have vanished, as have the dreams that lured the speaker away from that paradise. The wasteland of adult existence – the empty shore of "Heimweh II" – also goes unmentioned. Even the deep regret and despair of the second poem are now muted. Emotional pain gives way to confusion, then resignation, as the speaker strains to remember the distant past.

The text's ever more abstract imagery helps convey the effects of time's passage. The flowers [*Blumen*] and sun [*Sonne*] of the first stanza become fragrance [*Duft*] and brightness [*Glanz*] in the second stanza, and sweetness [*Schmelz*] and light [*Licht*] in the third. By the fourth stanza, the two images no longer represent distinct entities but rather serve as descriptions – fresh [*frisch*] and bright [*licht*] – of the speaker's old floral wreath, emblem of his youth. As memories grow hazier, the literal becomes figurative.

While the third poem shares certain structural traits with the second (four four-line stanzas, with three lines of iambic tetrameter and one of iambic trimeter), it is far more disjunctive. In the second poem, rhetorical questions and exclamations express angst; in the third, interjections express disorientation. Frequent temporal shifts add to the confusion. The first stanza switches between past and present, with memories interrupted by forgetfulness ("I don't know any more – what was it actually?") and fantasy ("I seem to see it still"). The first three lines of the second stanza focus on the past, but the fourth line again interjects present uncertainty ("What could have become of it?"). In the third stanza, the speaker persists in his obsessive search, but still without success. Finally, in the fourth stanza, he achieves a flash of understanding – recognition of what he has long sought, and of the quest's futility. The stanza begins with an undercurrent of bitter irony (the speaker mocking his own obsessive search) and closes in resignation.

Just as the three poems display broad similarities, so do Brahms's musical settings. As noted, each expresses nostalgia by introducing the folk-like traits of children's song into art song. Musical echoes among the three Lieder enhance their retrospective nature.

In "Heimweh I," Brahms combines qualities of folk song with subtleties of harmony, rhythm, and texture. The rocking motion of the piano's right hand in the opening measures creates the feel of a *Wiegenlied*, an impression that never entirely disappears, for all the song's artfulness.[69] Built from the sequential treatment of a descending four-note motif, the flowing left hand pattern supports the lullaby association through its resemblance to the melodic setting of "Wiege" in m. 7 (Example 4.1a). Other contributors to the work's *Volkstümlichkeit* include the repetition of the opening strophe, simple duple meter, "Zart bewegt" tempo marking, straight eighth-note rhythms at the start of the vocal line, and initial doubling of voice and bass line.

But the folk-like qualities of the song are more than matched by compositional artistry. Even within the first two musical strophes, various elements insinuate that the childhood world has disappeared – that the complexities of adult consciousness have displaced its simplicity. Intimations of mortality are heard in the descending thirds (a familiar Brahmsian death motif)[70] of the piano introduction and start of the vocal line. The chromatic inflection and minor coloring at "Wiege" suggest a memory of infancy clouded by disturbing thoughts. In mm. 10–12, syncopated rhythms impart tension. Temporary shifts to triple meter at the ends of the first two strophes slow the

Example 4.1a Brahms, "Heimweh I," Op. 63, no. 7, mm. 1–9

Example 4.1b Brahms, "Heimweh I," Op. 63, no. 7, mm. 34–39

pace and permit the repetition and emphasis of certain words ("das nicht, *das nicht* voll Träume hing" and "mir zu bei jedem, *jedem* Schritt").

With the third stanza, the shift of focus from past to present is reflected in changes to the original musical strophe, resulting in the form A A A'. As the protagonist rues his departure from childhood's paradise, the previously steady accompaniment breaks into fragments to produce a sobbing effect (mm. 35–36) (Example 4.1b). No longer does the vocal line begin by doubling the bass as in stanzas 1 and 2 (mm. 5–6 and 20–21). Now the voice alone sounds the melody, its separation from the accompaniment evoking a sense of isolation. Another striking alteration involves the vocal rhythm in the third measure of the strophe (m. 37). The exaggerated extension of the first syllable of "ganze" suggests a childlike assertion while also conveying anxiety.

Throughout the song, compositional complexity arises from textual repetitions involving diatonic melodic "corrections" – passages suggesting an attempt to keep painful emotions at bay. In mm. 7–9, the vocal line's chromatic F-natural at "Wiege" is immediately replaced by a diatonic F-sharp with the repetition of the phrase "wo meine Wiege ging." The minor coloration of the first statement cedes to major, implying a change in perspective, like a disturbing thought brushed aside. Similarly, in mm. 13–16, the descent from F-natural to E to D at "nicht voll Träume hing" is immediately restated as F-sharp – E – D, the mysterious fully diminished seventh harmony on the downbeat of m. 13 replaced by a brighter half-diminished seventh at m. 15. Textual repetitions in mm. 22–24, mm. 28–31, and mm. 36–39 engender further diatonic substitutions. The abundance of such passages keeps the prevailing mood from becoming overly somber.

Chromatic progressions also take the music beyond the realm of *Volks-Kinderlieder*. The first and second strophes include progressions that move through flat-III on the way to a full cadence in the dominant (mm. 10–16, 25–31). Introduced with a diminuendo from piano to pianissimo, these passages create an impression of interiority, of retreat to a deepened level of consciousness.[71] The progression to D is strengthened through the embellishment of *its* dominant (A) by upper and lower chromatic neighbors, B-flat and G-sharp. The flat-III of G thus functions locally as flat-VI of D. In the third strophe, the chromatic progression is magically transformed by the unexpected substitution of flat-VI for flat-III at the crucial word "Verlangen" in m. 42 (and more quickly in m. 44). Again the chromaticism is introduced by hushed dynamics that suggest thoughts turning inward. (For a quiet moment, the surprisingly thick chordal texture contributes to the seriousness of tone.) The flat-VI harmony emphasizes the meaning of "Verlangen" by functioning similarly to flat-III in the first two strophes: It intensifies the drive to the cadence. Now upper and lower chromatic neighbors, E-flat and C-sharp, embellish the *home* dominant (D).

The large-scale harmonic motion of the song – dominant prolongation that withholds resolution to the tonic until the final word of the text – creates intense yearning, the adult protagonist's "Sehnen" and "Verlangen." The four-measure piano introduction unfolds a dominant seventh harmony, descending to the dominant pitch D in a low register, two octaves below middle C. The dominant harmony is essentially sustained from the introduction to the same low D at m. 46, the end of the third stanza. (The resolutions to the tonic at the beginning of each strophe, occurring on weak beats and in a higher register, carry little structural weight; each time, the harmony glances off the tonic and heads back toward the dominant.) In the first two musical strophes, the harmony moves to a half cadence midway through the stanza (mm. 9, 24), and then to a full cadence in the dominant (mm. 16, 31). At the midpoint of the third strophe, instead of arriving at another half cadence in G, the music comes to a full cadence in D at the emphatic repetition of the phrase "not for the whole world!" The cadence sounds conclusive – Brahms rewrites the vocal line so that it descends to the first scale degree rather than hover around the fifth – but the key is wrong. The tonic remains elusive. Viewed more broadly, the full cadence in D major, like an enhanced half cadence, propels the harmony even more strongly to the tonic resolution in G at m. 47, intensifying the yearning that underlies the song.

Tonic harmony represents an obvious musical analogue for "home," in this case for the idyllic past of childhood.[72] Throughout "Heimweh I," the tonic seems to hover in the distance like wisps of memory.[73] Near the end of the song, it arrives in stages, with increasing degrees of stability, as if to show the protagonist closing in on his goal. Downbeat octave Gs sound in m. 44 but with scale degree 3 in the vocal part. G appears in the low bass register in m. 45 (at the word "ruhts"), but here it supports a diminished seventh harmony. Finally, in m. 47 the long delayed resolution occurs, coinciding with the final word of the text ("Feld").

How should this harmonic arrival be interpreted? The protagonist's lines "My yearning, my longing, / Dwells here in forest and field" suggest that he has not actually returned to the childhood paradise – the idyllic village – but rather remains on the outskirts; his yearning finds release in the surrounding woods and fields. A brief plagal cadence in the piano postlude (a transformation of the earlier lullaby music with the bass now holding fast to the tonic) confirms the tonic but also hints at religiosity in the final pronouncement.[74] Although the tonic has arrived, a chromatic descent in the alto line echoes the earlier chromatically enhanced yearning and offers a subtle reminder that death lies ahead. (The sounding of E-flat, associated with "Verlangen," against the diatonic F-sharp in m. 48 poignantly suggests that on some level emotional unrest persists.) Brahms seems to indicate that "home" has been reached only tenuously, through memory and imagination, an impression supported by the postlude's conclusion with the third scale degree in the upper voice.

Example 4.2a Brahms, "Heimweh II," Op. 63, no. 8, mm. 4–8

"Heimweh II" also joins characteristics of children's song and art song, but with an even greater emphasis on the latter; the musical expression of yearning now combines with sorrow and despair. In a slow 6/4 meter, swelling and receding motions in the piano and vocal line evoke images from both child and adult worlds: the rocking of an infant's cradle, water lapping against a barren shore, even "great waves of nostalgia which continually boom and sigh on the shore of reminiscence"[75] (Example 4.2a). The music projects an extraordinary lyricism, recalling the soothing strains of a lullaby. Annett Bruckmann has suggested that the two interior musical strophes (B and B'), constructed more simply than the outer strophes (A and A'), may be intended to reflect the simplicity of childhood. Here, the accompaniment doubles much of the vocal line.[76]

Yet throughout the song, elements of tension, suggesting the complexity of adult consciousness, lie just beneath the surface. In the first and fourth strophes, the bass moves down by step through the interval of a fourth (E to B) in the manner of a lament. As in "Heimweh I," descending thirds (e.g. mm. 1–4) and chromatic lines (mm. 3–8) infuse the sonic space with a vaguely ominous tone, as do diminished seventh arpeggios (mm. 5–6). Chromatic progressions (mm. 9–13) intensify the drive to the cadence. The unexpected addition of a seventh to the tonic chord on the downbeat of m. 13, echoing and intensifying the slightly delayed addition of a seventh to the tonic in m. 47 of "Heimweh I," forestalls emotional resolution, as does the weak-beat cadence at m. 14. The hidden chromatic descent (mm. 13–14) preceding the tonic arrival, now sunk into the bass register, insinuates even more sharply than the chromatic descent in "Heimweh I" that the path to the true "home" leads to death.

In the interior strophes, syncopated rhythms and hemiola patterns convey agitation. Chromaticism infuses both melody and bass. Moreover, whereas the outer strophes are harmonically closed (if weakly so) in the tonic, the two interior strophes enhance the sense of longing by prolonging the dominant harmony. (The F-sharp pedal tone in mm. 19–20 and 29–30 strengthens the full cadence in the dominant, B major, at the end of each stanza.)

Emotional angst peaks in the final strophe. While the setting of stanza 4 begins like that of stanza 1, m. 40 brings an abrupt change with its deceptive move to C followed by downward arpeggiation through F major (Example 4.2b). As the protagonist turns to face the barrenness of his present existence, the piano accompaniment forsakes the flowing rhythms in favor of a new broken octave pattern (another Brahmsian death motif)[77] whose hollow sound amplifies the sentiment of the text ("In vain I seek for fortune"). The change in texture, recalling that of m. 35 in "Heimweh I," highlights the abrupt disjunction.

The protagonist's despondency persists. Whereas in the first strophe the vocal line, having sounded the chromatic pitch C-natural (m. 9), soon reasserts the diatonic C-sharp (recalling the diatonic "corrections" of "Heimweh I"), in the fourth strophe it fails to do so. Measure 42, echoing the deceptive progression of mm. 39–40, evokes earlier moments of greater emotional control and suggests that the situation has changed. The voice concludes bleakly in E minor, as if having lost all hope.

Despair is pervasive, and yet the potent words "Vergebens" and "öder" are set to deceptive progressions, suggesting that the harmonic tension, and the emotional pain expressed through those words, will eventually subside. As if to confirm this, the postlude returns to the less anguished music of the opening. By cycling back to the mood, mode, and accompanimental patterns of the beginning, the postlude suggests that going home may be possible – a notion supported by the large-scale ternary structure of the song, with two outer strophes closed in the tonic and two inner ones prolonging the dominant.

As in "Heimweh I," however, one senses that the ultimate resting place has not been reached. Despite the major mode, the final cadence of "Heimweh

Example 4.2b Brahms, "Heimweh II," Op. 63, no. 8, mm. 39–47

II" resonates with emotional turmoil. At m. 44 (as in mm. 13–14, and the interludes and postlude of "Heimweh I"), Brahms adds a seventh to the chord of resolution and once again reaches a pure tonic through the chromatic descent of an inner voice, now heard beneath the ominous diminished seventh arpeggios. The tonic harmony eventually arrives, but not before a minor plagal cadence – a more somber version of the final plagal cadence in "Heimweh I." Even the last measure, a single rolled chord that condenses the arpeggiated motion of the song's accompaniment, is tinged with painful memories.

In certain respects, "Heimweh III" seems more closely connected to the child's world and *Volks-Kinderlieder* than does "Heimweh II." Its simple duple meter, frequent doubling of voice and accompaniment, refrain-like material at the end of each strophe, and predominant lightness of tone all

Example 4.3a Brahms, "Heimweh III," Op. 63, no. 9, mm. 1–6

convey a degree of *Volkstümlichkeit* greater than that of the intense second song (Example 4.3a). The mood is thus closer to, though not identical with, that of "Heimweh I."

Even the song's modified strophic structure (A B A' B') leans toward pure strophic repetitions, especially between the first and third strophes. More subtly, the second halves of the B sections (first the accompaniment alone, then both the accompaniment and the voice) borrow material from the A sections, altering harmonies and rhythms to provide greater unrest (cf. mm. 7–13 and 20–26). Moreover, the A and B sections contain similar harmonic progressions, moving through the dominant, minor dominant, flat subtonic, dominant, and tonic. (The progressions are not identical: the A sections, for example, also touch on the supertonic while the B sections move through the flat mediant.) Even the initial vocal melody of the two B sections derives from A section material. The descending eighth-note phrase (E E D B) in m. 15, then treated sequentially, is taken directly from the treble line of the piano accompaniment in the preceding measure, itself a recollection of both the concluding phrase of the vocal line in mm. 11–13 and the piano introduction (mm. 1–2). Brahms's use of developing variation helps unite all sections of the song.[78] Moreover, the refrain-like material at the end of each strophe enhances the folk-like effect, always leading the harmony back to the tonic. But once again the complexities of adult consciousness intrude. Rapid harmonic progressions, for example, help convey the protagonist's confusion as he contemplates his past. The effect is of disoriented searching, a confused quest for the happiness of youth.

The changing relationship between voice and accompaniment contributes to the song's complexity. When the protagonist thinks back upon the past, the upper line of the piano accompaniment generally doubles the voice, as in lines 1 and 3 of the first stanza ("As a boy I saw flowers blossoming – " and "I saw the sun shine above them – "). But the confused interjections of lines 2 and 4 ("I don't know any more – what was it actually?" and "I seem to see it still") are set differently, with the vocal line and accompaniment diverging. As present circumstances encroach on memory, the close connection between voice and accompaniment disappears, with textural complexity displacing the simpler expression of the preceding music. At several points in the song, the vocal line seems to get stuck on a certain pitch, unable to continue on the course set by the piano's melody (e.g. mm. 9 and 21–23). At other times, the voice presents the descending melodic line, but the piano does not (e.g. mm. 30–31).

The texture of mm. 46–47 produces a momentary emotional uplift. The joining of voice and piano in parallel sixths (a seeming compromise between exact doubling and complete independence) for the climactic phrase "so fresh, so bright, so dear" creates harmonic and emotional warmth for this final reflection on the cherished past. But the moment soon passes; the parallel sixths vanish as the harmony shifts from C major to A minor. Like a plaintive cry, the F-E half step motion in the vocal part (mm. 47–49) harkens back to the "Wiege" motif of "Heimweh I." Followed by a long chromatic descent in the piano, it projects the grief inherent in the final pronouncement "It was the glow of youth." That glow belongs to the irretrievable past (Example 4.3b).

Despite this painful recognition, the song ends with a feeling of gentle reassurance. In repeating the final line of text, the protagonist once again sings the refrain that concludes each of the first three stanzas (mm. 11–13, 24–26, 37–39, 50–52). The refrain reasserts the diatonic pitch F-sharp (mm. 50–51) – the final diatonic correction of the minicycle – transforming the plaintive F-E half step into a more comforting whole step before the final vocal descent to the tonic. In retrospect, the diatonic corrections that Brahms introduces into all three songs can be seen to foreshadow the uplifting mood with which he ends the cycle.

Considered together and in sequence, Brahms's settings form a distinct progression, different from the one suggested by the texts themselves: Whereas Groth's poems depict sequential stages of nostalgia, shifting the

Example 4.3b Brahms, "Heimweh III," Op. 63, no. 9, mm. 45–52

focus further and further from childhood, the musical settings create a large-scale arch shape. As Starobinski has observed, the first and third songs are lighter in tone than the second, the cycle's "center of gravity."[79] The first and third songs, he notes, both employ simple 2/4 meter, the second a weightier 6/4 time. Furthermore, the first and third both have a varied strophic form, while the second has a more complex ternary structure. Tension increases from the first song to the second, then relaxes from the second to the third: "Heimweh I," with its sustained dominant prolongation, creates a strong sense of yearning leading to a tenuous resolution; "Heimweh II," comprising an internal section of sustained dominant harmony bounded by lament-like sections in the tonic, compounds yearning with sorrow and despair; and "Heimweh III," whose four sections each return to the tonic after a period of harmonic wandering, offers a measure of relief.

Because "Heimweh II" is furthest removed from *Volks-Kinderlieder*, its protagonist seems furthest removed from childhood's paradise, emotionally if not temporally. Despair reaches a climax here, then subsides in the third song, and the emotional change is reflected in the two songs' endings. In "Heimweh II," the accompaniment eventually reaches the tonic major, but with no indication that the protagonist hears its arrival or recognizes its symbolic significance. Then in the third song the voice itself makes the final melodic correction to usher in the major mode and a concomitant sense of comfort.

The texts alone convey no sense of return. In the third text, although the image of the barren shore has disappeared, there is no revival of childhood joy, no message of solace. Even the final line "It was the glow of youth," where confusion gives way to clarity, offers no comfort. Brahms's settings, however, follow a different course, creating an impression of return in "Heimweh III" whereas the texts merely suggest that time has progressed. By imparting circularity to the trilogy, the music provides some relief. The emotional pains of old age, the third song seems to say, are less searing than those of middle age.

The competing linear and circular impulses of the texts and musical settings are reflected in the modified strophic forms of each song. This is perhaps most evident in "Heimweh II," whose music presses ahead, then doubles back on itself, albeit with significant alterations, to create an extended ternary form (A B B' A'). The inevitable passage of time ("Der Zeiten Wandel") – the path that led the child away from home and into adulthood – is countered by the contemplation of memories that in some fashion enable the adult to return ("Den Weg zurück). Fusion of linear and circular impulses both across the minicycle and within each song marks another kind of expressive duality, conjuring both child and adult worlds and the tension inherent in the effort to bridge them.

Competing impulses are also evident in the successive key relations of the songs: G major, E major, and A major. Tension rises with movement in the sharp direction and relaxes with the reverse. But while the third song lowers the level of emotional intensity, it does not revert to the key or mood of the first. Similarly, the tempo marking of the third song ("Etwas langsam") indicates a somewhat faster pace than that of the second ("Langsam") but without returning to that of the first ("Zart bewegt"). Brahms's setting of "Heimweh III" may suggest the possibility of return, but not to the point of origin.

The overall image suggested by the "Heimweh" trilogy is that of a spiral, advancing yet also circling. "Heimweh III" may project a lighter tone than "Heimweh II," but it is neither the dreaminess nor the childhood bliss of "Heimweh I" that we now hear. Textual and musical allusions to death throughout all three songs imply that that final state, so close at hand in "Heimweh III," is the "home" most desperately sought: Forest and field, a longing to rest, chromatic descents in both voice and piano, the minor mode setting of "Wiege," broken octaves, falling thirds – all point in this direction. Death, only partially resembling a child's peaceful sleep, signifies the ultimate return. Yearning for the peacefulness of the past inspires a more profound longing for the eternal serenity of the future.[80]

The key sequence supports this interpretation. Understood as a large-scale flat-VII – V – I progression (G – E – A), the succession of keys has a certain cadential logic. The drive to the cadence, i.e. to A, the key of the third song, is stronger than would be a return to G, the key of the first song (G – E – G, or I – VI – I). In reverting from four sharps to three, the third song resolves tensions that had built up in the first two songs and forms a fitting conclusion to the cycle. Ultimate acceptance of death as a release from life's emotional turmoil finds a musical parallel in harmonic resolution.

Given the frequency with which tonics turn into tonic sevenths in the trilogy, one might view the true harmonic goal of the minicycle as D, the key of death. (See, for example, the rapid transformation of the tonic A major into V_7/IV in m. 3 of "Heimweh III.") After all, the condition of old age portrayed by "Heimweh III" does not represent life's ultimate goal. The tonic A major of the third song, while resolving the tensions of the previous two songs, is not conclusive in dramatic terms; unrest may have eased, but the final resolution of earthly travails in the dissolution of death lies ahead. Following this interpretation, the background tonal concept for the trilogy could be read as IV (G) – V/V (E) – V (A) – [I (D)], the key of D hovering in the imagination as an unrealized aural/dramatic event, and yet another embodiment of the spiral-like pattern associated with Romantic *Heimweh*.

Brahms's "Heimweh" Lieder are reminiscent of Romantic expressions of a yearning for home. But is it reasonable to assume that this late nineteenth-century composer was aware of the rich philosophical and artistic tradition connected with the word *Heimweh*? Brahms was intimately familiar with Romantic writings. His enthusiasm for E. T. A. Hoffmann, whose complete works he owned, is well known.[81] Michael Musgrave's description of the contents of Brahms's personal library reveals that the composer also developed a keen interest in the works of many other late eighteenth- and early nineteenth-century literary and philosophical figures.[82] Over the years, he collected verses, stories, and novels by Eichendorff, Jean Paul, Arnim, Novalis, Hölderlin, Mörike, Tieck, Heine, Friedrich Hebbel, Kleist, and Kerner. He acquired essays and treatises by Christian Deitrich Grabbe, Ferdinand Freiligrath, Karl Leberecht Immermann, Hegel, Schopenhauer, and Schlegel, as well as poems and plays of Goethe, Schiller, Wieland, and Friedrich Maximilian Klinger. The handwritten notations he made in many of these volumes, as well as his various collections of quotations by poets, philosophers, and artists, reveal that he was closely acquainted with Romantic ideas.[83] Given that Brahms was an avid reader and life-long learner, it seems likely that he encountered the *Heimweh* concept in numerous contexts, such as poems by Eichendorff and Mörike, and Lieder by Schubert and Loewe.[84] Surely Brahms would have recognized the prevalence and importance of the concept, and he may well have intuited, if not consciously perceived, its characteristic spiral-like synthesis of oppositions leading to transcendent wholeness in the Romantic works he cherished.

While Brahms was indebted to Romantic writers and artists, his later works seldom express the unalloyed optimism associated with that movement at its peak. As Virginia Hancock notes, "the first of the songs often dubbed 'autumnal,' was written when he was only thirty-four years old."[85] It is natural that Brahms's "Heimweh" Lieder should temper the effect of the spiral they evoke. Rather than promise glorious transcendence, these songs, like other nostalgic works of Brahms's maturity, offer gentle assurance that life's inevitable conclusion will usher in a state of eternal serenity.

PART III

The lost world of folk song

In the late eighteenth and nineteenth centuries, folk song was revered in much the same manner as classical antiquity and childhood. Perhaps its most oft-remarked attribute was naturalness, a trait that, as we have seen, Schiller hailed in the culture of the ancient Greeks and Rousseau celebrated in children. The naturalness that Romantics likewise associated with the *Volk* stood in sharp contrast to the over-refinement and artificiality of cultivated society and its aesthetic products. The *Volkslied*, created (or at least adopted) by the German populace and transmitted orally from one generation to the next, was viewed as one of the most genuine expressions of the "purely human" and, like antiquity and childhood, became an object of ardent longing.[1] Romantic reverence for *Volkslieder* is evident in the elaborate frontispiece to volume 2 of Arnim and Brentano's folk song collection *Des knaben Wunderhorn* of 1808 (Figure 7).

Justus Thibaut, in his treatise *On Purity in Musical Art* (1825; *Über die Reinheit der Tonkunst*), extols the naturalness of folk song through a direct analogy to childhood.[2] The cultivated man will understandably choose to interact with other cultivated men, but he should not, Thibaut advises, lose feeling for the magic of innocence:

Perfect openness, sincerity, and truthfulness are the noblest traits of the human character. But education, and the circumstances of life, generally make a man more or less close, calculating, disingenuous, and deceitful; whereas a child stands before us with his virtues and his faults, a fresh and virgin specimen of nature's handiwork.

In Thibaut's view, the relation of the cultivated man to the child resembles that of art music to folk music. Just as society leads men to become dissemblers, so too does art music easily become unnatural:

It may be asserted, without exaggeration, that one half of our music is destitute of the natural element; a species of mathematics without a spark of life; a mere display for the honour and glory of nimble fingers; and such a compound of unwholesome ingredients, that it may seriously be asked whether it does not do us more harm than good.

The folk song represents a refreshing contrast to the sickly state of contemporary music: "[A]ll the songs that emanate from the people themselves, or

Figure 7 *Des knaben Wunderhorn*, vol. 2, ed. Achim von Arnim and Clemens Brentano (Heidelberg: Mohr und Zimmer, 1808), frontispiece.

are adopted by them and preserved as favourites, are, as a rule, pure and clear in character, like that of a child." Art music has become petrified, but folk music embodies the purity and potential of the young.

As Thibaut hints, folk song, like classical antiquity and childhood, was associated with an idealized past. Romantics looked back nearly two and a half millennia to the glorified culture of Periclean Athens. Childhood lay just a few decades away, but its paradisiacal nature seemed equally remote. Folk song evoked the Middle Ages, a broadly conceived period extending into the seventeenth century during which the bulk of *Volkslieder* were believed to have originated. (For Thibaut and others, whether a song actually derived from the common folk or was instead appropriated by them, during the Middle Ages or later, was of little consequence; what mattered was that it had stood the test of time, becoming firmly rooted in oral tradition.) Like fairy tales, ballads, legends, and romances, folk songs opened a window on what Romantics saw as a magnificent period in German history – a utopian Christian era long predating their own blighted, overly secular age, from which the "purely human" seemed to have disappeared.[3]

Romantic enthrallment with the medieval world was spurred by present conditions. The malaise afflicting Germans after the devastating Thirty Years' War had intensified during the eighteenth century as France's economic, political, and cultural supremacy became a source of increasing humiliation and resentment. To eighteenth-century German intellectuals and artists (many of whom came from the lower classes), the backwardness of the provincial German states was particularly dispiriting compared to France's glittering court society. Romantic nostalgia for the Middle Ages and its folk culture merged with the interrelated notions of *Bildung* and German nationalism. Like classical antiquity and childhood, the folk song was thought capable of restoring Germans to spiritual health and fostering national pride. Genuine, natural, unpretentious, sturdy, vibrant, venerable – the characteristic qualities of *Volkslieder* were widely recognized as the essence of what it meant to be German ("the truest reflection of the soul of a nation, of its character, of its capacity to feel," Carl Alexander wrote in 1834),[4] providing the foundation for a strong, unified German nation. Thibaut draws attention to the folk song's national significance:

Such songs almost invariably re-echo the emotions of vigorous, unperverted minds, and for that very reason have in various ways quite a peculiar value from their connection with great national events; and, dating from times when nations had all the innocence and freshness of youth, they seize with irresistible force upon minds which, however much warped, are still alive to true and genuine impulse.

Regaining the qualities of folk song was not just desirable but indispensable. Thibaut ends his essay on this point: "A return to simple and natural ways is daily becoming in every respect more and more necessary. Music, in truth, can boast but little of having escaped all share in the false tendencies of the age." Songs of the common folk could help remedy the fragmentation that beleaguered individuals and German society.

Besides naturalness, another parallel between folk song, classical antiquity, and childhood was the recognition of loss. Romantics were painfully aware of the vast distance separating their own cultivated society from the idealized world of the *Volk*, which, as Julian von Pulikowski writes, they sought "as a lost paradise."[5] Artists could try to infuse their works with the qualities of folk song, but its naiveté ultimately remained elusive.

The powerful lure of folk song during the late eighteenth and nineteenth centuries is manifest in the numerous *Volkslied* collections, newly composed *volkstümliche* Lieder, and *Kunstlieder* with folk-like elements, as well as in the emerging discipline of folk song scholarship. Although oral song traditions stretched back to medieval times, the *idea* of folk song was an invention of the Enlightenment. The driving force behind the eighteenth-century craze for the folk-like was Herder.[6] Herder, who coined the term "Volkslied," discussed the concept at length in his essay "Auszug aus einem Briefwechsel über Ossian und die Lieder alter Völker," published in his collection *Von deutscher Art und Kunst* of 1773.[7] Influenced by Rousseau's writings on the joint origins of language and music, the philosopher Johann Georg Hamann's veneration of folk cultures, Thomas Percy's *Reliques of Ancient English Poetry* (1765), and the poems of the reputed third-century Gaelic bard Ossian, Herder embarked on an ambitious program of gathering folk songs and ballads of many nationalities. He published the collection – poetic texts, but not the melodies to which they were commonly sung – in two parts under the title *Volkslieder* in 1778–79 (the title was later changed to *Stimmen der Völker in Liedern* when the collection was reissued posthumously in 1807). At the same time, he urged his literary contemporaries to track down additional folk songs through fieldwork and to infuse their own writings with the qualities of folk poetry – a double injunction to which Goethe, for one, responded with enthusiasm.

Not all of Herder's folk poems and ballads are "authentic," that is, derived from the general populace; the anthology includes, for example, texts by Shakespeare, Ossian (actually forgeries by the eighteenth-century Englishman James MacPherson), and Goethe. As folk song scholar Ernst Klusen explains, in Herder's view a *Volkslied* did not have to originate with uncultivated peoples; it did, however, need to be beautiful, widely sung, and (usually) old.[8] Unlike art works fashioned according to classical precepts, the folk song might involve irregular, rough, or primitive elements. Herder saw no need to elevate, smooth over, or improve upon the poems in his collection. He simply omitted those songs that, in his judgment, did not exhibit the traits he regarded as fundamental to the *Volkslied*. The collection thus reflects an idealized vision of the *Volk* and its art – to Klusen, a "Fiction"[9] – not an objective reporting of the full range of songs sung by the lower classes.

The traits that Herder regarded as essential to folk song differ markedly from the qualities he perceived in the cultivated poetry of his own time – artificial, stilted, rule-oriented works he deprecated as *Schlamm* (mud or slime) in contrast to the *Gold* of *Volkslieder*.[10] Nostalgia for a more natural, simple, and truthful art than that of contemporary society underlay his passion for *Volkslieder*, leading him to exclude from his collection most works of recent vintage. According to Klusen, "[Herder] saw the necessity of going back to the old times in order to discover the 'genuine folk song' in its original beauty and its true life among the Folk."[11] Songs that had long circulated among the *Volk*, he believed, could help restore integrity to art and society of the present.

Many new *Volkslied* collections appeared after Herder's pioneering effort, including those of Arnim-Brentano (1806–08), August Zarnack (1818–20), Friedrich Karl Freiherr von Erlach (1834–36), Zuccalmaglio and Kretzschmer (1838–41), Uhland (1844–45), Simrock (1851), and Ludwig Erk and Böhme (1893–94).[12] The nineteenth-century collections differ significantly from one another. Some, following Herder, include only the poetic texts, others both the texts and their accompanying melodies. They also diverge on the issue of authenticity. Both Brentano and Zuccalmaglio, for example, did not hesitate to alter, and on occasion even to create, some of the folk songs in their collections. Uhland and Erk each took a more scholarly approach, publishing the songs as they had encountered them. But while the collectors' methods and motivations varied, their dedication to preserving the wealth of German *Volkslieder* reflected shared nostalgia for an idealized national past – a time of natural, spontaneous expression of heartfelt feelings in which Germans could take deep pride. Herder's collecting activities were essentially cosmopolitan in spirit (a minority of the folk songs in his collection are German) while those of his successors had a nationalist bent.

Herder's passion for folk song inspired a number of late eighteenth-century poets, including Goethe, Gottfried August Bürger, Christian Friedrich Daniel Schubart, Claudius, Hölty, Voss, and the Stolberg brothers, to compose verse emulating the formal, stylistic, and expressive traits of folk poems and ballads. (Goethe's "Heidenröslein" is a well-known example.) This folk-like poetry attracted contemporary song composers, such as Schulz, Schubart, Zelter, and Reichardt, and, together with Herder's devotion to *Volkslieder*, inspired numerous musical settings in a similar folk-like style. Schulz's three volumes of *Lieder in Volkston*, which include many settings of texts by the above-named poets, were principally responsible for introducing folk-like musical elements – strophic form, melodic simplicity, symmetrical phrasing, rhythmic regularity, diatonic harmony, and subordinate accompaniments – into Lied composition.

Although Schulz was greatly influenced by Herder, he seems not to have been motivated by nostalgia (such as Herder experienced) so much as a kind of paternalistic humanism.[13] A champion of Enlightenment ideals, he composed his *Lieder im Volkston* to provide suitable music for the common folk to sing – songs demonstrating the "appearance of the familiar" (*Schein der Bekannten*) whose moral content made them worthy replacements for the disreputable street songs (*Gassenhauer* or *Pöbellieder*) that circulated among the lower classes. In adopting a folk-like style, he aimed to produce songs that anyone could sing, hopefully ensuring their broad popularity:

> In all these songs it is and remains my goal to sing more in the manner of the folk than in the manner of art, namely, so that even unpracticed lovers of song (as long as they don't completely lack a voice) can easily sing along and keep them in their memory. To this end, I have selected only those texts from our best lied poets that seem to me made for this folk singing *[Volksgesang]*, and sought in the melodies themselves for the greatest simplicity and comprehensibility, indeed sought in every way to attain the *appearance of the familiar [Schein des Bekannten]*, because I know from experience how helpful, even necessary, this appearance is to the quick reception of the volkslied. In this appearance of the familiar lies the entire secret of the *Volkston*.[14]

By creating *Lieder im Volkston* – seemingly artless, yet actually carefully crafted settings of texts by celebrated poets – the cultivated classes could help educate, and thereby improve the lives of, the populace. Achieving this goal required a certain degree of selectivity. As noted, Herder bypassed songs from the oral tradition that, for one reason or another, he deemed unworthy of his idealized notion of the *Volkslied*. Similarly, Schulz chose only those poetic texts whose moral content and aesthetic qualities he considered suitable to his broad humanitarian project, and composed musical settings geared specifically toward this end.

Schulz's *Lieder im Volkston* did in fact achieve great popularity, and were widely imitated in the late eighteenth century and even long into the nineteenth.[15] Tellingly, very few *volkstümliche Lieder* from the eighteenth century involve actual German folk poems, such as those in Herder's *Volkslieder*. (Herder's German translations of foreign poems and ballads did inspire a number of settings, perhaps, as J. W. Smeed speculates, because they exerted an "exotic fascination," or because they had "acquired something of a literary stamp by virtue of *being* translations.")[16] By far the most common approach of late eighteenth-century composers was to set texts written in the *manner* of folk song, that is, the folk-like poems of cultivated writers; the roughness and irregularities of authentic folk texts, evoking the crudities of the *Pöbel*, had little appeal to those aiming to create a repertory of songs that could educate the lower classes. Traditional folk tunes also received comparatively little attention during the eighteenth century. Sometimes poets wrote new words to existing folk songs (or folk song "parodies"), and composers occasionally penned accompaniments to traditional folk melodies.[17] On the whole, however, eighteenth-century poets and composers showed less interest in preserving the authentic *Volkslied* than in employing its idealized traits as an inspiration for their own more polished, folk-like works. As noted, even Herder, for all his devotion to *Volkslieder*, failed to include any melodies for the folk texts in his collection.

Around the turn of the nineteenth century, attitudes towards folk song began to shift. Carl Dahlhaus explains,

For Enlightenment thinkers, with their philanthropic leanings and never-ending attempts to intervene in the present, "noble simplicity" was to be found primarily in "folklike" songs that were written by composers and presented to the populace for the purpose of educating it. Not so the romantics, who were drawn to the past and felt that genuine folk song was to be discovered in songs which, it was thought, had emanated from the populace itself in a distant and eminently desirable bygone age.[18]

The failure of the French Revolution deflated many Enlightenment ideals, including the belief that the cultivated classes could (and should) improve the morality of the populace through education. To Romantics, this notion was misguided. The cultivated classes allegedly had more to learn from the common folk – whose culture, back in the Middle Ages, had produced the treasure of German *Volkslieder* – than vice versa. Jacob Grimm expressed a view shared by many of his contemporaries: "Men of old were greater, more pure, and holier than we are; there still shone in and around them the luster of godliness."[19] Thus, like Herder, Romantics looked upon the natural simplicity of folk song with nostalgia, as documented in Pulikowski's *Geschichte des Begriffes Volkslied im musikalischen Schrifttum*.[20] The rise of German nationalism in the early nineteenth century, however, led them to express their yearning with even greater intensity than had the Enlightenment era figure whose *Volkslieder* collection inspired them.

The Romantic idealization of both the medieval German past and nature ushered in a new period of reverence for folk song, intimated in the late eighteenth-century writings of Reichardt.[21] Within the realm of poetry, the *Volkslied* exerted greatest influence during the first three quarters of the nineteenth century. Numerous writers, including Uhland, Brentano, Eichendorff, Müller, Heine, Mörike, Geibel, Theodor Storm, and Keller, introduced folk-like traits into their verse. Many found particular inspiration in *Des knaben Wunderhorn*, which presented a wealth of folk poetry for emulation, transformation, or subtle evocation. In the area of music composition, the *Volkslied* remained influential (with varying degrees of intensity) well into the twentieth century, as reflected in arrangements of traditional folk songs, settings of both folk texts and folk-like texts, and art songs with folk-like elements. Beethoven, Schubert, Weber, Friedrich Silcher, Mendelssohn, Schumann, Franz, Brahms, Mahler, Humperdinck, Reger, and Armin Knab all demonstrated a strong attraction to the characteristic qualities of folk music.

Many writers have explored the influence of folk song on nineteenth-century German poets and composers, resulting in a wealth of broad-based as well as focused studies.[22] I will not here try to duplicate that material, but rather will merely introduce the following two chapters, which each examine the relation between folk song and art song in light of the lost paradise myth.

Chapter 5 concentrates on the intriguing phenomenon of songs-within-songs in Schubert's Lieder. Schubert's changing treatment of embedded songs over the course of his career draws attention to the variable musical awareness of Lied protagonists, evoking mankind's differing conditions before and after the Fall. Art songs exhibiting close ties to folk tradition, many with texts by eighteenth-century poets inspired by Herder, generally have protagonists who seem conscious of singing – a unity of thought and expression reminiscent of mankind's mythical existence in Eden. Schubert's later songs with Biedermeier era texts, however, typically involve self-conscious protagonists who, paradoxically, lack such musical awareness, suggesting a tragic rupture in the human psyche. In these works, the natural world of folk song hovers in the distance (in the sounds of embedded songs) as an object of intense longing.

Chapter 6 explores the influence of a well-known folk song motif – the human yearning to be a bird – on the Romantic Lied repertoire. While many aspects of folk song (structure, subject, tone, imagery, voice, concrete detail) help conjure the naturalness and simplicity for which Romantics longed, this particular wish motif held a special attraction, resonating with the lost paradise myth. According to Richard Heinberg, "Many traditions say that the First People had the capacity of flight, or had access to Heaven by means of a rope, tree, mountain, vine, or ladder . . . [I]n all cultures and eras flight and wings are symbolic of the freedom of the paradisal condition."[23] Songs from Reichardt to Mahler illustrate the continuous attraction of the *Voglmotif* throughout the nineteenth century, but also the gradual deflation of idealistic hopes.

5 | Schubert's songs-within-songs

"Listen to my song!" Orpheus commands. Before long, his lilting melody moves the assembled listeners to tears, and the legendary singer rejoices, promising them eternal bliss. A perennial operatic subject, the Orpheus myth appears in Schubert's "Lied des Orpheus," D. 474, within the confines of an art song; the famous episode before the entrance to Hades unfolds in just a few minutes of music. Orpheus – who sings throughout the work – announces his Lied, performs it, and then comments on the response of his audience. With four interior stanzas constituting the verses of Orpheus's Lied, the poetic text prompts the embedding of that song within a musical frame that both sets the scene for the legendary performance and reveals its powerful effect.

The multiple levels of musical discourse in D. 474 draw attention to the intriguing yet neglected phenomenon of songs-within-songs in Schubert's Lied oeuvre. The embedding of one work within another has a rich history in literary and musical domains.[1] Most closely related to Schubert's embedded songs are operatic serenades, lullabies, drinking songs, hymns, and other instances of what Edward Cone has termed "realistic" singing (that is, recognized as song by the operatic characters who sing and hear it).[2] Don Giovanni's "Deh vieni alla finestra" and Cherubino's "Voi che sapete" are two well-known examples. Operatic narratives also often possess reflexive properties similar to those of embedded literary works (e.g., a play-within-a-play). As Carolyn Abbate has discussed, beyond providing background information necessary to an understanding of the enacted drama, an operatic narrative might serve as an internal mirror of the larger work, clarifying the significance of dramatic developments.[3] At times, the embedded narrative might even seem to bring about those developments, story and enactment intertwining in a tangle of causation (e.g., the Count's narration of Cherubino's follies in the "Cosa sento" trio from *The Marriage of Figaro*).[4]

While the immense proportions and musico-dramatic complexities of opera make it highly suitable for musical embedding,[5] the art song represents a more surprising venue. Apart from extended ballads or cantata-like settings, the limited dimensions of Lieder would seem to hinder the embedding of one song within another. Yet Schubert often drew upon this technique, and his treatment of it illuminates a significant development in his Lied oeuvre: the increasing manifestation of Romantic alienation.[6]

Ranging from the obvious to the obscure, embedded songs occur in works from throughout Schubert's career. Although it is not possible to trace a straight chronology from simpler to more complex instances, a general trend nevertheless emerges. The earlier examples from the 1810s, when Schubert inclined towards texts from the 1770s and 80s (the early phase of Romanticism sometimes called the "Age of Sensibility"), are mostly explicit and serve a variety of functions.[7] As in "Lied des Orpheus," the embedding is openly announced in the text and/or music.

In the 1820s, however, as Schubert became increasingly attracted to Biedermeier era poetry, he employed the embedding technique with greater focus and subtlety. Many of the embedded songs from this later period share a single underlying purpose: to convey Lied protagonists' self-conscious alienation from an unspoiled natural world – perhaps the innocence of childhood, the beauty of the countryside, or the joy of new love. Although Biedermeier poets dwelled on many of the same subjects as earlier Romantic writers, including the separation of man and nature, divisions within the self, and death, times had changed. After the Congress of Vienna, the tide of idealism that had swept through the revolutionary years subsided. Still yearning for a return to naturalness but doubtful of the prospects for success, poets of the Restoration lowered their sights. Frustrated attempts to reunite oppositions led to nostalgia and sometimes madness. Many Biedermeier writers suffered from an agonizing sense of *Weltschmerz*. For Schubert, embedded songs proved a powerful means of expressing such painful emotions; multiple levels of musical discourse make audible the Lied protagonist's separation from the paradise for which he yearns.

Ironically, as Schubert's Lied protagonists became increasingly self-conscious, they seemed to lose touch with, and control of, their musicality; they became alienated from their own songs. Feeling incapable of singing (that is, of knowingly using song to serve some practical or emotional function in the manner of *Volkslieder*), they often allude to phantomlike songs: those they wish they could sing, once sang, or hear in nature. Although we perceive that the protagonists are singing throughout, they themselves might be aware, and perhaps dimly so, only of the songs they remember or imagine. They might show no inkling of their own musical discourse, a form of dramatic irony familiar, and likely borrowed, from opera. Schubert's later embedded songs thus assume a shadowy existence and are typically suffused with melancholy and nostalgia.

Embedded songs illuminate the expressive world of Lied protagonists – a subject about which Cone has expounded different views over the years and that merits reconsideration.[8] In doing so, they underscore the crucial role that consciousness, loss, memory, and nostalgia play in Schubert's late Lieder.[9] Various scholars have explored the centrality of these elements in his late instrumental works.[10] Given the frequent sharing of material between contemporaneous instrumental and vocal works, it is not surprising that Schubert's late Lieder should also foreground such elements.[11] Embedded songs give voice to some of Romanticism's most wrenching sentiments.

Embedded songs in Schubert's early Lieder: three examples

In Schubert's early works, embedded songs have different forms and functions. Sometimes the embedding is suggested through purely instrumental passages. Such is the case, for example, with "Der Sänger," D.149, composed in February 1815. The anonymous narrator of Goethe's six-stanza ballad (written *c.*1783) describes the arrival of a medieval minstrel at a magnificent royal court, where he sings to the king and assembled courtiers.[12] The narrator alludes to the minstrel's song in stanza 3 without including its lyrics.

Der Sänger drückt' die Augen ein	The minstrel closed his eyes
Und schlug in vollen Tönen;	And sang in resonant tones;
Die Ritter schauten mutig drein,	Resolutely the knights looked on,
Und in den Schoss die Schönen,	While the fair ladies looked down into their laps.
Der König, dem das Lied gefiel,	The king, pleased with the song,
Liess, ihn zu lohnen für sein Spiel,	Sent for a gold chain
Eine golden Kette holen.	To reward him for his singing.

Schubert sets the first two lines of stanza 3 as *secco* recitative (the piano drops out, effectively clearing the slate so that it can assume a new function in the succeeding measures). He then introduces eleven measures of music for piano alone (soon after recurring in a slightly varied version) – the interpolated "song" to which the king (and, implicitly, Schubert's listener, who will "reward" the composer with applause) responds with pleasure in the latter part of the stanza (Example 5.1).[13] This somewhat archaic-sounding instrumental music, a repeat of the piano introduction, plainly represents the minstrel's singing: it is perceived as such in both instances by characters in the narrative.[14] (The embedded music sounds archaic, but hardly medieval; it actually resembles the opening of a classical sonata allegro movement. In transforming the minstrel into a classical keyboard composer, Schubert turns "Der Sänger" into a subtle commentary on the old patronage system.)

Example 5.1 Schubert, "Der Sänger," D. 149, 2nd version, mm. 51–66.

While it may seem ironic that Schubert uses instrumental music as a stand-in for vocal music, he arguably had little choice since Goethe's text does not include the lyrics of the minstrel's song.[15] But Schubert also needed to distinguish the embedded song from the surrounding musical material. Since the anonymous narrator of the ballad (himself an implied minstrel) sings rather than speaks his tale, the shift to purely instrumental music helps to distinguish the minstrel's song of which he tells. The shift also focuses attention on the musical aspect of that song, for it is the music (rather than the words) that captures the king's attention and arouses his delight. In both the introduction and the interlude, the piano serves as an embodiment of the singer, projecting his voice and thereby implying the predominant role of music in the text-music relationship of song (a reversal of the usual 18th-century notion).[16] The fact that we hear the minstrel's music firsthand, rather than just hearing *of* it, conveys dramatic immediacy on the ballad's medieval court setting.

An embedded "song" *with* lyrics occurs in "Szene aus Faust," D.126, a Goethe setting composed in December 1814.[17] This dramatically conceived work alternates between passages of recitative for the Evil Spirit and Gretchen, who share the foreground of the cathedral scene, and chordal homophony for the choir, which intones select verses from *Dies irae* of the Latin requiem mass in the background.[18] Goethe's inclusion of these verses essentially compels their setting as an embedded "song" in D. 126, for the *Dies irae* is traditionally sung, not spoken. Accordingly, Schubert sets the choir music in sharp relief through its contrasting texture, meter, rhythm, tempo, dynamics, and tonality (Example 5.2). Because "Szene aus Faust" draws heavily on the musical vocabulary of opera, the interpolated requiem verses call to mind the "realistic" singing often heard in that medium.

The embedded choir music does more than establish the cathedral *mise en scène*. It also lends a sense of depth to the unfolding drama by subtly engaging its content. With verses dwelling on the terrors of Judgment Day, the intermittent choir music pricks Gretchen's conscience, magnifying her remorse at having entered into an illicit relationship with Faust, an affair that destroyed her innocence and indirectly caused her mother's death.

Chor:	Dies irae, dies illa,	The day of wrath, that fateful day,
	solvet saeclum in favilla.	will destroy the temporal world with flames.
...		
Chor:	Judex ergo cum sedebit,	Therefore when the judge sits,
	quidquid latet adparebit,	whatever is hidden will be manifest,
	nil inultum remanebit.	nothing will remain unpunished.
...		
Chor:	Quid sum miser tunc dicturus?	What will I say then in my sorrow?
	Quem patronum rogaturus?	Whom will I turn to for protection?
	Cum vix justus, cum vix justus	When even the just man, when even the just
	sit securus.	man is barely sure of salvation!
...		
Chor:	Quid sum miser tunc dicturus?	What will I say then in my sorrow?
	Quem patronum rogaturus?	Whom will I turn to for protection?[19]

Example 5.2 Schubert, "Szene aus Faust," D. 126, 2nd version, mm. 31–45

Like a Greek chorus, the choir, chanting in the background, offers an ironic commentary on the main line of dramatic action, intensifying its emotional force and casting a spotlight on the dire predicament of its focal character.

In "Lied des Orpheus," D. 474, composed in September 1816, the embedded song conveys the power of music to stir the emotions.[20] Jacobi's poem, written around 1770, communicates a strongly Christian message. Orpheus's lyre, which draws tears from a group of condemned souls, is the mouthpiece of an all-powerful God. Orpheus, representing Christ in hell (a subject derived from the liturgy of Holy Saturday), delivers a message of hope and divine forgiveness to those who heed his plea for pity. Schubert, however, makes no allusion to sacred compositional styles. Instead, he concentrates on the poem's dramatic presentational mode and inherent opportunities for vocal display; the song sounds like a cross between musical drama and a brilliant display piece. Just as Jacobi adapts the classical myth to suit his own purposes, Schubert alters the premise of the poetic text.[21]

Significantly, the eight-stanza poem is a dramatic monologue, not a dialogue:

Wälze dich hinweg, du wildes Feuer!	Roll back, savage fire!
Diese Saiten hat ein Gott gekrönt;	These strings have been crowned by a god;
Er, mit welchem jedes Ungeheuer,	With whom every monster
Und vielleicht die Hölle sich versöhnt.	And perhaps hell itself is reconciled.
Diese Saiten stimmte seine Rechte:	His right hand tunes these strings;
Fürchterliche Schatten, flieht!	Flee, dread shadows!
Und ihr winselnden Bewohner dieser Nächte,	And you, whimpering inhabitants of this darkness,
Horchet auf mein Lied!	Listen to my song!
Von der Erde, wo die Sonne leuchtet	From earth, where the sun
Und der stille Mond,	And the silent moon shine,
Wo der Tau das junge Moos befeuchtet,	Where dew moistens fresh moss,
Wo Gesang im grünen Felde wohnt;	Where song dwells in green fields;
Aus der Menschen süssem Vaterlande,	From the sweet country of mankind,
Wo der Himmel euch so frohe Blicke gab,	Where the heavens once looked upon you with joyful gaze,
Ziehen mich die schönsten Bande,	I am drawn by the fairest of ties,
Ziehet mich die Liebe selbst herab.	I am drawn down by love itself.
Meine Klage tönt in eure Klage;	My lament mingles with yours,
Weit von hier geflohen ist das Glück;	Happiness has fled far from here;
Aber denkt an jene Tage,	But remember those days,
Schaut in jene Welt zurück!	Look back into that world!
Wenn ihr da nur einen Leidenden umarmt,	If there you embraced but one sufferer,
O, so fühlt die Wollust noch einmal,	Then feel desire once more,
Und der Augenblick, in dem ihr euch erbarmt,	And may that moment when you took pity
Lindre diese lange Qual.	Soothe my long torment.
O, ich sehe Tränen fliessen!	O, I see tears flowing!
Durch die Finsternisse bricht	Through the darkness
Ein Strahl von Hoffnung; ewig büssen	A ray of hope breaks through; the good gods
Lassen euch die guten Götter nicht.	Will not let you atone for ever.
Götter, die für euch die Erde schufen,	The gods who created the earth for you
Werden aus der tiefen Nacht	Will call you from deep night
Euch in selige Gefilde rufen,	Into the Elysian fields
Wo die Tugend unter Rosen lacht.	Where virtue smiles amid roses.

Unlike Ranieri Calzabigi, the librettist of Gluck's opera *Orfeo ed Euridice* (1762), Jacobi assigns no speaking role to the inhabitants of Hades but instead gives Orpheus the task of conveying their presence.[22] As a result, precisely who constitutes Orpheus's audience is ambiguous. In stanza 2, Orpheus seems to address two different groups: the "dread shadows" (perhaps the Furies barring his entrance to the Underworld), whom he commands to flee, and "whimpering inhabitants of this darkness" (unnamed damned souls), whom he commands to listen. Neither stanzas 3–6 (the verses of Orpheus's "Lied") nor stanzas 7 and 8 (Orpheus's reaction to his audience's tears) further identify them. The ambiguity of address has important ramifications. Just as Orpheus is impersonated by the virtuoso singer who performs D. 474, the "whimpering inhabitants of this darkness" to whom Orpheus directs his song implicitly become Schubert's own listeners, whose sympathies are similarly stirred by the power of music.[23]

Schubert demonstrates music's effect on the emotions by borrowing a successful formula from Italian opera.[24] The first two stanzas of Jacobi's text, which establish both the infernal *mise-en-scène* and the heavenly source of Orpheus's musical magic, are set in the forthright, declamatory manner of an opening *scena*. The piano accompaniment announces Orpheus's resolve with its procession of accented octaves, dotted rhythms, and tremolos. The broad sweep of the vocal line, featuring several octave leaps, establishes Orpheus as a formidable musician, fearless in his pursuit (Example 5.3a).

Following the command "Listen to my song!" and a dramatic pause, Orpheus begins his "singing" – a *cantabile* section (marked "Ziemlich langsam") whose heightened lyricism stems from its triple meter, triplet rhythms, light accompaniment, and graceful melodic line (Example 5.3b). Although each of the four stanzas (3–6) presents new music rather than strophic repetitions, the cumulative effect is that of a lyrical Lied. The shift into the temporarily stable key area of A major at the beginning of Orpheus's embedded song contributes to the lyricism, particularly in contrast to the harmonically mobile opening *scena*, which moves from G-flat major to D-flat major to a half cadence in A minor. Orpheus wields his lyrical Lied like a weapon to win over the hearts of his listeners.

After a brief instrumental interlude whose descending lines evoke flowing tears, stanza 7 switches back to cut time, accelerates in tempo, and changes tonal direction, leading to B-flat major (mm. 74–93).[25] Orpheus has apparently concluded his "song." Whereas in stanzas 3–6 he plainly knows he is singing, in stanza 7 (as in stanzas 1 and 2) this no longer seems true. Like a *tempo di mezzo*, the music of stanza 7 interrupts the preceding lyricism and ushers in a new stage of the drama (Example. 5.3c).

Stanza 8, in which Orpheus triumphantly promises his listeners heavenly rewards, is set as a rousing *cabaletta*, turning Schubert's Lied into an exciting showpiece where attention focuses as much if not more on the actual singer as on the mythological character. Whether Orpheus now realizes he is singing is uncertain, for the dramatic scene has assumed a symbolic quality, with the

Example 5.3a Schubert, "Lied des Orpheus," D. 474, 2nd version, mm. 1–19

mythological character representing the virtuoso baritone who knowingly performs the work (Example 5.3d).

The song-within-a-song thus mirrors the song-as-a-whole, a simple form of *mise en abyme* which emphasizes the central message of the work.[26] Schubert must have hoped that the effect of Orpheus's song on the inhabitants of Hades would be duplicated by the effect of his own "Lied des Orpheus" on the residents of Vienna. This Orpheus, unlike Gluck's, seems far more concerned with the transformative power of music than with seeking his wife, who, tellingly, goes unmentioned. The ancient myth is recast as a modern tribute to the talent of the virtuoso performer, and the might of the musical god – perhaps Schubert himself – who, in Orpheus's words, "crowned the strings."[27]

Example 5.3b Schubert, ""Lied des Orpheus," D. 474, 2nd version, mm. 31–36

Embedded songs in Schubert's mature Lieder: three examples

Romantic subjectivity comes to the fore in Schubert's embedded songs from the 1820s. A good example is "Pause," the twelfth song of *Die schöne Müllerin*, composed in 1823. The miller lad's painful self-consciousness surfaces in his relationship to music, about which he is deeply ambivalent.[28] As he becomes increasingly aware of singing (a means of expression he initially denies), the sorrowful direction of his fate comes into focus. In this song, consciousness of singing involves the recognition of loss – the slipping away of imagined happiness.

To convey the miller's self-reflection, Schubert interpolates song-like music within a contrasting musical frame – a disjunction far less blatant than in "Lied des Orpheus," but audible. In the second stanza of Müller's text, the miller describes how he used to be able to express his ardent longing in playful song:

Meiner Sehnsucht allerheißesten Schmerz	The most ardent pangs of my longing
Durft' ich aushauchen in Liederscherz,	I could express in playful song,
Und wie ich klagte so süß und fein,	And as I lamented, so sweetly and tenderly,
Glaubt' ich doch, mein Leiden wär' nicht klein.	I believed my sorrows were not trifling.

Example 5.3c Schubert, "Lied des Orpheus," D. 474, 2nd version, mm. 74–84

Schubert's setting echoes the sound of those distant songs through the enhanced lyricism of both vocal line and piano accompaniment. The sighing eighth-note pairs (with voice and piano moving in harmonious parallel thirds) at "Meiner Sehnsucht" and the melodic flourish at "durft' ich aushauchen in Liederscherz" produce a songlike effect that contrasts sharply with the static, triadic "tune" of the first stanza (Example 5.4). The songful quality is enhanced by the balanced phrase structure of the passage, as well as the increased rhythmic and harmonic activity of the bass line. This music evokes Lieder from the past whose lyrics are missing.

The miller's denial that he is singing ("I can sing no more, my heart is too full") would seem to establish "Pause" as the antithesis of "Lied des Orpheus," whose vocal protagonist boldly announces his singing (or, for that matter, any Lied whose vocal protagonist consciously sings an embedded song). Yet "Pause" and "Lied des Orpheus" actually represent opposite

Example 5.3d Schubert, "Lied des Orpheus," D. 474, 2nd version, mm. 94–109

sides of the same coin. Whereas "Lied des Orpheus" highlights its musical embedding by calling attention to the "musical" nature of the embedded song, "Pause" does so by emphasizing the "un-musical" nature of its opening. In both works, the protagonist ostensibly begins by expressing himself in a manner other than song, suggested by declamatory or static musical material. Both works then shift into a more lyrical, song-like section. Orpheus obviously knows he is singing at this point, and the miller seems at least somewhat aware of mimicking his former songs. In both Lieder, the protagonist's awareness of singing in the final section is ambiguous, with interesting implications for an understanding of the song as a whole. In sum, the self-denying song "Pause" follows essentially the same structural pattern as the self-proclaiming song "Lied des Orpheus." Yet the musicality

Example 5.4 Schubert, "Pause," D. 795, no. 12, mm. 9–26

of "Pause" from beginning to end assumes a more shadowy, uncertain existence, reflecting the heightened subjectivity of Müller's text; the miller's ambivalence toward his own music-making points to the song's Biedermeier origins.

Why does the miller deny that he is singing? Why does he recoil from song? Singing is the manner of expression he associates with anguished longing, with his former sorrowful laments. To resume singing would imply a return to that emotional state. Once again he would experience the pain of unrequited love; the maiden would not love him after all. And so the miller insists that he can no longer sing, that his present joy is too great to be contained in song: "Ah, how great can my burden of joy be / That no song on earth will contain it?"

From the miller's perspective, it is important that the embedded song come to an end, that his musical memories be contained and not allowed to retain their grip on his imagination indefinitely. Suspecting perhaps that his great "burden of joy" might in fact be well suited to song (and ultimately not much different from the burden of his former longing), he tries to regain his speaking voice. Schubert's setting suggests this interpretation by reverting in m. 42 to the music of the opening. The return seems partly motivated by similarities between the opening lines of the two poetic stanzas: in both lines 1 and 11 the miller focuses on the lute hanging on the wall ("I have hung my lute on the wall" and "Rest now, dear lute, here on this nail." But line 11 takes the form of an imperative. Doubting the reality of his happiness, the miller intentionally distances himself from his instrument, hoping to prevent the return of his misery. The repetition of music from the opening intimates an effort to recapture his former self-assurance, to cast away doubts about the future.

Despite having laid his instrument aside, the miller worries that his lute will continue to make music and that he himself will resume singing. Nature does seem to conspire against him for, as he fears, the ribbon hanging from the lute flutters across the strings, producing a kind of natural (or supernatural) music in the remote, other-worldly key of A-flat major. The instrument calls to the voice, urging a continuation of song. The miller nervously ponders the implications: "Is this the echo of my love's sorrow, / Or could it be the prelude to new songs?" Schubert sets the first question in a declamatory, discordant manner, suggesting "love's sorrow." The second question, by contrast, receives a metrically regular, conventionally shaped, diatonic tune, mimicking the sound of "new songs."

While Müller's poem ends with two questions, Schubert's musical setting hints at an answer. The four-measure piano postlude, a repeat of mm. 5–8 of the piano prelude, in effect encapsulates the entire song within an expanded "prelude" (with mm. 1–4 and 5–8 on either end). This framing device suggests that "Pause" is not a conclusion to the miller's story but just a pause in the action, a prelude to songs yet unsung. "Pause" thus might be regarded as an embedded song within an expanded piano prelude to a larger work – the continuation of the song cycle. The answer to both of the miller's questions, therefore, is "yes"; "Pause" is both the echo of previous laments *and* the prelude to new songs. The miller's story will continue on its tragic course, as he himself comes to suspect. In the final analysis, there is little difference between the embedded "song" of mm. 20–32 (the miller's semi-conscious evocation of songs from the past) and the song as a whole. In both, music is allied with loss and sorrow.

The miller's attempt to distance himself from his lute – the physical symbol of his music making – exemplifies his divided sense of self. Leary of its alluring sounds, he seeks another mode of expression, to no avail. As he scrutinizes his own vocalism, his song becomes increasingly self-focused and angst-ridden. His self-consciousness is not like that of a mother who knowingly sings a lullaby to her child. Rather, the miller becomes ever more aware of singing despite himself, of having no control of his lute, his voice, or his fate. As if he had momentarily stepped outside the frame of the song, he seems to have heard his own music, and to recognize that he is a protagonist in someone else's Lied.

Schubert's beautiful spring song "Im Frühling," D. 882, composed in March 1826, moves, as Youens writes, into the realm of the "musical subjunctive."[29] The shift from sorrowful reality to serene imagination takes place in the song's final stanza, where the vocal protagonist, reflecting on bygone happiness, wishes to become a little bird who would sing about his lost love the summer through:

O wär ich doch ein Vöglein nur	Oh, if only I were a bird,
Dort an dem Wiesenhang,	There on the sloping meadow!
Dann blieb ich auf den Zweigen hier,	Then I would stay on these branches here,
Und säng ein süsses Lied von ihr,	And sing a sweet song about her
Den ganzen Sommer lang.	All summer long.

If he can no longer experience the bliss of requited love, at least he could sustain its memory through song. Expressed through the natural music of the birds, pain transmutes into beauty, misery into sweet lamentation. Schubert's pianissimo setting of the last stanza, which becomes even quieter in its concluding measures, seems to sound from afar, like a distant mirage. It is music of memory and imagination, infused with nostalgia and desire. It is the song the protagonist wishes he could sing – and, as he may ultimately realize, the song he has just sung.

Written by Ernst Schulze in March 1815 after a frustrated love affair, the poem associates springtime not with exuberance but rather loss and sorrow, an age-old conceit. Surrounded by the beauties of nature, the protagonist feels his unhappiness all the more acutely. In the first stanza, sitting quietly on a hillside observing the clear sky and playful breezes, he betrays his present suffering: "Where once, in the first rays of spring, / I was, oh, so happy" Although the signs of spring – flowers, fields, sun, and sky – are the same now as before, his emotional world has changed fundamentally. Stanza 5 offers a veiled explanation:

Es wandeln nur sich Will und Wahn,	Only will and whim change,
Es wechseln Lust und Streit,	And joy alternates with strife;
Vorüber flieht der Liebe Glück,	The happiness of love flies past,
Und nur die Liebe bleibt zurück,	And only love remains,
Die Lieb und ach, das Leid!	Love and, alas, sorrow.

Like a leaf tossed in the wind, the protagonist is buffeted between will and delusion, helpless to control his feelings or fate. His emotional pain erupts in the exclamation "and, alas, sorrow."

Schubert's musical setting softens that pain by sounding the very song the poetic protagonist wishes he could sing: the music expresses a sweet nostalgia that counterbalances the protagonist's angst. The feeling of nostalgia emerges from the musical structure, an unusual series of variations whose combination of constancy and change beautifully captures the poetic contrast between natural and human worlds, and whose altered repetitions invite retrospective listening.

The song divides into three large sections (A: mm. 1–16, B: mm. 17–32, C: mm. 33–50), each comprising two poetic stanzas. Within each large section and over the song as a whole, the music seems to reflect on itself, recalling yet also transforming what has come before. The first large section contains two sub-sections (A_1: mm. 1–9; A_2: mm. 10–16) corresponding to the first two poetic stanzas (Example 5.5a). The opening of A_2 recalls the opening of A_1 (the piano introduction), but now the vocal line enters early to complete the piano melody instead of waiting to introduce one of its own. The nine measures of A_1 are remolded into the seven measures of A_2. A_2 thus functions as a kind of musical reminiscence, paralleling the memory of happiness in mm. 8–9.

The single musical strophe that encompasses both A_1 and A_2 is repeated in varied form for stanzas 3 and 4 (B_1: mm. 17–25; B_2: mm. 26–32). Among the principal changes is the introduction of running sixteenth notes in the piano right hand and bouncing eighth notes in the left hand. The subtle syncopated rhythms in the inner voices of the piano in A_1 and A_2 have disappeared, suggesting undisturbed springtime joy. The protagonist willfully asserts that all is now as before, as proven by the constancy of nature. Yet the continual variations of the musical setting belie his certainty. B_2 transforms B_1, just as A_2 transformed A_1; thus the B section as a whole transforms the A section. Even before hearing the turbulent *minore* variation of stanza 5, one senses that this springtime *is* different, that the protagonist hides from what he knows to be true.

[Musical example: Schubert, "Im Frühling," D. 882, mm. 1–10, marked Andante, pp, with vocal text: "Still sitz' ich an des Hü-gels Hang, der Him-mel ist so klar, das Lüft-chen spielt im grü-nen Tal, wo ich beim er-sten Früh-lings-strahl einst, ach so glück-lich war, so glück-lich war; wo"]

Example 5.5a Schubert, "Im Frühling," D. 882, mm. 1–10

The veil of illusion is ripped off in section C, whose first subsection (C_1: mm. 33–40) exposes the anguish of human inconstancy, and whose second subsection (C_2: mm. 41–50) reveals the possibility of consolation through art. The shocking music of C_1 does not burst forth wholly unannounced. Its stormy, syncopated rhythms, conveying the pain of emotional truth, look back to the hidden syncopated patterns in section A (Example 5.5b). Likewise, its minor mode recalls the brief modulation to the minor in m. 9 at the protagonist's revealing "ach," which first hinted at the emotional chasm separating past from present. Even the temporary harmonic shift in C_1 into the region of the Neapolitan A-flat major – according to Youens, "one of Schubert's favored ways of darkening and intensifying the descent to

Example 5.5b Schubert, "Im Frühling," D. 882, mm. 33–36

tonic minor" – derives meaning from comparison with the corresponding shift in A_1 into the bright springtime region of the supertonic A major.[30]

The music of C_2 has if anything a more strongly retrospective character. G minor gives way to the original key of G major as the emotional turbulence begins to subside. As in A_2 and B_2, the vocal line enters a measure late with a continuation of the piano melody; C_2 thus recalls those earlier sections. It also recalls the sunny, if delusional, section B_1 through the running 16th notes of the piano's right hand part and the bouncing chords of the left hand. Moreover, the accompaniment features the syncopated rhythms heard in the stormy music of C_1 (and, before that, quietly sounding in the inner parts of section A). Schubert's music invites the listener to hear each variation in light of what has come before – a strategy appropriate for any variation form, but of particular significance to the musical setting of a text so gripped by the relation of past and present.

As noted, the setting of the last stanza moves into the realm of the musical subjunctive; over the course of the song, the protagonist's thoughts have shifted from "what was" to "what is" to "what could be." Measures 48–49, a seemingly purified version of B_1 and, by extension, the entire song (the syncopated rhythms and minor mode have disappeared), are especially imbued with this subjunctive quality (Example 5.5c). Here the protagonist seems to mimic the song of the birds, the song he says he *wishes* he could

Example 5.5c Schubert, "Im Frühling," D. 882, mm. 48–50

sing. But this imagined, embedded song sounds as a faint echo of the song as a whole. We know that the protagonist has been singing about his love from the start. In the closing measures of the song, the protagonist himself seems to become aware of this, a recognition that lends a special sweetness to the concluding music. The song's gentle ending suggests that he experiences the consolation of art. Through its retrospective nature and extraordinary musical lyricism, "Im Frühling" enables memories of the blissful past to calm the emotional turbulence of the present.

"Vor meiner Wiege," D. 927, composed in 1827–28, conveys Romantic subjectivity through an embedded lullaby whose lyrics are long forgotten and whose music seems more illusory than real.[31] The poetic text, written by Leitner in 1823, presents the ruminations of a speaker haunted by a divided sense of self. Standing before the cradle in which he once lay as a helpless infant, the speaker remembers the soothing lullabies his mother used to sing. Memories of the songs that comforted him as a child provide temporary respite from the pain and bitterness of his current existence. But soon his thoughts turn to his eventual demise, reawakening fear of helpless abandonment:

O Mutter, lieb' Mutter, bleib' lange noch hier!	O mother, dear mother, stay here a long time yet!
Wer sänge dann tröstlich von Engeln mir?	Who else would sing to me comforting songs of angels?
Wer küsste mir liebend die Augen zu	Who else would close my eyes lovingly with a kiss
Zur langen, zur letzten und tiefesten Ruh'?	For the long, last and deepest rest?

Terrified by the prospect of facing death alone with no loving maternal presence to calm his fears and lay him to eternal rest, he yearns to recapture the past, to re-hear his mother's mesmerizing music.

Schubert conveys the vocal protagonist's sense of alienation from the comforts of his infancy through contrasts between music of the past and of the present in a ternary (A B A') structure. Stanzas 1–2 (A), which expose the protagonist's current emotional state, are set in the somber key of B minor with music recalling the doleful "Wanderer" theme (Example 3.6a). The vocal line's frequent repetitions of the dominant pitch F♯ produce a monotonous effect suggesting hardness, coldness, and weariness. Transfixed by the sight of his old cradle, the protagonist remembers the miserable, isolated, and helpless condition in which he once lay within its narrow confines. Occasional forays into the relative major provide the only suggestions of emotional warmth. (In mm. 6–8, his mood seems to brighten momentarily as he first thinks of his infancy. In mm. 17–19, the move to D major suggests the flicker of sympathy he feels for the helpless baby he once was.) The protagonist's bitterly worded description in stanzas 1–2 says as much about his present state of mind as about his former self, for he remains miserable, isolated, and helpless.

At the start of stanza 3, as the protagonist remembers his mother's enchanting lullabies, a sharply contrasting section (B) in B major begins (Example 3.6b). The vocal melody, formerly broken into short, halting phrases, stretches into a long lyrical line. The piano accompaniment is likewise transformed by the introduction of continuous triplet rhythms in the inner parts. This music is clearly intended to evoke the soothing strains of a lullaby. Interestingly, the words of the embedded lullaby music are not those of his mother's songs but rather a continuation of his self-reflective narrative:

Dann lachte ich saugend zu ihr empor,	Then I laughed up at her as I suckled,
Sie sang mir von Rosen und Engeln vor,	And she sang to me of roses and angels;
Sie sang und sie wiegte mich singend in Ruh,	She sang and with her singing lulled me to sleep,
Und küsste mir liebend die Augen zu.	And with a kiss lovingly closed my eyes.
Sie spannte aus Seide, gar dämmerig grün,	She spread a cool tent of dusky green silk
Ein kühliges Zelt hoch über mich hin.	Above me.
Wo find ich nur wieder solch friedlich Gemach?	Where shall I find such a peaceful chamber again?
Vielleicht, wenn das grüne Gras mein Dach!	Perhaps when the green grass is my roof!

Schubert takes his cue from the protagonist's several-fold reference to his mother's singing, not, as with "Szene aus Faust" and "Lied des Orpheus," the quotation of embedded song lyrics. ("Vor meiner Wiege" also differs from "Der Sänger," which similarly lacks such lyrics. The embedded "song"

Example 5.6 Schubert, "Vor meiner Wiege," D. 927, mm. 55–70

in "Vor meiner Wiege" is not purely instrumental, like that of "Der Sänger," but rather sung to words other than the original lullaby lyrics.) The musical aspect of the embedded song makes itself immediately felt, while the verbal aspect hovers in the imagination.

Whereas the beginning of the B major Wiegenlied in m. 27 is clearly delineated (its comforting sound anticipated by the modulation into F♯ major at the end of stanza 2), the ending is not. In the last two lines of stanza 4, as the protagonist's memory of maternal love yields to feelings of fearful isolation, the lullaby music gradually dissipates (Example 5.6). The vocal melody loses its long-spun, flowing character by breaking into fragments (mm. 51–64). The piano accompaniment becomes ever thinner in texture, the triplet rhythms disappearing bit by bit until the music loses all momentum. Lyricism gives way to declamatory recitative as the protagonist envisions his own death: "Where shall I find such a peaceful chamber again? / Perhaps when the green grass is my roof!" The return of the B minor opening music (A') for the final stanza helps to signal the emotional and temporal shift from blissful past into troubled present.

Several changes Schubert makes to the opening music as re-heard in the fifth stanza shed light on his interpretation of Leitner's poem. As before, the first three vocal phrases hover around the dominant pitch F♯, producing a monotonous effect. The last vocal phrase ("For the long, last and deepest rest?"), however, traces a broad melodic arch and concludes on B, first supported by a cadential progression in the tonic minor (mm. 72–73), and then repeated in the tonic major (mm. 74–76). By having the vocal line ultimately come to rest on the first scale degree, rather than the fifth, Schubert seems to indicate that the protagonist's long, last sleep will indeed by restful. The shift into the parallel major at the repeat of his last phrase recalls the tonality of the embedded lullaby, and suggests a degree of hopefulness that his yearning to be re-enveloped by the warmth and security of maternal love at life's end may be rewarded. The two-measure piano postlude, a mixed-mode plagal cadence with an accented minor subdominant chord resolving to a pianissimo major tonic chord, encapsulates both the terrors and the peacefulness of death. The final resolution to B major, the key of the lullaby, insinuates a positive outcome, with the divided self re-united in eternal comfort. Whereas Leitner's poem ends unresolved with the protagonist's question, Schubert's setting introduces an element of hope.

The ternary structure of "Vor meiner Wiege," with embedded lullaby music flanked by two quasi-declamatory sections, raises an intriguing question: does the vocal protagonist realize he is singing? Does he hear in the two A sections, and especially in the more lyrical B section, the music through which he expresses himself – either his own vocal line or the piano accompaniment? Or does the B section music signal "lullaby" only to Schubert's audience?

Because the B section comprises lullaby music without lullaby lyrics, it makes sense to think of these lyrical sounds as distant musical memories, not an actual lullaby that the protagonist consciously sings. Perhaps without fully realizing it, he expresses his thoughts through music reminiscent of the songs that his mother used to sing (remembering the music but not the words). We cannot really know whether he hears himself singing, and whether he realizes that, like a mother singing to her child, he has momentarily comforted himself in doing so. In the quasi-declamatory A sections, it seems likely (that is, at least until the last vocal phrase in each) that the protagonist is mostly unaware of singing. Indeed, it is the presumed absence of song – those comforting lullabies from the past – that symbolizes the intensity of his present despair. And yet, as Schubert's audience knows, the protagonist is singing throughout. To what extent does this fact shed light on his predicament?

While a definitive answer may elude us, it seems significant that "Vor meiner Wiege" displays a symmetrical "song form," rather than, say, a through-composed structure. Balancing two quasi-declamatory sections on either side of a contrasting middle section creates a song-like effect that supports the notion that, at least subconsciously, the protagonist perceives the music. "Vor meiner Wiege," if not an actual lullaby, nevertheless has a soothing effect, offering the protagonist (and the listener) a certain release from worldly cares.

Observations

The preceding analyses shed light on the changing nature of musical embedding in Schubert's Lieder. Let us begin with some observations about Schubert's early works. First, as noted, in Lieder of the 1810s, embedded songs take different forms (purely instrumental or vocal passages) and serve a variety of functions (conveying dramatic immediacy, establishing a particular *mise en scène*, lending depth to an unfolding drama, offering ironic commentary on the action, and expressing the power of music, among others). In addition, embedded songs in Schubert's early Lieder generally belong to familiar vocal genres of folk and sacred musical traditions: minstrel song, requiem, lament, hymn, lullaby, serenade, and so forth. Schubert transforms these genres by implanting them within a larger musical context, as occurs with embedded numbers in opera – which indeed likely served as the principal model for these frequently operatic-sounding works. An embedded song may itself be identifiable as a lullaby, while the overall work is best described as a dramatic scene, ballad, or simply Lied. Within the frame of the larger work, the embedded lullaby is one step removed from its original function of lulling a child to sleep. The artistic representation of that function contributes to the stylization that governs the work.

Finally, the texts of these early songs do not convey the subjective stance of their speakers – the explicit or implicit narrators who ostensibly quote the embedded songs. We get little sense of who these speakers are or what they feel about the subjects they relate. No narrative commentary, exclamations, reflections, or asides project an individualized, subjective voice. The narrator might "speak" in the 3rd person, as in "Der Sänger," or submerge his or her voice, as in "Szene aus Faust." Either way, the text presents a straightforward rendering of events, with our attention drawn to the poetic content rather than to the speaker who presents it.

These several observations are less applicable to Schubert's embedded songs from the 1820s. The Biedermeier poetry that captivated Schubert in his final decade typically features a heightened degree of subjectivity. Seized by self-consciousness, the speaker dwells on his relation to the content of his verse; his views and emotions, his sense of self, color the mode of presentation. Often, loss and estrangement arise from the speaker's evocation of another world, more natural or simple than his own, through the reference to some distant song. Usually the embedded material evokes no particular vocal genre, like lullaby or lament, but just "song" in general. Music of memory and imagination resounds like an echo in the mind of the speaker, evoking an idyllic world, far-removed from the tortured present.

As "Pause," "Im Frühling," and "Vor meiner Wiege" illustrate, the embedded song-like material might not constitute an actual song that the protagonist is fully conscious of singing. Indeed, the song-like material, often signaled by the shift from a declamatory to a lyrical style, might best be described as a trace of songs the protagonist remembers having heard or sung, or an imagined realization of songs he wishes he could sing. The embedded "song" assumes a shadowy existence. Of related significance, the words of the embedded material might not constitute ostensible song lyrics (like stanzas 3–6 of "Lied des Orpheus"). There might be no obvious disjunction between the verses of the embedded and framing songs. Instead, it might be the protagonist's mere reference to song that prompts the musical lyricism.

Curiously, the protagonist might associate "song" with comforting *or* painful emotions; hence, using song as a means of self-expression may or may not seem desirable, and the protagonist may or may not wish to be singing. Consequently, he is supremely interested in his own relationship to the distant songs of memory and imagination conjured by the embedded music and to what they represent. His self-consciousness inheres in this relationship. As with Schubert's earlier songs-within-songs, the relation between the embedded and the framing songs is crucial to an understanding of the work. In the later works, however, the protagonist himself reflects on this relation; it is not left implicit as in earlier Lieder.

While the protagonist dwells self-consciously on his relationship to those distant songs, he may not be aware of expressing himself through music. During the song-like passages, he might seem partially conscious of doing so, but during framing sections he seems oblivious to the musicality (in both voice and piano) of his expression. He could actually insist that he is *not* singing. To further complicate matters, the beginning and/or ending of the embedded song-like material may not be clearly delineated; instead, it may transition gradually into the musical frame. The lack of a clear boundary between the embedded and framing songs suggests that the protagonist experiences varying degrees of self-awareness. All of these factors impart nebulousness to the embedded songs of Schubert's later years.

Lied protagonists: competing conceptions

These observations lead us to reconsider the expressive world inhabited by Lied protagonists. In his influential study *The Composer's Voice* (1974), Cone argues that the vocal persona of a Lied "adopts the original simulation of the poetic persona and adds another of his own: he 'composes,' not the words alone, but the vocal line as well."[32] Nevertheless, Cone asserts, most Lied personae should not be thought of as "singing." While the actual singer sings, the vocal persona is usually "speaking" his thoughts. The persona is generally unaware of both singing and being accompanied; he hears neither his own vocal melody nor the piano's music. He chooses his words consciously, but the musical components of his expression – both vocal and instrumental – belong to his subconscious.

Nearly two decades later, Cone revised his views. In "Poet's Love or Composer's Love" (1992), a study which attempts to apply insights about opera to Lieder, Cone asserts that there is little distinction between times when the vocal persona is supposedly singing, and times when he is not.[33] Many songs, Cone notes, involve characters who knowingly adopt song as a means of expression. Such works include stylized ballads (which simulate traditional forms of public performance), persuasive or rhetorical songs (such as hymns, serenades, or lullabies), and "pure natural songs expressing simple emotions" (e.g., singing for joy or for sorrow).[34] These are not merely the thoughts of the persona, but songs written or improvised by him. Cone states that it is "more the rule than the exception" that Lied personae know they are singing, that they are conscious of words and music (both vocal melody and piano accompaniment). This is obviously the case in works like Schubert's "Ständchen" but is also true of more subtle examples like the songs in *Die schöne Müllerin*.[35] The protagonist of a Lied, simply put, is "a composer."[36]

Neither Cone's initial nor revised conceptions of vocal personae capture the rich complexity of expressive discourse in Schubert's Lieder. We can better understand this complexity by introducing a historical dimension to

[musical notation]

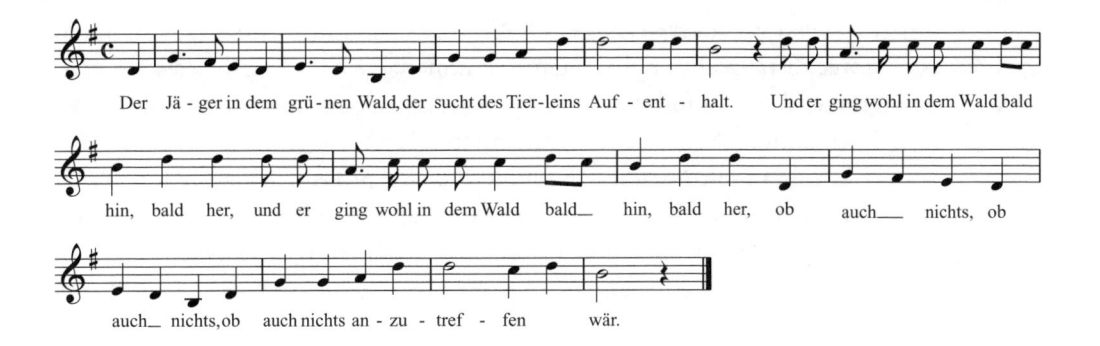

Der Jä-ger in dem grü-nen Wald, der sucht des Tier-leins Auf-ent-halt. Und er ging wohl in dem Wald bald hin, bald her, und er ging wohl in dem Wald bald hin, bald her, ob auch nichts, ob auch nichts, ob auch nichts an-zu-tref-fen wär.

Mein Hündlein hab ich stets bei mir,
in diesem grünen Waldrevier:
Und mein Hündelein, das jagt,
und mein Herz, das lacht,
meine Augen leuchten hell und klar.

Ich sing mein Lied aus voller Brust,
der Hirsch tut einen Satz vor Lust:
Und der Fink, der pfeift
und der Kuckuck schreit,
und die Hasen, kratzen sich am Bart.

Und als ich in den Wald rein kam,
traf ich ein schönes Mägdlein an:
Ei, wie kommst du in den Wald hinein,
du strahlenäugig Mägdelein,
ei, wie kommst du in den Wald hinein?

Du sollst nicht länger bleiben hier
in diesem grünen Waldrevier:
Bleibe du bei mir als Jägerin,
du strahlenäugig Mägdelein,
bleib du bei mir als meine Braut!

Example 5.7 "Der Jäger in dem grünen Wald" (traditional)

the discussion, conjoining ideas about the relation of folk song and art song, Schubert's changing poetic preferences, and musical embedding.

The personae of many German folk songs loosely fit Schiller's definition of the naïve; they seem to exist in a world where singing is as natural as breathing, and convey their thoughts, feelings, desires, and stories with little or no self-reflection.[37] (In this context, "persona" refers to the archetypal self – perhaps a huntsman, mother, or lover – that emerges through the words, music, and function of a communal folk song passed down orally through the generations. It might also signify a collective self, e.g., a group of students, soldiers, or children, who sing together in unison.) In "Der Jäger in dem grünen Wald," a traditional folk song whose textual and musical variants were sung throughout Germany during the eighteenth and nineteenth centuries, emotional expression derives from the subject material – the activity of hunting – not the persona's self-conscious ruminations about that material (Example 5.7).[38] The joy of hunting (whether for animals or maidens) is conveyed through both words and music; there is no sense of ironic distance, but rather a natural immediacy. The song displays the general tendency of folk songs "to let things speak for themselves without the intervention of the poet as commentator."[39]

While unselfconscious, the hunter-singer projects an awareness of the musical medium through which he expresses himself; his song seems central to his identity. In some folk songs, as in this variant of "Der Jäger in dem grünen Wald," the persona makes reference to his or her singing ("I sing my song at full voice"), while in others an awareness of singing is implicit. Either way, the music typically serves some clear function. The persona uses song spontaneously – not deliberately or skeptically – to lull a child to sleep, woo a lover, celebrate the arrival of spring, tell a story, or lament the dead. In "Der Jäger in dem grünen Wald," to hunt is to feel joy, and to feel joy is to sing.

The notion of folk song's deep-rooted connection to human nature originated with Herder. In his influential essays *Treatise on the Origin of Language* (1772: *Abhandlung über den Ursprung der Sprache*) and *Excerpt from an Exchange of Letters on Ossian and the Songs of Ancient Folk* (1773; *Auszug aus einem Briefwechsel über Ossian und die Lieder alter Völker*), Herder claims that the ancient folk poetry of all cultures has a close affinity with music.[40] In his view, both poetry and music are associated, as German and Comparative Literature scholar Jane K. Brown writes, with "the pre-rational aspects of the soul. This is both the oldest part of our mental being and the part that in each of us comes before reflective mental activity. Music and song do not simply express emotion ... [T]hey are the voice of the spontaneous self underlying all linguistic expression.[41] Folk song personae never seem at odds with their own singing; the spontaneity with which they adopt music as a means of expression confirms their fundamental unity with the world they inhabit.

As interest in folk traditions surged in the later eighteenth century (with strong impetus from Herder's passionate investigations), many Lied composers sought to emulate the qualities of folk song. The songs in Schulz's collection *Lieder im Volkston*, evincing the "appearance of the familiar," could be sung with or without accompaniment, in the drawing room or in the fields. Simple strophic settings written on two staves (vocal line, bass line, and sometimes an inner part moving in parallel thirds or sixths with either of these), the songs project a sense of musical awareness resembling that of folk songs. Because the right hand of the piano part doubles the vocal line, it is difficult to imagine the vocal persona as incognizant of the accompaniment. As eighteenth-century paintings, sentimental novels, and other sources indicate, most songs of the period were performed by one person; singer and accompanist were the same.[42] Under these conditions, it would indeed be nearly impossible to envision the vocal persona as oblivious to the music. (Only when accompaniments grew more substantial and complex – beginning around the turn of the nineteenth century – did it become common for Lieder to be performed by both a singer and an accompanist, a change reflected in the increasing use of three staves. Paradoxically, as composers devoted greater attention to the accompaniment, Lied personae seemed to become increasingly unaware of it, as well as of their own singing.)

The impression of Lied personae's musical awareness in folk-like songs was fostered by a pair of related beliefs with wide currency in the late eighteenth century: the music of a Lied should essentially "clothe" the poem, and poetry needs music to bring it to life.[43] Words and music, it was thought, should never work at cross-purposes. The close relationships between many eighteenth-century poets and the composers who set their poems (e.g., Voß and Schulz, Zumsteeg and Matthisson, Goethe and both Reichardt and Zelter) parallel – and helped bring about – the intimate connection between words and music in *volkstümliche* Lieder.

A few of Schubert's Lieder, such as "Wiegenlied," D. 498, and "Am Brunnen vor dem Tore" (the first vocal strophe of D. 911, no. 5) passed into the oral tradition, achieving the status of authentic folk song. Many more, like "Heidenröslein," D. 257, simulate folk song but in a subtly stylized manner. The vocal protagonists engage in impersonation uncharacteristic of genuine *Volkslieder*. As Kramer has discussed, the protagonist of "Heidenröslein" assumes the role of a storyteller who relates a lighthearted tale of deflowering.[44] We recognize a degree of contrivance behind the song's folk-like charm stemming from both the artistry of Goethe's poem and certain elements of Schubert's musical setting (e.g., the vocal line's high G's, lying at the upper limit of the average female's comfortable range). That is, we sense a consciousness outside the boundaries of the simulated song – someone who enacts the telling of a tale, perhaps as an expression of nostalgia for "the simple life, a life free of modern perplexities," or a "pretense of innocence."[45] Kramer writes, "When we hear the high note, we can hear the demands of art music imposing themselves in the carefree realm of folk music. Thanks to the high note, the folk tone becomes self-conscious."[46] Tellingly, for all its folk-like traits, Schubert's "Heidenröslein" has not entered the repertory of folk song, unlike the less artful settings of Reichardt (1793) and Heinrich Werner (1827) (Examples 5.8a and 5.8b). Schubert's version is not learned by German school children; its

Example 5.8a Reichardt, "Heidenröslein"

Example 5.8b Werner, "Heidenröslein"

accompaniment, while simple, is not negligible. There is a "knowingness" about the song that tells us this is not a spontaneously created and delivered story but a carefully crafted and performed one.[47]

In the mid-1810s, after a period of dramatic ballad composition, Schubert became attracted to *volkstümliche* Lieder like "Heidenröslein." Between 1814 and 1816, he wrote around a hundred strophic songs, many evoking the *Volkston*. Most of them employ poetic texts from the 1770s and 80s in which the vocal protagonist's subjectivity is evident but not excessive; a delicate balance prevails in the relation between the self and the outer world. These include many settings of Klopstock, Matthisson, Hölty, Kosegarten, Johann Gaudenz von Salis-Seewis, and Claudius, as well as some of Schiller and Goethe. Unadorned melodies, natural vocal rhythms, diatonic harmonies, negligible accompaniments, and strophic repetitions evoke the simplicity of folk song. Texts in which the protagonist's subjective perspective plays a more prominent role tend to receive more artful settings. Although simple in comparison to many of Schubert's later songs, they could not be mistaken for actual folk songs. An excellent example is "Nähe des Geliebten," D. 162, a Goethe setting from 1815 which, as Frisch has discussed, exemplifies Schubert's transformation of the *Volkston*.[48]

While many of Schubert's settings from the mid-1810s strike a balance between naturalness and artfulness, settings from the 1820s tilt toward the latter. Estrangement from the natural world corresponds with estrangement from music. If the protagonists show any awareness of their own song, they also recognize that they have little control over it. In "Pause," the miller comes to suspect that he is singing and to understand that he commands neither his means of self-expression nor his destiny. The protagonist of "An die Leyer," D. 737, wants to sing songs of war, but his lyre continually plays songs of love. In "Sehnsucht," D. 879, the protagonist laments that his songs don't work, then eventually "discovers" a song and feels he can sing again. The protagonist of "Im Walde," D. 834, would like to sing with the birds but must keep silent. One of the best examples is "Einsamkeit," D. 911, no. 12. Trudging through the woods, alternately despondent and enraged, the protagonist is so alienated from the natural world that he shows no awareness of using song – a natural means of expression – to convey his thoughts and emotions.

For the Biedermeier protagonist, evoking a more natural kind of music within the frame of his own unacknowledged song may be the closest union he can achieve with the natural world. Incapable of the intimate and unselfconscious relationship to music experienced by folk song personae, he can sing with apparent naturalness only through an act of impersonation – by quoting the songs of others, remembering songs he himself once sang, or imagining songs he wishes he could sing.

The preceding discussion suggests a way of reconciling Cone's competing conceptions of Lied personae – his initial view that most Lied personae are not conscious of either singing or being accompanied and his revised view that most Lied personae are singing-poets who consciously compose (or improvise) both words and music. Broadly speaking, Cone's *second* conception applies well to many of Schubert's settings from the 1810s (as well as some later settings), whose eighteenth-century texts convey less intense subjectivity and in numerous cases represent overt attempts to emulate or evoke the *Volkston*. Although their artistic complexity transcends the *Volkston* to varying degrees, many of these earlier settings show close enough ties to folk song that traditional genre designations (serenade, lullaby, etc.) still seem appropriate.

Cone's *first* conception, on the other hand, aptly describes many of Schubert's Biedermeier settings, whose texts convey protagonists' anguished self-consciousness. These songs, often best identified simply as "Lieder" or "Gesänge" rather than serenades, lullabies, etc., seem only distantly related to folk song, sometimes evoking it through musical embedding.

Although they may not realize it, the protagonists do express themselves through song; they have not lapsed into actual speaking, as in melodrama. Nevertheless, as Lied protagonists became increasingly conscious of their alienation from the natural world, they showed less awareness of their own musicality. This observation pertains to works with or without embedded songs.

All of Schubert's Lieder might be said to involve musical embedding. In a *volkstümliche* Lied, such as "Heidenröslein," the embedded folk-like material comprises most of the work and the frame reveals itself only minimally and subtly. In more musically complex settings, like "Nähe des Geliebten," aesthetic qualities have a more important role; the works engage familiar folk traditions even while standing apart from them. We sense that the subjective/aesthetic frame has expanded in relation to the embedded material; our attention is drawn to the consciousness that reflects upon and transforms that material. As Lied protagonists become increasingly self-conscious, the frame assumes greater prominence and the embedded song-like material correspondingly less. In works like "Pause" and "Im Frühling," the protagonists show at most minimal consciousness of singing.[49] In settings like "Einsamkeit," one might argue, the frame expands to fill the entire work, displacing musical embedding entirely. The protagonists of these Lieder show essentially no awareness of the musical medium through which they express themselves, so extreme is their alienation. But even a folk song, such as Schubert's "Wiegenlied," if performed in concert, can be understood as an embedded song, i.e., a conscious enactment of the singing of an authentic lullaby. An aesthetic frame is implied, as if the folk song as a whole were enclosed in quotation marks.[50]

Without undermining the historical argument linking protagonists' heightened musical awareness with Schubert's earlier settings and diminished awareness with his later ones, in songs from throughout his career, the richness of musical expression involves shifting degrees of consciousness. As embedded songs reveal, vocal protagonists often pass through different states, at certain times ostensibly speaking, at other times singing, quoting, reminiscing, or imagining. They can be fully aware, semi-aware, barely aware, or wholly unaware of their music making.

Cone seems to have recognized this variability from the start. In *The Composer's Voice*, after developing his conception of Lied personae over the span of two chapters, he writes, "Our model has done its work; let us dismiss it. In the last analysis, there is only one literary analogue rich enough and complex enough to come near serving as a model for accompanied song or for opera . . . It is the mixed form par excellence: the nameless genre of *Ulysses* . . . [H]ere narrative, dramatic, and esoteric techniques are combined; here conscious and subconscious persistently interpenetrate each other."[51] While Schubert's earlier Lieder tend to suggest greater musical awareness than his later ones, works from throughout his life display fluctuations that exemplify the rich expressiveness of art song.

6 | On wings of song from Reichardt to Mahler

"Mondnacht," the fifth song in Schumann's Eichendorff *Liederkreis*, Op. 39, and one of the most beloved works in the Romantic Lied repertoire, combines poetry and music to intimate paradise regained. The uniting of the two media is but one of multiple couplings in the work. On a cosmic level, the sky bends to kiss the earth ("Es war, als hätt' der Himmel / Die Erde still geküßt"), beautifully suggested by the descending treble line of the piano introduction and merging of the pitches B and C♯ from the great expanse of over four octaves (m. 1) to the intimacy of a major second (m. 6). The alternating E's and B's (identified in German as E and H) in the bass line of mm. 10–13 repeatedly spell out *Ehe* (marriage), as if to confirm the music's symbolic nature (Example 6.1). On a human level, the protagonist's soul leaves its earth-bound body, ascending to greet the heavens with wings that carry it over the quiet land as if flying home ("als flöge sie nach Haus") – an image conveyed by the voice's rising tessitura in the third stanza and eventual descent to the home pitch. In this rendering of universal serenity, every sense of division or separation is overcome.

The combination of flight imagery and subjunctive tense evoking a return to paradise echoes a similar formulation from the repertory of German folk song. The traditional *Volkslied* "Wenn ich ein Vöglein wär," which enjoyed considerable popularity throughout the nineteenth century, draws upon the same two elements, as do several other folk songs.[1] "Mondnacht," however, involves far greater artistic complexity, evident in its use of the past subjunctive tense (less common than the present subjunctive) and consequent fusion of memory and imagination. Whereas "Wenn ich ein Vöglein wär" concerns the plight of separated lovers, "Mondnacht" portrays the spiritual striving of a human soul. The art song evokes the folk song yet transcends it.

Flight imagery illuminates the relation between "Mondnacht" and "Wenn ich ein Vöglein wär" – and between art song and folk song more generally. In recalling a certain moment, the protagonist of "Mondnacht" describes feeling *as if* his soul were flying home. The creation of the song represents another sort of imaginary flight, experienced by both poet and composer. Mirroring the protagonist's airborne journey, Eichendorff and Schumann fashion words and music *as if* returning to the realm of folk song – the

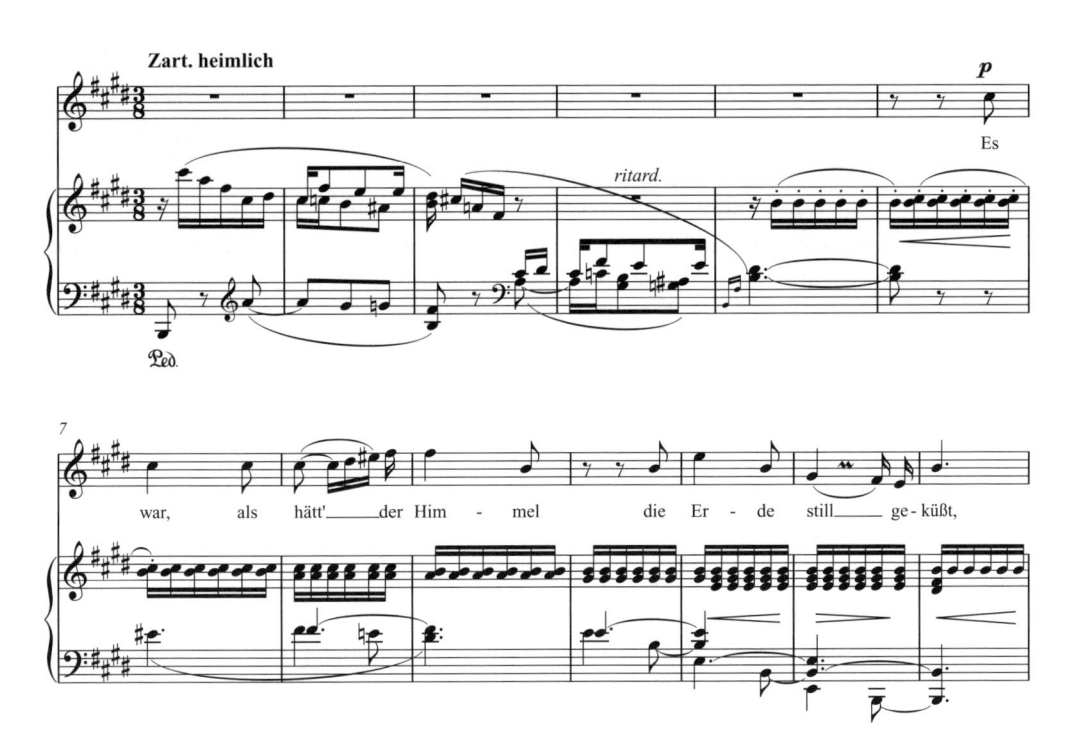

Example 6.1 Schumann, "Mondnacht," Op. 39, no. 5, mm. 1–13

Romantic art song's ostensible "home." They express themselves *as if* with the naturalness of birds, or, in the Romantics' idealized conception, the common folk. In both words and music, qualities of folk song are coupled with compositional artistry, suggesting the elusive intermediary state – somewhere between reality and illusion – of the subjunctive tense. Eichendorff combines the folk-like "wishing-to-be-a-bird" motif and simple structural traits with an unusual verb tense and classical allusion (the cosmic uniting of sky and earth evoking the mythical marriage of the primal Greek gods Ouranos and Gaia). Schumann in turn combines musical repetitions (five of the song's six vocal phrases are nearly identical) with discreet dissonances (e.g., the simultaneous sounding of E♯ and E in m. 8) and subtle alterations (the transformation of the oft heard antecedent vocal phrase into a consequent in the third stanza). "Mondnacht" might thus be viewed as an aesthetic marriage of *Volk* and *Kunst*; it evokes a simple, natural mode of musico-poetic expression without forsaking artistic complexity. In aspiring toward – but not copying – folk song, Schumann's Lied conveys a higher level unity, and far greater profundity, than "Wenn ich ein Vöglein wär" and other *Volkslieder*.

The "wishing-to-be-a-bird" motif (henceforth *Voglmotif*) captivated German Romantics, as indicated by the many allusions to "Wenn ich ein Vöglein wär" in early ninetenth-century literary and musical works.[2] Its appeal lay to a great extent in its easy adaptation as a means to express Romantic yearning for transcendence, or "freedom from earthbound restraint."[3] The speaker of "Wenn ich ein Vöglein wär" pines to be a bird so that he may fly to his distant beloved. In Romantic works, however, flight imagery often engages multiple meanings, from the physical to the metaphysical.

This chapter examines the *Voglmotif* in Romantic Lieder as a way of illuminating the powerful attraction of folk song, a "lost paradise" to many nineteenth-century observers. After reviewing the absorption of "Wenn ich ein Vöglein wär" into late eighteenth- and nineteenth-century German culture, we will turn to the *Voglmotif* in art song, paying attention to its varied expression in both words and music. Discussion will center on works in which the vocal protagonist explicitly yearns to be a bird (in some cases involving direct verbal or musical quotations from the folk song). Some of these works express longing for transcendence but offer no resolution. Others, like "Mondnacht," intimate the protagonist's eventual success or failure – the former most common in early nineteenth-century settings, the latter in subsequent works. As a pendant to this discussion, and a fitting conclusion to the book as a whole, we will consider songs that engage the *Voglmotif* on a more abstract level. In certain Lieder, humans are symbolized by birds, with human yearning sublimated. And in a special few, the image of a human or bird in flight is replaced by that of song itself. As poetry and music take to the air, escaping all restraints, we recognize the art song's miraculous ability to lead us back to paradise.

"Wenn ich ein Vöglein wär": musical settings and literary allusions

The earliest extant source of the anonymous text for "Wenn ich ein Vöglein wär" is a *Flugblatt* of 1756: *Vier Weltliche Schöne Lieder, [. . .] Jedes in seiner eigenen Melodey. Gedruckt im 1756sten Jahr*, no. 2.[4] The most familiar version of the song appeared two decades later in Herder's *Volkslieder* collection of 1778 (I, 231, no. 12) under the title "Der Flug der Liebe."[5]

Wenn ich ein Vöglein wär,	If I were a little bird,
Und auch zwei Flügein hätt',	And had two little wings,
Flög ich zu dir;	I would fly to you;
Weil es aber nicht kann seyn,	But because that cannot be,
Bleib ich allhier.	I stay right here.

Bin ich gleich weit von dir,	Although I am far from you,
Bin ich doch im Schlaf bei dir,	I am with you in sleep,
Und red' mit dir:	And speak with you;
Wenn ich erwachen tu,	But when I am jarred awake,
Bin ich allein.	I am alone.
Es vergeht keine Stund' in der Nacht,	No hour in the night passes
Da mein Herze nicht erwacht,	When my heart doesn't awake
Und an dich gedenkt,	And think of you,
Daß du mir viel tausendmal	That many thousand times you
Dein Herz geschenkt.	Gave me your heart.

Although Herder published only the words of the song, he noted, under the designation *Deutsch*, "The melody fits the contents, light and yearning." Nearly thirty years later, Arnim and Brentano included a nearly identical version of the text in the first volume of *Des knaben Wunderhorn*, now with the opening line serving as the title. Thereafter, the song, or variants thereof, appeared in nearly every nineteenth-century collection of German *Volkslieder*, evidence of its broad popularity.[6] Its appeal extended to the literary elite. Goethe, in his review of *Wunderhorn*, described "Wenn ich ein Vöglein wär" as "uniquely beautiful and true."[7] Heine also praised the song, writing "all moonlight, an abundance of moonlight, engulfing the soul, stands in the Lied" and including the text in his *Romantischen Schule*.[8]

Because neither the *Flugblatt* nor Herder's *Volkslieder* includes music, it is uncertain how "Wenn ich ein Vöglein wär" was sung during the eighteenth century (and perhaps earlier). In 1800, however, the melody that was to become most closely associated with the text was published (together with the words) by Reichardt in his Liederspiel *Lieb und Treue*. There the song is identified as a "Schweizervolkslied" and presented as a vocal duet over a simple bass line (Example 6.2).[9] Although each poetic stanza comprises five lines, the tune extends through twelve measures (divided into six two-measure phrases), with the fourth textual line repeated. The melodic range is confined to a fifth. Some nineteenth-century folk song collections, following Reichardt's model, present "Wenn ich ein Vöglein wär" as a duet, with the second voice entering in a pseudo-canon in the third measure (and again in the ninth).[10] Elsewhere, the song appears with only a single-line melody.[11]

Numerous composers wrote solo song settings (with piano accompaniment) of the "Vöglein" text, either devising new melodies, or duplicating or varying Reichardt's tune: Weber (Op. 54, no. 6; 1818), Georg Henschel (Op. 24, no. 6; 187-?), Adolph Jensen (Op. 1, no. 5; 1859), Friedrich Kücken, Heinrich Proch, and Carl Wilhelm. Duet settings were composed by Schumann (Op. 43, no. 1; 1840), Ferdinand Hiller, and Wilhelm Taubert, choral settings by Silcher, Brahms (an arrangement for unaccompanied women's

[Musical example: Langsam, 3/4. Lyrics: "Wenn ich ein Vög-lein wär', und auch zwei Flüg-lein hätt', flög ich zu dir, weil's a-ber nit kann seyn, weil's a-ber nit kann seyn, bleib' ich all hier"]

* Second voice enters

Example 6.2 Reichardt, "Schweizervolkslied" from *Lieb und Treue*

chorus of Schumann's setting)[12] and Reger (a setting entitled "Liebchens Bote" arranged for unaccompanied mixed and all-male choruses).[13] According to Max Friedländer, 15 of the nearly 60 settings of "Wenn ich ein Vöglein wär" were written for *Männerchor*.[14]

There are also settings whose words alter or echo the *Wunderhorn* text. Beethoven's "Ruf vom Berge: Wenn ich ein Vöglein wär" for solo voice and piano (WoO 147; 1816) employs a text by Friedrich von Treitschke that begins with the first stanza of the *Wunderhorn* version, and then extends the wish motive from birds to other elements, such as stars, brooks, and breezes.[15] Louis Spohr's "Lied aus Aslauga's *Ritter*" (Op. 41, no. 2; 1815), employing a text by Friedrich Heinrich Karl, Freiherr de La Motte-Fouqué, adopts a similar strategy, with the narrator knight wishing first to be a bird, then a flower. In Franz Abt's *Kinderlied* "Vöglein so klein möcht ich wohl sein" (1870?), a setting of a poem by Georg Christian Dieffenbach, the youthful protagonist initially yearns to be a little bird, then in succeeding stanzas a little fish and a little hare, before cheerfully accepting the necessity of remaining a child, "joyful and free." In the *Kinderlied* "Wenn ich ein Vöglein wär" published in the collection *Kling-Klang Gloria* of 1921, the third stanza expresses a child's wish not to be separated from its mother:

Einsam dann weine ich,	Alone then I cry,
Nenne im seufzen dich,	Sighing, I call for you,
Doch du bleibst fern.	But you remain far away.
Mutter, o Mutter mein,	Mother, oh my mother,
Bleib' nicht mehr fern.	Do not stay away any longer.

Silcher's folk-like setting "Ach, wie ist's möglich dann," with words by Wilhelmine von Chézy, alludes to the *Wunderhorn* text in its last stanza:[16]

Wär' ich ein Vögelein,	If I were a little bird,
wollt' ich bald bei dir sein,	I would want to be with you soon,
scheut' Folk und Habicht nicht,	I wouldn't fear people and hawks,
flog' schnell zu dir!	But would fly quickly to you!
Schöß' mich ein Jäger tot,	If a hunter shot me dead,
sänk' ich in deinen Schoß,	And I sank into your lap;
säh'st du mich traurig an,	And you looked sadly at me,
gern stürb' ich dann!	Then I would gladly die!

"Wenn ich ein Vöglein wär" not only inspired folk-like settings but also influenced more elevated art works, both literary and musical. Outside the folk realm, the song proved protean in character. Depending on its context and formulation, it could express nostalgia, humor, irony, or anguish. Even the briefest allusion to its well-known opening was inevitably fraught with meaning.

Literary references abound. In the "Forest and Cave" scene from Part I of Goethe's *Faust* (the scene immediately preceding that of Gretchen at her spinning wheel), Mephistopheles taunts Faust with an image of the forsaken girl, who sits alone in her room pining for her lover: "She has been waiting pitifully long; / Stands by the window, sees the clouds, so free, / Across the city ramparts flee, / Were I a little bird, thus goes her song, / Day after day, and half the night. / Now she will be serene, more often blue, / Sometimes shed tear on tear, / Then be in fair good cheer, / And always loving you."[17] The folk song reference emphasizes Gretchen's simple nature, underscores the anguish she feels in being separated from her lover, and hints that there will be no happy reunion.

Heine employs the same folk song reference in his poetic parody "Ich steh auf des Berges Spitze" (1822–24), but to very different effect.[18] As the *Voglmotif* develops over four stanzas, the narrator's initially light self-mockery leads to a biting conclusion which casts aspersion on the loved one as much as the narrator himself.

Ich steh auf des Berges Spitze,	I stand on the mountain peak,
Und werde sentimental.	And become sentimental.
'Wenn ich ein Vöglein wäre!'	"If I were a little bird!"
Seufz ich viel tausendmal.	I sigh many thousand times.
Wenn ich eine Schwalbe wäre,	If I were a swallow,
So flög ich zu dir, mein Kind,	I would fly to you, my child,
Und baute mir mein Nestchen	And build myself a little nest
Wo deine Fenster sind.	Where your windows are.

Wenn ich eine Nachtigall wäre,	If I were a nightingale,
So flög ich zu dir, mein Kind,	I would fly to you, my child,
Und sänge dir nachts meine Lieder	And nightly I would sing you my songs
Herab von der grünen Lind.	Down from the green linden tree.
Wenn ich ein Gimpel wäre,	If I were a loon,
So flög ich gleich an dein Herz;	I would fly right to your heart;
Du bist ja hold den Gimpeln,	For you are dear to the loony,
Und heilest Gimpelschmerz.	And heal their loony pain.

In the narrative poem "Der weiße Elefant" (from *Romanzero*, 1851), Heine again alludes to the folk song, but with humor predominating. A lovesick Indian elephant, pining for a lovely Parisian countess, utters what by the mid nineteenth century had become a hackneyed phrase.

Sehnsucht verzehrt ihn seit jener Stund,	Yearning consumes ever since that hour,
Und er, der vormals so froh und gesund,	And he, who had been so cheerful and healthy,
Er ist ein vierfüßiger Werther geworden,	Has become a four-footed Werther,
Und träumt von einer Lotte im Norden.	And dreams of a Lotte in the north.
Geheimnisvolle Sympathie!	Mysterious sympathy!
Er sah sie nie und denkt an sie.	He never saw her yet thinks of her.
Er trampelt oft im Mondschein umher	He often tramples around in the moonlight
Und seufzet: wenn ich ein Vöglein wär!	And sighs, "if I were a little bird!"

Quotations from "Wenn ich ein Vöglein wär" also appear in several works by Eichendorff. In the novella *Aus dem Leben eines Taugenichts* (1826), as the "good-for-nothing" narrator finally arrives in Rome (chapter 7) with no idea where to turn, he starts to sing a suggestive variation of the familiar folk song before an on-looker interrupts.

Wenn ich ein Vöglein wär',	If I were a little bird,
Ich wüßt wohl, wovon ich sänge,	I would know just what I was singing about,
Und auch zwei Flügeln hätt',	And if I had two little wings,
Ich wüßt' wohl, wohin ich mich schwänge!	I would know just where to wing to!

The passage is but one of many allusions in the work to the narrator's bird-like nature.[19] Another varied quotation appears in Eichendorff's historical drama *Ezelin von Romano* (1828). In Act V, scene ii, Mercutio begins to sing a spiritual song but then unintentionally slips into the opening lines of the folk song:

Wenn mich der Engel Heer	If the angelic host
Führt auf der Tugend Bahn –	Led me on the path of virtue –
Wenn ich ein Vög'lein wär',	If I were a little bird,
Und auch zwei Flügel hätt' –	And had two wings –

Composers too were drawn to the folk song. As noted, Reichardt included both words and music in his *Liederspiel Liebe und Treue* (1800); prompted by the sound of hunting horns playing the tune, members of a loving family circle sing the song for entertainment. A half century later, the song again appeared in a musical drama – Schumann's opera *Genoveva*, Op. 81 (1850) – but with far greater symbolic significance. In Act II, Genoveva and Golo begin to sing the familiar folk song as a duet (Schumann uses his duet setting of the text from 1840). For each character, the song assumes a different meaning. Genoveva, who has been left under Golo's care while her husband Siegfried is off at war, sings with loving thoughts of her distant spouse; the words of the song (which she has suggested they sing to block out noise from the carousing servants) give voice to her own sentiments. Golo, who secretly loves Genoveva, perceives the song's message of separation as pertaining to his own predicament. Before completing the third verse, he loses control and breaks into a passionate recitative. The folk song duet dissolves as Golo confesses his feelings.

Like numerous well-known operatic melodies, the traditional tune of "Wenn ich ein Vöglein wär" also served as thematic material for a variety of purely instrumental works, such as etudes for piano (Henselt), violin (Oser), and harp (Oberthür). Indeed, the song echoes throughout nineteenth-century art culture, revealing the powerful attraction of folk song in general, and this one in particular. "Wenn ich ein Vöglein wär" exerted perhaps its greatest influence in the realm of *Kunstlieder*. As one of the most popular songs in the cherished repertory of German *Volkslieder*, it quickly came to assume the character of a lost idyllic world, an object of yearning that acted like a polestar in guiding Lied poets and composers in their creative efforts. The *Voglmotif* found a new home in both the words and music of art song.

The Voglmotif in art song: the quest for transcendence

Just as various folk-like song settings evoke "Wenn ich ein Vöglein wär," so do works whose textual and musical traits, as well as performance and publishing history, confer upon them the status of art song. An example is Schubert's "Der Knabe," D. 692, composed in 1820 with a poetic text drawn from Friedrich Schlegel's *Abendröthe* cycle (Part I).[20] The opening line quotes the beginning of the folk song almost exactly. As in *Kinderlieder*, the poetic speaker is a child – the boy of the title.

Der Knabe	The Boy
Wenn ich nur ein Vöglein wäre,	If only I were a bird,

Ach wie wollt', ich lustig fliegen,	Ah, how joyfully I would fly,
Alle Vögel weit besiegen.	Far outstripping all other birds.
Wenn ich so ein Vogel bin,	If I were a bird
Darf ich alles haschen	I could get everything
Und die höchsten Kirschen naschen;	And nibble the highest cherries.
Fliege dann zur Mutter hin.	Then I'd fly back to mother.
Ist sie bös in ihrem Sinn,	If she were angry
Kann ich lieb mich an sie schmiegen,	I could nestle sweetly up to her
Ihren Ernst gar bald besiegen.	And soon overcome her sternness.
Bunte Federn, leichte Flügel,	Coloured feathers, light wings,
Dürft' ich in der Sonne schwingen,	I could flap them in the sunlight,
Daß die Lüfte laut erklingen,	So that the air resounded loudly,
Weiß nichts mehr von Band und Zügel.	I would no longer be curbed and shackled.
Wär' ich über jene Hügel,	If I were beyond those hills,
Ach dann wollt', ich lustig fliegen,	Ah, how joyfully I would fly,
Alle Vögel weit besiegen.	Far outstripping all other birds.

Example 6.3   Schubert, "Der Knabe," D. 692, mm. 6–9

From the speaker's perspective, flight signifies freedom – from deprivation, loneliness, sadness, and every kind of physical and auditory restraint. Soaring with the birds would enable him to escape the miseries of a schoolboy's confinement.

Reed has written that Schubert's setting is a "delightful essay in the vernacular manner."[21] The music certainly exhibits folk-like qualities, such as diatonic harmonies (the first 33 measures contain only tonic and dominant), simple rhythms, horn calls, and exact phrase repetitions (Example 6.3). Yet "Der Knabe" also includes more artful musical elements that, together with Schlegel's poetic ventriloquism, distinguish it from geniune folk song: a piano introduction, interludes, and postlude, multiple accompaniment patterns, affective mode switches (mm. 34–37), key changes, and rhythmic augmentation (cf. mm. 1–19 and mm. 64–91). The return of the opening music in extended note values for the last three lines of text serves several purposes. It creates an aesthetically pleasing, rounded musical structure while also suggesting that the boy's yearning for freedom remains a fantasy. But his outlook at the end of the song is not the same as at the beginning. As the song nears its conclusion, exuberance yields to wistfulness; the restatement of the opening music in augmented rhythms betrays recognition of a chasm separating fantasy from reality. "Der Knabe" is an art song masquerading as a folk song; it expresses Romantic sentiments in a lighthearted vein through the voice and vocabulary of youth. The artful qualities of the song (both text and music) suggest that the school boy's wishes are a cover for adult yearning.

A more intricate example is "Die Stille," the fourth song from Schumann's Eichendorff *Liederkreis*, Op. 39.[22] In this work, the last stanza, rather than the first, recalls "Wenn ich ein Vöglein wär."

Die Stille	*Silence*
Es weiß und rät es doch keiner,	Not a soul knows or guesses
Wie mir so wohl ist, so wohl!	how happy, happy I am!
Ach, wüßt es nur einer, nur einer,	Oh, if only *one* were to know it,
Kein Mensch es sonst wissen soll.	then no other should.
So still ist's nicht draußen im Schnee,	The snow outside's not so silent,
So stumm und verschwiegen sind	nor so mute and silent
Die Sterne nicht in der Höh,	the stars on high,
Als meine Gedanken sind.	as are my thoughts.
Ich wünscht, ich wär ein Vöglein	Would I were a bird
Und zöge über das Meer,	and might fly over the sea,
Wohl über das Meer und weiter,	over the sea and on,
Bis daß ich im Himmel wär!	Until I were in heaven!

As in "Der Knabe," bird flight symbolizes freedom, but here involving the expression of emotion. Flying serves as a metaphor for the revelation of concealed feelings, the utterance of the ineffable.[23] The poetic speaker wishes to be able to disclose her secret joy, to share it with "just one," but remains even more silent than the frozen landscape of winter, reflected in the icy articulation of the accompaniment (Example 6.4a). While commentators have often assumed that her repressed ecstasy results from being in love, only the first poetic stanza makes any reference (and a veiled one at that) to the existence of a beloved. Schumann further obscures the issue by omitting the poem's third stanza, which depicts two larks flying together up into the sky (an image suggesting not only a love relationship but also the achievement of transcendence). Although in its original narrative context the poem concerned a hidden love between two characters,[24] and Eichendorff later included it in the "Spring and Love" section of his collected verse, in Schumann's setting the words seem to point beyond the world of

Example 6.4a Schumann, "Die Stille," Op. 39, no. 4, mm. 1–4

human relationships. The vocal protagonist's desire to become a bird, to fly "over the sea and on, / Until I were in heaven!" suggests a yearning for transcendence.[25] In following the image of celestial flight with a repeat of the first poetic stanza (mm. 25–34), Schumann invests that stanza with new meaning, the line "Oh, if only *one* were to know it" now a subtle reference to divinity; the beloved to whom the narrator wishes to communicate her most deeply concealed feelings is God.[26]

Repeating the first stanza serves another important purpose: it turns the stanza beginning "Would I were a bird" into an enclosed middle section (mm. 17–24) with a distinct character. This section, more than those on either end, suggests the exuberance of unrestricted flight; here the music soars (Example 6.4b). The tempo increases ("Etwas lebhafter" replaces the earlier heading, "Nicht schnell, immer sehr leise"), as does the rhythmic activity of the accompaniment. The vocal line sails gracefully over a prolonged dominant 9th harmony, and horn calls (mm. 21–22), traditionally associated with expansive landscapes, convey distance. When the opening material returns in m. 25, however, the feeling again becomes one of restraint. As in the song's first section, the third section offers only hints of the protagonist's concealed emotional intensity (e.g., vocal leaps at "wohl" in mm. 3 and 27 and "Einer" in mm. 6 and 30, and bursts of diminished 7th harmony in mm. 6 and 30).

If the middle section represents a moment of emotional release in which the protagonist finally articulates a yearning for transcendence (expressed through the folk-like *Voglmotif*), it does so as the result of a musical process initiated in the song's first section. The middle section's melodic theme, beginning with a rising half step and falling arpeggio, derives from material of the first section, as if a hidden emotion were finally brought to light. Its emergence is gradual. In mm. 1 and 4, rising half step motion gives shape to the principal melody (sounding in both the vocal line and piano

Example 6.4b Schumann, "Die Stille," Op. 39, no. 4, mm. 17–24

accompaniment); the slight forward thrust created by rising half steps both prevents melodic stagnancy and insinuates yearning. In mm. 8 and 10, the rising half step motive again sounds, first in the accompaniment, then echoing at the start of the succeeding vocal phrases. In m. 12, Schumann adds the falling arpeggio, but the expanded motif occurs only in the accompaniment, like a thought or feeling buried in the subconscious. Finally, beginning with the anacrusis to m. 17, the vocal line (prompted by a rising half step in the accompaniment) presents the full melody: the concealed emotion surfaces and takes to the air.

The moment of expressive liberation soon passes. At m. 25, Schumann thrusts the protagonist back into a state of emotional restraint by repeating the first poetic stanza. (Although the text is identical, the music is slightly modified so as to lead to the tonic.) In the piano postlude, both the registral descent and the silencing of the voice confirm that the protagonist's flight of emotion – and, by extension, the song itself – has come to an end.

If "Der Knabe" and "Die Stille" evoke "Wenn ich ein Vöglein wär" through overt textual echoes, other works reveal its influence more obliquely. The folk song's impact on the art song repertory is primarily evident in allusions to the *Voglmotif*, rather than textual or musical quotations. (Aside from Schumann's duet version of "Wenn ich ein Vöglein wär," almost no composers drew upon the folk song's most well-known melody.) As noted, poems and musical settings from the early nineteenth century tend to present the *Voglmotif* in a positive manner, with the protagonist's wish fulfilled to some degree. As the century progressed, however, writers and composers engaged the *Voglmotif* with greater pessimism. In Romantic Lieder of the middle and later nineteenth century, yearning for transcendence remains an important theme, but is generally portrayed as an insatiable human drive.

Goethe's poem "Sehnsucht" ("Was zieht mir das Herz so?"; before 18 December 1802), set by Zelter (1802 unpub), Reichardt (1805 pub), Beethoven (1810), Schubert (1814), Fanny Mendelssohn (1839), and even the young Wolf (1875), draws upon the *Voglmotif* to present an ecstatic vision of love's union. The poetic speaker, drawn outdoors by irresistible longing, finds himself imaginatively joining a passing flock of ravens. Acquiring the birds' dual capabilities of flight and song enables him to approach and attract the attention of his beloved.

Sehnsucht	*Yearning*
Was zieht mir das Herz so?	What tugs so at my heart?
Was zieht mich hinaus?	What pulls me outside?
Und windet und schraubt mich	What wrenches, wrests me
Aus Zimmer und Haus?	from room and house?
Wie dort sich die Wolken	How, there, the clouds
Um Felsen verziehn!	disperse about the rocks!
Da möcht ich hinüber,	Over them would I go,
Da möcht ich wohl hin!	thither would I go!
Nun wiegt sich der Raben	The ravens swing by
Geselliger Flug;	in companionable flight;
Ich mische mich drunter	I mingle with them,
Und folge dem Zug.	and follow their course.
Und Berg und Gemäuer	And mountain and ruin,
Umfittichen wir;	about them we wing;
Sie weilet da drunten,	below there she tarries,
Ich spähe nach ihr.	for her I keep watch.
Da kommt sie und wandelt;	Now she comes walking;
Ich eile sobald,	I hasten at once,
Ein singender Vogel,	a bird in song,
Zum buschigen Wald.	to the bushy wood.
Sie weilet und horchet	She lingers and listens
Und lächelt mit sich:	and smiles to herself:
"Er singet so lieblich	"He sings so sweetly,
Und singt es an mich."	and for me he sings."
Die scheidende Sonne	The sun, departing,
Vergüldet die Höhn;	makes golden the hills;

Die sinnende Schöne,	that pensive fair one
Sie läßt es geschehn.	lets it be so.
Sie wandelt am Bache	She walks by the brook,
Die Wiesen entlang,	over the meadows,
Und finster und finstrer	and darker and darker
Umschlingt sich der Gang;	the path twists its way;
Auf einmal erschein ich,	all at once I appear,
Ein blinkender Stern,	a shining star,
"Was glänzet da droben,	"What glitters up there,
So nah und so fern?"	so near and so far?"
Und hast du mit Staunen	And when, with amazement,
Das Leuchten erblickt,	you've sighted the gleam,
Ich lieg dir zu Füßen,	I will lie at your feet,
Da bin ich beglückt!	and be content!

In presenting the speaker's transformations as means to reach the beloved, Goethe aligns his treatment of the *Voglmotif* with that of "Wenn ich ein Vöglein wär"; the desire to become like a bird, satisfied through the creative imagination, is motivated by the speaker's devotion to a particular woman. At the same time, his *Sehnsucht* extends beyond the world of human relationships. His yearning draws him progressively into the realm of the celestial, where he becomes a twinkling star. Although both the bird's song and the star's light find their way to the woman, providing a conduit for the speaker's passionate sentiments, the course of his imaginative flight – from a domestic dwelling to the rocky outdoor landscape to the treetops to the starry firmament – also suggests a perhaps sublimated longing to transcend earthly (human) existence.

Beethoven's modified strophic setting, Op. 83, no. 2, conveys the poetic speaker's vision of blissful fulfillment without complexity. The *Allegretto* tempo gives the music a sprightly feel. The speaker's imaginative transformation is intimated through text-painting: hints of bird song in the trills of m. 12 and its various recurrences, and the suggestion of bird flight in the 16th notes of mm. 15–18 (Example 6.5). To underscore the vocal protagonist's hopefulness, Beethoven switches from the song's predominant tonality of B minor to B major at the start of the last stanza. If the song's major mode ending does not confirm the fulfillment of longing, it at least preserves the protagonist's fantasy (Example 6.5). Goethe's adaptation of the *Voglmotif*, presented through music whose bouncy eighth-note vocal rhythms, mostly syllabic declamation, and 6/8 meter give it a folklike air, exemplifies the spirit of optimism that prevailed in the early years of the nineteenth century.

Example 6.5 Beethoven, "Sehnsucht," Op. 83, no. 2, mm. 10–16

Schubert's setting, D. 123, less folklike than Beethoven's, borrows the musical language of dramatic ballad settings to convey the transcendent vision of Goethe's poem. The song has an episodic structure, employing frequent changes of tempo, key, rhythm, and texture to illustrate textual imagery, including that linked to the *Voglmotif*. At the beginning of the setting, for example, Schubert conveys a gradual acceleration of physical movement (the protagonist's imagined transition from an earth-bound to aerial state) through a shift from declamatory recitative (mm. 2–5) to an arioso passage in 6/8 meter and *Mässig* tempo (mm. 5–9) to a yet more melodious section whose 12/8 meter, *Ziemlich geschwind* tempo, and lyrical accompaniment pattern of continuous eighth-note arpeggios evoke the graceful flight of the birds (mm. 10ff).[27] The melodic sequence of mm. 10–13 emphasizes the parallel between the vocal protagonist and the ravens whose soaring inspires his fantasy (Example 6.6).

Like Beethoven's setting, Schubert's not only illustrates the birds' flight but also mimics their song. After a short passage of recitative in which the protagonist announces his transformation ("I hasten at once, / a bird in song, / to the bushy wood"), six chirping measures of treble trills, scales, and arpeggios (mm. 24–29) sound in the piano alone – an embedded "song" indicating that the protagonist can indeed warble like a bird. In the song's final measures, an extended scalar descent in the treble line of the

Example 6.6 Schubert, "Sehnsucht," D. 123, mm. 10–13

piano illustrates his culminating pose of loving worship at the feet of the beloved.

In "Sehnsucht" ("Ach, aus dieses Tales Gründen"; 1802), Schiller engages what he perceived as the fundamental tension characterizing modern civilization. In many of his essays and poems, he depicts the modern world as un-poetic, artificial, restricted, and anguished. Yet despite the problems wrought by culture, Schiller held out hope that man, through strenuous effort and unwavering faith in human progress, could escape his bondage and achieve a more exalted existence. In certain poems, such as "Der Pilgrim" (1803; set by Schubert in 1823), he expresses despair over man's ability to transcend his limitations: "I am no nearer my goal. // Ah, no bridge will take me there; / Ah, the sky above me / Will not touch the earth, / And the There is never here!" "Sehnsucht," however, through use of the *Voglmotif*, presents the goal as attainable. In the first stanza, the speaker yearns for wings to help him escape the dismal valley of the present and fly to the distant paradise he envisions. Unlike Goethe, Schiller makes no mention of a loved one from whom the speaker is separated. Here the *Voglmotif* represents a means for humanity to reach its potential.

Ach, aus dieses Tales Gründen,   Ah, if only I could find a way out
Die der kalte Nebel drückt,   From the depths of this valley,
Könnt ich doch den Ausgang finden,   Oppressed by cold mists,

Ach wie fühlt ich mich beglückt!	How happy I would feel!
Dort erblick ich schöne Hügel,	Yonder I see lovely hills,
Ewig jung und ewig grün!	Ever young and ever green!
Hätt ich Schwingen, hätt ich Flügel,	If I had pinions, if I had wings
Nach den Hügeln zög ich hin.	I would fly to those hills.

The second stanza and the beginning of the third evoke the idyllic pastoral world. Midway through the third stanza, the fantasy is interrupted, the protagonist bemoaning the treacherous waters that separate him from his ideal. The poem then concludes with a positive, if not wholly reassuring, message: man can reach that distant shore, unassisted by the gods, through unflinching courage and commitment.

Einen Nachen seh ich schwanken,	I see a boat pitching,
Aber ach! Der Fährmann fehlt.	But, alas! there is no boatman.
Frisch hinein und ohne Wanken,	Jump in without hesitation!
Seine Segel sind beseelt.	The sails are billowing.
Du mußt glauben, du mußt wagen,	You must trust, and you must dare,
Denn die Götter leihn kein Pfand,	For the gods grant no pledge;
Nur ein Wunder kann dich tragen	Only a miracle can convey you
In das schöne Wunderland.	To the miraculous land of beauty.

Schubert set Schiller's poem twice, once in 1813 (D. 52) and again in 1821 (D. 636).[28] Both settings employ an episodic form and text-painting to convey poetic ideas and imagery. The later version, however, does so with greater assurance, originality, and success, and will thus form the focus of the following discussion. Like Schiller, Schubert expresses confidence in man's capacity to overcome his earthly limitations. The music gives aural expression to the formidable challenges he faces: in mm. 70ff, swirling 16th-note motion in the accompaniment evokes the "raging torrent." The music also hints at man's ability to fly out of the oppressive valley, or, in the altered imagery of the third and fourth stanzas, to cross the treacherous sea. Schubert sets the line "If I had pinions, if I had wings" (mm. 25–26) over a sustained A7 harmony (V7/V in the local key of G major), creating forward momentum that, together with continuous 8th note rhythms and the rising tessitura of the vocal line, suggests an aerial ascent (Example 6.7a). (In the 1813 version, by contrast, he sets the line over a rhythmically static A major harmony, or III/F. Apart from the abrupt harmonic shift, only two rising arpeggios in the piano's upper register evoke the protagonist's imagined flight; the vocal line has a downward trajectory.)

Another means of conveying optimism involves progressive tonality. In setting the first stanza, Schubert distinguishes the real and ideal worlds through tonal contrasts: B minor for the former ("Ah, if only I could find

Example 6.7a Schubert, "Sehnsucht," D. 636, mm. 25–28

a way out / From the depths of this valley, / Oppressed by cold mists"), G major for the latter ("Yonder I see lovely hills, / Ever young and ever green!"). Forays into keys more remote from the original B minor tonic, including B-flat major, A-flat major, and E-flat major (all in stanza 2, which focuses on the ideal world), intimate the daunting distance that must be traversed to reach human fulfillment. The song concludes with an energetic, cabaletta-like section in E major (borrowed from the 1813 version of the song), reached by way of an enharmonic shift in m. 86 at the critical moment of recognition ("But, alas! there is no boatman."): humanity needs to steer its own course (Example 6.7b). By ending the song in E major, rather than returning to B minor, Schubert insinuates that man has begun his transcendental journey.

Mayrhofer's "Sehnsucht," set by Schubert in 1817 (D. 516), establishes a similar contrast between the real and the ideal. Bird-like flight into the realm of imagination – or perhaps death – represents a ray of hope to the poetic speaker, miserable despite, or because of, the abundant springtime beauty surrounding him. But whereas Schiller's "Sehnsucht" concludes with an inspiring imperative ("You must trust, and you must dare") to humankind, Mayrhofer's ends far less positively, with an acknowledgement of personal defeat.

Sehnsucht
Der Lerche wolkennahe Lieder
Erschmettern zu des Winters Flucht,
Die Erde hüllt in Samt die Glieder,
Und Blüten bilden rote Frucht.

Nur du, o sturmbewegte Seele,
Nur du bist blütenlos, in dich gekehrt,
Und wirst in goldner Frühlingshelle
Von tiefer Sehnsucht aufgezehrt.

Longing
The songs of the cloud-soaring lark
Ring out as winter flees;
The earth wraps her limbs in velvet,
And red fruit forms from the blossoms.

You alone, storm-tossed soul,
Do not flower; turned in on yourself,
You are consumed by deep longing
Amid spring's golden radiance.

Example 6.7b Schubert, "Sehnsucht," D. 636, mm. 85–93

Nie wird, was du verlangst, entkeimen	What you crave will never burgeon
Dem Boden, Idealen fremd,	From this earth, alien to ideals,
Der trotzig deinen schönsten Träumen	Which defiantly opposes its raw strength
Die rohe Kraft entgegenstemmt.	To your fairest dreams.
Du ringst dich matt mit seiner Härte,	You grow weary struggling with its harshness,
Vom Wunsche heftiger entbrannt,	Ever more inflamed by the desire
Mit Kranichen ein strebender Gefährte,	To journey to a kinder land,
Zu wandern in ein milder Land.	As aspiring companion to the cranes.

The speaker does not express yearning to become one of the birds – he is too alienated from their joyfulness for that – but only to accompany them on their journey; Mayrhofer's idealism had limits.

Schubert's musical setting counters the poetic pessimism. As in "Sehnsucht," D. 636, the music differentiates the vocal protagonist's bitter emotional world from the idyllic land he envisions, while also suggesting the possibility of traversing the distance between them. The harshness of reality is conveyed through various means: major-minor shifts (mm. 13, 20–21), heavy chordal textures (mm. 14–15), chromatic descents (m. 17), insistent repeated octaves (mm. 24–27, 30–33), downbeat dissonances (mm. 25–26, 30–32), and pounding accents (mm. 28–33). By contrast, the "kinder Land" for which the protagonist longs is evoked through major modes, diatonic writing, lighter textures, horn calls, and hushed dynamics. Once again, bird flight and song (merging in the imagery of line 1) hold promise of human fulfillment. As Youens notes, the larks sing in the "trills and sixteenth-note darting-and-swooping passaggi" of the piano's treble in mm. 6–13; the vocal line forms a duet with this bird song, the two parts becoming more closely aligned as the first stanza nears its end.[29]

The bird song disappears, however, at the start of the second stanza, as the protagonist dwells on his isolation and hopeless longing. Not until midway through the fourth stanza does another countermelody appear. At mention of the cranes' journey, the vocal line moves in tandem with the treble line of the piano, creating a gentle succession of horn calls – the "figure most emblematic of 'home' to nineteenth-century German listeners"[30] – in the pastoral key of G major (Example 6.8). Chromaticism yields to diatonicism, insistent octaves to lulling single notes. Thus in Schubert's setting, the protagonist's yearning to accompany birds to the idyllic land becomes a reality – a *musical* reality – with a sense of fulfillment no less satisfying than had the protagonist, like a fairy-tale character, suddenly sprouted wings. The increasing separation of the piano's treble and bass lines in the song's final measures provides yet another suggestion of transcendence, as if the protagonist had taken to the sky, leaving behind his earthly troubles (echoing in the chromatic E-flats of mm. 40–41).[31]

To these Lieder that employ the *Voglmotif* to convey optimism about man's capacity for transcendence, one might add Schubert's "Im Frühling," D. 882, the 1826 Schulze setting discussed in chapter 5. The last stanza sounds the familiar theme:

O wär ich doch ein Vöglein nur	Oh, if only I were a bird,
Dort an dem Wiesenhang!	There on the sloping meadow!
Dann blieb ich auf den Zweigen hier,	Then I would stay on these branches here,
Und säng ein süsses Lied von ihr,	And sing a sweet song about her
Den ganzen Sommer lang.	All summer long.

Example 6.8 Schubert, "Sehnsucht," D. 516, mm. 33–42

Schulze employs the *Voglmotif* without alluding to the power of flight. But the ability to *sing* like a bird has similar metaphorical implications. Singing, the poem suggests, also enables one to escape earthly reality, and thus represents a special form of flight. (As we have seen, many poems emphasize birds' dual capacities). Singing about his lost love could allow the protagonist to transcend his emotional pain. Schulze's poem ends in a hypothetical mode, with the protagonist's yearning. As noted, Schubert's setting may be the very song the protagonist wishes he could sing; the Lied as a whole represents a magnification of the imagined bird song in the last three measures (Example 5.5c). Schubert transforms the poem's conditional tense into an implied indicative, with the protagonist's wish fulfilled in a new transcendent reality encompassing both loss and consolation.

The *Voglmotif* of "Wenn ich ein Vöglein wär" echoes in art songs from the mid and late nineteenth century. Some, like "Mondnacht," enact the fulfillment of Romantic yearning. On the whole, however, both the words and music of later nineteenth-century settings convey emotions ranging from restrained hopefulness to despair. In Schumann's "Die Stille," for example, only the central section hints at the exhuberance of flight, or emotional release. A more salient example is his "Sehnsucht," Op. 51, no. 1 (1840).[32] Geibel's poetic text projects both yearning and recognition of its futility. The paradisiacal world to which the vocal protagonist alludes recalls Mignon's "Land wo die Citronen blühn": a beautiful, blossoming, bountiful region in the sunny south.[33] It is not a present place but a past era upon which the protagonist fixates. The vanished age of classical antiquity and the protagonist's own lost youth merge in his outburst, and he laments that neither a bird's wings nor song itself can lead him back to the time of innocence and hope.

Sehnsucht	*Longing*
Ich blick in mein Herz und ich blick in die Welt,	I look into my heart, and then I look into the world;
Bis vom schwimmenden Auge die Träne mir fällt;	and the tears fall from my eyes.
Wohl leuchtet die Ferne mit goldenem Licht,	Far-off lands shine in the golden light;
Doch hält mich der Nord, ich erreiche sie nicht.	but the north holds me prisoner.
O die Schranken so eng und die Welt so weit,	My life is so narrow and the world so wide;
Und so flüchtig die Zeit, und so flüchtig die Zeit!	And time so fleeting, and time so fleeting!
Ich weiß ein Land, wo aus sonigem Grün	I know a land where the grapevines bloom
Um versunkene Tempel die Trauben blühn,	among sunny foliage around ruined temples,
Wo die purpurne Woge das Ufer besäumt,	where the purple waves foam on the shore,
Und von kommenden Sängern der Lorbeer träumt;	and the laurel dreams of poets to come.
Fern lockt es und winkt dem verlangenden Sinn,	Far lands shine and beckon to my yearning mind;
Und ich kann nicht hin, kann nicht hin!	and I cannot go, I cannot go!
O hätt ich Flügel, durchs Blau der Luft,	Oh for wings to cleave through the blue of the sky;
Wie wollt ich baden im Sommerduft,	how I should bathe in the fragrance of summer.
Doch umsonst! und Stunde auf Stunde entflieht,	But all in vain; the hours pass by.

Betraure die Jugend, begrabe das Lied.	Mourn for lost youth; bury the songs.
O die Schranken so eng, und die Welt so weit,	My life is so narrow and the world so wide;
Und so flüchtig die Zeit, und so flüchtig die Zeit!	And time so fleeting, and time so fleeting![34]

To evoke the beautiful far-off lands (e.g., mm. 6–7, 14–23), Schumann draws on major modes, diatonic harmonies, a middle vocal range, stepwise melodic motion, quiet dynamics, and a light accompaniment. The harsh reality of the present is suggested by the song's principal D minor tonality, an ominous-sounding half-step motif (between C and D-flat, or scale degrees 5 and flat-6; mm. 8–9, 29–30), and low vocal registers (mm. 8–9). The intensity of the protagonist's yearning finds expression in the eruption of 32nd notes in alternating hands of the piano during the song's opening and closing measures, and in the driving repeated chords in triplet rhythms throughout the accompaniment. Large ascending vocal leaps (mm. 9–11, 25–27, 35) and a generally rising tessitura contribute to the sense of striving. But yearning is in vain. Instead of ending, like Schubert's setting of Mayrhofer's "Sehnsucht," with a musical evocation of paradise, Schumann's song returns to the passionate 32nd note passage, leading to an emphatic cadence in D minor (Example 6.9). Each of the three poetic stanzas concludes with an expression of despair (the third stanza repeating the last two lines of the first stanza), and Schumann's musical setting injects no hopefulness; human transcendence is shown to be a chimera.

Schumann's "Flügel! Flügel!," Op. 37, no. 8, a Rückert setting from 1841, concludes with an implicit warning about the catastrophic consequences of man's reckless yearning to "fly": an image of the mythological Icarus plummeting into the sea. The first five stanzas convey obsession with the concept of flight through the language's heightened emotionalism (reflected in Schumann's tempo marking "Leidenschaftlich") and incessant repetitions of the word *Flügel*. What begins in exuberance, however, ends in despondency. Regret and bitterness in response to lost happiness transform the protagonist's expression of yearning into an elegy.

Flügel! Flügel!	*Wings! Wings!*
Flügel! Flügel! um zu fliegen	Wings, wings, to fly
Über Berg und Tal,	over hill and dale;
Flügel, um mein Herz zu wiegen	wings, to set my heart floating
Auf des Morgens Strahl!	on the dawn sunlight!
Flügel, übers Meer zu schweben	Wings, to soar over the seas
Mit dem Morgenrot,	with the sunrise;

Example 6.9 Schumann, "Sehnsucht," Op. 51, no. 1, mm. 33–39

Flügel, Flügel übers Leben,
Über Grab und Tod!

Flügel, wie sie Jugend hatte,
Da sie mir entflog,
Flügel wie des Glückes Schatten
Der mein Herz betrog!

Flügel, nachzufliehn den Tagen,
Die vorüber sind!

wings, wings to soar through life,
over death and the grave!

Wings such as my youth had,
now flown away;
wings like the illusion of happiness
that deceived my heart!

Wings, to fly after the days
now fled;

Flügel! Freuden einzujagen,	wings, to track down the joys
Die entflohn im Wind.	now blown away in the wind!
Flügel, gleich den Nachtigallen	Wings like nightingales,
Wann die Rosen blühn,	when the roses fade,
Aus dem Land, wo Nebel wallen,	to fly in search of them away
Ihnen nachzuziehn! Flügel! Flügel!	from this land of mists! Wings, wings![35]

Schumann's music races along in 6/8 meter with alternating quarter- and eighth-note rhythms – more evocative, perhaps, of galloping than flight, but nevertheless conveying an appropriate sense of urgency. The vocal line's extended phrases and occasional octave leaps add to the impression of frenetic striving. Soon, however, the harmony darkens, moving from the opening key of B major through several minor key regions (g♯, c♯, f♯, b) as the protagonist becomes consumed with the painful loss of happiness.

With the arrival of stanza 6, focus turns to destitute present reality, captured in the F♯ minor tonality, the accompaniment's reduction to a single line of syncopated chords, and the music loss of lyricism.

Ach! von dem Verbannungsstrande,	Oh! From this shore of exile
Wo kein Nachen winkt,	with no ship in sight,
Flügel, Flügel nach deim Heimatlande,	oh for wings to bear me back to the homeland
Wo die Krone blinkt!	where my crown is shining.

In the following two stanzas, which together with stanza 6 form the slow, common time middle section of Schumann's song, the protagonist's yearning for escape through the power of flight becomes reinvigorated. As in "Wenn ich ein Vöglein wär," nighttime dreams represent a possible solution.

Freiheit, wie zum Schmetterlinge	Oh for freedom, as the chrysalis splits
Raupenleben reift,	to release the butterfly
Wenn sich dehnt des Geistes Schwinge	when the spirit of Nature
Und die Hüll entstreift!	moves!
Oft in stillen Mitternächten	Often in silent midnights
Fühl' ich mich empor	I feel myself wafted aloft
Flügeln von des Traumes Mächten	by the power of dream
Zu dem Sternen-Tor.	to the gateway of the stars!

Gentle cascades of parallel thirds and sixths, a temporary harmonic turn to A major, and a vocal ascent to a climactic high A (the highest pitch in the song) intimate the possibility of transcendence through the magic of dreams.

But the illusion of restored happiness is short-lived; night yields to day. The return of the galloping rhythms in 6/8 for the song's final two stanzas suggests the over-weaning nature of the protagonist's desires. He strives for transcendence, and crashes into the tumultuous sea of earthly passions.[36]

Doch gewachsene Gefieder	Yet the plumage resplendent
In der Nächte Duft,	at night
Mir enttraüfeln seh ich's wieder	falls from me by day
An des Morgens Luft.	in the morning's breeze.
Sonnenbrand den Fittich schmelzet,	The burning sun melts my pinions,
Ikar stürzt ins Meer,	Icarus plunges headlong into the sea;
Und der Sinne Brausen wälzet	and in the roaring waves of sensual life
Überm Geist sich her.	the spirit is drowned.

Fortissimo dynamics, vocal chromaticism, and off-beat accents in the accompaniment convey emotional turbulence. The accompaniment's final descent into a low register during the lengthy postlude and its firm conclusion in the key of F♯ minor confirm the tragic outcome (Example 6.10). All hope has been expunged.

A more muted expression of despair conveyed through both words and music is Brahms's "Auf dem Schiffe," Op. 97, no. 2, composed by May 1885 to a text by Christian Reinhold. The poem describes a bird in flight, then reveals the envy of the ship-bound speaker watching its joyful course.

Auf dem Schiffe	*On the Ship*
Ein Vögelein	A little bird
Fliegt über den Rhein	Flies over the Rhein
Und wiegt die Flügel	And cradles its wings
Im Sonnenschein,	In the sunshine;
Sieht Rebenhügel	It sees vine-clad hills
Und grüne Flut	And green waves
In goldner Glut, –	In a golden glow;
Wie wohl das tut,	How fine it feels
So hoch erhoben	To be borne so high aloft
Im Morgenhauch!	In the morning breeze!
Beim Vöglein droben	If only I too could
O wär ich auch!	Fly high above with that bird![37]

Brahms signals the poetic shift from objective description to emotional identification through rhythmic, textural, and harmonic changes. The first seven lines are set to lively music in 3/8 meter whose consistent rhythmic pattern, built from a repeated triplet figure, suggests the rapid fluttering of a bird's wings (mm. 1–28). As the vocal protagonist imagines

Example 6.10 Schumann, "Flügel! Flügel!," Op. 37, no. 8, mm. 80–104

the delightful sensation of flying, the accompaniment slips into a series of ascending 16th-note arpeggios (mm. 29–44), as if mimicking the act of taking flight. Although the fluttering opening material returns briefly at the final reference to the bird (mm. 45–48), the remainder of the song, exposing the protagonist's deep yearning through a textual echo of "Wenn ich ein Vöglein wär," unfolds in straight 16th notes. The protagonist longs to soar with the bird, but the disappearance of the fluttering accompaniment pattern in m. 49 signals the futility of his desire.

Other aspects of the setting play a similar role. In mm. 47–48, just after the return of the major mode opening material, the harmony unexpectedly shifts

Example 6.11 Brahms, "Auf dem Schiffe," Op. 97, no. 2, mm. 44–63

to a minor seventh sonority, emphasizing that the bird is *droben*, distant, beyond reach (Example 6.11). The crucial G-natural, which darkens the preceding E dominant 7th harmony, sounds again high up in the vocal line at the protagonist's climactic outcry "o," insinuating his sorrowful awareness of human limitations. The unaccompanied restatement of the outcry on the single note C♯ in m. 54 emphasizes his isolation. A sustained tonic pedal in the accompaniment's low register (mm. 49–53), contrasting with extended sections of dominant prolongation during earlier flying-fantasy parts of the song, seems to confirm his earth-bound existence, as does the final vocal descent (from a high G-natural in m. 48 to A in m. 59). The emphatic statement of tonic harmony in the song's last measures extinguishes further dreams of flight.

Mahler's "Ging heut' Morgen übers Feld," the second song in the cycle *Lieder eines fahrenden Gesellen* of 1883–84 (text by Mahler himself), differs from the preceding examples in containing neither an explicit expression of yearning nor any reference to flying. It is related, however, in conveying pessimism about man's ability to commingle with birds and other elements of nature. The vocal protagonist can no more perceive the beauty of the natural world than partake in the birds' joyfulness.

Ging heut Morgen übers Feld,	I walked the fields this morning,
Tau noch auf den Gräsern hing;	dew still hung upon the grass;
Sprach zu mir der lustge Fink:	the merry finch said to me:
"Ei, du! Gelt? Guten Morgen! Ei gelt? Du!	"Why, good morning. Don't you agree –
Wird's nicht eine schöne Welt? schöne Welt!?	does not the world grow fair?
Zink! Zink! schön und flink!	Tweet! Tweet! Bright and fair!
Wie mir doch die Welt gefällt!"	How pleasing to me the world is!"
Auch die Glockenblum am Feld	And the bluebell at the field's edge,
Hat mir lustig, guter Ding	merrily, in good spirits,
Mit dem Glöckchen klinge, kling,	ding-dong with its tiny bell
Ihren Morgengruß geschellt:	rang out its morning greeting:
"Wird's nicht eine schöne Welt? schöne Welt!?	"Does not the world grow fair?
Kling! Kling! Schönes Ding!	Ding-dong. Beautiful thing.
Wie mir doch die Welt gefällt! Hei-a!"	How pleasing to me the world is!"
Und da fing im Sonnenschein	And then, in the sun,
Gleich die Welt zu funkeln an;	the world at once began to sparkle;
Alles, alles, Ton und Farbe gewann im Sonnenschein!	all, all gained tone and colour in the sun.
Blum und Vogel, groß und klein!	Flower and bird, great and small,
Guten Tag, guten Tag! Ist's nicht eine schöne Welt?	Good day, good day! Is the world not fair?
Ei du! Gelt!? Schöne Welt!?	Why, don't you agree – the world is fair?
Nun fängt auch mein Glück wohl an?!	Will my happiness now begin?!
Nein! Nein! Das ich mein, mir nimmer blühen kann!	No! No! The happiness I mean will never bloom!

The rising line in jaunty quarter note rhythms at the song's opening recalls the cheerful walking gait of Schubert's "Das Wandern." Like the miller lad, Mahler's protagonist sets off on a trek through nature, singing music with a folk-like air. In this vibrant world of finches and bluebells, everything shimmers with beauty. As dawn breaks over the glistening fields, chimes ring and melodies jingle. As if the entire *Die schöne Müllerin* cycle had been compressed into a single song, however, what begins in hopefulness concludes in despondency. In the third vocal strophe, set in the non-diatonic key of B major, or VI/D, bass ostinatos and a gradual deceleration of tempo together suggest a cessation of wandering as the protagonist surveys the natural world around him. In setting the last two lines, Mahler holds out the sprightly opening melodic motif (symbolizing man's excursion into nature's realm) as a kind of dream vision, an illusion of happiness. With the protagonist's final assertion that his lot will always be one of misery, the familiar tune echoes faintly and slowly before fading into nothingness (Example 6.12).

The preceding examples bear witness to the deflation of Romantic ideals in the latter half of the nineteenth century. While Romantic *topi* such as the *Voglmotif* – borrowed from and conveying longing for folk culture – retained appeal in the mid and late nineteenth century, they were rarely presented with the optimism characterizing many early Romantic works. In the post-Romantic era, an ability to soar beyond the boundaries of human existence, to sing with the naturalness and simplicity of birds or the common *Volk*, seemed hopelessly remote, inspiring melancholy and nostalgia.

Certain Lieder, however, tell a different and more uplifting story. If the unappeasable longing in "Wenn ich ein Vöglein wär" and numerous art songs is central to Romanticism, the fulfillment of that desire occasionally finds expression in works involving a poetic abstraction – the symbolic representation of humans by birds, or the human acquisition of birdlike features. Here, the subjunctive tense disappears, as if wish had become reality. In Heine's "Aus meine Tränen sprießen," set by Schumann (1840), Fanny Mendelssohn (1838), Rimsky-Korsakov (1866), Mussorgsky (1866), and Borodin (1870), for example, the speaker's sighs become a choir of nightingales which, he claims, will fly to his beloved's window to enchant her with sweet yet sorrow-laden serenades.[38] In Felix Schumann's "Meine Liebe ist grün," the text for Brahms's Op. 63, no. 5 (1873), the speaker's soul has the wings of a nightingale and flits through the lilacs singing love-intoxicated songs. Eichendorff's "Im Abendrot," which Strauss set as the last of his *Vier letzte Lieder* (1948), depicts two larks ascending into the hazy sky, tracing the path to transcendence sought by the poetic speaker and his wife, who stand together at the precipice of death after life's long journey. In the song's final moments, Strauss quotes the transfiguration theme from *Tod und Verklärung* to assure the listener that the couple's wish has been fulfilled.

At a yet greater level of abstraction are those works in which neither human protagonists nor symbolic avians but rather song itself takes flight, and it is here that the consolatory powers of music become most apparent.

Example 6.12 Mahler, "Ging heut' Morgen übers Feld," *Lieder eines fahrenden Gesellen*, no. 2, mm. 103–127

Although humans remain subject to physical, temporal, and other restrictions of earthly existence, their songs, like a set of wings, grant them access to transcendent freedom. In these works, the linguistic figure of synecdoche, whereby songs are used to represent the humans who sing them, in effect reopens the gates to paradise, offering comfort, even blissfulness, to legions of sufferers. Mendelssohn's famous Heine setting "Auf dem Flügel des Gesanges," Op. 34, no. 2 (1833–34), employs the figure in a largely positive context – as a means to woo a lover: "On wings of song, / dearest, will I bear you away, / away to the Ganges meadows, / where I know the nicest place... // There let us sink down / beneath the palm tree, / and drink in love and peace, / and dream a blissful dream." Brahms's song "Meine Lieder," Op. 106, no. 4 (1888), with words by Adolf Frey, draws upon a similar image of musical flight but directs focus toward the past rather than the future, creating a mood of melancholic nostalgia: "When my heart begins to make music, / when it unfolds the wings of melody, / then I see hovering back and forth before me / pale joys, unforgotten, / and the shadows of cypress trees. / My songs sound dark!"[39]

It is fitting to conclude with a return to Schubert, whose songs played such a crucial inspirational role both to those who witnessed their creation and to those who later carried on the Romantic Lied tradition. "An die Musik," D. 547, (1817), a setting of a poem by his close friend Schober that was likely inspired by the blissful experience of hearing Schubert's works during the difficult Metternich era, produces exactly the magical effect that its words describe. Song carries the self-conscious protagonist, the performers, and the listeners – *as if* with wings – to "a better world." "An die Musik," like so many Romantic Lieder, owes its enduring appeal to the glimmer of transcendence offered by art.

Du holde Kunst, in wieviel grauen Stunden,	Beloved art, in how many a bleak hour,
Wo mich des Lebens wilder Kreis umstrickt,	When I am enmeshed in life's tumultuous round,
Hast du mein Herz zu warmer Lieb entzunden,	Have you kindled my heart to the warmth of love,
Hast mich in eine bessre Welt entrückt!	And borne me away to a better world!
Oft hat ein Seufzer, deiner Harf entflossen,	Often a sigh, escaping from your harp,
Ein süsser, heiliger Akkord von dir	A sweet, celestial chord
Den Himmel bessrer Zeiten mir erschlossen,	Has revealed to me a heaven of happier times,
Du holde Kunst, ich danke dir dafür!	Beloved art, for this I thank you!

Notes

Introduction: Seeking lost paradise

1 From Franz Schubert, "Die Götter Griechenlands," D. 677. Unless otherwise noted, English translations of texts for Schubert Lieder are borrowed from Richard Wigmore, *Schubert: The Complete Song Texts* (New York: Schirmer Books, 1998) and translations of texts for Lieder by composers apart from Schubert are borrowed from Dietrich Fischer-Dieskau, comp., *The Fischer-Dieskau Book of Lieder* (New York: Limelight Editions, 1995). Other translations, unless a source is cited, are mine.
2 From Robert Schumann, "Aus alten Märchen winkt es," Op. 48, no. 15.
3 There is a vast literature on nostalgia in nineteenth-century European culture. Linda Hutcheon cites many studies in "Irony, Nostalgia, and the Postmodern," in *Methods for the Study of Literature as Cultural Memory*, eds. Raymond Vervliet and Annemarie Estor (Amsterdam: Rodopi, 2000), pp. 189–207.
4 See, for example, Peter Russell, *The Themes of the German Lied From Mozart to Strauss* (Lewiston: The Edwin Mellen Press, 2002), pp. 355–66; Harry Seelig, "The Literary Context: Goethe as Source and Catalyst," in *German Lieder in the Nineteenth Century*, ed. Rufus Hallmark (New York: Schirmer Books, 1996), pp. 13–14; and Deborah Stein and Robert Spillman, *Poetry Into Song: Performance and Analysis of Lieder* (New York: Oxford University Press, 1996), p. 14. The lost paradise myth has been explored in many disciplines. Particularly informative studies include: John Ashton and Tom Whyte, *The Quest for Paradise: Visions of Heaven and Eternity in the World's Myths and Religions* (New York: Harper-Collins, 2001); Richard Heinberg, *Memories and Visions of Paradise: Exploring the Universal Myth of a Lost Golden Age*, rev. ed (Wheaton, IL: Quest Books, 1995); Mario A. Jacoby, *Longing for Paradise: Psychological Perspectives on an Archetype*, trans. Myron B. Gubitz (Boston: Sigo Press, 1985, orig. German edn 1980); and John Armstrong, *The Paradise Myth* (London: Oxford University Press, 1969). Studies of Romanticism treating the subject include: Isaiah Berlin, *The Roots of Romanticism*, ed. Henry Hardy (Princeton University Press, 1999); Herbert Lindenberger, "Theories of Romanticism: From a Theory of Genre to the Genre of Theory," in *The History in Literature: On Value, Genre, Institutions* (New York: Columbia University Press, 1990), pp. 61–84; Virgil Nemoianu, *The Taming of Romanticism: European Literature and the Age of Biedermeier* (Cambridge, MA: Harvard University Press, 1984); M. H. Abrams, *Natural Supernaturalism: Tradition and Revolution in Romantic Literature* (New York: W. W. Norton, 1971);

Geoffrey H. Hartman, "Romanticism and 'Anti-Self-Consciousness,'" in *Romanticism and Consciousness: Essays in Criticism*, ed. Harold Bloom (New York: W. W. Norton, 1970), pp. 46–56; Arthur O. Lovejoy, "On the Discrimination of Romanticisms," *Proceedings of the Modern Langue Association* 39 (1924), 229–53. The myth is likewise addressed within studies of musical Romanticism, e.g., Charles Rosen, *The Romantic Generation* (Cambridge, MA: Harvard University Press, 1995); John Daverio, *Nineteenth-Century Music and the German Romantic Ideology* (New York: Schirmer Books, 1993); Carl Dahlhaus, *Nineteenth-Century Music*, trans. J. Bradford Robinson (Berkeley: University of California Press, 1989); Leon Plantinga, *Romantic Music: A History of Musical Style in Nineteenth-Century Europe* (New York: W. W. Norton, 1984).

5 Ashton and Whyte, *The Quest for Paradise*, p. 33.
6 Hesiod, *Works and Days*, trans. Richard Lattimore (Ann Arbor: University of Michigan Press, 1959), 31–33.
7 Ashton and Whyte, *The Quest for Paradise*, 33.
8 Genesis 2:15–17.
9 See, for example, Ashton and Whyte, *The Quest for Paradise*; Heinberg, *Memories and Visions of Paradise*; Mircea Eliade, *Myths, Dreams and Mysteries* (New York: Harper and Row, 1967); Eliade, *Patterns in Comparative Religion* (New York: New American Library, 1974).
10 See chapter 4 of Heinberg, *Memories and Visions of Paradise*, and chapter 3 of Eliade, *Myths, Dreams and Mysteries*.
11 Heinberg, *Memories and Visions of Paradise*, p. 3.
12 Ibid., p. 98.
13 David Blayney Brown, *Romanticism* (London: Phaidon, 2001), p. 364.
14 The phrase "eine beßre Welt" is taken from the text, by Franz von Schober, to Schubert's song "An die Musik," D. 547.
15 Friedrich Schiller, "Letters on the Aesthetic Education of Man," in *Essays*, ed. Walter Hinderer and Daniel O. Dahlstrom, trans. Dahlstrom (New York: The Continuum Publishing Co., 1993), p. 98.
16 Friedrich Schiller, "On Naïve and Sentimental Poetry," in *Essays*, ed. Walter Hinderer and Daniel O. Dahlstrom, trans. Dahlstrom (New York: The Continuum Publishing Co., 1993), p. 200.
17 Schiller, "On Naïve and Sentimental Poetry," pp. 179, 195–97.
18 Jane K. Brown, "The Poetry of Schubert's Songs," in *Schubert's Vienna*, ed. Raymond Erickson (New Haven: Yale University Press, 1997), p. 193.
19 Schiller, "On Naïve and Sentimental Poetry," pp. 194–95.
20 Ibid., pp. 180–81.
21 Ibid., pp. 194–95.
22 Ibid., pp. 214–15.
23 Lindenberger, "Theories of Romanticism," p. 63.
24 Schiller, "On Naïve and Sentimental Poetry," pp. 228–29.
25 Ibid., pp. 228.

26 Ibid., p. 193.
27 Ibid., p. 181.
28 Schiller, "Letters on the Aesthetic Education of Man," p. 99.
29 Leslie Sharpe, *Friedrich Schiller: Drama, Thought and Politics* (Cambridge University Press, 1991), p. 145.
30 Hartman, "Romanticism and 'Anti-Self-Consciousness,'" p. 54.
31 See, for example, Arthur O. Lovejoy, "Schiller and the Genesis of German Romanticism," in *Essays in the History of Ideas* (New York: George Braziller, Inc., 1955), pp. 207–27. First published in *Modern Language Notes* 35 (1920), 1–10, 134–46.
32 Hartman, "Romanticism and 'Anti-Self-Consciousness,'" p. 48.
33 Ibid., p. 51.
34 Ibid., pp. 51–52.
35 Heinrich von Kleist, "The Puppet Theater," in *Selected Writings*, ed. and trans. David Constantine (London: J. M. Dent, 1997), p. 416.
36 Susan Youens, *Schubert: Die schöne Müllerin* (Cambridge University Press, 1992), p. 30. Youens attributes the phrase to Carl Schorske in *Fin-de-siècle Vienna* (New York: Alfred A. Knopf, 1980), p. 221.
37 *Literary Encyclopedia*, s.v., "German Romanticism" (www.litencyc.com/php/stopics.php?rec=true&UID=1353)
38 As cited in Robert Pascall, "'My Love of Schubert – No Fleeting Fancy': Brahms's Response to Schubert," *Schubert Durch die Brille: Internationales Franz Schubert Institut – Mitteilungen* 21 (June 1998), 51.
39 "Songs are sailing such an erroneous course nowadays that one cannot impress the ideal too sharply on oneself. And that's what folk-song is for me." Letter from Brahms to Clara Schumann of 27 January 1860. *Johannes Brahms: Life and Letters*, selected and annotated by Styra Avins, trans. Josef Eisinger and Styra Avins (Oxford University Press, 1997), p. 212.

Part I: The lost world of antiquity

1 Fani-Maria Tsigakou, *Through Romantic Eyes: European Images of Nineteenth-Century Greece From the Benaki Museum, Athens* (Alexandria, VA: Art Services International, 1991), p. 14.
2 Jeremy McInerney, "Ethnic Identity and *Altertumswissenschaft*," in *Prehistory and History: Ethnicity, Class and Political Economy*, ed. David W. Tandy (Montreal: Black Rose Books, 2001), p. 86.
3 Johann Joachim Winckelmann, *Reflections on the Imitation of Greek Works in Painting and Sculpture*, trans. Elfriede Heyer and Roger C. Norton (La Salle, IL: Open Court, 1987), p. 5.
4 George S. Williamson, *The Longing for Myth in Germany: Religion and Aesthetic Culture from Romanticism to Nietzsche* (The University of Chicago Press, 2004), p. 38.

5 "Da die Götter menschlicher noch waren, / Waren Menschen göttlicher." Schiller, first version of "Die Götter Griechenlands," lines 191–92 (stanza 24).
6 See, for example, David S. Ferris, *Silent Urns: Romanticism, Hellenism, Modernity* (Stanford University Press, 2000); David Gress, *From Plato to Nato: The Idea of the West and its Opponents* (New York: The Free Press, 1998); Suzanne L. Marchand, *Down from Olympus: Archaeology and Philhellensim in German, 1750–1970* (Princeton University Press, 1996); Josef Chytry, *The Aesthetic State: A Quest in Modern German Thought* (Berkeley: University of California Press, 1989); Helene M. Kastinger Riley, *Das Bild der Antike in der Deutschen Romantik* (Amsterdam: John Benjamins B/. V., 1981); Henry Hatfield, *Aesthetic Paganism in German Literature: From Winckelmann to the Death of Goethe* (Cambridge, MA: Harvard University Press, 1964); Humphry Trevelyan, *Goethe and the Greeks* (Cambridge University Press, 1941); Walther Rehm, *Griechentum und Goethezeit: Geschichte eines Glaubens* (Leipzig: Dieterich, 1936); Eliza Marian Butler, *The Tyranny of Greece over Germany* (Boston: Beacon Press, 1935); Rudolf Sühnel, *Die Götter Griechenlands und die deutsche Klassik* (Würzburg: Verlag Konrad Triltsch, 1935).
7 Hatfield, *Aesthetic Paganism in German Literature*, p. 16.
8 Ibid., p. 53.
9 Schiller, "On Naïve and Sentimental Poetry," p. 193.
10 The lines are taken from stanzas 4 and 7 of Hölderlin's poem "Brot und Wein." As cited in Gress, *From Plato to Nato*, pp. 66–7.
11 August William Schlegel, *A Course of Lectures on Dramatic Art and Literature*, trans. John Black (London: Bell and Daldy, 1871), pp. 26–27.
12 McInerney, "Ethnic Identity and *Altertumswissenschaft*," p. 89. See also Marchand, *Down from Olympus*, p. 6.
13 Schlegel's *Gespräch über die Poesie* and the closing section of Schelling's *System des transcendentalen Idealismus*, both published in the spring of 1800, call for a "new mythology." On the early Romantic attraction to myth, see Williamson, *The Longing for Myth in Germany*, pp. 19–71.
14 Friedrich Schlegel, *Dialogue on Poetry and Literary Aphorisms*, trans. Ernst Behler and Roman Struc (University Park, PA: The Pennsylvania State University Press, 1968), pp. 86–7.
15 Ibid., p. 88.
16 Fragment 116 of the journal *Athenaeum* (1798).
17 See Frederick C. Beiser, *The Romantic Imperative: The Concept of Early German Romanticism* (Cambridge, MA: Harvard University Press, 2003).
18 Friedrich Sengle, *Biedermeierzeit: Deutsche Literatur im Spannungsfeld Zwischen Restauration und Revolution 1815–1848*, vol. 1 (Stuttgart: J. B. Metzler, 1971), pp. 355–56.
19 Marchand, *Down from Olympus*, pp. 16–24.
20 Ibid., p. 35.
21 Ibid., pp. xix–xx.

22 Wilhelm von Humboldt, *Geschichte des Verfalls und Unterganges der griechischen Freistaaten*. As cited in McInerney, "Ethnic Identity and *Altertumswissenschaft*," p. 85.
23 Ibid., p. 33.
24 Fritz Graf, in *Griechische Mythologie* (Munich: Artemis, 1987), p. 15, argues that during the later nineteenth century, ancient Greece held a strong grip on German spiritual life. As cited in McInerney, "Ethnic Identity and *Altertumswissenschaft*," p. 109.
25 Gress, *From Plato to Nato*, p. 68.
26 Ibid., pp. 67–69.

1: Schubert's Greek revival

This is a revised version of a full chapter that appears as "Mayrhofer, Schubert, and the Myth of 'Vocal Memnon'" in *Unknown Schubert*, ed. Lorraine Byrne and Barbara Reul (Aldershot: Ashgate, 2008) © 2008.

1 Otto Erich Deutsch, ed., *Schubert: Memoirs by his Friends* (New York: Macmillan, 1958), p. 131.
2 Deutsch, ed., *Schubert: Memoirs by his Friends*, p. 132.
3 Schubert referred privately to Vogl as the "Greek bird" ("der griechische Vogel"). Otto Erich Deutsch, ed., *Schubert: Die Dokumente seines Lebens* (Kassel: Bärenreiter, 1964), p. 66.
4 Deutsch, ed., *Schubert: Memoirs by his Friends*, p. 226. I borrow the term *Antikenlieder* from Otto Weinreich's "Franz Schuberts Antikenlieder," *Deutsche Vierteljahresschrift für Literaturwissenschaft und Geistesgeschichte* 13 (1935), 91–117.
5 For documentary references to Schubert's and Vogl's performances of songs with classical themes, see Otto Erich Deutsch, ed., *The Schubert Reader: A Life of Franz Schubert in Letters and Documents* (New York: W. W. Norton, 1947), pp. 188–89, 207–08, 400, 404, 407, 753.
6 On Schubert's *Antikenlieder*, see: Lorraine Byrne, "Goethe, Schubert and the Greeks," in *Schubert's Goethe Settings* (Aldershot: Ashgate, 2003), pp. 78–100; Russell, *The Themes of the German Lied*, pp. 315–21; Ilija Dürhammer, "Deutsch- und Griechentum: Johann Mayrhofer und Theodor Körner," *Schubert 200 Jahre, Schloß Achberg: "Ich lebe und componire wie ein Gott" – Schuberts Leben und Schaffen* (Heidelberg: Braus, 1997), pp. 21–24; Michael Raab, "Arten von Zusammenhang in Schuberts Liedbearbeitungen," *Schubert-Jahrbuch* (1997), pp. 85–94; Susan Youens, "Chromatic Melancholy: Johann Mayrhofer and Schubert," in *Schubert's Poets and the Making of Lieder* (Cambridge University Press, 1996, pbk ed. 1999), pp. 151–227; David Gramit, "Schubert and the Biedermeier: The Aesthetics of Johann Mayrhofer's 'Heliopolis,'" *Music and Letters* 74 (1993), 355–82; Graham Johnson, "Schubert and the Classics" (notes accompanying *The Hyperion Schubert Edition*, vol. 14, CDJ33014, 1992), pp. 2–39; Reinhold Hammerstein, "'Schöne Welt, wo bist du?': Schiller, Schubert und die Götter Griechenlands,"

in *Musik und Dichtung*, ed. Michael von Albrecht and Werner Schubert (Frankfurt am Main: Peter Lang, 1990), pp. 305–30; Werner Thomas, "Schillergedicht und Schubertlied," *Schubert-Studien* (Frankfurt am Main: Verlag Peter Lang, 1990), pp. 7–80; Werner Thomas, "Schuberts Lied 'Antigone und Oedip' im Licht der Antikenrezeption um 1800," *Schubert-Studien* (Frankfurt am Main: Verlag Peter Lang, 1990), pp. 81–114; Nicholas Temperley, "Schubert and Beethoven's Eight-Six Chord," *19th-Century Music* 5/2 (Fall 1981), 142–54; Bok-Joo Jhong, *German Solo Song Settings by Reichardt, Schubert, and Wolf of Goethe Poems Based on Classical Mythology* (Ph. D. diss., Indiana University, 1978); Weinreich, "Franz Schuberts Antikenlieder"; Leopold Hirschberg, "Franz Schubert und die Antike," *Neue Jahrbücher für Wissenschaft und Jugendbildung* 4 (1928), 677–93; Ludwig Scheibler, "Franz Schuberts einstimmige Lieder, Gesänge und Balladen mit Texten von Schiller," *Die Rheinlande* (April–Sept. 1905), 131–36, 163–69, 231–39, 270–74, 311–15; 353–56.

7   J. A. Smeed, *German Song and its Poetry 1740–1900* (London: Croom Helm), and Russell, *The Themes of the German Lied*, pp. 29–32.

8   Besides "Ganymed" (1794) and "Prometheus" (1809), other Reichardt settings of Goethe texts with classical subjects include: "Felsen stehen gegründet, aus *Euphrosyne*" (1809), "Tiefer liegt die Nacht um mich her, aus *Euphrosyne*" (1809), "Lass dich geniessen, aus *Prosperina*" (1801), "Lied der Parzen" (1798), "Monolog der Iphigenia" (1798), and "Aeneas zu Dido." Loewe's Anacreontic settings include "An die Grille" (1835), "Auf sich selbst" (1815?; after Anacreon's 11th Ode), "An die Leier" (1815?; after Anacreon's 1st Ode), and "Auf sich selbst" (1815?; after Anacreon's 24th Ode).

9   See Max Friedlaender, *Das deutsche Lied im 18. Jahrhundert*, vol. 1, part 2 (Hildesheim, Georg Olms, 1962), pp. 298–99, 310.

10 Russell, *The Themes of the German Lied*, p. 318.

11 Deutsch, ed., *Schubert: Memoirs by his Friends*, p. 21.

12 Graham Johnson, "Schubert and the Classics," pp. 2–3. See also David Gramit, *The Intellectual and Aesthetic Tenets of Franz Schubert's Circle: Their Development and Their Influence on His Music* (Ph.D. diss., Duke University, 1987), pp. 26–29.

13 The Linz circle included Josef and Anton Spaun, Josef Kenner, Johann Mayrhofer, and Anton Ottenwalt. Others friends who sympathized with the circle's educational and aesthetic aims were Franz Schober, Johann Senn, and Franz Bruchmann. On the circle, including the influence of Herder, Schiller, and Goethe, see Gramit, *The Intellectual and Aesthetic Tenets*, pp. 31–74.

14 Ibid., p. 42.

15 Johnson, "Schubert and the Classics," p. 5.

16 As cited and translated in Gramit, *The Intellectual and Aesthetic Tenets*, pp. 51–52.

17 Through-composed songs include "Antigone und Oedip," "Elysium," "Fragment aus dem Aeschylus," "Ganymed," "Gruppe aus dem Tartarus," "Hektors Abschied," "Iphigenia," "Lied des Orpheus," "Memnon," "Orest auf Tauris,"

and "Prometheus." Songs with rounded forms include "Atys," "Der Atlas," "Die Götter Griechenlands," "Fahrt zum Hades," and "Philoktet." "Dithyrambe" has a strophic form.

18 Songs with recitative are "Antigone und Oedip," "Fahrt zum Hades," "Fragment aus dem Aeschylus," "Hektors Abschied," "Klage der Ceres," "Prometheus," and "Uraniens Flucht." *Antikenlieder* with an arioso style (either throughout or in isolated passages) include "Der entsühnte Orest," "Freiwilliges Versinken," "Iphigenia," "Lied des Orpheus," "Lied eines Schiffers an die Dioskuren," "Orest auf Tauris," and "Prometheus." The opening of "Antigone und Oedip" resembles an operatic aria.

19 For example, the operatic oracle *topos* is evoked in "Antigone und Oedip," "Orest auf Tauris," and "Memnon." Horn calls, more common in Romantic Lieder, occur in "Antigone und Oedip," "Iphigenia," and "Lied des Orpheus."

20 Songs with progressive tonality include "Fahrt zum Hades," "Freiwilliges Versinken," "Ganymed," "Hektors Abschied," "Iphigenia," "Lied des Orpheus," "Orest auf Tauris," and "Prometheus." Songs with unified tonal schemes include "Antigone und Oedip," "Atys," "Fragment aus dem Aeschylus," "Die Götter Griechenlands," and "Lied eines Schiffers an die Dioskuren."

21 On the quasi-classical nature of Schubert's late Mayrhofer settings "Aus Heliopolis I," "Aus Heliopolis II," "Abendstern," and "Auflöung," see Johnson, "Schubert and the Classics," pp. 6–7.

22 Letter of 7 March 1822. *Diary and Letters of Wilhelm Müller*, ed. Philip Schuyler Allen and James Taft Hatfield (The University of Chicago Press, 1903), p. 102.

23 The *Iliad* does not mention Memnon, and the *Odyssey* makes only passing reference. Ancient writers who mention Memnon include Apollodorus, Diodorus Siculus, Hesiod, Hyginus, Ovid, Pausanias, Flavius Philostratus, Pindar, Quintus Smyrnaeus, Strabo, and Tryphiodorus.

24 Quintus of Smyrna, *The War at Troy: What Homer Didn't Tell*, trans. Frederick M. Combellack (Norman: University of Oklahoma Press, 1968), pp. 59–60. Quintus of Smyrna may have drawn on the eighth-century BC poem *Aethiopis* by Arctinus of Miletus.

25 John Boardman, *The Archaeology of Nostalgia: How the Greeks Re-created Their Mythical Past* (London: Thames and Hudson, 2002), pp. 118–23.

26 The ancient geographer Strabo from Amasya, who visited Egypt in 25–24 BC and claims to have heard the sound himself, thought that it might have been fabricated to attract tourists. Boardman, *The Archaeology of Nostalgia*, p. 122. According to Susi Jeans and Arthur W. J. G. Ord-Hume, in antiquity "[h]ydraulically blown organ pipes were used to imitate birdsong, as well as to produce the awe-inspiring sound emitted by Memnon's statue at Thebes. For the latter, solar heat was used to siphon water from one closed tank into another, thereby producing compressed air for sounding the pipes" (*The New Grove Dictionary of Music and Musicians*, s.v. "water organ," www.grovemusic.com (accessed 28 November 2006).

27 Vivant Denon, *Travels in Upper and Lower Egypt During the Campaigns of General Bonaparte in That Country*, vol. 2 (New York: Heard and Forman, 1803), pp. 251–52.
28 E.g., James B. V. Thomson, Victor Hugo, John Keats, Alfred Lord Tennyson, Edgar Allan Poe, Oliver Wendell Holmes, Bulwer Lytton, Charles G. D. Roberts, Sándor Petöfi, Oscar Wilde, and Conrad Aiken.
29 The first review, by an unknown author, was published 19 January 1822 in the Vienna *Allgemeine musikalische Zeitung* (Deutsch, *The Schubert Reader*, pp. 206–07).
30 The second review (of Schubert's Lieder Opp. 1–7), written by Friedrich von Hentl, appeared on 23 March 1822 in the *Wiener Zeitschrift für Kunst* (Deutsch, *The Schubert Reader*, p. 217).
31 Youens, *Schubert's Poets*, pp. 175–83.
32 Ibid., p. 182. Mayrhofer's poetic speakers include such mythological figures as Orestes, Hector, Achilles, Antigone, Oedipus, Philoktet, Endymion, Antigone, and Iphigenia.
33 Translation borrowed from Fischer-Dieskau, comp., *The Fischer-Dieskau Book of Lieder*, pp. 298–99.
34 Walther Dürr, "Schubert in Seiner Welt," in *Schubert Handbuch*, ed. Walther Dürr and Andreas Krause (Kassel: Bärenreiter, 1997), p. 25.
35 For an in-depth discussion of the Memnon myth's relation to Romantic poetry, see Bettine Menke, *Prosopopoiia: Stimme und Text bei Brentano, Hoffmann, Kleist und Kafka* (Munich: Wilhelm Fink, 2002), pp. 217–60 and 367–429.
36 The poem is "Letzte Mahungsworte des Waldbruders," published posthumously in: Johann Mayrhofer, *Gedichte von Johann Mayrhofer. Neue Sammlung. Aus dessen Nachlasse mit Biographie und Vorwort*, ed. Ernst Freiherr von Feuchtersleben (Vienna: Ignaz Klang, 1843), pp. 251–52.
37 As translated in Youens, *Schubert's Poets*, pp. 171–74. Bauernfeld's poem, first appearing in his *Buch von uns Wienern in lustig-gemütlichen Reimlein*, was later published (in a revised form) under the title "Ein Wiener Censor" in his collected works: Eduard von Bauernfeld, *Gesammelte Schriften*, vol. 11, *Reime und Rhythmen* (Vienna: Wilhelm Braumüller, 1873).
38 Ibid., p. 180. As support, Youens cites the poem "Unter Antiken," published in: Johann Mayrhofer, *Gedichte* (Vienna: Friedrich Volke, 1824), p. 143.
39 Novalis, *Schriften*, vol. 2: *Das philosophische Werk* I, ed. Richard Samuel, Hans-Joachim Mähl, and Gerhard Schulz (Stuttgart: W. Kohlhammer, 1981), p. 373.
40 Ibid. See also Georg Wilhelm Friedrich Hegel, *Vorlesungen über die Ästhetik I* (Frankfurt am Main: Suhrkamp, 1970), p. 462.
41 Menke, *Prosopopoiia*, p. 218.
42 György Fogarasi, "Reverberations of Romanticism: Petöfi's Figure of Memnon," *Kakanien Revisited* (Jan. 17, 2002), p. 4, www.kakanien.ac.at/beitr/fallstudie/GFogarasi1/pdf (accessed 28 November 2006).
43 Gramit, "Schubert and the Biedermeier."

44 On Mayrhofer's hypochondria, see Schubert's letter to his friends of 8 September 1818. Deutsch, *The Schubert Reader*, p. 100.
45 Schubert dedicated his "Memnon" setting to Vogl on its publication on commission (Op. 6, no. 1) in August 1821 by Cappi and Diabelli.
46 Deutsch, *Schubert: Memoirs by his Friends*, p. 21.
47 Ibid., p. 363.
48 Ibid., p. 59
49 Reinhold Hammerstein, *Die Stimme aus der anderen Welt: Über die Darstellung des Numinosen in der Oper von Monteverdi bis Mozart* (Tutzing: Hans Schneider, 1998).
50 Ibid.
51 One might regard "Memnon" as a one-way dialogue. A poem entitled "Aurora" appears directly after "Memnon" in the 1824 collection of Mayrhofer's poetry. Schubert did not set it.
52 Lawrence Kramer, *Franz Schubert: Sexuality, Subjectivity, Song* (Cambridge University Press, 1998), p. 66.
53 The autograph manuscript [Vienna, *Stadt- und Landesbibliothek*, MH 2064] is dated November 1819. Schubert penciled in several small changes to create the second version of the song. Nicholas Rast speculates that Schubert made the changes in 1824 while working on the A Minor String Quartet, Op. 29, which uses some of the same musical material. Nicholas Rast, "'Schöne Welt, wo bist du?': Motiv and Form in Schubert's A Minor String Quartet," in *Schubert the Progressive: History, Performance Practice, Analysis*, ed. Brian Newbould (Burlington, VT: Ashgate, 2003), p. 86. The second version of "Die Götter Griechenlands" was published posthumously in 1848/49 in volume 42 of the *Nachgelassene musikalische Dichtungen*.
54 For example, Richard Kramer describes the second version's ending as "cause for regret" in *Distant Cycles: Schubert and the Conceiving of Song* (The University of Chicago Press, 1994), p. 53.
55 The through-composed form of "Ganymed" and rounded form of "Der Atlas" support this observation.
56 See, for example, Hammerstein, "'Schöne Welt, wo bist du?,'" p. 309; Hirschberg, "Franz Schubert und die Antike," p. 688; and Weinreich, "Franz Schuberts Antikenlieder," p. 112.
57 See Gramit, *The Intellectual and Aesthetic Tenets*, p. 229; Johnson, "Schubert and the Classics," p. 9; and Rast, "'Schöne Welt, wo bist du?'" p. 86.
58 Gramit, *The Intellectual and Aesthetic Tenets*, p. 230.
59 Sharpe, *Friedrich Schiller*, p. 100.
60 Ibid., p. 104.
61 Ibid., p. 98.
62 In a letter of 1 September 1788 to his friend Christian Gottfried Körner, Schiller wrote, "Mache dich doch an einige Strophen aus den Göttern Griechenlands; Du könntest mich recht damit regaliren. Sie sind gewiß sehr singbar, und einige

leiden auch sehr die musikalische Behandlung. Du könntest mich und meine hiesigen Freunde ordentlich glücklich dadurch machen." *Schillers Briefe, Kritische Gesamtausgabe*, ed. V. F. Jonas, vol. 2 (Stuttgart, 1983), p. 11. Cited in Hammerstein, "'Schöne Welt, wo bist du?,'" p. 307.
63 Ibid., p. 308.
64 John Reed, *The Schubert Song Companion* (Manchester University Press: 1985), p. 164.
65 Hammerstein, "'Schöne Welt, wo bist du?,'" p. 319.
66 Temperly, "Schubert and Beethoven's Eight-Six Chord," p. 150.
67 Raab, "Arten von Zusammenhang," p. 88.
68 Temperly, "Schubert and Beethoven's Eight-Six Chord," pp. 152–53.
69 Hammerstein, "'Schöne Welt, wo bist du?'" p. 312.
70 Gramit, *The Intellectual and Aesthetic Tenets*, p. 232, and Temperly, "Schubert and Beethoven's Eight-Six Chord," p. 152.
71 Hammerstein, "'Schöne Welt, wo bist du?'" p. 314.
72 Thomas, "Schillergedicht und Schubertlied," p. 36.
73 Raab, "Arten von Zusammenhang," p. 88.
74 Gramit, *The Intellectual and Aesthetic Tenets*, p. 232.
75 Ibid.
76 Hammerstein, "'Schöne Welt, wo bist du?,'" p. 314.
77 Ibid., p. 318.

2: Goethe, Wolf, and the lure of immortality

1 Russell, *The Themes of the German Lied*, pp. 321–25.
2 Brahms used Hölderlin's poem "Hyperions Schicksalslied" as the text for his *Schicksalslied* for chorus and orchestra, Op. 54 (1871). Nineteenth-century Lied settings of Hölderlin's poetry include Theodor Fröhlich's "Rückkehr in die Heimat" (1830) and Peter Cornelius's "Sonnenuntergang" (1862).
3 The twentieth century saw an explosion of interest in Hölderlin's verse, reflected in approximately seventy-five song settings.
4 Wilhelm Müller, *Gedichte von Wilhelm Müller: Vollständige Kritische Ausgabe*, ed. James Taft Hatfield (Berlin: B. Behr, 1906; Nedeln/Liechtenstein: Kraus Reprint, 1968), pp. 183–234. For documentary evidence of Müller's sympathy for the Greeks, see *Diary and Letters of Wilhelm Müller*, pp. 98–99.
5 Russell, *The Themes of the German Lied*, pp. 316–17.
6 See, for example, Kerner's "Die Äolsharfe in der Ruine"; Uhland's "Distichen"; Grillparzer's "Campo vaccino"; Heine's "Frühlingsfeier,"; Mörike's "Antike Poesie," "An eine Äolsharfe," and "Erinna an Sappho"; Nietzsche's "Dionysos-Dithyramben" and "Klage der Ariadne"; Dehmel's "Venus mater"; Schmidt's "Sapphische Ode"; and Bodmann's "Gesang der Apollopriesterin."
7 Georg Friedrich Daumer, *Polydora, ein weltpoetisches Liederbuch*, vol. 1 (Frankfurt am Main: Literarische Anstalt, 1855), pp. V–VI, XI.

8 E.g., Ludwig Heinrich Christoph Hölty, Johann Wolfgang von Goethe, Johann Heinrich Voß, Friedrich von Matthisson, Friedrich Hölderlin, Karl August Graf von Platen-Hallermünde, Nikolaus Lenau, Emanuel August Geibel, Heinrich Leuthold, and Hans Schmidt. Differences between German and Greek made direct imitation impossible, as Susan Youens discusses in "Elegies Within Elegies: 'Anakreons Grab' from the *Goethe-Lieder* of Hugo Wolf," *Journal of Research in Singing and Applied Vocal Pedagogy* 10/2 (June 1987): 36–37.

9 The classical meters and forms in these songs are associated with ancient Greek poets Asklepiades, Pherekrates, Glykon, and Sappho. Brahms's interest in the classical world is manifest in his travels to Italy and Sicily, fascination with ancient art and sculpture, purchase of numerous Latin and Greek writings (in translation) for his personal library, and decision in 1860 to learn Latin, which enabled him to read odes by Horace. He produced three large choral works on classical themes – *Schicksalslied*, Op. 54 (Hölderlin, 1871), *Nänie*, Op. 82 (Schiller, 1881), and *Gesang der Parzen*, Op. 89 (Goethe, 1883).

10 "An Aphrodite" (1835; Op. 9, ix, 4; Sappho, translated by Carl von Blankensee) and "An die Grille" (1835; Op. 9, ix, 5; Anacreon, translated by Carl von Blankensee).

11 Russell, *The Themes of the German Lied*, p. 324.

12 Ibid.

13 Ibid.

14 Wolf valued his classical Lieder, placing "Prometheus," "Ganymed," and "Grenzen der Menschheit" together prominently at the conclusion of his Goethe songbook. Relevant studies of Wolf's Lieder include: Lawrence Kramer, "Decadence and Desire: The Wilhelm Meister Songs of Wolf and Schubert," *Nineteenth-Century Music* 10 (1987): 229–42; Kramer, "Hugo Wolf: Subjectivity in the Fin-de-Siècle Lied," in *German Lieder in the Nineteenth Century*, ed. Rufus Hallmark (New York: Schirmer Books, 1996), pp. 186–217; Amanda Glauert, *Hugo Wolf and the Wagnerian Inheritance* (Cambridge University Press, 1999); Susan Youens, *Hugo Wolf and his Mörike Songs* (Cambridge University Press, 2000); Youens, *Hugo Wolf: The Vocal Music* (Princeton University Press, 1992); Youens, "Tradition and Innovation: The Lieder of Hugo Wolf," in *The Cambridge Companion to the Lied*, ed. James Parsons (Cambridge University Press, 2004), pp. 204–22.

15 The passage appears in a review, dated 23 November 1884, of a performance by the Vienna Court Opera of Gluck's *Iphigénie en Tauride*. *The Music Criticism of Hugo Wolf*, trans. and ed. Henry Pleasants (New York: Holmes and Meier, 1979), p. 82.

16 Ibid., p. 155.

17 As cited in Glauert, *Hugo Wolf and the Wagnerian Inheritance*, p. 13.

18 Hans von Wolzogen, *Bayreuther Blätter* 13 (1890). See the press notice for Wolf's Goethe songs at the end of the June issue. As cited in Glauert, *Hugo Wolf and the Wagnerian Inheritance*, p. 14.

19 Years later, Nietzsche published harsh criticisms of his earlier work. See his "Attempt at a Self-Criticism" which prefaces the 1886 edition.
20 Friedrich Nietzsche, *The Birth of Tragedy and The Case of Wagner*, trans. Walter Kaufmann (New York: Vintage Books, 1967), p. 123.
21 Glauert, *Hugo Wolf and the Wagnerian Inheritance*, p. 16.
22 Ibid., p. 79.
23 Ibid.
24 Eduard Hanslick: *Fünf Jahre Musik [1891–1895] (Der "Modernen Oper" VII. Teil.)* (Berlin: Allgemeiner Verein für Deutsche Litteratur, 1896), p. 271. Wolf had previously immersed himself in the poetry of Heine, Eichendorff, and Mörike.
25 Nietzsche, *The Birth of Tragedy and The Case of Wagner*, p. 164.
26 Ibid., pp. 181–85.
27 Friedrich Eckstein, *Alte unnennbare Tage: Erinnerungen aus siebzig Lehr- und Wanderjahren* (Vienna, Herbert Reichner Verlag, 1936), p. 195.
28 Nietzsche, *The Birth of Tragedy and The Case of Wagner*, pp. 161–62.
29 Ibid., p. 160.
30 Christopher Hatch, "Some Things Borrowed: Hugo Wolf's *Anakreons Grab*," *The Journal of Musicology* 17 (Summer 1999), 420.
31 Wolf composed "Anakreons Grab" in Vienna on 4 November 1888.
32 Frank Walker, *Hugo Wolf: A Biography* (Princeton University Press, 1968), pp. 213–14. The public concert took place in the Bösendorfersaal on 15 December 1888. The singer was Ferdinand Jäger, the pianist Wolf himself. The program also included Wolf's Mörike settings "Fussreise," "Der Jäger," "Peregrina I," and "Der Tambour"; the Goethe setting "Der Rattenfänger"; the Eichendorff settings "Der Soldat I" and "Seemanns Abschied"; and the Reinick setting "Gesellenlied," as well as Beethoven's *Piano Sonatas*, Opp. 53 and 106, and the *Variations*, Op. 35.
33 Hugo Wolf, *Letters to Melanie Köchert*, ed. Franz Grasberger, trans. Louise McClelland Urban (New York: Schirmer Books, 1991), p. 211.
34 Hatch, "Some Things Borrowed," p. 420.
35 Glauert, *Hugo Wolf and the Wagnerian Inheritance*.
36 Wolf orchestrated "Anakreons Grab" in 1890, and then again (after the first version had been lost) in 1893.
37 Wolf, *Letters to Melanie Köchert*, p. 88. Letter of 8 January 1894.
38 Ibid., p. 91. Letter of 9 January 1894.
39 As quoted in Walker, *Hugo Wolf*, p. 333.
40 Walker, *Hugo Wolf*, pp. 186–87.
41 Susan Youens, "The Song Sketches of Hugo Wolf," *Current Musicology* 44 (1990), 9.
42 As quoted in Walker, *Hugo Wolf*, p. 225.
43 Rosen, *The Romantic Generation*, p. 124. Hatch refers to this passage of Rosen's on p. 423 (note 8) of his article "Some Things Borrowed."

44 Both Anacreon's poetry and the *Anacreontea* appear in: *Greek Lyric,* trans. David A. Campbell, vol. 2: *Anacreon, Anacreontea, Choral Lyric from Olympus to Alcman* (Cambridge, MA: Harvard University Press, 1988).
45 Patricia A. Rosenmeyer, *The Poetics of Imitation: Anacreon and the Anacreontic Tradition* (Cambridge University Press, 1992), p. 2.
46 *Greek Lyric,* pp. 79–80.
47 Ibid., pp. 169–70.
48 Ibid., pp. 211–12.
49 Ibid., p. 213.
50 Rosenmeyer, *The Poetics of Imitation,* pp. 1–3.
51 Ibid., pp. 1–6.
52 Trevelyan, *Goethe and the Greeks,* p. 10.
53 See Johann Wolfgang von Goethe, *Gedichte,* ed. Erich Trunz, vol. 2 (Hamburg: Fischer, 1964), pp. 14–24, 171–78.
54 Trevelyan, *Goethe and the Greeks,* p. 53.
55 Ibid., p. 69.
56 On the function, structural traits, and literary evolution of ancient epigrams, see Peter Jay, ed., *The Greek Anthology and Other Ancient Greek Epigrams* (New York: Oxford University Press, 1973), pp. 10–13.
57 Trevelyan, *Goethe and the Greeks,* p. 118.
58 Goethe did, however, substitute light and heavy stresses for the short and long syllables of ancient Greek poetry.
59 Goethe may also have been familiar with Klopstock's German epigrams in antique meters (written beginning in 1774).
60 See Ernst Beutler, "Die Renaissance der Anthologie in Weimar," in *Das Epigramm: Zur Geschichte einer Inschriftlichen und Literarischen Gattung,* ed. Gerhard Pfohl (Darmstadt: Wissenschaftliche Buchgesellschaft, 1969), pp. 352–415.
61 Goethe's earliest epigram in elegiac metre ("Versuchung") dates from 1 June 1781.
62 See Goethe's letter (no. 782) addressed to Herder and dated "Ende November 1784." Johann Wolfgang von Goethe, *Briefe der Jahre 1764–1786,* ed. Ernst Beutler (Zürich: Artemis Verlag, 1951), p. 818.
63 Trevelyan, *Goethe and the Greeks,* pp. 115–16.
64 Goethe's epigrams differed from earlier eighteenth-century epigrams not only in borrowing antique forms but also in projecting an elegiac rather than witty tone. As Johann Wolfgang von Goethe, *Gedichte,* ed. Erich Trunz, vol. 1 (Munich: C. H. Beck, 1981), p. 620.
65 Goethe, *Gedichte,* ed. Trunz, vol. 1, p. 620.
66 On Goethe's changes and additions to the ancient epigrammatic models, see Beutler, "Die Renaissance der Antholgie in Weimar," p. 388.
67 Sepulchral Epigram No. 23, by Antipater of Sidon, in *The Greek Anthology,* trans. W. R. Paton, vol. 2 (London: William Heinemann; New York: G. P. Putnam's Sons, 1917), p. 17. The German version is Epigram No. 19 in Book 1 of Herder's *Blumen*

aus der griechischen Anthologie gesammlet. Herders Sämtliche Werke, ed. Redlich, vol. 26, p. 15.

68 Sepulchral Epigram No. 24, by Simonides (?), in *The Greek Anthology*, trans. Paton, vol. 2, p. 17. The German version is Epigram No. 11 in Book 3 of Herder's *Blumen aus der griechischen Anthologie gesammlet. Herders Sämtliche Werke*, ed. Redlich, vol. 26, p. 31.

69 Sepulchral Epigram No. 31, by Dioscorides, in *The Greek Anthology*, trans. Paton, vol. 2, p. 21. The German version is Epigram No. 20 in Book 5 of Herder's *Blumen aus der griechischen Anthologie gesammlet. Herders Sämtliche Werke*, ed. Redlich, vol. 26, p. 51.

70 Goethe may also have known other "Anakreons Grab" epigrams in the full *Greek Anthology*.

71 Erwin Panofsky, "*Et in Arcadia Ego*: Poussin and the Elegiac Tradition," in *Meaning in the Visual Arts* (The University of Chicago Press, 1955, Phoenix ed. 1982), p. 313.

72 Ibid., p. 313.

73 On eighteenth-century usage of the expression, see Georg Büchmann, *Geflügelte Worte: Der Zitatenschatz des deutschen Volkes* (Berlin: Verlag der Haude and Spenerschen Buchhandlung, 1926), pp. 441–42.

74 Although "Anakreons Grab" appears as the twenty-ninth of the fifty-one settings in Wolf's Goethe songbook, it was actually the sixth of these settings by date of composition. The first five Goethe settings that Wolf composed during this period include: "Harfenspieler I" (27 October 1888), "Harfenspieler II" (29 October), "Harfenspieler III" (30 October), "Philine" (30 October), and "Spottlied" (2 November). "Der Schäfer" was composed on the same day as "Anakreons Grab." Wolf had composed several previous solo song settings of Goethe texts (both published and unpublished) during the 1870s and 80s.

75 Of the five Goethe settings that preceded "Anakreons Grab," four have texts previously set by other composers, and these settings may have inspired Wolf. As is well known, Wolf generally set poems others had set only if he found the earlier songs deficient. "Spottlied" (written two days before "Anakreons Grab"), "Anakreons Grab," and "Der Schäfer" (written the same day as "Anakreons Grab") had not previously been set.

76 Hatch, "Some Things Borrowed," pp. 426–37.

77 Youens, "The Song Sketches of Hugo Wolf."

78 Between February and April 1821, Schubert composed Lieder with texts exclusively by Goethe. (Or so Schubert thought. The texts of the two "Suleika" songs were actually written by Marianne von Willemer, with whom Goethe had a short and intense tryst, but were published in Goethe's *West-östlicher Divan* of 1819.) The autograph manuscript of Schubert's setting of "Grenzen der Menschheit" is dated March 1821. The song was published in January 1832 in book 14 of the Schubert *Nachlass*.

79 In 1864, Josef von Spaun defended Schubert's setting of "Grenzen der Menschheit." Deutsch, ed., *Schubert: Memoirs of his Friends*, p. 365.
80 Translation borrowed from Wigmore, *Schubert: The Complete Song Texts*, pp. 223–24.
81 The poems were not all written at the same time: "Prometheus" and "Ganymed" both date from 1774, "Das Göttliche" from 1783.
82 Job 36:32; 37:3 and 16:12. Byrne, *Schubert's Goethe Settings*, pp. 131, 481.
83 The following discussion thus departs from the argument of Carl Conway Moman, Jr. (*A Study of the Musical Settings by Franz Schubert and Hugo Wolf for Goethe's "Prometheus," "Ganymed," and "Grenzen der Menschheit"* [Ph.D. diss., Washington University, 1980]), p. 108), who claims that Schubert and Wolf set the text similarly.
84 John Reed claims the song is almost unrealizable in performance. Reed, *The Schubert Song Companion*, pp. 249–50.
85 Youens notes that Wolf would have "associated enchained, broken-chordal augmented triads with the first movement of Liszt's Faust Symphony." Youens, "Tradition and Innovation," p. 214. On augmented triads as a motif in Wolf's music, see Eric Sams, *The Songs of Hugo Wolf* (Bloomington: Indiana University Press, 1992), p. 30.
86 This interpretation assumes that Goethe intended the word "sich" rather than "sie" in line 40 of the poem. Goethe's manuscript has "sie," but the first printing of the poem (in the *Schriften* of 1789) and all subsequent printings substitute "sich." Both Schubert and Wolf employ "sich," which imparts to the "Geschlechter" (rather than the gods) a more active role in attaining immortality through their endless chain. See commentary by Erich Trunz in Goethe, *Gedichte*, ed. Trunz, vol. 1, pp. 558–59.
87 "Ganymed" was published by Diabelli in June 1825 as Op. 19, no. 3; Schubert dedicated the setting (without permission) to Goethe. "Grenzen der Menschheit" was published in January 1832 in Book 14 of the *Nachlass*. "Prometheus" was published in early 1850 in Book 47 of the *Nachlass*. Both "Grenzen der Menschheit" and "Prometheus" were both written for bass voice.
88 In 1831, Anton Schindler wrote that "Grenzen der Menschheit" was one of numerous Schubert songs that enchanted Beethoven in his final days. Deutsch, ed., *Schubert: Memoirs by his Friends*, p. 307.
89 Franz von Hartmann notes a Schubertiade performance of "Grenzen der Menschheit" in his diary entry of 21 April 1827. He does not mention "Ganymed" or "Prometheus." Deutsch, ed. *The Schubert Reader*, p. 630. The Schubert documents contain no other references to performances of "Grenzen der Menschheit."
90 The only intervening setting was "Königlich Gebet," composed on January 7th.
91 Wolf's Goethe songbook was published by Lacom of Vienna in 1890.
92 Sams, *The Songs of Hugo Wolf*, p. 245.
93 Walker, *Hugo Wolf*, p. 252.
94 Ibid., p. 253.

95 Ibid.
96 Ibid., p. 254.
97 Kramer, "Hugo Wolf: Subjectivity in the Fin-de-Siècle Lied," pp. 200–01.
98 Youens, "Tradition and Innovation," p. 214.
99 Ibid., p. 216.

Part II: The lost world of childhood

1 Schiller is inconsistent on whether childhood exemplifies the naïve. In one passage of *On Näive and Sentimental Poetry* he writes, "Naïveté is a *childlikeness*, where it is no longer expected, and precisely for that reason it cannot be attributed to actual childhood in the strictest sense" (p. 184). Later, however, he notes, "the naïve manner of thinking can thus never be a property of a degenerate human being; it can only be an attribute of children and people with a childlike disposition" (p. 187).
2 The chronological association of antiquity and childhood engages what is commonly known as the "Law of Recapitulation." As Ellen Key writes in *The Century of the Child* (New York: Putnam, 1909), "The development of the child . . . answers in miniature to the development of mankind as a whole" (p. 222). The theory, aspects of which can be traced back to St. Augustine, found a strong proponent in the philosopher August Comte (1798–1857). See George Boas, *Essays on Primitivism and Related Ideas in the Middle Ages* (Baltimore: Johns Hopkins University Press, 1978, 1948) and Boas, *The Cult of Childhood* (London: The Warburg Institute, University of London, 1966), pp. 60–79.
3 Renewed interest in classical antiquity had, of course, also helped launch the Renaissance, perhaps making "rediscovered" a more appropriate term.
4 Philippe Ariès, *L'Enfant et la vie familiale sous l'ancien régime* (Paris: Plon, 1960), published in English as *Centuries of Childhood* (London: J. Cape, 1962). See also Lawrence Stone, *The Family, Sex and Marriage in England 1500–1800* (London: Weidenfeld and Nicholson, 1977).
5 Linda Pollock, *Forgotten Children: Parent–Child Relations from 1500 to 1900* (Cambridge University Press, 1983).
6 See, for example, Hugh Cunningham, *The Children of the Poor: Representations of Childhood since the Seventeenth Century* (Oxford, UK and Cambridge, MA: Blackwell, 1991), pp. 1–3, and James Christen Steward, *The New Child: British Art and the Origins of Modern Childhood, 1730–1830* (Berkeley: University Art Museum and Pacific Film Archive, University of California, Berkeley, 1995), pp. 81–83.
7 Louise Chawla, *In the First Country of Places: Nature, Poetry, and Childhood Memory* (Albany: State University of New York Press, 1994), p. 33.
8 Ibid., p. 38.
9 Ibid.
10 As quoted in Boas, *The Cult of Childhood*, pp. 42–43.

11 "Childe-hood," lines 35–36. *The Works of Henry Vaughan*, ed. L. C. Martin (Oxford: Clarendon Press, 1914), vol. 2. As quoted in Chawla, *In the First Country of Places*, p. 38.
12 As cited in Peter Coveney, *The Image of Childhood* (Baltimore, MD: Penguin Books, 1967), p. 44.
13 Jean-Jacques Rousseau, *Émile, Or Treatise on Education*, trans. William H. Payne (Amherst, NY: Prometheus Books, 2003), p. 1.
14 Coveney, *The Image of Childhood*, p. 42.
15 See Steward, *The New Child*.
16 Rousseau, *Émile*, pp. 43–44.
17 Numerous sources describe the emergence of idealized childhood during the late eighteenth and early nineteenth centuries. See, for example: Boas, *The Cult of Childhood*; Marilyn R. Brown, ed., *Picturing Children: Constructions of Childhood Between Rousseau and Freud* (Aldershot: Ashgate, 2002); Chawla, *In the First Country of Places*; Coveney, *The Image of Childhood*; Cunningham, *The Children of the Poor*; Hans-Heino Ewers, *Kindheit als poetische Daseinform: Studien zur Entstehung der romantischen Kindheitsutopie im 18. Jahrhundert* (Munich: Wilhelm Fink Verlag, 1989); Anne Higgonet, *Pictures of Innocence: The History and Crisis of Ideal Childhood* (London, Thames and Hudson Ltd., 1998); Annette Kreutziger-Herr, "Die Kindheit als Paradies: Musikalische Romantik und mythische Verklärung," *Neue Züricher Zeitung* (8–9 Feb.1997), 68; Kreutziger-Herr, "Nichts als Kinderkram?" *Hamburger Jahrbuch für Musikwissenschaft* 16 (1999), 209–35; Kreutziger-Herr, "Zwischen Idealisierung und Entzauberung: Kindheitsbilder in der Musik des 19. und 20. Jahrhunderts," in *Jung und wild: zur kulturellen Konstruktion von Kindheit und Jugend* (Berlin: D. Reimer, 1996), pp. 90–115; Judith Plotz, *Romanticism and the Vocation of Childhood* (New York: Palgrave, 2001).
18 E.g., Jean Paul, Hölderlin, Novalis, Brentano, Eichendorff, Hoffmann, the Grimm brothers, Tieck, Schopenhauer, Uhland, Kleist, Mörike, Tieck, Varnhagen, Chamisso, Wordsworth, Blake, Coleridge, Lamb, Southey, Dickens, Eliot, Anderson, Swinburne, Hugo, Emerson, Whitman, and Dickinson.
19 Schiller, *On Naïve and Sentimental Poetry*, p. 182.
20 Coveney, *The Image of Childhood*, p. 55.
21 Schopenhauer, "Vom Genie," in *Die Welt als Wille und Vorstellung*.
22 Schiller, *On Naïve and Sentimental Poetry*, pp. 180–81.
23 E.g., Mark 10: 14–15: "Suffer the little children to come unto me, and forbid them not: for of such is the kingdom of God. / Verily I say unto you, Whosoever shall not receive the kingdom of God as a little child, he shall not enter therein." The opposite lesson is suggested by I Corinthians (13: 11), where St. Paul famously states: "When I was a child, I spake as a child, I understood as a child, I thought as a child: but when I became a man, I put away childish things."
24 Gotter, "Elegie bei einer Wiege"; Eichendorff, "Bin ich denn nicht auch ein Kind gewesen?"; Groth, "O wüßt ich doch den Weg zurück"; Novalis, "Wie selig war

die Zeit der Knabenspiele"; Heine, "Mein Kind, wir waren Kinder"; Rückert, "Aus der Jugendzeit"; Hoffmann von Fallersleben, "So singe wieder, immer wieder."
25 See Cunningham, *The Children of the Poor*.
26 Ibid., pp. 151–52.
27 Coveney, *The Image of Childhood*, pp. 291–92.
28 Ibid., pp. 301.

3: Sleep and death in Schubert's lullabies

1 Sengle, *Biedermeierzeit*, vol. 1, pp. 61–3 ("Lob des Hauses"). Sengle discusses Biedermeier reverence for the family, as well as the perceived holiness of mother and child, on pp. 20–25, and 59–60.
2 Bonnie S. Anderson and Judith P. Zinsser, *A History of Their Own: Women in Europe from Prehistory to the Present*, vol. 2 (New York: Harper and Row, 1988), pp. 129–32.
3 According to Sengle, Karl Immermann, an observer of his own Biedermeier era, regarded the family as "ein 'Himmelreich' auf Erden." Sengle, *Biedermeierzeit*, vol. 1, p. 20.
4 Leon Botstein, "Realism Transformed: Franz Schubert and Vienna," in *The Cambridge Companion to Schubert*, ed. Christopher Gibbs (Cambridge University Press, 1997), pp. 31–33; Lorrraine Gorrell, *The Nineteenth-Century German Lied* (Portland: Amadeus Press, 1993), pp. 58–62, 169–73; Alice M. Hanson, *Musical Life in Biedermeier Vienna* (Cambridge University Press, 1985), pp. 117–26.
5 Leon Botstein discusses the intimacy of Biedermeier domestic music-making in connection with courtship and friendship. Botstein, "Realism Transformed," p. 32.
6 Two insightful studies of *Wiegenlieder* are Thomas Freitag's *Kinderlied – Von der Vielfalt einer musikalischen Liedgattung* (Frankfurt am Main: Peter Lang, 2001), pp. 139–61, and Emily Gerstner-Hirzel's *Das volkstümliche deutsche Wiegenlied: Versuch einer Typologie der Texte* (Schweizerische Gesellschaft für Volkskunde) (Basel: G. Krebs, 1984). On infancy as a lost paradise (including the views of Sigmund Freud and Carl Jung), see Heinberg, *Memories and Visions of Paradise*, pp. 193–95, and Jacoby, *Longing for Paradise*, pp. 25–35.
7 Franz Magnus Böhme includes 130 German folk lullabies in his encyclopedic collection *Deutsches Kinderlied und Kinderspiel: Volksüberlieferungen aus allen Landen deutscher Zunge* (Leipzig: Breitkopf and Härtel, 1897), pp. 1–38.
8 C. F. J. Girschner, "Über Wiegen- und Spinnerlieder," *Berliner Allgemeine musikalische Zeitung* 2 (1828), 16. The writer is presumably Karl Friedrich J. Girschner (born in Spandau in 1794), a piano pedagogue in Berlin.
9 The text of "Eia popeia" appears in Achim von Arnim and Clemens Brentano's folk song collection *Des knaben Wunderhorn*. Carl Maria von Weber's setting of "Eia popeia" (1810) appears under the title "Walte Gott Vater" in Böhme, *Deutsches Kinderlied und Kinderspiel*, p. 22.

10 Johann Stephan Schütze, "Über Wiegenlieder,"*Caecilia* (1825), 269–71.
11 E.g., Herder, Gleim, Campe, Jacobi, Claudius, Goethe, Schiller, Tieck, von Arnim, Brentano, Mayrhofer, Ottenwalt, Körner, Leitner, Müller, Seidl, Eichendorff, Lenau, Hoffmann von Fallersleben, Rückert, and Reinick. See Dieter Richter, ed., *Kindheit im Gedicht: Deutsche Verse aus acht Jahrhunderten*, (Frankfurt am Main: Fischer, 1992); Walter Flemmer, ed., *Bin ich denn nicht auch ein Kind gewesen?: Deutsche Gedichte über Kinder* (Munich: Piper, 1986). Hoffmann von Fallersleben devotes an entire section of his poetry collection (*Gedichte* [Leipzig: Brocknaus, 1834]) to *Wiegenlieder*. On the prevalence of Biedermeier *Wiegenlieder*, see Sengle, *Biedermeierzeit*, vol. 2, pp. 523–24.
12 On the rise of interest in folk song during the late eighteenth century, see Russell, *The Themes of the German Lied*, pp. 23–50; Arnold Feil, *Franz Schubert: Die schöne Müllerin, Winterreise*, trans. Ann C. Sherwin (Portland: Amadeus, 1988), pp. 11–14. On the publication of music in domestic periodicals, see Bonny H. Miller, "A Mirror of Ages Past: The Publication of Music in Domestic Periodicals," *NOTES: Quarterly Journal of the Music Library Association* 50/3 (March 1994), 883–901.
13 Matthew Head, "'If the Pretty Little Hand Won't Stretch': Music for the Fair Sex in Eighteenth-Century Germany," *Journal of the American Musicological Society* 52/2 (Summer 1999), 235–44. See also Susan Youens, *Schubert's Late Lieder: Beyond the Song Cycles* (Cambridge University Press, 2002), pp. 249–52.
14 On Reichardt's lullaby collection, see Head, "'If the Pretty Little Hand Won't Stretch,'" pp. 235–44; Youens, *Schubert's Late Lieder*, pp. 252–57; Freitag, *Kinderlied*, pp. 139–40, 153–54.
15 Johann Friedrich Reichardt, *Wiegenlieder für gute deutsche Mütter* (Leipzig: Gerhard Fleischer der Jüngere, 1799), preface, p. i. For Rousseau's influence on Reichardt, see Head, "'If the Pretty Little Hand Won't Stretch,'" pp. 237–39.
16 Ibid., preface, pp. iii–iv.
17 Ibid., preface, p. iv.
18 Head, "'If the Pretty Little Hand Won't Stretch,'" pp. 237–39.
19 On the relation of eighteenth-century *Affektenlehre* and song composition, see Smeed, *German Song and Its Poetry*, pp. 7–10.
20 Gerstner-Hirzel, *Das volkstümliche deutsche Wiegenlied*, p. 10.
21 Ibid., p. 18.
22 Ibid., pp. 9–46.
23 Freitag, *Kinderlied*, p. 148. Gerstner-Hirzel, *Das volkstümliche deutsche Wiegenlied*, p. 10.
24 A small selection of folk lullabies appears in Ludwig Erk's and Franz Magnus Böhme's *Deutscher Liederhort: Auswahl der vorzüglicheren Deutschen Volkslieder nach Wort und Weise aus der Vorzeit und Gegenwart* (Leipzig: Breitkopf und Härtel, 1894), vol. 3, pp. 579–82. Folk-like lullabies are included in Franz Magnus Böhme's *Volksthümliche Lieder der Deutschen im 18. und 19. Jahrhundert* (Lepizig: Brietkopf and Härtel, 1895; Hildesheim and New York: Georg Olms; Wiesbaden:

Brietkopf and Härtel, 1970), pp. 464–67. See also Friedländer, *Das deutsche Lied im 18. Jahrhundert.*

25 See Gerstner-Hirzel, *Das volkstümliche deutsche Wiegenlied*, pp. 10–18.

26 On the occasional introduction of menacing, sorrowful, frightening, even sadistic elements into the lullaby, see Gerstner-Hirzel, *Das volkstümliche deutsche Wiegenlied*, pp. 18–27.

27 Reichardt, *Wiegenlieder für gute deutsche Mütter*, preface, pp. i–ii.

28 Reichardt notes these possibilities in his preface. *Wiegenlieder für gute deutsche Mütter*, preface, pp. v–vi.

29 Head, "'If the Pretty Little Hand Won't Stretch,'" p. 237. Head provides a complete listing of the songs, along with their first lines, authors, meters, keys, and forms, on p. 236.

30 Ibid. Head discusses the diverse poetic content of Reichardt's *Wiegenlieder* on pp. 235–37.

31 Art song lullabies were written by Schubert, Weber, Mendelssohn, Schumann, Mussorgsky, and Brahms, among others. Composers of piano lullabies include, most notably, Schumann, Mendelssohn, Chopin, Liszt, Balakirev, Grieg, Brahms, and Debussy. There are also lullabies for piano duet, chamber ensemble, orchestra, and other performing forces. For a list of vocal and instrumental lullabies, see Herbert Schneider, "Berceuse," *Die Musik in Geschichte und Gegenwart*, vol. 1 (Kassel: Bärenreiter, 1994), pp. 1398–1402.

32 See, for example, Walter Frisch, "Schubert's *Nähe des Geliebten* (D. 162): Transformation of the *Volkston*," in *Schubert: Critical and Analytical Studies*, ed. Walter Frisch (Lincoln: University of Nebraska Press, 1st pbk. ed. 1996), pp. 174–99; Heinrich W. Schwab, *Sangbarkeit, Popularität und Kunstlied: Studien zu Lied und Liedästhetik der mittleren Goethezeit 1770–1814* (Regensburg: Gustav Bosee Verlag, 1965); Walter Wiora, *Das deutsche Lied: Zur Geschichte und Ästhetik einer musikalischen Gattung* (Wolfenbüttel and Zürich: Karl Heinrich Möseler Verlag, 1971).

33 Matthew Head links Reichardt's lullabies to "masculine psychological needs." Head, "'If the Pretty Little Hand Won't Stretch,'" p. 243.

34 Böhme, ed., *Volksthümliche Lieder der Deutschen im 18. und 19. Jahrhundert*, p. 467.

35 Schubert's *Wiegenlieder* published during his lifetime are "Schlummerlied" ("Schlaflied"), Op. 24, no. 2 (pub. 27 Oct. 1823, Sauer and Leidesdorf), and "Des Baches Wiegenlied," Op. 25, no. 20 (pub. Feb.–Aug. 1824, Sauer and Leidesdorf). "Wiegenlied," Op. 105, no. 2 (pub. 21 Nov. 1828, Czerny) and "Vor meiner Wiege," Op. 106, no. 3 (pub. Spring 1828, Lithographic Institute, Vienna) were published shortly after Schubert's death and, according to John Reed, were probably proofread by him. Reed, *The Schubert Song Companion*, p. 504.

36 Some lullaby texts were composed by women, e.g., Luise Hensel's "Nächtliches Wiegenlied," Agnes Graf zu Stollberg's "Schlummre, Bübchen, schlummr' im

Schoß," Friederike Brun's "Schlaf, Kindlein, schlafe sanft und süß," and Anne Bothwell's old Scottish "Balow, my babe, ly stil and sleipe!"

37 Numerous poems on the subject of children and childhood – including remembered youth – were penned by nineteenth-century male writers. See Richter, ed., *Kindheit im Gedicht: Deutsche Verse aus acht Jahrhunderten.*

38 Of course, many Schubert Lieder besides lullabies draw an association between sleep and death, e.g., "Totenkranz für ein Kind," D. 275, "Grablied für die Mutter," D. 616, "Nachtstück," D. 672, "Nachthymne," D. 687, "Todtengräberweise," D. 869, "Das Marienbild," D. 623, "Ellens Gesang I," D. 837, and "Ellens Gesang II," D. 838.

39 Botstein, "Realism Transformed," pp. 26–31.

40 Ibid., p. 28.

41 Almost every poetry collection of the Biedermeier age contained poetic laments on the death of children. Sengle, *Biedermeierzeit*, vol. 2, p. 522–23. A selection of poems on the death of children appears in *Kindheit im Gedicht*, ed. Richter, pp. 155–216.

42 No members of Schubert's immediate circle of friends died during the 1810s or 20s, but the members did suffer from the deaths of several relatives and acquaintances.

43 Graham Johnson, "Death and the Composer." Liner notes to *The Hyperion Schubert Edition* vol. 11 CDJ33011 (1991), p. 81.

44 See Karl Michael Komma, "'Gib mir deine Hand': zu Franz Schuberts Musik vom Tode," *International Journal of Musicology* 3 (1994), 133–49; Johnson, "Death and the Composer," pp. 3–9. As Johnson discusses, Schubert's preoccupation with death seems to have been most intense shortly after he contracted syphilis. Two years later, he apparently had come to terms with it. Johnson, "Death and the Composer," p. 8.

45 Homer describes Sleep (Hypnos) and Death (Thanatos) as twins in Book 16 of the *Iliad*. In the *Theogony* (211–12 and 756), Hesiod says that the goddess Night gave birth in a single generation to the gods Fate, Doom, Dreams, Sleep, and Death. The sleep-death topos also appears in Virgil's *Aeneid* (6, 278) and other ancient writings. For additional background on the sleep-death topos, as well as its manifestation in Wagner's *Ring* cycle, see Jeffrey L. Buller, "Sleep in the *Ring*," *The Opera Quarterly* 12/2 (Winter 1995/95), 3–22.

46 Christoph Wolff, "Schubert's 'Der Tod und das Mädchen'": Analytical and Explanatory Notes on the Song D531 and the Quartet D810," in *Schubert Studies: Problems of Style and Chronology*, ed. Eva Badura-Skoda and Peter Branscombe (Cambridge University Press, 1982), p. 145.

47 As quoted in Hatfield, *Aesthetic Paganism in German Literature*, p. 28.

48 Ibid., p. 29.

49 *The Apology, Phaedo and Crito of Plato*, trans. Benjamin Jowett (New York: P. F. Collier and Son, 1937), pp. 8–9.

50 As quoted in Hatfield, *Aesthetic Paganism in German Literature*, pp. 28–29.

51 Translation borrowed from Friedrich Schiller, *The Poems and Ballads of Schiller*, trans. Sir Edward Bulwer Lytton (Edinburgh: Williams Blackwood and Sons, 1852), p. 278. These lines open the ninth stanza of the second version of the poem (fashioned from the fourteenth and fifteenth stanzas of the first version).
52 Hatfield, *Aesthetic Paganism in German Literature*, p. 30.
53 Translation borrowed from Novalis, *Hymns to the Night*, trans. Mabel Cotterell (London: Phoenix Press, 1948), p. 41.
54 Translation borrowed from Novalis, *Hymns to the Night*, trans. Cotterell, pp. 55–57.
55 Reed, *The Schubert Song Companion*, p. 438.
56 Claudius's lullabies appear in *Matthias Claudius Werke: Asums Omnia Sua Secum Portans oder Sämtliche Werke des Wandsbecker Boten* (Stuttgart: J. G. Cotta'sche Buchhandlung Nachfolger, 1966), pp. 44, 88–89, 91, 935–39, 950–51.
57 Sometimes male writers assumed the voice of a mother in their lullaby texts, as evidenced by the third and fourth songs in Reichardt's *Wiegenlieder für gute deutsche Mutter*.
58 Susan Youens, "Metamorphoses of a Melody: Schubert's 'Wiegenlied,' D. 498 in Twentieth-Century Opera," *The Opera Quarterly* 2/2 (Summer 1984), 39.
59 John Reed writes that in Schubert Lieder the key of A-flat major is "associated with secret happiness and private joy, and with a secure and reciprocated love," as well as with "faith in the power of Nature to revive and renew." Reed, *The Schubert Song Companion*, p. 492.
60 Youens, "Metamorphoses of a Melody," pp. 38–39.
61 "The simple 'Slumber Song' (Op. 24, No. 2), must for the sake of logic endure a few desperate modulations toward the middle." The author, possibly G. W. Fink, appeared in the Leipzig *Allgemeine musikalische Zeitung* on 24 Jun 1824. The review is of Schubert's songs Opp. 21, 22, 23, and 24, most of which the author criticizes as not being true songs. "Schlaflied" comes closer than some in his estimation. Deutsch, *The Schubert Reader*, p. 354.
62 Translation borrowed from Reed, *The Schubert Song Companion*, pp. 112–13.
63 The A' section sets a repetition of the last two lines of the second stanza.
64 For discussion of D. 304 in the context of Körner's life, see Youens, *Schubert's Poets*, pp. 140–41.
65 Ibid., p. 141.
66 Reed, *The Schubert Song Companion*, p. 438.
67 On the chorale's influence on Lieder, see Smeed, *German Song and Its Poetry*, pp. 33–37.
68 Youens, *Schubert's Poets*, p. 141.
69 Feil, *Franz Schubert: Die schöne Müllerin, Winterreise*, p. 83.
70 Thrasybulos G. Georgiades, *Schubert: Musik und Lyrik* (Göttingen: Vandenhoeck and Ruprecht, 1967), p. 318. See also Feil, *Franz Schubert: Die schöne Müllerin, Winterreise*, 83. Georgiades explores the relationship between "Des Baches Wiegenlied" and "Das Wandern" on pp. 305–18.

71 Youens, *Schubert: Die schöne Müllerin*, p. 111.
72 Feil claims that the line "du bist zu Haus" actually has a "*spoken* effect amid the flow of the singing." Feil, *Franz Schubert: Die schöne Müllerin, Winterreise*, p. 83.

4: Brahms's spiral journey back home

The discussion of Brahms's "Heimweh" Lieder in this chapter was published as "The Spiral Journey Back Home: Brahms's 'Heimweh' Lieder," *Journal of Musicology*, 22, no. 3 (July 2005): 454–89 © 2005 Regents of the University of California.

1 On piano works involving childhood, see especially Isabel Eicker, *Kinderstücke: An Kinder adressierte und über das Thema der Kindheit komponierte Alben in der Klavierliteratur des 19. Jahrhunderts* (Kassel: Gustav Bosse, 1995). See also Ian Sharp, *Classical Music's Evocation of the Myth of Childhood* (Lewiston, NY: The Edwin Mellon Press, 2000); Kreutziger-Herr, "Nichts als Kinderkram?"; Petra Weber-Bockholdt, "Kinder in der Musik des 19. Jh.: Schumann's *Kinderszenen*, Bizets *Jeux d'enfants* und Mussorgskijs *Detskaja*," in *Kunst-Gespräche: Musikalische Begegnungen zwischen Ost und West*, ed. Peter Andraschke and Edelgard Spaude (Freiburg im Breisgau: Rombach, 1998), pp. 425–40; Kreutziger-Herr, "Zwischen Idealisierung und Entzauberung: Kindheitsbilder in der Musik des 19. und 20. Jahrhunderts."
2 Kreutziger-Herr, "Nichts als Kinderkram?," p. 217.
3 On *Kinderlieder*, see Russell, *The Themes of the German Lied*, pp. 153–66; Freitag, *Kinderlied*; Katharina Schilling-Sandvoss, "Kinderlieder des 18. Jahrhunderts als Ausdruck der Vorstellungen vom Kindsein," in *Geschlechtsspezifische Aspekte des Musiklernens* (Essen: Blaue Eule, 1996), pp. 170–89; Edward F. Kravitt, "Innovation and the Kinderlied," in *The Lied: Mirror of Late Romanticism* (New Haven: Yale University Press, 1996), pp. 132–41; Emily Gerstner-Hirzel, "Das Kinderlied," in *Handbuch des Volksliedes*, vol 1: *Die Gattungen des Volksliedes*, ed Rolf Wilhelm Brednich, Lutz Röhrich, Wolfgang Suppan (Munich: Wilhelm Fink, 1973), pp. 923–67.
4 Appendix to volume III. The songs were not entirely authentic: Brentano rewrote some of the texts.
5 Böhme, ed., *Deutsches Kinderlied und Kinderspiel*, introduction, p. XVI.
6 The categories are not mutually exclusive. Songs composed for children, for example, might enter the oral tradition of *Volks-Kinderlieder*. The oral tradition also includes many songs about children and childhood.
7 According to Gerstner-Hirzel, *Kunst-Kinderlieder* first appeared in German-speaking lands during the sixteenth century. Gerstner-Hirzel, "Das Kinderlied," p. 937. Gerstner-Hirzel discusses the relation between *Kunst-Kinderlieder* and *Volks-Kinderlieder* on pp. 937–41.
8 See Schilling-Sandvoss, "Kinderlieder des 18. Jahrhunderts."
9 Christian Felix Weiße, *Lieder für Kinder*, 3rd edn (Leipzig: Weidmann, 1770).

10 For Burmann's *Kinderlied* collections, see the following note.
11 See, for example, Gottlob Wilhelm Burmann's *Gottlob Wilhelm Burmanns kleine Lieder für kleine Mädchen: Zur Bildung tugendhafter und edler Herzen* (1773), *Kleine Lieder für kleine Jünglinge: Text und Musick von Gottlob Wilhelm Burmann* (1777); Johann Adoph Scheibe's *Kleine Lieder für Kinder zur Beförderung der Tugend* (1766, 1768); Johann Adam Hiller's *Lieder für Kinder, vermehrte Auflage. Mit neuen Melodieen von Johann Adam Hiller* (1769) and *Sammlung der Lieder aus dem Kinderfreunde, die noch nicht componirt waren, mit neuen Melodien* (1782); Gottlob Gottwald Hunger's *Lieder für Kinder mit neuen Melodien von Gottlob Gottwald Hunger* (1772); Johann Friedrich Reichardt's *Lieder für Kinder aus Campes Kinderbibliothek mit Melodieen, bey dem Klavier zu singen* (1781, 1787, 1790), *Wiegenlieder für gute deutsche Mütter* (1798), and *Lieder für die Jugend.* (1799); Georg Carl Claudius's *Lieder für Kinder mit neuen sehr leichten Melodieen* (1780); Carl Spazier's *Einfache Clavierlieder* (1790); and Karl Gottlieb Horstig's *Kinder-Lieder und Melodien* (1798).
12 Schilling-Sandvoss, "Kinderlieder des 18. Jahrhunderts," pp. 177–79.
13 Reichardt, *Wiegenlieder für gute deutsche Mutter*, preface, pp. v–vi.
14 Opp. 37, 63, 75, 91, 135, 138, 154b, 196, 270, 285.
15 *Lieder für Kinder und Kinderfreunde am Clavier: Frühlingslieder* (Vienna: Ignaz Alberti, 1791). Mozart's "Sehnsucht nach dem Frühlinge," K.596, appears as song no. 1; "Im Frühlingsanfang," K 597, under the title "Dankesempfindung gegen den Schöpfer des Frühlings," as no. 14; and "Das Kinderspiel," K. 598, as no. 24. Three similarly titled Lied collections oriented to the summer, fall, and winter seasons were published in Vienna around the same time, but only the *Frühlingslieder* and *Winterlieder* collections are extant. See also *Deutsche Lieder für Jung und Alt* (Berlin: Realschulbuchhandlung, 1818), ed. Lisa Feurzeig (Middleton, WI: A-R editions, 2002).
16 Georges Starobinski, in "Brahms et la nostalgie de l'enfance: Volks-Kinderlieder, berceuses et Klaus-Groth-Lieder," *Acta Musicologica* 74/2 (2002), 141–94, cites as an example Christian Adolf Overbeck's collection *Fritzchens Lieder* of 1781 (p. 150). See also Freitag, *Kinderlied*, pp. 91–110.
17 There is no sharp distinction between the two categories. Schumann's "Mignon," a setting of Goethe's "Kennst du das Land" that appears as the last song in the progressively arranged *Lieder-Album für die Jugend*, Op. 79, for example, is as aesthetically rich and demanding as many art songs, appealing to adult performers and listeners. Peter Cornelius's six *Weihnachtslieder* express both child and adult perspectives on Christmas. Moreover, a *Kinderlied* presented in a concert hall by professional musicians can create the effect of art music.
18 Schilling-Sandvoss, "Kinderlieder des 18. Jahrhunderts," pp. 174–75.
19 On the lullaby as a special form of the *Kinderlied*, see Freitag, *Kinderlied*, pp. 139–61.
20 With some songs, such as Schubert's "Wiegenlied," D. 498, it is difficult to tell whether poetic reference to the child's "death" is to be understood literally or

metaphorically. In Zelter's "Auf den Tod eines Kindes," the speaker is actually a dead child who consoles its grieving mother. In Schumann's "Wiegenlied am Lager eines kranken Kindes" (Op. 78, no. 4, duet for soprano and tenor), lullaby verges on lament.

21 Russell, *The Themes of the German Lied*, p. 164.
22 The song appeared in Claudius's *Lieder für Kinder* of 1780.
23 Translation borrowed from Reed, *The Schubert Song Companion*, p. 319.
24 On Brahms's devotion to children, see Joseph Viktor Widmann, *Johannes Brahms in Erinnerung* (Basel: Amerbach-Verlag, 1947 [1898]), p. 25. Starobinki claims that Brahms's attraction to the subject of childhood in his song settings was partly fueled by his own lack of children (Starobinski, "Brahms et la nostalgie," p. 170).
25 Starobinski surveys Brahms's *Volks-Kinderlieder* and various berceuses, including Op. 49, no. 4 (Starobinski, "Brahms et la nostalgie," pp. 142–45, 155–69).
26 The first public performance of the song was by Luisa Dustmann-Meyer and Clara Schumann in Vienna in December 1869.
27 Starobinski, "Brahms et la nostalgie," p. 145.
28 "Nachklang," Op. 59, no. 4, might perhaps be included in this group, given its close textual and musical ties to "Regenlied," Op. 59, no. 3. "Nachklang," however, makes no mention of childhood, and is primarily concerned with the emotional present.
29 See, for example, Eric Sams, *The Songs of Johannes Brahms* (New Haven: Yale University Press, 2000), pp. 206–10; Annett Bruckmann, "'O wüßt ich doch den Weg zurück . . .': Ein Beitrag zum Brahmsschen Liedschaffen," *Jahresgabe – Klaus Groth-Gesellschaft* 34 (1992), 15–35; Gerd Sannemüller, "Die Lieder von Johannes Brahms auf Gedichte von Klaus Groth," *Jahresgabe – Klaus-Groth-Gesellschaft* 16 (1972), 29–30; and Max Friedländer, *Brahms's Lieder: An Introduction to the Songs for One and Two Voices* (London: Oxford University Press, 1928), pp. 111–13.
30 The widespread preference for the second song was foreshadowed by the early reaction of Brahms's friend Theodore Billroth. See *Billroth und Brahms im Briefwechsel*, ed. C. A. T. Gottlieb-Billroth (Berlin: Urban and Schwarzenberg, 1935), p. 212. According to Max Kalbeck, the popularity of the second song was largely responsible for the tendency to disregard the unity of the trilogy (*Johannes Brahms*, 4 vols. [Berlin: Deutsche Brahms Gesellschaft, 1904–15] 3: 39).
31 Some writers assert that the nine songs of Op. 63 together constitute a cycle. See, for example, Timothy L. Jackson's discussion in *The Compleat Brahms: A Guide to the Musical Works of Johannes Brahms*, ed. Leon Botstein (New York: Norton, 1999), p. 251. In "Brahms et la nostalgie," Starobinski discusses tonal connections among the last five songs of Op. 63. Both Starobinski and Kalbeck touch on the unity of the three "Heimweh" Lieder.
32 Exactly when Brahms composed "Heimweh I," Op. 63, no. 7, and "Heimweh III," Op. 63, no. 9, is uncertain, although Margit McCorkle notes that the latter

may have been written by December 1873. "Heimweh II," Op. 63, no. 8, dates from the summer of 1874. Margit McCorkle, *Johannes Brahms: Thematisch-Bibliographisches Werkverzeichnis* (Munich: Henle, 1984), p. 269. Brahms mentioned the three songs in a letter (to the poet Klaus Groth) of September 1874.

33 On musical expressions of the pastoral fantasy, see Thomas Keith Nelson, *The Fantasy of Absolute Music* (Ph.D. diss., University of Minnesota, 1998).

34 Virginia Hancock identifies all nine of Brahms's Op. 63 Lieder as "lyric songs, or *Kunstlieder*" rather than either "folklike songs" or "hybrid songs" ("songs with folk or folklike texts set in a manner more characteristic of art songs while retaining *volkstümlich* qualities"). Virginia Hancock, "Johannes Brahms: Volkslied/Kunstlied," in *German Lieder in the Nineteenth Century*, ed. Rufus Hallmark (New York: Schirmer, 1996), pp. 123–24. One could describe the three "Heimweh" songs as *Kunstlieder* that employ *Kindheit* and *Volkstümlichkeit* as topics. Heather Platt discusses Brahms's attraction to folk song in "Hugo Wolf and the Reception of Brahms's Lieder," in *Brahms Studies*, vol. 2 (Lincoln: University of Nebraska Press, 1998), pp. 91–111.

35 Starobinski, "Brahms et la nostalgie," pp. 145–47.

36 According to John Daverio, "One can often detect 'minicycles' of songs on texts by the same poet embedded within what appear to be heterogeneously grouped lieder. It was Brahms's practice to begin with clusters such as these, which were only later assembled into larger 'bouquets' just prior to publication." John Daverio, "The Song Cycle: Journeys Through a Romantic Landscape," in *German Lieder in the Nineteenth Century*, ed. Rufus Hallmark (New York: Schirmer, 1996), p. 294.

37 Daverio writes, "Frequently the minicycles on a single author's work share not only poetic imagery but musical material as well" (Daverio, "The Song Cycle," p. 294).

38 Walter Frisch, "'You Must Remember This': Memory and Structure in Schubert's String Quartet in G Major, D. 887," *Musical Quarterly* 84 (2000), 582–602.

39 Among Brahms's songs that present death as a welcome refuge from life are "Herbstgefühl," Op. 48, no. 7; "Schwermut," Op. 58, no. 5; "Todessehnen," Op. 86, no. 6; "Der Tod, das ist die kühle Nacht," Op. 96, no. 1; and "Auf dem Kirchhofe," Op. 105, no. 4.

40 Daniel Beller-McKenna, "Brahms on Schopenhauer: The *Vier ernste Gesänge*, Op. 121, and Late Nineteenth-Century Pessimism," in *Brahms Studies*, vol. 1, ed. David Brodbeck (Lincoln: University of Nebraska Press, 1994), pp. 170–88.

41 Abrams, *Natural Supernaturalism*.

42 In discussing the generic multiplicity hailed by Friedrich Schlegel as a fundamental trait of modern romantic art, Daverio states, "[Brahms's] works afford us many examples of this 'quieter,' but no less instructive side of the Romantic imperative" (Daverio, *Nineteenth-Century Music and the German Romantic Ideology*, p. 138).

43 Klaus Groth (1819–99), the first German writer to produce a significant body of poetry in *Plattdeutsch*, or Low German, is generally regarded as the founder of north German *Mundartdichtung*. Brahms opted to set the poet's *Hochdeutsch* verse. He found the three "Heimweh" poems in Groth's collection *Hundert Blätter: Paralipomena zum Quickborn* (1854). The poems appear sequentially on pp. 44–45 of *Klaus Groth Sämtliche Werke* (Heide in Holstein: Boyens, 1981). Brahms, who owned a copy of Groth's *Hundert Blätter*, eventually set ten of Groth's poems. Brahms's solo songs with texts by Groth include "Regenlied," WoO 23 (composed by 1872); "Regenlied," Op. 59, no. 3 (1873); "Nachklang," Op. 59, no. 4 (1873); "Mein wundes Herz," Op. 59, no. 7 (1873); "Dein blaues Auge," Op. 59, no. 8 (1873); "Heimweh I," Op. 63, no. 7 (*c.* 1873); "Heimweh II," Op. 63, no. 8 (1874); "Heimweh III," Op. 63, no. 9 (*c.* 1873); "Komm bald," Op. 97, no. 5 (1885); "Wie Melodien," Op. 105, no. 1 (1886); and "Es hing der Reif," Op. 106, no. 3 (1888). WoO 23 and Op. 59, no. 4 use the same text.

44 Letter of September 1874. Avins, ed., *Johannes Brahms: Life and Letters*, pp. 469–70. For German original, see *Briefe der Freundschaft: Johannes Brahms – Klaus Groth*, ed. Volquart Pauls (Heide in Holstein: Westholsteinische Verlangsanstalt Boyens and Co., 1956), p. 83. Despite his dissatisfaction with the second song, Brahms must have taken pride in its composition, for he signed and dated the original manuscript, but not those of the other two "Heimweh" songs. Klaus Groth, in a letter to Brahms of 10 December 1874, wrote that upon first hearing both he and his wife particularly liked the second song, although he would reserve further judgment until he had studied them more carefully (Pauls, ed., *Briefe der Freundschaft*, pp. 86–87). No further mention of the songs appears in the published correspondence.

45 Letter of 27 September 1874. Avins, ed., *Johannes Brahms: Life and Letters*, p. 470. For German original, see Pauls, ed., *Briefe der Freundschaft*, pp. 83–84).

46 Brahms apparently delayed making a decision until at least late October 1874. On 23 October he wrote to his friend Billroth, "Zu den drei Grothschen Liedern hätte ich gern einen gemeinsamen Titel oder drei Überschriften. Fällt Dir etwas ein, so wüßte ich's gern gleich (sie sind im Stich)." That same day Billroth responded, "Es ist doch wohl bedenklich Gedichten Überschriften zu geben, wenn der Dichter es nicht selber getan; er wird wohl seine Gründe dazu gehabt haben; warum hast Du Dich nicht direct an ihn gewandt? Mir fällt nichts Gutes dazu ein. Am verzeihlichsten wäre es, den Titel aus den Gedichten selbst zu nahmen; da dachte ich etwa an 'Jugendglanz'; doch was der Dichter darunter in diesen Gedichten verstanden wissen will, ergibt sich eigentlich erst aus den Gedichten selbst. Ich dachte einen Moment an 'Selige Zeit'; doch das erinnert wieder an 'O se – elig, o se – elig, ein Kind noch zu sein!' Ich rate daher davon ab, oder den Titel durch den Dichter selbst bestimmen zu lassen" (Gottlieb-Billroth, ed., *Billroth und Brahms im Briefwechsel*, pp. 210–12). Brahms presented all nine Lieder of op. 63 (plus op. 64) to the publisher C. F. Peters of Leipzig on 5 October 1874.

47 The autograph manuscripts of the songs offer further evidence for the importance of their numerical sequence. The first and third songs appear together in an unsigned and undated manuscript (Cambridge, Fitzwilliam Museum), but in reverse order. On the top left corner of p. 1^r is written "(Groth N.3)" and on the top left corner of p. 2^r "(Groth N.1)." The second song appears in a signed and dated manuscript (New York, The Pierpont Morgan Library, The Mary Flagler Cary Music Collection). On top middle of p. 1^r is written "Claus Groth" [in blue:] (N2). Although Brahms may have composed "Heimweh III" before the other two songs, he clearly attached significance to their ultimate order (McCorkle, *Johannes Brahms: Thematisch-Bibliographisches Werkverzeichnis*, p. 270).

48 Imogen Fellinger, "Cyclic Tendencies in Brahms's Song Collections," in *Brahms Studies: Analytical and Historical Perspectives*, ed. George S. Bozarth (Oxford: Clarendon Press, 1990), p. 381.

49 An additional piece of evidence: In 1873 Brahms composed a setting of Groth's poem "Regenlied," which in the collection *Hundert Blätter* follows immediately after the third "Heimweh" poem. Although "Regenlied" also involves nostalgia for childhood, Brahms did not group it with the "Heimweh" songs in op. 63; instead, "Regenlied" was published as Op. 59, no. 3.

50 Groth himself had written poems entitled "Heimweh" and "Sehnsucht," both of which appear in *Hundert Blätter*.

51 Of course, Groth may not have fully understood Brahms's joint conception of the three songs. In *Hundert Blätter*, the three poems (none of which is given a title) appear consecutively but are not grouped into a single unit through a common heading or any other means.

52 Youens's *Schubert's Late Lieder*, p. 155. Youens discusses Romantic *Heimweh* on pp. 151–89. Additional studies include: Dieter Arendt, "Das romantische *Heimweh* nach der blauen Blume: Oder, Der Traumweg 'nach Hause,'" *Etudes-Germaniques* 51/2 (1996), 261–81; Renate Bebermeyer, "Aus dem Leben eines Wortes: *Heimweh*," *Sprachspiegel: Schweizerische Zeitschrift für deutsche Muttersprache* 42 (1986), 139–44; Karin Lorenz-Lindemann, "Die liebe Gegend schwarzumzogen: *Heimweh* als Verheissung," *Jahrbuch der Eichendorff Gesellschaft (Aurora)* 49 (1989), 151–61; and Fritz Ernst, *Vom Heimweh* (Zurich: Fretz and Wasmuth, 1949).

53 Bebermeyer, "Aus dem Leben eines Wortes: *Heimweh*," pp. 139–43.

54 Ibid., p. 141.

55 Berlin, *The Roots of Romanticism*, p. 104.

56 Abrams, *Natural Supernaturalism*, p. 182.

57 Novalis, *Schriften*, vol. 3: *Das philosophische Werk II*, ed. Richard Samuel (Stuttgart: W. Kohlhammer, 1960), p. 434. The statement appears as fragment no. 857 in the "Dritte Gruppe" of *Das Allgemeine Brouillon (Materialien zur Enzyklopädistik 1798/99)*.

58 Schiller, "On Naïve and Sentimental Poetry," p. 192.

59 Schiller, *Schillers Werke*, vol. 17 (Weimar: Böhlaus, 1943–), pp. 505–06.
60 Schiller, "On Naïve and Sentimental Poetry," p. 193.
61 For discussion of Goethe, Coleridge, Schelling, and Hegel on this issue, see Abrams, *Natural Supernaturalism*, pp. 183–87.
62 Abrams, *Natural Supernaturalism*, pp. 183–84. Abrams discusses the "spiral journey back home" on pp. 190–92.
63 Kreutziger-Herr, "Nichts als Kinderkram?," p. 217.
64 See Abrams, *Natural Supernaturalism*.
65 On the Biedermeier era, see Gramit, "Schubert and the Biedermeier"; Carl Dahlhaus, "Romantik und Biedermeier: Zur musikgeschichtlichen Charakteristik der Restaurationszeit," *Archiv für Musikwissenschaft* 31 (1974), 22–41; and Sengle, *Biedermeierzeit*, 3 vols. For changes in the cultural climate after 1850, see Dahlhaus, "Neo-Romanticism," in *Between Romanticism and Modernism: Four Studies in the Music of the Later Nineteenth Century*, trans. Mary Whittall (Berkeley: University of California Press, 1980), pp. 1–18; and Dahlhaus, *Realism in Nineteenth-Century Music*, trans. Mary Whittall (Cambridge University Press, 1985).
66 Groth's "Heimweh" texts. Translations (modified) by Stanley Appelbaum. *Johannes Brahms: Complete Songs for Solo Voice and Piano, Series II* (New York: Dover Publications, Inc., 1979), p. xviii.
67 Schiller's reference to the "more fortunate sister who remained at home with her mother, while we stormed out into an alien world, arrogantly confident of our freedom" supports this inference.
68 The concept of romantic irony, including the sudden destruction of illusion, has been explored especially in relation to the works of Robert Schumann. For a discussion of romantic irony in the music of Brahms, see Peter Jost's "Brahms und die romantische Ironie zu den 'Romanzen aus L. Tieck's Magelone' Op. 33," *Archiv für Musikwissenschaft* 47 (1990), 27–61.
69 On the song's lullaby effect, see Sams, *The Songs of Johannes Brahms*, p. 207, and Starobinski, "Brahms et la nostalgie," p. 184.
70 See, for example, the opening measures of *Vier ernste Gesänge*, op. 121, no. 3 (at the words "O Tod, o Tod"), or mm. 26–28 of "Feldeinsamkeit," Op. 86, no. 2 (at the phrase "mir ist, als ob ich längst gestorben bin").
71 On the role of dynamics in evoking the past or suggesting interiority, see Frisch, "'You Must Remember This,'" p. 593, and Scott Burnham, "Schubert and the Sound of Memory," *Musical Quarterly* 84 (Winter 2000), pp. 659, 661. Burnham notes that harmonic motion in the flat direction can produce similar effects (p. 662). On the "Arcadian Poetics" of flat-VI, see chapters 3 and 4 of Nelson's *The Fantasy of Absolute Music*.
72 Nicholas Marston discusses the relation of tonic and "home" in Schubert's music in "Schubert's Homecoming," *Journal of the Royal Musical Association* 125 (2000), 248–70. See also Charles Fisk, *Returning Cycles: Contexts for the Interpretation of Schubert's Impromptus and Last Sonatas*

(Berkeley: University of California Press, 2001) and Janet Schmalfeldt, "Coming Home" (Keynote Address, Twenty-Sixth Annual SMT Conference), *Music Theory Online* 10/1 (February 2004) (http://www.societymusictheory.org/mto/issues/mto.04.10.1/mto.04.10.1.schmalfeldt).

73 For discussion of the relation between music and memory in Schubert's instrumental music, see articles by Leon Botstein, Walter Frisch, John Daverio, John M. Gingerich, Charles Fisk, and Scott Burnham in *The Musical Quarterly* 84 (Winter 2000), 531–36, 581–663.

74 On plagal closes in various Brahms songs that express unrequited love and longing, see Heather Platt, "Unrequited Love and Unrealized Dominants," *Intégral* 7 (1993), 119–48. Platt concentrates on songs in which a plagal cadence substitutes for the expected final authentic cadence. In "Heimweh I" (and "Heimweh II"), however, a plagal cadence follows the final authentic cadence.

75 Sams, *The Songs of Johannes Brahms*, p. 208.

76 Bruckmann, "'O wüßt ich doch den Weg zurück . . . ,'" p. 30.

77 See again mm. 26–27 of Brahms's setting of "Feldeinsamkeit" ("mir ist, als ob ich längst gestorben bin"), in which octave sonorities descend by thirds.

78 On Brahms's use of developing variation, see Arnold Schoenberg, "Brahms the Progressive," *Style and Idea* (New York: Philosophical Society, 1950), pp. 398–441, and Walter Frisch, *Brahms and the Principle of Developing Variation* (Berkeley: University of California Press, 1984).

79 Starobinski, "Brahms et la nostalgie," p. 184. See also Lucien Stark, *A Guide to the Solo Songs of Johannes Brahms* (Bloomington: Indiana University Press, 1995), p. 198.

80 Kalbeck recognized a metaphorical link between home and death, attributing its appeal to Brahms to the composer's yearning for his dead parents (Kalbeck, *Johannes Brahms*, 3: 39).

81 See Siegfried Kross, "Brahms and E. T. A. Hoffmann," *19th-Century Music* 5 (1982), 193–200.

82 Michael Musgrave, *A Brahms Reader* (New Haven: Yale University Press, 2000), pp. 177–78.

83 For a description of Brahms's handwritten notes in the books of his personal library, see Kurt Hofmann, *Die Bibliothek von Johannes Brahms* (Hamburg: Wagner, 1974). For Brahms's collection of quotations, see Johannes Brahms, *The Brahms Notebooks: The Little Treasure Chest of the Young Kreisler: Quotations from Poets, Philosophers, and Artists Gathered by Johannes Brahms*, ed. Carl Krebs, trans. Agnes Eisenberger (Hillsdale, N.Y.: Pendragon, 2003).

84 Schubert composed "Das Heimweh," D. 456; "Totengräbers Heimweh," D. 842; and "Das Heimweh," D. 851. Carl Loewe, Luise Reichardt, Karl Gottlieb Reissiger, and Fanny Mendelssohn all wrote songs entitled either "Heimweh" or "Das Heimweh." The list of possibly influential works expands when one considers songs with related titles and themes. Brahms composed a song entitled "Heimkehr," Op. 7, no. 6.

85 Hancock, "*Johannes Brahms*: Volkslied/Kunstlied," p. 139. The designated song is "Herbstgefühl," Op. 48, no. 7. As Hancock notes, "some of Brahms's songs are upbeat, e.g. 'Botschaft,' Op. 47, no. 1; 'O liebliche Wangen,' Op. 47, no. 4; 'Meine Liebe ist grün,' Op. 63, no. 5; and 'Ständchen,' Op. 106, no. 1" (p. 132). These Lieder, however, are more exceptional than normative.

Part III: The lost world of folk song

1 On the idea of folk song during the nineteenth century, see Dahlhaus, *Nineteenth-Century Music*, pp. 105–111.
2 Anton Friedrich Justus Thibaut, "On Popular Melodies," in *On Purity in Musical Art*, trans. W. H. Gladstone (London: John Murray, 1877), pp. 66–82. German original: Ant[on] Friedr[ich] Just[us] Thibaut, "Über Volksgesänge," in *Über die Reinheit der Tonkunst* [Heidelberg, 1825], 7th ed. (Freiburg i.B.: J. C. B. Mohr, 1893), pp. 33–41.
3 Julian von Pulikowski, *Geschichte des Begriffes Volkslied im musikalischen Schrifttum: Ein Stück deutscher Geistesgeschichte* (Wiesbaden: Dr. Martin Sändig oHG, 1970), p. 459.
4 Carl Alexander, "Über das Volkslied," *Neue Zeitschrift für Musik* 1 (1834), 234. As quoted in Pulikowski, *Geschichte des Begriffes Volkslied im musikalischen Schrifttum*, p. 464.
5 Pulikowski, *Geschichte des Begriffes Volkslied*, p. 462.
6 On Herder's involvement with folk song, see Ernst Klusen, *Volkslied: Fund und Erfindung* (Cologne: Hans Gerig, 1969), pp. 132–38.
7 Johann Gottfried Herder, "Auszug aus einem Briefwechsel über Ossian und die Lieder alter Völker," in *Schriften zur Ästhetik und Literatur 1767–1781*, ed. Gunter E. Grimm (Frankfurt am Main: Deutscher klassiker Verlag, 1993), pp. 447–97.
8 Klusen, *Volkslied*, pp. 133–34.
9 Ibid., pp. 134–35.
10 Ibid., p. 134.
11 Ibid.
12 Achim von Arnim and Clemens Brentano, *Des knaben Wunderhorn: Alte deutsche Lieder* (Heidelberg, 1806, 1808); August Zarnack, *Deutsche Volkslieder in Volksweisen*, 2 parts (Berlin, 1818–20); Friedrich Karl Freiherr von Erlach, *Die Volkslieder der Deutschen: Eine vollständige Sammlung der vorzüglichen deutschen Volkslieder von der Mitte des fünfzehnten bis in die erste Hälfte des neunzehnten Jahrhunderts* (Mannheim, 1834–36); Anton Wilhelm von Zuccalglio and August Kretzschmer, *Deutsche Volkslieder mit ihren Originalweisen*, 2 vols. (Berlin, 1838–41); Johann Ludwig Uhland, *Alte hoch- und nieder-deutsche Volkslieder* (1844–45); Karl Simrock, *Die deutschen Volkslieder* (Frankfurt am Main, 1851); Ludwig Erk, *Deutscher Liederhort: Auswahl der vorzüglicheren deutschen Volkslieder, nach Wort und Weise aus der Vorzeit und Gegenwart und fortgesetzt von Franz M. Böhme*, 3 vols. (Leipzig, 1893–94).

13 See David Gramit, "The Dilemma of the Popular: the *Volk*, the Composers, and the Culture of Art Music," in *Cultivating Music: The Aspirations, Interests, and Limits of German Musical Culture, 1770–1848* (Berkeley: University of California Press, 2002), pp. 63–92. On the *Volkston*, see also Margaret Mahony Stoljar, *Poetry and Song in Late Eighteenth Century Germany: A Study in the Musical "Sturm und Drang"* (London: Croom Helm, 1985), and Smeed, *German Song and Its Poetry*, pp. 20–37.

14 Johann Abraham Peter Schulz, preface to the second edition of *Lieder im Volkston bey dem Claviere zu singen* (Berlin: Georg Jacob Decker, 1785). As translated in Gramit, "The Dilemma of the Popular," pp. 66–67. The German original appears in Friedlaender, *Das deutsche Lied im 18. Jahrhundert*, volume 1, part 1, p. 256.

15 On Schulz's imitators, see Smeed, *German Song and Its Poetry*, pp. 29–32.

16 Ibid., p. 33.

17 See, for example, my discussion of "Schäfers Klagelied" in *Schubert's Dramatic Lieder* (Cambridge University Press, 1993), pp. 98–115.

18 Dahlhaus, *Nineteenth-Century Music*, p. 108.

19 As quoted in Pulikowski, *Geschichte des Begriffes Volkslied*, pp. 464–65.

20 Nostalgia was not the only attitude toward folk song expressed by nineteenth-century writers, as the second part of Pulikowski's book emphasizes.

21 Gramit, "The Dilemma of the Popular," pp. 74–79.

22 See, for example, Russell, "The Effect of Folk-Song on German Poetry" and "The Effect of Folk-Song on Song Composers," in *The Themes of the German Lied*, pp. 29–36; Edward F. Kravitt, "The Volkstümlich Song and Its Composers," in *The Lied: Mirror of Late Romanticism* (New Haven: Yale University Press, 1996), pp. 113–23; Smeed, *German Song and Its Poetry*, pp. 156–72; Walter Wiora, "Die Anknüpfung an Volkstraditionen in der romantischen Liedkomposition," in *Das deutsche Lied* (Wolfenbüttel and Zurich: Möseler, 1971), pp. 119–34; Max Kommerell, "Das Volkslied und das deutsche Lied," in *Dame Dichterin und andere Essays* (Munich: Deutscher Taschenbuch Verlag, 1967), pp. 7–64; and Schwab, *Sangbarkeit, Popularität und Kunstlied*. Among the more focused studies are: Matthias Schmidt, "Komponierte Uneinholbarkeit: Anmerkungen zum 'Volkston' der *Wunderhorn*-Lieder," in *Gustav Mahler und das Lied: Referate des Bonner Symposions 2001* (Frankfurt am Main: Lang, 2003), pp. 51–68; Frisch, "Schubert's *Nähe des Geliebten* (D. 162): Transformation of the *Volkston*"; Hancock, "Johannes Brahms: *Volkslied/Kunstlied*"; Christopher Lewis, "Gustav Mahler: Romantic Culmination," in *German Lieder in the Nineteenth Century*, ed. Rufus Hallmark (New York: Schirmer Books, 1996), pp. 218–49; Siegmund Helms, *Die Melodiebildung in den Liedern von Johannes Brahms und ihr Verhältnis zu Volksliedern und volkstümlichen Weisen* (Berlin, Ph.D. diss., 1968); Werner Morik, *Johannes Brahms und Sein Verhältnis zum Deutschen Volkslied* (Tutzing: Hans Schneider, 1965).

23 Heinberg, *Memories and Visions of Paradise*, p. 67.

5: Schubert's songs-within-songs

A condensed version of this chapter was published as "Mirrors, Memories, and Mirages: Songs-Within-Songs in Schubert's Lieder," *Journal of Musicological Research*, 26, no. 1 (2007): 1–32 © 2007. Reproduced by permission of Taylor and Francis Group, LLC, www.taylorandfrancis.com.

1 On embedding (also known as "inclusion" or "*mise en abyme*") in literature, see: Tzetan Todorov, "A Poetic Novel," in *Genres in Discourse*, trans. Catherine Porter (Cambridge University Press, 1990), pp. 56–58; Lucien Dällenbach, *The Mirror in the Text*, trans. Jeremy Whiteley with Emma Hughes (The University of Chicago Press, 1989); Alastair Fowler, *Kinds of Literature: An Introduction to the Theory of Genres and Modes* (Cambridge, MA: Harvard University Press, 1982), pp. 179–81, 216–21; and Rosalie L. Colie, *The Resources of Kind: Genre Theory in the Renaissance*, ed. Barbara K. Lewalski (Berkeley: University of California Press, 1973), pp. 119–20. On embedding in Schumann's *Fantasie*, Op. 17, see Daverio, *Nineteenth-Century Music and the German Romantic Ideology*, p. 36.

2 Edward T. Cone, "The World of Opera and Its Inhabitants," in *Music: A View from Delft* (University of Chicago Press, 1989), p. 126.

3 Carolyn Abbate, *Unsung Voices: Opera and Musical Narrative in the Nineteenth Century* (Princeton University Press, 1991), pp. 61–118.

4 Ibid., p. 97. See also Gerard Loubinoux, "Le Chant dans le Chant: À la Recherche d'une Mémoire Mythique," in *Opéra, Théatre, Une Mémoire Imaginaire* (Paris: Herne, 1990), pp. 77–89.

5 On the comparable quality of literary epics, see Northrup Frye, *Anatomy of Criticism* (Princeton University Press, 1957), p. 324.

6 Two related studies are Lawrence Kramer's "Beyond Words and Music: An Essay on Songfulness," in *Musical Meaning: Toward a Critical History* (Berkeley: University of California Press, 2002), pp. 51–67, and chapter 5 ("Song") of his *Music and Poetry: The Nineteenth Century and After* (Berkeley: University of California Press, 1984).

7 For an overview of Schubert's changing poetic preferences, see Jane K. Brown, "In the Beginning Was Poetry," in *The Cambridge Companion to the Lied*, ed. James Parsons (Cambridge University Press, 2004), pp. 12–32; Brown, "The Poetry of Schubert's Songs," in *Schubert's Vienna*, ed. Raymond Erickson (New Haven: Yale University Press, 1997), pp. 183–213; and Walther Dürr, "Schubert's Songs and Their Poetry: Reflections on Poetic Aspects of Song Composition," in *Schubert Studies: Problems of Style and Chronology*, ed. Eva Badura-Skoda and Peter Branscombe (Cambridge University Press, 1982), pp. 1–24. For more in-depth discussions of Schubert's poets, see Youens's *Schubert's Poets* and *Schubert's Late Lieder*.

8 See Edward T. Cone, *The Composer's Voice* (Berkeley: University of California Press, 1974), and Cone, "Poet's Love or Composer's Love," in *Music and Text:*

Critical Inquiries, ed. Steven Paul Scher (Cambridge University Press, 1992), pp. 177–92. Cone's views will be discussed in the final section of this chapter.

9 Schubert's attraction to these subjects was surely magnified by the onset of his syphilis in 1822 and subsequent premonitions of death.

10 As noted, a significant portion of the Winter 2000 issue (vol. 84/4) of *The Musical Quarterly* is devoted to this subject.

11 See Appendix III ("Thematic and Stylistic Links Between the Songs and the Instrumental Works") in Reed's *The Schubert Song Companion*, pp. 494–98. See also, Youens, *Schubert's Late Lieder*.

12 The poem was later included in the 1795 edition of *Wilhelm Meisters Lehrjahre*, Book II, Chapter 11, where the Harper, paralleling the minstrel in the ballad, sings it to guests at the inn. On the novelistic context of "Der Sänger" and settings by Reichardt, Schubert, and Wolf, see Amanda Glauert, "'Ich singe, wie der Vogel singt': Reflections on Nature and Genre in Wolf's Setting of Goethe's *Der Sänger*," *Journal of the Royal Musical Association* 125 (2000), 271–86.

13 The present discussion refers to Schubert's second version of the work. The first version also includes the interpolated "song," but is twenty-two measures shorter. An earlier example of instrumental music substituting for song occurs in mm. 23–26 of Mozart's Lied "Das Veilchen."

14 Although the listener will not initially perceive the dramatic significance of the piano introduction, the first stanza makes clear that the music represents the sound of the minstrel's song as he approaches the castle gates. In the first version of "Der Sänger," Schubert writes the phrase "in der Ferne" over the music of m.1, confirming that the "song" should be understood there as sounding from afar.

15 In stanza 3, the minstrel's song apparently occurs somewhere between the end of line 2 ("Und schlug in vollen Tönen") and the beginning of line 5 ("Der König, dem das Lied gefiel").

16 Throughout the song, the music of the piano accompaniment serves a variety of narrative functions, e.g., depicting physical action, creating atmosphere, and portraying character.

17 The text is drawn from Goethe's first sketch of *Faust*, written before 1775. In the final version of the drama, it constitutes Scene 20 of Part I.

18 In Schubert's first version of "Szene aus Faust," the music is written on two staves throughout, with the vocal line appearing in the treble staff and the piano accompaniment in the bass staff. The choir's music, written in four-part harmony with words printed between the two staves, presents an interpretive challenge; it is not clear whether Schubert intended one vocalist to sing just the uppermost line or multiple vocalists to sing all four lines. It is also not clear whether Schubert intended one or two singers for the parts of the Evil Spirit and Gretchen, although the ranges differ to some extent. Schubert's second version of the song, which devotes a separate staff to the vocal part, dispels the ambiguities. As in "Death and the Maiden," "Antigone und Oedip," "Der Müller und der Bach," and other

songs with multiple, identifiable vocal protagonists, only one singer is called upon to sing all dramatic roles (including the uppermost line of the choir's four-part harmony, now clearly assigned to the piano). The song thus to some extent resembles narrative songs like "Erlkönig," with a single narrator quoting different characters in his story, although in "Szene aus Faust" the presumed narrator never speaks in his or her own voice.

19 Translation by Stanley Appelbaum. *Schubert's Songs to Texts by Goethe*, ed. Eusebius Mandyczewski (New York: Dover Publications, Inc., 1979), p. xii.
20 Schubert's enthusiasm for the Orpheus myth dates from his years at the Vienna *Stadtkonvikt*. Deutsch, ed., *Schubert: Memoirs by his Friends*, p. 59, and Deutsch, ed., *The Schubert Reader*, pp. 870, 880. The composition of *Lied des Orpheus* may also reflect the influence of Italian composer Antonio Salieri (in turn influenced by Gluck), with whom Schubert was then studying.
21 One might argue that Schubert's setting does support the text's Christian message – the triumphant musical ending reflecting Orpheus's promise of redemption to those who have exercised pity. This interpretation, however, does not account for the fact that our attention is increasingly drawn to the vocal talents of the actual singer who performs D. 474.
22 In different versions of the Greek myth, Orpheus's singing charms one or more of the following: Charon, Cerberus, the Shades, the Furies, Pluto and Prosperine. In Schubert's setting, although the inhabitants of Hades do not speak directly, the piano evokes their lamentation through the flowing, descending lines in the treble at mm. 51ff (coinciding with the words "Meine Klage tönt in eure Klage").
23 Perhaps the composer intended to draw a subtle parallel with the "whimpering inhabitants" of Vienna during a period of "darkness" imposed by Metternich.
24 "Lied des Orpheus" exists in two versions. The first version, written in common time with the final section in D major, poses greater vocal challenges than the more practical second version, written in *alla breve* time with passages from the middle and end of the song transposed down a fifth and third, respectively. The following discussion refers to the second version.
25 In the more difficult first version of the song, the music of stanza 7 modulates to D major, rather than B-flat major.
26 For discussion of *mise en abyme* relations, see Dällenbach, *The Mirror in the Text*.
27 On the connection between Schubert and Orpheus, see Eric Sams, "Notes on a Magic Flute: the Origins of the Schubertian Lied," *Musical Times* 119 (1978), 949.
28 The text of "Pause," along with those of the other *Die schöne Müllerin* songs, was first published in 1821. Wilhelm Müller conceived the poems several years earlier in conjunction with a party game involving a group of young men and women in Berlin. See Susan Youens, *Schubert, Müller and Die schöne Müllerin* (Cambridge University Press, 1997), and Youens, *Schubert: Die schöne Müllerin*.
29 Youens, *Schubert's Poets*, p. 291.

30 Ibid., p. 291.
31 This song is also discussed in chapter 3.
32 Cone, *The Composer's Voice*, p. 23. Responses to and elaborations on *The Composer's Voice* by Marion Guck, Charles Fisk, Fred Everett Maus, James Webster, and Alicyn Warren appear in *College Music Symposium* 29 (1989).
33 Cone, "Poet's Love or Composer's Love?" Cone applies to Lieder ideas from his study "The World of Opera and Its Inhabitants." For responses to Cone's "World of Opera," see: Peter Kivy, "Opera Talk: A Philosophical 'Phantasie'" *Cambridge Opera Journal* 3/1 (Mar. 1991), 63–77; David Rosen, "Cone's and Kivy's 'World of Opera'" *Cambridge Opera Journal* 4/1 (Mar. 1992), 61–74; and Ellen Rosand, "Operatic Ambiguities and the Power of Music," *Cambridge Opera Journal* 4/1 (Mar. 1992), 75–80.
34 Cone, "Poet's Love or Composer's Love?," p. 178.
35 According to Cone, when the persona of "Pause" "hangs his lute on the wall, singing 'Ich kann nicht mehr singen, mein Herz ist zu voll,' he confirms his own status as a musician, just as his rhyming insistence that he can no longer rhyme ('Weiss nicht wie ich's in Reime zwingen soll') implies that he is equally a poet" (Cone, "Poet's Love or Composer's Love?," p. 180). Even the *Winterreise* protagonist, Cone claims, is to some extent conscious of singing, as suggested by the reference to his Lieder in "Der Leiermann."
36 Ibid., p. 192.
37 Schiller, "On Naïve and Sentimental Poetry."
38 "Der Jäger in dem grünen Wald" appears in *Deutscher Lieder*, ed. Ernst Klusen (Frankfurt am Main: Insel, 1980), pp. 100–01. See also Erk, *Deutscher Liederhort*, vol. 3, pp. 311–12.
39 Smeed, *German Song and its Poetry*, p. 165.
40 "War also die erste Menschensprache Gesang: so wars Gesang, der ihm so natürlich, seinen Organen und Naturtrieben so angemessen war, als der Nachtigallengesang ihr selbst, die gleichsam eine schwebende Lunge ist, und das war – eben unsre tönende Sprache." Johann Gottfried Herder, "Über den Ursprung der Sprache," in *Werke*, vol. 2, ed. Wolfgang Pross (Munich: Carl Hanser, 1987), p. 294.
41 Brown, "In the Beginning Was Poetry," p. 20.
42 Smeed, *German Song and its Poetry*, p. 63.
43 According to J. N. Forkel (*Musikalisch-kritische Bibliothek*, I, 1778, 212), the relationship between music and words should resemble that between garment and soul. J. A. P. Schulz (Preface to the 2nd edition of *Lieder im Volkston*, 1784) writes that a good song has a melody that "fits the declamation and the metre of the text as a garment fits the body." Cited in Smeed, *German Song and its Poetry*, p. 79. On Goethe's view that modern folk poetry was meant to be sung, see Byrne, *Schubert's Goethe Settings*, p. 10.
44 Kramer, "Beyond Words and Music: An Essay on Songfulness." For discussion of both Goethe's poem "Heidenröslein" and Schubert's setting, see also Byrne,

Schubert's Goethe Settings, pp. 209–12. On the role of the singer in narrative ballads, see Georgiades, *Schubert: Musik und Lyrik*, pp. 208–9.

45 Kramer, "Beyond Words and Music," p. 61.
46 Ibid., pp. 60–1.
47 Marshall Brown, discussing skeptical negation in lyric poetry, writes, "The lyric . . . communicates both emotion and a knowingness about emotion. A poem is not a primal cry from the heart. The precision of utterance removes it from the immediacy of exclamation." Marshall Brown, "Negative Poetics: On Skepticism and the Lyric Voice," *Representations* 86 (Spring 2004), 129. On this issue, see also Kommerell's "Das Volkslied und das deutsche Lied."
48 Walter Frisch, "Schubert's 'Nähe des Geliebten' (D.162): Transformation of the *Volkston*." See also Georgiades, *Schubert: Musik und Lyrik*, pp. 47–57.
49 For discussion of "music-making" by the wanderer and organ grinder at the end of "Der Leiermann," D. 911, no. 24, see Richard Kramer, *Distant Cycles*, pp. 182–83.
50 Lawrence Kramer uses the image of quotation marks around the "folksong atmosphere" of "Heidenröslein" to help convey the self-consciousness of the work (Kramer, "Beyond Words and Music: An Essay on Songfulness," p. 60).
51 Cone, *The Composer's Voice*, p. 37.

6: On wings of song from Reichardt to Mahler

1 Several folk songs in *Des knaben Wunderhorn* express yearning to be a bird: "Der Falke" (I 63), "Wenn ich ein Vöglein wär" (I 231), "Der Berggesell" (III 25), "Liebeswünsche" (III 84), and the *Kinderlied* "Ach wenn ich doch ein Täublein wär" (KL 93d). Of these, "Wenn ich ein Vöglein wär" was the most well known during the nineteenth century, its title (and opening line) becoming a familiar catch phrase and the song itself appearing in innumerable *Volkslied* collections. The following discussion will concentrate on "Wenn ich ein Vöglein wär" and its treatment of the *Voglmotif*. Apart from the *Kinderlied*, the other songs also concern separated lovers.
2 On the wish motive (including the wish to become a bird) in ancient Greek and modern German poetry, and the relationship between the two repertories, see Alfred Biese, "Einige Wandlungen des Wunschmotivs in antiker und moderner Poesie," *Zeitschrift für vergleichende Litteraturgeschichte* (Berlin: A. Haack, 1886–87), pp. 411–25. On *Wunschlieder*, see also Ludwig Uhland, ed., *Alte hoch- und niederdeutsche Volkslieder mit Abhandlung und Anmerkungen*, vol. 3 (Stuttgart: Cotta, no date), pp. 213–35.
3 John Smeed, "'Wenn ich ein Vöglein wär': From *Flugblatt* to Opera," in *German Studies at the Millennium*, ed. Neil Thomas (Durham, England: University of Durham, 1999), p. 108.

4 Berne, *Stadtbibliothek*, Engelmann, 136, no. 2. Despite the title's claim, the music is not provided. See Smeed, "'Wenn ich ein Vöglein wär': From *Flugblatt* to Opera," 95–6, and Barbara James, "'Wenn ich ein Vöglein wär . . . ': Neues zur Datierung des Liedes," *Jahrbuch für Volksliedforschung* 32 (1987), pp. 127–28.

5 Herder's version has three stanzas while the *Flugblatt*'s has five. Stanzas 1 and 3 of Herder's version derive from stanzas 1 and 2, respectively, of the *Flugblatt* text. Stanza 2 of Herder's version is without precedent in the *Flugblatt* text. Smeed suggests that both the *Flugblatt* and Herder's version may have been based on a pre-existing folk song. Smeed, "'Wenn ich ein Vöglein wär': From *Flugblatt* to Opera," 97. According to Max Friedländer, the text was likely well known before its printing, and may have influenced the composition of a Lied by Hölty of 1775 ("Ich träumt ich war ein Vögelein / Und flog auf ihren Schooß"). Friedländer, *Das deutsche Lied im 18. Jahrhundert*, vol. 2, p. 152.

6 Smeed, "'Wenn ich ein Vöglein wär': From *Flugblatt* to Opera," pp. 97–98.

7 As quoted in Erk, ed., *Deutscher Liederhort*, vol. 2, p. 333.

8 Ibid.

9 Reichardt had employed the tune with different words in his *Lieder mit Melodien zum Gebrach der Loge* of 1784, no. 4, as well as in the overture to his Singspiel *Jery und Bätely* of 1790. Max Friedländer speculates that Mozart may have had the melody in mind when writing Zerlina's aria "Vedrai carino" in *Don Giovanni* in 1787. Friedländer, *Das deutsche Lied im 18. Jahrhundert*, vol. 2, p. 151.

10 See, for example, *Deutsche Lieder für Jung und Alt*, ed. Feurzeig, p. 208, and *Die deutschen Volkslieder mit ihren Singweisen*, ed. Ludwig Erk and Wilhelm Irmer, vol. 1, part 2 (Berlin: Plahn'schen Buchhandlung, 1838; Hildesheim; New York: Georg Olms Verlag, 1982), pp. 4–5.

11 See Erk, ed., *Deutscher Liederhort*, vol. 2, p. 333.

12 Johannes Brahms, *Volksliedbearbeitungen für Frauenchor*, ed. Siegmund Helms (Kassel: Bärenreiter, 1970), 34 (no. 27: "Wenn ich ein Vöglein wär").

13 Max Reger, *Sechs ausgewählte Volkslieder für gemischten Chor bearbeitet*, no. 5 (Jos. Aibl Verlag, 1899) and *Fünf ausgewählte Volkslieder für Männerchor bearbeitet*, no. 2 (Jos. Aibl Verlag, 1899).

14 Friedländer, *Das deutsche Lied im 18. Jahrhundert*, vol. 2, p. 151.

15 Smeed notes that there are "further sentimental reworkings of 'Wenn ich ein Vöglein wär' by Heinrich Proch (*c.* 1840), Otto Banck and J. Körnlein (both early 1840s), Hoffman von Fallersleben (*c.* 1850) and Ernst Kleinpaul (1870)." Smeed, "'Wenn ich ein Vöglein wär': From *Flugblatt* to Opera," p. 99.

16 According to Erk and Böhme, the text, a transformation of the old folk song, was written by Helmine Chézy around 1824. Erk and Böhme provide another melody which they attribute to Friedrich Kücken, supposedly composed in 1827, "aber vom Volke zurechtgesungen worden" (Erk, ed., *Deutscher Liederhort*, vol. 2, 373). The song appeared in *Kücken-Album*, vol. 2, no. 11 (Leipzig, F. Kistner's Verlag).

17 Johann Wolfgang von Goethe, *Faust: A Tragedy*, trans. Walter Arndt (New York: W. W. Norton, 1976), p. 81.
18 "Ich steh auf des Berges Spitze" appears in Heine's *Buch der Lieder*, Lyrisches Intermezzo No. 53, 1822–24. Another poetic parody, by Ferdinand Freiherrn von Biedenfeld, entitled "Die Wünsche," appeared in the *Rheinblüten* in 1822. Biedenfeld's poem is reprinted on p. 379 of Heinrich Heine, *Buch der Lieder* (Munich: Goldmann, 1992).
19 See Gero von Wilpert, "Der ornithologische Taugenichts: Zum Vogelmotiv in Eichendorffs Novelle," in *Ansichten zu Eichendorff: Beiträge der Forschung 1958 bis 1988*, ed. Alfred Riemen (Sigmaringen: Jan Thorbecke Verlag, 1988), pp. 277–95.
20 The poem was written in 1800/01.
21 Reed, *The Schubert Song Companion*, p. 112.
22 Composed in 1840. Also set by Felix Mendelssohn-Bartholdy (Op. 99, no. 6; 1842). The poem dates from 1815.
23 See David Ferris, *Schumann's Eichendorff Liederkreis and the Genre of the Romantic Cycle* (Oxford University Press, 2000), pp. 212–16.
24 The poem appears in chapter 14 of Eichendorff's novel *Ahnung und Gegenwart* (1815), where it is sung by Erwine, a girl who dresses in male clothing to meet her secret lover Friedrich. Dietrich Fischer-Dieskau, *Robert Schumann Words and Music: The Vocal Compositions*, trans. Reinhard G. Pauly (Portland: Amadeus, 1988), pp. 74–75.
25 See Ferris's discussion of human spiritual striving in Schumann's Eichendorff Liederkreis in: *Schumann's Eichendorff Liederkreis*, pp. 213–16.
26 See Joseph von Eichendorff, *Gedichte Versepen*, ed. Hartwig Schultz (Frankfurt am Main: Deutscher Klassiker Verlag, 1987), p. 932.
27 A similar rhythmic pattern is used to illustrate the girl's wandering in mm. 42ff.
28 The poem was also set to music by Ferdinand Ries ("Sehnsucht," Op. 35, no. 4; 1811 pub).
29 Youens, *Schubert's Poets*, p. 196.
30 Ibid., p. 198.
31 Ibid.
32 Schumann had high regard for this song. On 9 August 1840, he wrote to Clara about this work, "I have written a song in these last few days that I think will make a special appeal to you; it strikes me as quite exceptionally inventive." As quoted in Eric Sams, *The Songs of Robert Schumann* (Bloomington: Indiana University Press, 1993), p. 159.
33 Sams notes that the song also evokes Schubert's "Des Mädchens Klage," "Aus Heliopolis I," and "Der Wanderer." Sams, *The Songs of Robert Schumann*, p. 159. Johanna Mathieux Kinkel's setting of the text is titled "Sehnsucht Nach Griechenland" (Op. 6, no. 1; 1837).
34 Translation borrowed from Sams, *The Songs of Robert Schumann*, p. 159.
35 Translation borrowed from Sams, *The Songs of Robert Schumann*, p. 182.

36 According to Fischer-Dieskau, "This was a fear that plagued both the composer and the poet." Fischer-Dieskau, *Robert Schumann: Words and Music*, p. 115.
37 Translation borrowed from Eric Sams, *The Songs of Johannes Brahms* (New Haven: Yale University Press, 2000), p. 294.
38 The settings of Rimsky-Korsakov, Mussorgsky, and Borodin are in Russian.
39 Translation borrowed from Sams, *The Songs of Johannes Brahms*, p. 311.

References

Pre-1900 titles

Alexander, Carl. "Über das Volkslied." *Neue Zeitschrift für Musik* 1 (1834), 233–35.

Arnim, Ludwig Achim von, and Clemens Brentano, eds. *Des Knaben Wunderhorn: Alte deutsche Lieder.* 3 vols. Heidelberg: Mohr und Zimmer, 1806–08. Kommentierte Gesamtausgabe. Edited by Heinz Rölleke. Stuttgart: Philipp Reclam Jun., 1987.

Bauernfeld, Eduard von. *Gesammelte Schriften.* Vol. 11. *Reime und Rhythmen.* Vienna: Wilhelm Braumüller, 1873.

Biese, Alfred. "Einige Wandlungen des Wunschmotivs in antiker und moderner Poesie." In *Zeitschrift für vergleichende Litteraturgeschichte*, pp. 411–25. Berlin: A. Haack, 1886–87.

Böhme, Franz Magnus, ed. *Deutsches Kinderlied und Kinderspiel: Volksüberlieferungen aus allen Landen deutscher Zunge.* Leipzig: Breitkopf and Härtel, 1897.

———, ed. *Volksthümliche Lieder der Deutschen im 18. und 19. Jahrhundert.* Leipzig: Breitkopf and Härtel, 1895.

Brahms, Johannes. *The Brahms Notebooks: The Little Treasure Chest of the Young Kreisler: Quotations from Poets, Philosophers, and Artists Gathered by Johannes Brahms.* Edited by Carl Krebs. Translated by Agnes Eisenberger. Hillsdale, NY: Pendragon, 2003.

———. *Johannes Brahms: Complete Songs for Solo Voice and Piano.* Series II. New York: Dover Publications, Inc., 1979.

———. *Johannes Brahms: Life and Letters.* Edited by Styra Avins. Translated by Josef Eisinger and Styra Avins. Oxford University Press, 1997.

———. *Volksliedbearbeitungen für Frauenchor.* Edited by Siegmund Helms. Kassel: Bärenreiter, 1970.

Burmann, Gottlob Wilhelm. *Kleine Lieder für kleine Jünglinge: Text und Musick von Gottlob Wilhelm Burmann.* Berlin and Königsberg: G. J. Decker and G. L. Hartung, 1777.

———. *Gottlob Wilhelm Burmanns kleine Lieder für kleine Mädchen: Text und Musick von Gottlob Wilhelm Burmann.* Berlin and Königsberg: G. J. Decker and G. L. Hartung, 1773.

Campbell, David A., trans. *Greek Lyric.* Vol. 2. *Anacreon, Anacreontea, Choral Lyric from Olympus to Alcman.* Cambridge, MA: Harvard University Press, 1988.

Claudius, Georg Carl. *Lieder für Kinder mit neuen sehr leichten Melodieen.* Frankfurt am Main: Heinrich Ludwig Brönner, 1780.

Claudius, Matthias. *Matthias Claudius Werke: Asums Omnia Sua Secum Portans oder Sämtliche Werke des Wandsbecker Boten.* Stuttgart: J. G. Cotta, 1966.

Daumer, Georg Friedrich. *Polydora, ein weltpoetisches Liederbuch.* Vol. 1. Frankfurt am Main: Literarische Anstalt, 1855.

Denon, Vivant. *Travels in Upper and Lower Egypt During the Campaigns of General Bonaparte in That Country.* 2 vols. New York: Heard and Forman, 1803.

Eichendorff, Joseph von. *Gedichte Versepen.* Edited by Hartwig Schultz. Frankfurt am Main: Deutscher Klassiker Verlag, 1987.

Erk, Ludwig. *Deutscher Liederhort. Auswahl der vorzüglicheren deutschen Volkslieder, nach Wort und Weise aus der Vorzeit und Gegenwart und fortgesetzt von Franz M. Böhme.* 3 vols. Leipzig: Breitkopf und Härtel, 1893–94.

Erk, Ludwig, and Wilhelm Irmer, eds. *Die deutschen Volkslieder mit ihren Singweisen.* 3 vols. Berlin: Plahn'schen Buchhandlung, 1838; Hildesheim; New York: Georg Olms Verlag, 1982.

Erlach, Friedrich Karl Freiherr von. *Die Volkslieder der Deutschen: Eine vollständige Sammlung der vorzüglichen deutschen Volkslieder von der Mitte des fünfzehnten bis in die erste Hälfte des neunzehnten Jahrhunderts.* Mannheim: H. Hoff, 1834–36.

Fallersleben, Hoffmann von. *Gedichte.* Leipzig: Brockhaus, 1834.

Feurzeig, Lisa, ed. *Deutsche Lieder für Jung und Alt.* Berlin: Realschulbuchhandlung, 1818. Middleton, WI: A–R editions, 2002.

Forkel, Johann Nikolaus. *Musikalisch-kritische Bibliothek.* 3 vols. Gotha: C. W. Ettinger, 1778–79.

Girschner, C. F. J. "Über Wiegen- und Spinnerlieder," *Berliner Allgemeine musikalische Zeitung* 2 (1828), 16.

Goethe, Johann Wolfgang von. *Faust: A Tragedy.* Translated by Walter Arndt. New York: W. W. Norton, 1976.

    Gedichte. Edited by Erich Trunz. Vol. 1. Munich: C. H. Beck, 1981.

    Gedichte. Edited by Erich Trunz, Vol. 2. Hamburg: Fischer, 1964.

Gottlieb-Billroth, C. A. T., ed. *Billroth und Brahms im Briefwechsel.* Berlin: Urban and Schwarzenberg, 1935.

Groth, Klaus. *Klaus Groth Sämtliche Werke.* Heide/Holstein: Westholsteinische Verlagsanstalt Boyens and Co., 1981.

Hanslick, Eduard. *Fünf Jahre Musik [1891–1895] (Der "Modernen Oper" VII. Teil.)* Berlin: Allgemeiner Verein für Deutsche Litteratur, 1896.

Hegel, Georg Wilhelm Friedrich. *Werke.* Vols. 13–15. *Vorlesungen über die Ästhetik.* Frankfurt am Main: Suhrkamp, 1971, 1986.

Heine, Heinrich. *Buch der Lieder.* Munich: Goldmann, 1992.

Herder, Johann Gottfried Herder. "Auszug aus einem Briefwechsel über Ossian und die Lieder alter Völker." In *Schriften zur Ästhetik und Literatur 1767–1781,* 447–97. Edited by Gunter E. Grimm. Frankfurt am Main: Deutscher klassiker Verlag, 1993.

Blumen aus der griechischen Anthologie gesammlet. Herders Sämtliche Werke. Vol. 26. Edited by Carl Redlich. Berlin: Weidmannsche Buchhandlung, 1882.

"Über den Ursprung der Sprache." In *Werke*, vol. 2. Edited by Wolfgang Pross. Munich: Carl Hanser, 1987.

Hesiod, *The Works and Days. Theogony. The Shield of Herakles.* Edited and translated by Richard Lattimore. Ann Arbor: University of Michigan Press, 1959.

Hiller, Johann Adam. *Lieder für Kinder, vermehrte Auflage. Mit neuen Melodieen von Johann Adam Hiller.* Leipzig: Weidmanns Erben und Reich, 1769.

Sammlung der Lieder aus dem Kinderfreunde, die noch nicht componirt waren, mit neuen Melodien von Johann Adam Hiller. Leipzig: Siegfried Lebrecht Crusius, 1782.

Horstig, Karl Gottlieb. *Kinder-Lieder und Melodien* Leipzig, 1798.

Humboldt, Wilhelm von. "Geschichte des Verfalls und Unterganges der griechischen Freistaaten." In *Sechs ungedruckte aufsätze über das klassische Altertum.* Edited by Albert Leitzmann. Nendeln: Kraus, 1968, 1896.

Hunger, Gottlob Gottwald. *Lieder für Kinder mit neuen Melodien von Gottlob Gottwald Hunger.* Leipzig: Weidmanns Erben und Reich, 1772.

Jay, Peter, ed., *The Greek Anthology and Other Ancient Greek Epigrams.* New York: Oxford University Press, 1973.

Kleist, Heinrich von. "The Puppet Theater." In *Selected Writings.* Edited and translated by David Constantine. London: J. M. Dent, 1997.

Lieder für Kinder und Kinderfreunde am Clavier: Frühlingslieder. Vienna: Ignaz Alberti, 1791.

Mayrhofer, Johann. *Gedichte.* Vienna: Friedrich Volke, 1824.

Gedichte von Johann Mayrhofer. Neue Sammlung. Aus dessen Nachlasse mit Biographie und Vorwort. Edited by Ernst Freiherr von Feuchtersleben. Vienna: Ignaz Klang, 1843.

Müller, Wilhelm. *Diary and Letters of Wilhelm Müller.* Edited by Philip Schuyler Allen and James Taft Hatfield. The University of Chicago Press, 1903.

Gedichte von Wilhlem Müller: Vollständige Kritische Ausgabe. Edited by James Taft Hatfield. Berlin: B. Behr, 1906; Nedeln/Liechtenstein: Kraus Reprint, 1968.

Nietzsche, Friedrich. *The Birth of Tragedy and The Case of Wagner.* Translated by Walter Kaufmann. New York: Vintage Books, 1967.

Novalis. *Hymns to the Night.* Translated by Mabel Cotterell. London: Phoenix Press, 1948.

Schriften: Die werke Friedrich von Hardenbergs. 6 vols. Edited by Paul Kluckhohn and Richard Samuel. Stuttgart: W. Kohlhammer Verlag, 1960.

Paton, W. R., trans. *The Greek Anthology.* Vol. 2. London: William Heinemann; New York: G. P. Putnam's Sons, 1917.

Pauls, Volquart, ed. *Briefe der Freundschaft: Johannes Brahms – Klaus Groth.* Heide in Holstein: Westholsteinische Verlangsanstalt Boyens and Co., 1956.

Plato, *The Apology, Phaedo and Crito of Plato.* Translated by Benjamin Jowett. New York: P. F. Collier and Son, 1937.

Quintus of Smyrna, *The War at Troy: What Homer Didn't Tell*. Translated by Frederick M. Combellack. Norman: University of Oklahoma Press, 1968.

Reger, Max. *Fünf ausgewählte Volkslieder für Männerchor bearbeitet*. Jos. Aibl Verlag, 1899.

Sechs ausgewählte Volkslieder für gemischten Chor bearbeitet. Jos. Aibl Verlag, 1899.

Reichardt, Johann Friedrich. *Lieder für die Jugend*. Leipzig, 1799.

Lieder für Kinder aus Campes Kinderbibliothek mit Melodieen, bei dem Klavier zu singen. Parts 1 and 2. Hamburg: Heroldschen Buchhandlung; Berlin: Erk 1781. Part 3. Wolfenbüttel: Schulbuchhandlung; Berlin: Erk, 1787. Part 4. Braunschweig: Schulbuchhandlung; Berlin: Erk, 1790.

Reichardt, Johann Friedrich. *Wiegenlieder für gute deutsche Mütter*. Leipzig: Gerhard Fleischer der Jüngere, 1798.

Rousseau, Jean-Jacques. *Émile, Or Treatise on Education*. Translated by William H. Payne. Amherst, NY: Prometheus books, 2003.

Scheibe, Johann Adolph. *Kleine Lieder für Kinder zur Beförderung der Tugend*. Flensburg: Johann Christoph Korte; Vienna: Hofbibliothek, 1766, 1768.

Schelling, Friedrich Wilhelm Joseph von. *Sämmtliche Werke*. Stuttgart, Augsburg: J. G. Cotta, 1856–61.

Schiller, Friedrich. *Essays*. Edited by Walter Hinderer and Daniel O. Dahlstrom. Translated by Dahlstrom. New York: Continuum, 1993.

The Poems and Ballads of Schiller. Translated by Sir Edward Bulwer Lytton. Edinburgh: Williams Blackwood and Sons, 1852.

Schillers Briefe, Kritische Gesamtausgabe. 7 vols. Edited by Fritz Jonas. Stuttgart: Deutsche Verlags-Anstalt, 1892–96.

Schillers Werke. Edited by Julius Petersen and Gerhard Fricke. Weimar, H. Böhlaus Nachf., 1943–2003.

Schlegel, August William. *A Course of Lectures on Dramatic Art and Literature*. Translated by John Black. London: Bell and Daldy, 1871.

Schlegel, Friedrich. *Dialogue on Poetry and Literary Aphorisms*. Translated by Ernst Behler and Roman Struc. University Park and London: The Pennsylvania State University Press, 1968.

Geschichte der alten und neuen Literatur [1815]. Vol. 6 of *Kritische Friedrich-Schlegel-Ausgabe*. Edited by Ernst Behler with Jean-Jacques Anstett and Hans Eichner. Munich: F. Schöningh, 1958–2002.

Gespräch über die Poesie. 1800. Stuttgart: J. B. Metzler, 1968.

Schopenhauer, Arthur. *Die Welt als Wille und Vorstellung*. 2 vols. Edited by Julius Frauenstädt. Leipzig: F. A. Brockhaus, 1891.

Schubert, Franz. *Schubert's Songs to Texts by Goethe*. Edited by Eusebius Mandyczewski. New York: Dover Publications, Inc., 1979.

Schulz, Johann Abraham Peter. *Lieder im Volkston bei dem Claviere zu singen*. 2nd edn. Berlin: Georg Jacob Decker, 1785.

Schütze, Johann Stephan. "Über Wiegenlieder." *Caecilia* (1825), 269–71.

Simrock, Karl, ed. *Das deutsche Kinderbuch.* Frankfurt am Main: [s.n.], 1848.
  Die deutschen Volkslieder. Frankfurt am Main, 1851.
Spazier, Carl. *Einfache Clavierlieder.* Berlin: in Commission der neuen Berl. Musikhandlung und der Akadem. Kunst- und Buchhandlung, 1790.
Thibaut, Anton Friedrich Justus. *On Purity in Musical Art.* Translated by W. H. Gladstone. London: John Murray, 1877.
  Über die Reinheit der Tonkunst. Heidelberg, 1825. 7th edn. Freiburg i.B.: J. C. B. Mohr, 1893.
Uhland, Ludwig, ed., *Alte hoch- und niederdeutsche volkslieder mit Abhandlung und Anmerkungen.* 1844–45. Stuttgart: Cotta, 1893.
Vaughan, Henry. *The Works of Henry Vaughan.* Edited by L. C. Martin. 2 vols. Oxford: Clarendon Press, 1914.
Weiße, Christian Felix. *Lieder für Kinder,* 3rd ed. Leipzig: Weidmann, 1770.
Widmann, Joseph Viktor. *Johannes Brahms in Erinnerung.* Berlin: Gebrüder Paetel, 1898. Basel: Amerbach-Verlag, 1947.
Wiener Allgemeine musikalische Zeitung. Vienna: Böhlaus, 1813.
Wiener Zeitschrift für Kunst, Literatur, Theater und Mode. Vienna: A Strauss, 1816–1846.
Winckelmann, Johann Joachim. *Reflections on the Imitation of Greek Works in Painting and Sculpture.* Translated by Elfriede Heyer and Roger C. Norton. La Salle, IL: Open Court, 1987.
Wolf, Hugo. *Letters to Melanie Köchert.* Edited by Franz Grasberger. Translated by Louise McClelland Urban. New York: Schirmer Books, 1991.
  The Music Criticism of Hugo Wolf. Translated and edited by Henry Pleasants. New York: Holmes and Meier, 1979.
Zarnack, August. *Deutsche Volkslieder in Volksweisen,* 2 parts. Berlin, 1818–20.
Zuccalmaglio, Anton Wilhelm von, and August Kretzschmer. *Deutsche Volkslieder mit ihren Originalweisen,* 2 vols. Berlin: Vereinsbuchhandlung, 1838–41.

Post-1900 titles

Abbate, Carolyn. *Unsung Voices: Opera and Musical Narrative in the Nineteenth Century.* Princeton University Press, 1991.
Abrams, M. H. *Natural Supernaturalism: Tradition and Revolution in Romantic Literature.* New York: W. W. Norton, 1971.
Anderson, Bonnie S., and Judith P. Zinsser. *A History of Their Own: Women in Europe from Prehistory to the Present.* 2 vols. New York: Harper and Row, 1988.
Arendt, Dieter. "Das romantische *Heimweh* nach der blauen Blume: Oder, Der Traumweg 'nach Hause.'" *Études-Germaniques* 51/201 (April–June 1996), 261–81.
Ariès, Philippe. *L'Enfant et la vie familiale sous l'ancien régime.* Paris: Plon, 1960. Published in English as *Centuries of Childhood.* London: J. Cape, 1962.
Armstrong, John. *The Paradise Myth.* London: Oxford University Press, 1969.

Ashton, John and Tom Whyte. *The Quest for Paradise: Visions of Heaven and Eternity in the World's Myths and Religions.* New York: HarperCollins, 2001.

Bebermeyer, Renate. "Aus dem Leben eines Wortes: *Heimweh.*" *Sprachspiegel: Schweizerische Zeitschrift für deutsche Muttersprache* 42/5 (October 1986), 139–44.

Beiser, Frederick C. *The Romantic Imperative: The Concept of Early German Romanticism.* Cambridge: Harvard University Press, 2003.

Beller-McKenna, Daniel. "Brahms on Schopenhauer: The *Vier ernste Gesänge*, Op. 121, and Late Nineteenth-Century Pessimism." In *Brahms Studies*, vol. 1, pp. 170–88. Edited by David Brodbeck. Lincoln: University of Nebraska Press, 1994.

Berlin, Isaiah. *The Roots of Romanticism.* Edited by Henry Hardy. Princeton University Press, 1999.

Beutler, Ernst. "Die Renaissance der Anthologie in Weimar." In *Das Epigramm: Zur Geschichte einer Inschriftlichen und Literarischen Gattung*, pp. 352–415. Edited by Gerhard Pfohl. Darmstadt: Wissenschaftliche Buchgesellschaft, 1969.

Boardman, John. *The Archaeology of Nostalgia: How the Greeks Re-created Their Mythical Past.* London: Thames and Hudson, 2002.

Boas, George. *The Cult of Childhood.* London: The Warburg Institute, University of London, 1966.

Essays on Primitivism and Related Ideas in the Middles Ages. 1948. New York: Octagon Books, 1978.

Botstein, Leon. "Memory and Nostalgia as Music-Historical Categories." *The Musical Quarterly* 84/4 (Winter 2000), 531–36.

"Realism Transformed: Franz Schubert and Vienna." In *The Cambridge Companion to Schubert*, pp. 15–35. Edited by Christopher Gibbs. Cambridge University Press, 1997.

Breivik, Magnar. "The Representation of Sleep and Death in Berg's *Piano Songs*, op. 2." In *Encrypted Messages in Alban Berg's Music*, pp. 109–35. Edited by Siglind Bruhn. New York: Garland, 1998.

Brown, David Blayney. *Romanticism.* London: Phaidon, 2001.

Brown, Jane K. "In the Beginning Was Poetry." In *The Cambridge Companion to the Lied*, pp. 12–32. Edited by James Parsons. Cambridge University Press, 2004.

"The Poetry of Schubert's Songs." In *Schubert's Vienna*, pp. 183–213. Edited by Raymond Erickson. New Haven: Yale University Press, 1997.

Brown, Marilyn R., ed. *Picturing Children: Constructions of Childhood Between Rousseau and Freud.* Aldershot: Ashgate, 2002.

Brown, Marshall. "Negative Poetics: On Skepticism and the Lyric Voice." *Representations* 86 (Spring 2004), 120–40.

Bruckmann, Annett. "'O wüßt ich doch den Weg zurück . . .' – Ein Beitrag zum Brahmsschen Liedschaffen." *Jahresgabe – Klaus Groth-Gesellschaft* 34 (1992), 9–38.

Büchmann, Georg. *Geflügelte Worte: Der Zitatenschatz des deutschen Volkes*. Berlin: Verlag der Haude and Spenerschen Buchhandlung, 1926.

Buller, Jeffrey L. "Sleep in the *Ring*." *The Opera Quarterly* 12/2 (Winter 1995/95), 3–22.

Burnham, Scott. "Schubert and the Sound of Memory." *The Musical Quarterly* 84/4 (Winter 2000), 655–63.

Butler, Eliza Marian. *The Tyranny of Greece over Germany*. Boston: Beacon Press, 1935.

Byrne, Lorraine. *Schubert's Goethe Settings*. Aldershot: Ashgate, 2003.

Chawla, Louise. *In the First Country of Places: Nature, Poetry, and Childhood Memory*. Albany: State University of New York Press, 1994.

Chytry, Josef. *The Aesthetic State: A Quest in Modern German Thought*. Berkeley: University of California Press, 1989.

Colie, Rosalie L. *The Resources of Kind: Genre Theory in the Renaissance*. Edited by Barbara K. Lewalski. Berkeley: University of California Press, 1973.

Cone, Edward T. *The Composer's Voice*. Berkeley: University of California Press, 1974.

    "Poet's Love or Composer's Love." In *Music and Text: Critical Inquiries*, pp. 177–92. Edited by Steven Paul Scher. Cambridge University Press, 1992.

    "The World of Opera and Its Inhabitants." In *Music: A View from Delft*, pp. 125–38. University of Chicago Press, 1989.

Coveney, Peter. *The Image of Childhood*. Baltimore, MD: Penguin Books, 1967.

Cunningham, Hugh. *The Children of the Poor: Representations of Childhood since the Seventeenth Century*. Oxford, UK and Cambridge, MA: Blackwell, 1991.

Dällenbach, Lucien. *The Mirror in the Text*. Translated by Jeremy Whiteley with Emma Hughes. The University of Chicago Press, 1989.

Dahlhaus, Carl. "Neo-Romanticism." In *Between Romanticism and Modernism: Four Studies in the Music of the Later Nineteenth Century*, pp. 1–18. Translated by Mary Whittall. Berkeley: University of California Press, 1980, pbk. 1989.

    Nineteenth-Century Music. Translated by J. Bradford Robinson. Berkeley: University of California Press, 1989.

    Realism in Nineteenth-Century Music. Translated by Mary Whittall. Cambridge University Press, 1985.

    "Romantik und Biedermeier: Zur musikgeschichtlichen Charakteristik der Restaurationszeit." *Archiv für Musikwissenschaft* 31 (1974), 22–41.

Daverio, John. *Nineteenth-Century Music and the German Romantic Ideology*. New York: Schirmer Books, 1993.

    "'One More Beautiful Memory of Schubert' Schumann's Critique of the Impromptus, D. 935." *The Musical Quarterly* 84/4 (Winter 2000), 604–18.

    "The Song Cycle: Journeys Through a Romantic Landscape." In *German Lieder in the Nineteenth Century*, pp. 279–312. Edited by Rufus Hallmark. New York: Schirmer, 1996.

Deutsch, Otto Erich, ed. *Schubert: Die Dokumente seines Lebens*. Kassel: Bärenreiter, 1964.
Schubert: Memoirs by his Friends. New York: Macmillan, 1958.
The Schubert Reader: A Life of Franz Schubert in Letters and Documents. New York: W. W. Norton, 1947.
Draheim, Joachim. *Vertonungen antiker Texte vom Barock bis zur gegenwart (mit einer Bibliographie der Vertonungen für den Zeitraum von 1700–1987)*. Amsterdam: B. R. Grüner, 1981.
"Die Welt der Antike in den Liedern von Johannes Brahms." In *Brahms als Liedkomponist: Studien zum Verhältnis von Text und Vertonung*, pp. 47–64. Stuttgart: Franz Steiner, 1992.
Dürhammer, Ilija. "Deutsch- und Griechentum: Johann Mayrhofer und Theodor Körner." In *Schubert 200 Jahre, Schloß Achberg: "Ich lebe und componire wie ein Gott" – Schuberts Leben und Schaffen*, pp. 21–24. Heidelberg: Braus, 1997.
Dürr, Walther. "Schubert's Songs and Their Poetry: Reflections on Poetic Aspects of Song Composition." In *Schubert Studies: Problems of Style and Chronology*. Edited by Eva Badura-Skoda and Peter Branscombe, pp. 1–24. Cambridge University Press, 1982.
Dürr, Walther, and Andreas Krause, eds. *Schubert Handbuch*. Kassel: Bärenreiter, 1997.
Eckstein, Friedrich. *Alte unnennbare Tage: Erinnerungen aus siebzig Lehr- und Wanderjahren*. Vienna: Herbert Reichner Verlag, 1936.
Eicker, Isabel. *Kinderstücke: An Kinder adressierte und über das Thema der Kindheit komponierte Alben in der Klavierliteratur des 19. Jahrhunderts*. Kassel: Gustav Bosse, 1995.
Eliade, Mircea. *Myths, Dreams and Mysteries*. New York: Harper and Row, 1967.
Patterns in Comparative Religion. New York: New American Library, 1974.
Ernst, Fritz. *Vom Heimweh*. Zurich: Fretz and Wasmuth, 1949.
Ewers, Hans-Heino. *Kindheit als poetische Daseinform: Studien zur Entstehung der romantischen Kindheitsutopie im 18. Jahrhundert*. Munich: Wilhelm Fink Verlag, 1989.
Feil, Arnold. *Franz Schubert: Die schöne Müllerin, Winterreise*. Translated by Ann C. Sherwin. Portland: Amadeus, 1988.
Fellinger, Imogen. "Cyclic Tendencies in Brahms's Song Collections." In *Brahms Studies: Analytical and Historical Perspectives.*, pp. 379–88. Edited by George S. Bozarth. Oxford: Clarendon Press, 1990.
Ferris, David. *Schumann's Eichendorff Liederkreis and the Genre of the Romantic Cycle*. Oxford University Press, 2000.
Ferris, David S. *Silent Urns: Romanticism, Hellenism, Modernity*. Stanford University Press, 2000.
Fischer-Dieskau, Dietrich, comp. *The Fischer Dieskau Book of Lieder*. English translations by George Bird and Richard Stokes. New York: Limelight Editions, 1995.

Robert Schumann Words and Music: The Vocal Compositions. Translated by Reinhard G. Pauly. Portland: Amadeus, 1988.

Fisk, Charles. "Questions about the Persona of Schubert's 'Wanderer' Fantasy." *College Music Symposium* 29 (1989), 19–30.

Returning Cycles: Contexts for the Interpretation of Schubert's Impromptus and Last Sonatas. Berkeley: University of California Press, 2001.

"Schubert Recollects Himself: The Piano Sonata in C Minor, D.958." *The Musical Quarterly* 84/4 (Winter 2000), 635–54.

Flemmer, Walter, ed., *Bin ich denn nicht auch ein Kind gewesen?: Deutsche Gedichte über Kinder.* Munich: Piper, 1986.

Fogarasi, György. "Reverberations of Romanticism: Petőfi's Figure of Memnon," *Kakanien Revisited* (Jan. 17, 2002), 1–5.

Fowler, Alastair. *Kinds of Literature: An Introduction to the Theory of Genres and Modes.* Cambridge, MA: Harvard University Press, 1982.

Freitag, Thomas. *Kinderlied – Von der Vielfalt einer musikalischen Liedgattung.* Frankfurt am Main: Peter Lang, 2001.

Friedländer, Max. *Brahms's Lieder: An Introduction to the Songs for One and Two Voices.* London: Oxford University Press, 1928.

Das deutsche Lied im 18. Jahrhundert. 2 volumes. Stuttgart: J. G. Cotta, 1902. Hildesheim: Georg Olms, 1962.

Frisch, Walter. *Brahms and the Principle of Developing Variation.* Berkeley: University of California Press, 1984.

"Schubert's *Nähe des Geliebten* (D. 162): Transformation of the *Volkston*." In *Schubert: Critical and Analytical Studies*, pp. 175–99. Edited by Walter Frisch, Lincoln and London: University of Nebraska Press, 1st pbk. ed. 1996.

"'You Must Remember This': Memory and Structure in Schubert's String Quartet in G Major, D. 887." *The Musical Quarterly* 84/4 (Winter 2000), 582–603.

Frye, Northrup. *Anatomy of Criticism.* Princeton University Press, 1957.

Georgiades, Thrasybulos G. *Schubert: Musik und Lyrik.* Göttingen: Vandenhoeck and Ruprecht, 1967.

Gerstner-Hirzel, Emily. "Das Kinderlied." In *Handbuch des Volksliedes.* Vol 1. *Die Gattungen des Volksliedes*, pp. 923–67. Edited by Rolf Wilhelm Brednich, Lutz Röhrich, and Wolfgang Suppan. Munich: Wilhelm Fink, 1973.

Das volkstümliche deutsche Wiegenlied: Versuch einer Typologie der Texte (Schweizerische Gesellschaft für Volkskunde). Basel: G. Krebs, 1984.

Gingerich, John M. "Remembrance and Consciousness in Schubert's C Major String Quintet, D. 956." *The Musical Quarterly* 84/4 (Winter 2000), 619–34.

Glauert, Amanda. *Hugo Wolf and the Wagnerian Inheritance.* Cambridge University Press, 1999.

"'Ich singe, wie der Vogel singt': Reflections on Nature and Genre in Wolf's Setting of Goethe's *Der Sänger.*" *Journal of the Royal Musical Association* 125 (2000), 271–86.

Gorrell, Lorraine. *The Nineteenth-Century German Lied*. Portland: Amadeus Press, 1993.

Graf, Fritz. *Griechische Mythologie*. Munich: Artemis, 1987.

Gramit, David. "The Dilemma of the Popular: the *Volk*, the Composers, and the Culture of Art Music." In *Cultivating Music: The Aspirations, Interests, and Limits of German Musical Culture, 1770–1848*, 63–92. Berkeley: University of California Press, 2002.

The Intellectual and Aesthetic Tenets of Franz Schubert's Circle: Their Development and Their Influence on His Music. Ph.D. diss., Duke University, 1987.

"Schubert and the Biedermeier: The Aesthetics of Johann Mayrhofer's 'Heliopolis,'" *Music and Letters* 74 (1993), 355–82.

Gress, David. *From Plato to Nato: The Idea of the West and its Opponents*. New York: The Free Press, 1998.

Guck, Marion. "Beethoven as Dramatist." *College Music Symposium* 29 (1989), 8–18.

Hammerstein, Reinhold. "'Schöne Welt, wo bist du?': Schiller, Schubert und die Götter Griechenlands." In *Musik und Dichtung*, pp. 305–30. Edited by Michael von Albrecht and Werner Schubert. Frankfurt am Main: Peter Lang, 1990.

Die Stimme aus der Anderen Welt: Über die Darstellung des Numinosen in der Oper von Monteverdi bis Mozart. Tutzing: Hans Schneider, 1998.

Hancock, Virginia. "Johannes Brahms: *Volkslied/Kunstlied*." In *German Lieder in the Nineteenth Century*, pp. 119–52. Edited by Rufus Hallmark. New York: Schirmer Books, 1996.

Hanson, Alice M. *Musical Life in Biedermeier Vienna*. Cambridge University Press, 1985.

Hartman, Geoffrey H. "Romanticism and 'Anti-Self-Consciousness.'" In *Romanticism and Consciousness: Essays in Criticism*, pp. 46–56. Edited by Harold Bloom. New York: W. W. Norton, 1970.

Hatch, Christopher. "Some Things Borrowed: Hugo Wolf's *Anakreons Grab*." *The Journal of Musicology* 17 (Summer 1999), 420–37.

Hatfield, Henry. *Aesthetic Paganism in German Literature: From Winckelmann to the Death of Goethe*. Cambridge, MA: Harvard University Press, 1964.

Head, Matthew. "'If the Pretty Little Hand Won't Stretch' Music for the Fair Sex in Eighteenth-Century Germany." *Journal of the American Musicological Society* 52/2 (Summer 1999), 235–44.

Heinberg, Richard. *Memories and Visions of Paradise: Exploring the Universal Myth of a Lost Golden Age*. Revised edition. Wheaton, IL: 1995.

Helms, Siegmund. *Die Melodiebildung in den Liedern von Johannes Brahms und ihr Verhältnis zu Volksliedern und volkstümlichen Weisen*. Ph.D. diss., Berlin, 1968.

Higgonet, Anne. *Pictures of Innocence: The History and Crisis of Ideal Childhood*. London, Thames and Hudson Ltd., 1998.

Hirsch, Marjorie Wing. *Schubert's Dramatic Lieder*. Cambridge University Press, 1993.

Hirschberg, Leopold. "Franz Schubert und die Antike." *Neue Jahrbücher für Wissenschaft und Jugendbildung* 4 (1928), 677–93.

Hoeckner, Berthold. "Schumann and Romantic Distance." *Journal of the American Musicological Society* 50/1 (1997), 55–132.

Hofmann, Kurt. *Die Bibliothek von Johannes Brahms.* Hamburg: Wagner, 1974.

Hutcheon, Linda. "Irony, Nostalgia, and the Postmodern." In *Methods for the Study of Literature as Cultural Memory*, pp. 189–207. Edited by Raymond Vervliet and Annemarie Estor. Amsterdam: Rodopi, 2000.

Jackson, Timothy L. "9 Lieder und Gesänge, Opus 63." In *The Compleat Brahms: A Guide to the Musical Works of Johannes Brahms*, pp. 251–54. Edited by Leon Botstein. New York: W. W. Norton, 1999.

Jacoby, Mario A. *Longing for Paradise: Psychological Perspectives on an Archetype.* Translated by Myron B. Gubitz. Boston: Sigo Press, 1985. Originally published in German as *Sehnsucht nach dem Paradies.* Fellbach (West Germany): Bonz, 1980.

James, Barbara. "'Wenn ich ein Vöglein wär . . .': Neues zur Datierung des Liedes," *Jahrbuch für Volksliedforschung* 32 (1987), 127–28.

Jhong, Bok-Joo. *German Solo Song Settings by Reichardt, Schubert, and Wolf of Goethe Poems Based on Classical Mythology.* Ph.D. diss., Indiana University, 1978.

Johnson, Graham. "Death and the Composer." Liner notes to *The Hyperion Schubert Edition.* Vol. 11. CDJ33011 (1991).

———. "Schubert and the Classics." Liner notes to *The Hyperion Schubert Edition.* Vol. 14, CDJ33014 (1992).

Jost, Peter. "Brahms und die romantische Ironie zu den 'Romanzen aus L. Tieck's Magelone' Op. 33." *Archiv für Musikwissenschaft* 47/1 (1990), 27–61.

Kalbeck, Max. *Johannes Brahms.* 4 vols. Vienna: Deutsche Brahms-Gesellschaft, 1904–15.

Key, Ellen. *The Century of the Child.* New York: Putnam, 1909.

Kivy, Peter. "Opera Talk: A Philosophical 'Phantasie.'" *Cambridge Opera Journal* 3/1 (Mar. 1991), 63–77.

Klusen, Ernst, ed. *Deutscher Lieder.* Frankfurt am Main: Insel, 1980.

———. *Volkslied: Fund und Erfindung.* Cologne: Hans Gerig, 1969.

Komma, Karl Michael. "'Gib mir deine Hand': Zu Franz Schuberts Musik vom Tode." *International Journal of Musicology* 3 (1994), 133–49.

Kommerell, Max. "Das Volkslied und das deutsche Lied." In *Dame Dichterin und andere Essays*, pp. 7–64. Munich: Deutscher Taschenbuch Verlag, 1967.

Kramer, Lawrence. "Beyond Words and Music: An Essay on Songfulness." In *Musical Meaning: Toward a Critical History*, pp. 51–67. Berkeley: University of California Press, 2002.

———. "Decadence and Desire: The Wilhelm Meister Songs of Wolf and Schubert." *Nineteenth-Century Music* 10 (1987), 229–42.

———. *Franz Schubert: Sexuality, Subjectivity, Song.* Cambridge University Press, 1998.

"Hugo Wolf: Subjectivity in the Fin-de-Siècle Lied." In *German Lieder in the Nineteenth Century*, pp. 188–217. Edited by Rufus Hallmark. New York: Schirmer Books, 1996.

Music and Poetry: The Nineteenth Century and After. Berkeley: University of California Press, 1984.

Kramer, Richard. *Distant Cycles: Schubert and the Conceiving of Song*. The University of Chicago Press, 1994.

Kravitt, Edward F. "Innovation and the Kinderlied." In *The Lied: Mirror of Late Romanticism*, pp. 132–41. New Haven: Yale University Press, 1996.

"The Volkstümlich Song and Its Composers." In *The Lied: Mirror of Late Romanticism*, pp. 113–23. New Haven: Yale University Press, 1996.

Kreutziger-Herr, Annette. "Die Kindheit als Paradies: Musikalische Romantik und mythische Verklärung," *Neue Zürcher Zeitung* 32 (8–9 Feb. 1997), 68.

"Nichts als Kinderkram?" *Hamburger Jahrbuch für Musikwissenschaft* 16 (1999), 209–35.

"Zwischen Idealisierung und Entzauberung: Kindheitsbilder in der Musik des 19. und 20. Jahrhunderts." In *Jung und wild: zur kulturellen Konstruktion von Kindheit und Jugend*, pp. 90–115. Berlin: D. Reimer, 1996.

Kross, Siegfried. "Brahms and E. T. A. Hoffmann." *19th-Century Music* 5/3 (Spring 1982), 193–200.

Lewis, Christopher. "Gustav Mahler: Romantic Culmination." In *German Lieder in the Nineteenth Century*, pp. 218–49. Edited by Rufus Hallmark. New York: Schirmer Books, 1996.

Lindenberger, Herbert. "Theories of Romanticism: From a Theory of Genre to the Genre of Theory." In *The History in Literature: On Value, Genre, Institutions*, pp. 61–84. New York: Columbia University Press, 1990.

Lorenz-Lindemann, Karin. "Die liebe Gegend schwarzumzogen: *Heimweh* als Verheissung." *Jahrbuch der Eichendorff Gesellschaft (Aurora)* 49 (1989), 151–61.

Loubinoux, Gerard. "Le Chant dans le Chant: À la Recherche d'une Mémoire Mythique." In *Opéra, Théatre, Une Mémoire Imaginaire*, pp. 77–89. Paris: Herne, 1990.

Lovejoy, Arthur O. "On the Discrimination of Romanticisms." *Proceedings of the Modern Langue Association* 39 (1924), 229–53.

"Schiller and the Genesis of German Romanticism." In *Essays in the History of Ideas*, pp. 207–27. New York: George Braziller, Inc., 1955. First published in *Modern Language Notes* 35 (1920), 1–10, 134–46.

Marchand, Suzanne L. *Down from Olympus: Archaeology and Philhellenism in Germany, 1750–1970*. Princeton University Press, 1996.

Marston, Nicholas. "Schubert's Homecoming," *Journal of the Royal Musical Association* 125 (2000), 248–70.

Maus, Fred Everett. "Agency in Instrumental Music and Song." *College Music Symposium* 29 (1989), 31–43.

McCorkle, Margit L. *Johannes Brahms: Thematisch-Bibliographisches Werkverzeichnis.* Munich: G. Henle Verlag, 1984.

McInerney, Jeremy. "Ethnic Identity and Altertumswissenschaft." In *Prehistory and History: Ethnicity, Class and Political Economy*, pp. 85–112. Edited by David W. Tandy. Montreal: Black Rose Books, 2001.

Menke, Bettine. *Prosopopoiia: Stimme und Text bei Brentano, Hoffmann, Kleist und Kafka.* Munich: Wilhelm Fink Verlag, 2002.

Miller, Bonny H. "A Mirror of Ages Past: The Publication of Music in Domestic Periodicals." *NOTES: Quarterly Journal of the Music Library Association* 50/3 (March 1994), 883–901.

Moman, Carl Conway, Jr. *A Study of the Musical Settings by Franz Schubert and Hugo Wolf for Goethe's "Prometheus," "Ganymed," and "Grenzen der Menschheit."* Ph.D. diss., Washington University, 1980.

Morik, Werner. *Johannes Brahms und Sein Verhältnis zum Deutschen Volkslied.* Tutzing: Hans Schneider, 1965.

Most, Glenn W., ed. *Disciplining Classics – Altertumswissenschaft als Beruf.* Göttingen: Vandenhoeck and Ruprecht, 2002.

Motte, Diether de la. "Traum, Schlaf und Tod: Die andere Zeit in Liedern von Robert Schumann." In *Zeit in der Musik – Musik in der Zeit: 3. Kongreß für Musiktheorie, 10. – 12. Mai 1996, Hochschule für Musik und Darstellende Kunst in Wien*, pp. 15–21. Edited by Diether de la Motte. Frankfurt am Main: Peter Lang, 1997.

Musgrave, Michael. *A Brahms Reader.* New Haven: Yale University Press, 2000.

Nägele, Rainer. "Poetic Revolution." In *A New History of German Literature*, pp. 511–16. Edited by David E. Wellbery. Cambridge, MA: The Belknap Press of Harvard University Press, 2004.

Nelson, Thomas Keith. *The Fantasy of Absolute Music.* Ph.D. diss., University of Minnesota, 1998.

Nemoianu, Virgil. *The Taming of Romanticism: European Literature and the Age of Biedermeier.* Cambridge, MA: Harvard University Press, 1984.

Panofsky, Erwin. "*Et in Arcadia Ego*: Poussin and the Elegiac Tradition." In *Meaning in the Visual Arts*, pp. 295–320. The University of Chicago Press, 1955, Phoenix ed., 1982.

Pascall, Robert. "'My Love of Schubert – No Fleeting Fancy': Brahms's Response to Schubert," *Schubert Durch die Brille: Internationales Franz Schubert Institut – Mitteilungen* 21 (June 1998), 39–60.

Plantinga, Leon. *Romantic Music: A History of Musical Style in Nineteenth-Century Europe.* New York: W. W. Norton, 1984.

Platt, Heather. "Hugo Wolf and the Reception of Brahms's Lieder." In *Brahms Studies*, vol. 2, pp. 91–111. Edited by David Brodbeck. Lincoln: University of Nebraska Press, 1998.

"Unrequited Love and Unrealized Dominants." *Intégral* 7 (1993), 119–48.

Plotz, Judith. *Romanticism and the Vocation of Childhood.* New York: Palgrave, 2001.

Pollock, Linda. *Forgotten Children: Parent-Child Relations from 1500 to 1900*. Cambridge University Press, 1983.
Poos, Heinrich. "Hugo Wolfs Klavierlied 'An den Schlaf': Eine ikonographische Studie." *Musik-Konzepte* 75 (1992), 3–36.
Prosl, Helga. *Der Freundeskreis um Anton von Spaun: Ein Beitrag zur Geistesgeschichte von Linz in der Biedermeierzeit (1811–1827)*. Ph.D. diss., Leopold-Franzens Universität, Innsbruck, 1951.
Pulikowski, Julian von. *Geschichte des Begriffes Volkslied im musikalischen Schrifttum: Ein Stück deutscher Geistesgeschichte*. Wiesbaden: Dr. Martin Sändig oHG, 1970.
Raab, Michael. "Arten von Zusammenhang in Schuberts Liedbearbeitungen." *Schubert-Jahrbuch* (1997), 85–94.
Rast, Nicholas. "'Schöne Welt, wo bist du?': Motiv and Form in Schubert's A Minor String Quartet." In *Schubert the Progressive: History, Performance Practice, Analysis*, pp. 81–88. Edited by Brian Newbould. Burlington, VT: Ashgate, 2003.
Reed, John. *The Schubert Song Companion*. Manchester University Press, 1985.
Rehm, Walther. *Griechentum und Goethezeit: Geschichte eines Glaubens*. Leipzig: Dieterich, 1936.
Richter, Dieter, ed., *Kindheit im Gedicht: Deutsche Verse aus acht Jahrhunderten*. Frankfurt am Main: Fischer, 1992.
Riley, Helene M. Kastinger. *Das Bild der Antike in der Deutschen Romantik*. Amsterdam: Benjamins, 1981.
Rosand, Ellen. "Operatic Ambiguities and the Power of Music." *Cambridge Opera Journal* 4/1 (Mar. 1992), 75–80.
Rosen, Charles. *The Romantic Generation*. Cambridge, MA: Harvard University Press, 1995.
Rosen, David. "Cone's and Kivy's 'World of Opera.'" *Cambridge Opera Journal* 4/1 (Mar. 1992), 61–74.
Rosenmeyer, Patricia A. *The Poetics of Imitation: Anacreon and the Anacreontic Tradition*. Cambridge University Press, 1992.
Russell, Peter. *The Themes of the German Lied from Mozart to Strauss*. Lewiston: The Edwin Mellon Press, 2002.
Sams, Eric. "Notes on a Magic Flute: the Origins of the Schubertian Lied." *Musical Times* 119 (1978), 947–49.
  The Songs of Hugo Wolf. Bloomington: Indiana University Press, 1992.
  The Songs of Johannes Brahms. New Haven: Yale University Press, 2000.
  The Songs of Robert Schumann. Bloomington: Indiana University Press, 1993.
Sannemüller, Gerd. "Die Lieder von Johannes Brahms auf Gedichte von Klaus Groth." *Jahresgabe – Klaus-Groth-Gesellschaft* 16 (1972), 23–35.
Scheibler, Ludwig. "Franz Schuberts einstimmige Lieder, Gesänge und Balladen mit Texten von Schiller." *Die Rheinlande* (April–Sept. 1905), 131–36, 163–69, 231–39, 270–74, 311–15; 353–56.

Schilling-Sandvoss, Katharina. "Kinderlieder des 18. Jahrhunderts als Ausdruck der Vorstellungen vom Kindsein." In *Geschlechtsspezifische Aspekte des Musiklernens*, pp. 170–89. Essen: Blaue Eule, 1996.

Schmalfeldt, Janet. "Coming Home" [Keynote Address, Twenty-Sixth Annual SMT Conference]. *Music Theory Only* 10/1 (February 2004). www.societymusictheory.org/mto/issues/mto.04.10.1/ mto.04.10.1.schmalfeldt

Schmidt, Matthias. "Komponierte Uneinholbarkeit: Anmerkungen zum 'Volkston' der *Wunderhorn*-Lieder." In *Gustav Mahler und das Lied: Referate des Bonner Symposions 2001*, pp. 51–68. Frankfurt am Main: Lang, 2003.

Schoenberg, Arnold. "Brahms the Progressive." In *Style and Idea*, pp. 398–441. New York: Philosophical Society, 1950.

Schorske, Carl. *Fin-de-siècle Vienna*. New York: Alfred A. Knopf, 1980.

Schwab, Heinrich W. *Sangbarkeit, Popularität und Kunstlied: Studien zu Lied und Liedästhetik der mittleren Goethezeit 1770–1814*. Regensburg: Gustav Bosse Verlag, 1965.

Schwarmath, Erdmute. *Musikalischer Bau und Sprachvertonung in Schuberts Liedern*. Tutzing: H. Schneider, 1969.

Seelig, Harry. "The Literary Context: Goethe as Source and Catalyst." In *German Lieder in the Nineteenth Century*, pp. 1–30. Edited by Rufus Hallmark. New York: Schirmer Books, 1996.

Sengle, Friedrich. *Biedermeierzeit: Deutsche Literatur im Spannungsfeld Zwischen Restauration und Revolution 1815–1848*. 3 vols. Stuttgart: J. B. Metzler, 1971, 1972.

Sharp, Ian. *Classical Music's Evocation of the Myth of Childhood*. Lewiston, NY: The Edwin Mellon Press, 2000.

Sharpe, Lesley. *Friedrich Schiller: Drama, Thought and Politics*. Cambridge University Press, 1991.

Smeed, J. W. *German Song and its Poetry 1740–1900*. London: Croom Helm, 1987.

Smeed, John. "'Wenn ich ein Vöglein wär': From *Flugblatt* to Opera." In *German Studies at the Millennium*, pp. 95–108. Edited by Neil Thomas. Durham, England: University of Durham, 1999.

Stark, Lucien. *A Guide to the Solo Songs of Johannes Brahms*. Bloomington and Indianapolis: Indiana University Press, 1995.

Starobinski, Georges. "Brahms et la nostalgie de l'enfance: *Volks-Kinderlieder*, berceuses et *Klaus-Groth-Lieder*." *Acta musicologica* 74/2 (July–Dec. 2002), 141–94.

  "Les Kinderszenen Op. 15 de Schumann: Composantes littéraires et biographiques d'une genèse." *Revue de musicologie* 88/2 (2002), 361–88.

Stein, Deborah, and Robert Spillman. *Poetry Into Song: Performance and Analysis of Lieder*. New York: Oxford University Press, 1996.

Steward, James Christen. *The New Child: British Art and the Origins of Modern Childhood, 1730–1830*. Berkeley: University Art Museum and Pacific Film Archive, University of California, Berkeley, 1995.

Stoljar, Margaret Mahony, *Poetry and Song in Late Eighteenth Century Germany: A Study in the Musical "Sturm und Drang."* London: Croom Helm, 1985.

Stone, Lawrence. *The Family, Sex and Marriage in England 1500–1800*. London: Weidenfeld and Nicholson, 1977.

Sühnel, Rudolf. *Die Götter Griechenlands und die deutsche Klassik*. Würzburg: Konrad Triltsch, 1935.

Temperley, Nicholas. "Schubert and Beethoven's Eight-Six Chord." *19th Century Music* 5/2 (Fall 1981), 142–54.

Thomas, Werner. "Schillergedicht und Schubertlied." In *Schubert-Studien*, pp. 7–80. Frankfurt am Main: Peter Lang, 1990.

"Schuberts Lied 'Antigone und Oedip' im Licht der Antikenrezeption um 1800." In *Schubert-Studien*, pp. 81–114. Frankfurt am Main: Peter Lang, 1990.

Todorov, Tzetan. *Genres in Discourse*. Translated by Catherine Porter. Cambridge University Press, 1990.

Trevelyan, Humphry. *Goethe and the Greeks*. Cambridge University Press, 1941.

Tsigakou, Fani-Maria. *Through Romantic Eyes: European Images of Nineteenth-Century Greece From the Benaki Museum, Athens*. Alexandria, VA: Art Services International, 1991.

Turchin, Barbara. "The Nineteenth-Century Wanderlieder Cycle." *The Journal of Musicology* 5/4 (Autumn 1987), 498–525.

Walker, Frank. *Hugo Wolf: A Biography*. Princeton University Press, 1968.

Warren, Alicyn. "The Camera's Voice." *College Music Symposium* 29 (1989), 66–74.

Wasselin, Christian. "La Jerusalem Perdue." *Musical: Revue du Theatre Musical de Paris-Chatelet – L'Orchestre, France* 6 (January–March 1988), 8–15.

Weber-Bockholdt, Petra. "Kinder in der Musik des 19. Jh.: Schumann's *Kinderszenen*, Bizets *Jeux d'enfants* und Mussorgskijs *Detskaja*." In *Kunst-Gespräche: Musikalische Begegnungen zwischen Ost und West*, pp. 425–40. Edited by Peter Andraschke and Edelgard Spaude. Freiburg im Breisgau: Rombach, 1998.

Webster, James. "Cone's 'Personae' and the Analysis of Opera." *College Music Symposium* 29 (1989), 44–65.

Weinreich, Otto. "Franz Schuberts Antikenlieder," *Deutsche Vierteljahresschrift für Literaturwissenschaft und Geistesgeschichte* 13 (1935), 91–117.

Wigmore, Richard. *Schubert: The Complete Song Texts*. New York: Schirmer Books, 1988.

Williamson, George S. *The Longing for Myth in Germany: Religion and Aesthetic Culture from Romanticism to Nietzsche*. The University of Chicago Press, 2004.

Wilpert, Gero von. "Der ornithologische Taugenichts: Zum Vogelmotiv in Eichendorffs Novelle." In *Ansichten zu Eichendorff: Beiträge der Forschung 1958 bis*

1988, pp. 277–95. Edited by Alfred Riemen. Sigmaringen: Jan Thorbecke Verlag, 1988.

Wiora, Walter. "Die Anknüpfung an Volkstraditionen in der romantischen Liedkomposition." In *Das deutsche Lied*, pp. 119–34. Wolfenbüttel and Zurich: Möseler, 1971.

Das deutsche Lied: Zur Geschichte und Ästhetik einer musikalischen Gattung. Wolfenbüttel and Zürich: Karl Heinrich Möseler Verlag, 1971.

Wolff, Christoph. "Schubert's 'Der Tod und das Mädchen': Analytical and Explanatory Notes on the Song D531 and the Quartet D810." In *Schubert Studies: Problems of Style and Chronology*, pp. 143–71. Edited by Eva Badura-Skoda and Peter Branscombe. Cambridge University Press, 1982.

Youens, Susan. "Elegies Within Elegies: 'Anakreons Grab' from the *Goethe-Lieder* of Hugo Wolf." *Journal of Research in Singing and Applied Vocal Pedagogy* 10/2 (June 1987), 31–42.

Hugo Wolf and his Mörike Songs. Cambridge University Press, 2000.

Hugo Wolf: The Vocal Music. Princeton University Press, 1992.

"Metamorphoses of a Melody: Schubert's 'Wiegenlied,' D. 498 in Twentieth-Century Opera." *The Opera Quarterly* 2/2 (Summer 1984), 35–48.

Schubert: Die schöne Müllerin. Cambridge University Press, 1992.

Schubert, Müller and Die schöne Müllerin. Cambridge University Press, 1997.

Schubert's Late Lieder. Cambridge University Press, 2002.

Schubert's Poets and the Making of Lieder. Cambridge University Press, 1996, pbk ed. 1999.

"The Song Sketches of Hugo Wolf." *Current Musicology* 44 (1990), 5–37.

"Tradition and Innovation: the Lieder of Hugo Wolf." In *The Cambridge Companion to the Lied*, pp. 204–22. Edited by James Parsons. Cambridge University Press, 2004.

Index

Abbate, Carolyn 182
Abrams, M. H. 150
Abt, Franz 218
Aeschylus 11
Alexander, Carl 175
Anacreon 36, 64, 65, 66, 73–88
Anacreontea 73–75
Anderson, Hans Christian 109
Antipater of Sidon 77, 78
Apollodorus 6
Apollonian 27, 66, 82, 87
Ariès, Phillipe 101
Ariosto 11
Arnim, Achim von 25, 140, 170, 173, 177, 217

Barrie, James M. 109
Bauernfeld, Eduard von 33–34, 46–47
Beethoven, Ludwig von 36, 60, 67, 71, 85, 88, 120, 180
  "Abendlied unterm gestirnten Himmel" 18
  Gellert Lieder 9
  "Mailied" 17
  "Ruf vom Berge: Wenn ich ein Vöglein wär" 218
  "Sehnsucht" 226, 227–28
Beller-McKenna, Daniel 150
Berg, Alban 64
Berlin, Isaiah 152
Blake, William 106
Blankensee, Carl von 65
Bodmann, Emanuel, Freiherr von 64, 65
Böhme, Franz Magnus 117–18, 140–41, 177
Borodin, Alexander 243
Botstein, Leon 120
Brahms, Johannes 15, 21, 22, 65, 72, 110, 146–71, 180
  "Abenddämmerung" 147, 148
  Alto Rhapsodie 150
  "An eine Aolshärfe" 32, 64, 65
  "Auf dem Schiffe" 239–41
  "Die Kränze" 64, 65
  "Die Mainacht" 64, 65
  "Die Schale der Vegessenheit" 64, 65

Ein deutsches Requiem 150
  "Feldeinsamkeit" 17
  "Geistliches Wiegenlied" 144, 147
  "Gestillte Sehnsucht" 144, 147
  "Heimweh" Lieder, nos. 1–3 18, 147, 148–71
  "Junge Lieder I: Meine Liebe ist grün" 243
  "Meine Lieder" 245
  "Mit vierzig Jahren" 147, 148
  "Regenlied" 147, 148
  "Ruhe, Süßliebchen" 147
  "Sapphische Ode" 64, 65
  Vier ernste Gesänge 150
  Volks-Kinderlieder 142, 147, 148
  "Wenn ich ein Vöglein wär" 218
  "Wie bist du meine Königen" 17
  "Wiegenlied" 147, 148
Brentano, Clemens 25, 44, 104, 140, 152, 173, 177, 180, 217
Brown, Jane K. 208
Bruchmann, Franz 34, 35
Bruckmann, Annett 163
Bruckner, Anton 9
Bürger, Gottfried August 177
Burmann, Gottlob Wilhelm 141, 144, 145
Busoni, Ferruccio Benvenuto
  "Berceuse élégiaque: Des Mannes Wiegenlied am Sarge seiner Mutter" 118
Byron, Lord George Gordon 25

Calzabigi, Ranieri 188
Chamisso, Adelbert von 25
Cherubini, Luigi 33
Chézy, Wilhelmine von 219
Claudius, Georg Carl 141, 145
Claudius, Matthias 121, 123, 127, 177, 210
Coleridge, Samuel Taylor 10, 107, 153
Collin, Matthäus von 41
Cone, Edward 182, 184, 206, 211–13
Cornelius, Peter
  Trauer und Trost, no. 1: "Trauer" 18
  Weihnachtslieder 9
  "Wiegenlied" 144
Coveney, Peter 109

Dahlhaus, Carl 179
Dante Alighieri 28
Daumer, Georg Friedrich 64, 65
Dehmel, Richard 64, 65
Denon, Vivant 42–43
"Der Jäger in dem grünen Wald" (traditional) 207–08
Des knaben Wunderhorn 113, 140, 147, 173, 177, 180, 217, 218, 219
Diabelli, Anton 55
Dickens, Charles 109
Dieffenbach, Georg Christian 218
Dionysian 27, 31–32, 66, 71, 82, 87–88
Dionysius 66
Dioscorides 77, 78–79
Dvorak, Antonin
  Biblical Songs 9

Earle, John 102
Eckstein, Friedrich 69
Edda 28
Eichendorff, Joseph von 9, 15, 68, 105, 106, 108, 152, 170, 171, 180, 214–15, 220, 223–25, 243
Erk, Ludwig 177
Erlach, Friedrich Karl Freiherr von 177

Feil, Arnold 136
Fellinger, Imogen 151
Ferrand, Eduard (B. Eduard Schulz) 147
Fichte, Johann Gottlieb 14, 31
Fischer-Dieskau, Dietrich 131
Förster, Friedrich 147
Franz, Robert 180
  "Cupido, loser Knabe" 32, 64
Freiligrath, Ferdinand 170
Freud, Sigmund 109–10
Frey, Adolf 245
Friedländer, Max 218
Friedrich, Caspar David 15
Frisch, Walter 149, 210

Gainsborough, Thomas 103
Garden of Eden 5, 6, 8, 10
Geibel, Emmanuel August 64, 147, 180, 235–36
Gerstenberg, Georg Friedrich von 34, 35
Gerstner-Hirzel, Emily 114
Gesner, J. M. 28
Gessner, Salomon 75
Girschner, C. F. J. 112, 114, 115, 117, 118, 138
Glauert, Amanda 68
Gleim, Johann Ludwig Wilhelm 75

Gluck, Christoph Willibald 19, 33, 36, 49–50, 63, 67, 188, 190
Goethe, Johann Wolfgang von 3, 11, 15, 19, 26, 27, 28, 30, 32, 33, 34, 35, 37, 40, 44, 48, 58, 63, 64, 65, 66, 68, 69–71, 72, 73, 75–99, 122, 147, 153, 170, 176, 177, 178, 184–87, 209, 210, 217, 219, 226–29
Golden Age, Greek 5, 6
Götz, Johann Nikolaus 75
Gotter, Friedrich Wilhelm 108
Grabbe, Christian Dietrich 170
Gramit, David 37, 56
Greek Anthology 73, 76–80
Gress, David 32
Grillparzer, Franz 31, 65
Grimm, Jacob 15, 25, 179
Grimm, Wilhelm 15, 25
Groth, Klaus 108, 147, 150–52, 154–55, 167

Hagedorn, Friedrich von 75
Hamann, Johann Georg 176
Hammerstein, Reinhold 59
Hancock, Virginia 171
Handel, George Frideric 50
Hanslick, Eduard 67, 69
Hartman, Geoffrey 13, 15
Hatch, Christopher 71, 72, 80, 82, 85, 88
Haydn, Franz Joseph 36
Head, Matthew 116
Hebbel, Friedrich 170
Hegel, Georg Wilhelm Friedrich 14, 26, 44, 59, 152, 153, 170
Heinberg, Richard 181
Heine, Heinrich 1, 8, 15, 34, 35, 40, 41, 64, 65, 68, 108, 170, 180, 217, 219–20, 243, 245
Heinse, Wilhelm 28
Hemsterhuis, Frans 47
Henschel, Georg 217
Herder, Johann Gottfried 10, 26, 27, 28, 37, 44, 58, 69, 75–77, 79, 81, 116, 121–22, 149, 176–80, 208, 216–17
Hesiod 5–6, 7
Heyne, Christian Gottlob 28
Hiller, Ferdinand 217
Hiller, Johann Adam 141
Hitler, Adolf 32
Hoffmann, E. T. A. 15, 170
Hoffmann von Fallersleben, August Heinrich 108, 147
Hölderlin, Friedrich 14, 26, 27–28, 31, 44, 59, 63–64, 147, 170
Hölty, Ludwig Heinrich Christoph 64, 65, 177, 210

Holzapfel, Anton 50
Homer 5, 6, 11, 26, 28, 41, 75, 91
Horstig, Karl Gottlieb 141, 142
Humboldt, Wilhelm von 26, 28, 30, 31
Humperdinck, Engelbert 142, 180
Hunger, Gottlob Gottwald 141

Immermann, Karl Leberecht 170

Jacobi, Johann Georg 34, 35, 75, 81, 187–90
Jensen, Adolph 217
Joachim, Josef 147
Johnson, Graham 120
Joseph II, Holy Roman Emperor 16
Julianus, Prefect of Egypt 77

Kalbeck, Max 72
Kant, Immanuel 10
Kauffmann, Emil 72
Keller, Gottfried 147, 180
Kerner, Justinus 65, 170
Kinkel, Johanna Mathieux 64
Kleist, Heinrich von 15, 16, 25, 170
Klingemann, Ernst August 44
Klinger, Friedrich Maximilian 170
Klopstock, Friedrich Gottlieb 69, 210
Klusen, Ernst 176–77
Knab, Armin 180
Köchert, Melanie 71, 142
Körner, Theodor 34, 35, 118, 132–33
Kosegarten, Gotthard Ludwig 44, 210
Kramer, Lawrence 52, 98–99, 209
Kretzschmer, August von 148, 177
Kücken, Friedrich 217

La Motte-Fouqué, Friedrich Heinrich Karl, Freiherr de 218
Lawrence, Sir Thomas 103
Leitner, Karl Gottfried von 41, 118, 134–36, 147, 200–04
Lessing, Gotthold Ephraim 77, 121–22
Lindenberger, Herbert 12
Liszt, Franz
    "Jugendglück" 146
Locke, John 103
Loewe, Carl Gottfried 36, 65, 142, 171
    "An Aphrodite: Ode der Sappho" 32, 64, 65
    "An die Grille" 64, 65
    "An die Leier" 64
    "An die Muse: Hymn an die Kalliope" 64
    "Auf sich selbst ('Es sagen mir')" 64
    "Auf sich selbst ('Weil ich steblich')" 64

"Der alte Goethe" 147
"Ganymed" 64
"Jugend und Alter" 147
Lully, Jean-Baptiste 50

Mahler, Gustav 15, 63, 67, 180, 181
    "Ging heut' Morgen übers Feld" 242–43
    "Ich bin der Welt abhanden gekommen" 17
    Kindertotenlieder 145
    Das Lied von der Erde, no. 6: "Der Abschied" 18
    "Um Mitternacht" 18
Marchand, Suzanne 30
Marpurg, Friedrich Wilhelm 34
Matthisson, Friedrich von 36, 147, 209, 210
Mayreder, Rosa 68
Mayrhofer, Johann 19, 33, 34, 35, 41, 44–48, 49, 50, 53, 64, 118, 119, 126–27, 231–33, 236
McInerney, Jeremy 28
Mendelssohn, Fanny 111, 119
    "Aus meine Tränen sprießen" 243
    "Die Mainacht" 64, 65
    "Sehnsucht" 226
Mendelssohn, Felix 63, 180
    "Auf dem Flügel des Gesanges" 245
    "Bei der Wiege" 144
    "O Jugend, o schöne Rosenzeit" 147
Metastasio, Pietro 34, 35
Metternich, Prince Clemens von 16, 31, 38, 111
Monteverdi, Claudio 50
Moore, Gerald 131
Mörike, Eduard 8, 64, 65, 67, 68, 105, 108, 152, 170, 171, 180
Mozart, Wolfgang Amadeus 19, 36, 49, 50, 63, 67, 117
    "Das Kinderspiel" 143, 144
    "Im Frühlingsanfang" 143
    "Sehnsucht nach dem Frühling" 143, 144
Müller, Wilhelm 15, 41, 64, 118, 136–39, 180, 191–96
Musgrave, Michael 170
Mussorgsky, Modest 243

Napoleon Bonaparte 38, 42
National Socialism 32
Nazarenes, German 9
Nietzsche, Friedrich 31–32, 63, 65, 66, 67, 68, 69–70, 82, 88, 147
    "Aus der Jugendheit" 147
Novalis (Friedrich von Hardenberg) 9, 14, 25, 44, 47, 56, 59, 108, 152–53, 170
    Hymnen an die Nacht 9, 47, 48, 122–23

Index

Ossian (James MacPherson) 176
Ottenwalt, Anton 38, 118, 119, 129–32

Panofsky, Erwin 80
Percy, Thomas 176
Pfitzner, Hans 64
Pindar 6, 75, 91
Plato 6, 26, 75
Pollock, Linda 101
Poussin, Nicolas 80–81
Proch, Heinrich 217
Pulikowsky, Julian von 176, 179
Pyrker, Johann Ladislaus 41

Quintus of Smyrna 41–42

Rameau, Jean-Philippe 50
Ramler, Karl Wilhelm 75
Reed, John 59, 133, 222
Reger, Max 180, 218
   "Mariä Wiegenlied" 145
Reichardt, Johann Friedrich 34–36, 113–14, 115–17, 118, 141, 142, 143–44, 178, 180, 181, 209, 217, 221, 226
   "Sehnsucht" 226
Reichardt, Luise 119
Reign of Terror, French 13, 16
Reil, Johann Anton Friedrich 147
Reinecke, Carl 142
Reinhold, Christian 239–41
Reynolds, Sir Joshua 103
Rheinberger, Joseph 142
Richter, Jean Paul 14, 44, 170
Rimsky-Korsakov, Nikolay 243
Risorgimento, Italian 25
Rosen, Charles 72, 87
Rosenmeyer, Patricia 73
Rossini, Gioachino 50
Rousseau, Jean Jacques 10, 102–04, 113, 140, 141, 144, 173, 176
Rückert, Friedrich 108, 145, 147, 236–39
Runge, Philipp Otto 15
Russell, Peter 66
Rust, Friedrich Wilhelm 36

Salis-Seewis, Johann Gaudenz von 210
Sams, Eric 98
Sappho 64, 65, 66
Scarlatti, Alessandro 50
Schack, Adolf Friedrich, Graf von 147
Scheibe, Johann Adolph 141
Schelling, Friedrich 14, 16, 28, 152, 153

Schiller, Friedrich 1, 3, 8, 10–14, 19, 23, 26, 27, 28, 30, 34, 35, 37, 44, 53, 55, 56–59, 81, 101, 104, 107, 116, 122, 153, 170, 173, 207, 210, 229–31
   On the Aesthetic Education of Man 10
   On Naïve and Sentimental Poetry 10, 23
Schinkel, Karl Friedrich 19
Schlegel, August Wilhelm 14, 28
Schlegel, Friedrich 9, 14, 16, 26, 28–29, 30, 48, 56, 170, 221–23
Schleiermacher, Friedrich 14
Schmidt, Hans 64, 65
Schober, Franz von 33, 245
Schoeck, Othmar
   "Jugendgedenken 147
Schopenhauer, Arthur 31, 66, 107, 170
Schubart, Christian Friedrich Daniel 177, 178
Schubert, Elisabeth (née Vietz) 120
Schubert, Franz 15, 21–22, 32, 33–62, 63, 64, 67, 70, 71, 85, 88, 110, 111, 116, 118–20, 123–39, 144, 145, 171, 180, 182–213, 245
   Adrast 36
   "Am Brunnen vor dem Tore" 209
   "Am Fenster" 119
   "Amphiaraos" 35, 39
   "An die Leyer" 35, 211
   "An die Musik" 245
   "An Schwager Kronos" 34, 35
   "Antigone und Oedip" 35, 39
   "Atys" 35, 39
   "Aus Heliopolis I" 35, 39
   "Aus Heliopolis II" 35
   "Das Lied im Grünen" 17, 147
   "Das Rosenband" 17
   "Das Wandern" 136, 138, 242, 243
   "Das Wirtshaus" 18
   "Der Atlas" 18, 35, 39, 40
   "Der entsühnte Orest" 35, 39
   "Der Knabe" 145, 221–23, 225
   "Der Knabe in der Wiege" 118, 129–32, 133, 144
   "Der Kreuzzug" 18
   "Der Leidende" 18
   "Der Lindenbaum" 18
   "Der Musensohn" 35
   "Der Pilgrim" 18, 229
   "Der Sänger" 184–86, 201–02, 204
   "Der Sieg" 35, 39
   "Der Tod und das Mädchen" 50, 51, 127, 138
   "Der Vater mit dem Kind" 146
   "Der Wanderer" 9, 18, 34
   "Der zürnenden Diana" 34, 35, 39
   "Des Baches Wiegenlied" 118, 136–39, 144

"Des Fischers Liebesglück" 17
"Die Bürgschaft" (D. 246) 35
Die Bürgschaft (D. 435) 36
"Die Götter Griechenlands" 1–3, 4, 35, 39–41, 53–62, 71
"Die junge Nonne" 9, 18
"Die Knabenzeit" 146
Die schöne Müllerin 18, 34, 136, 191, 206, 242, 243
"Die vier Weltalter" 35
"Dithyrambe" 35, 39
"Einsamkeit" 17, 211, 212
"Ellens Gesang III (Ave Maria)" 9
"Elysium" 8, 35, 39
"Fahrt zum Hades" 35, 39
"Fragment aus dem Aeschylus" 35, 39
"Freiwilliges Versinken" 35, 39
"Freude der Kinderjahre" 146
"Frühlingstraum" 17, 60
"Ganymed" 18, 32, 34, 35, 39, 40, 97
"Grenzen der Menschheit" 35, 39, 88–97
"Gruppe aus dem Tartarus" (D. 396) 35
"Gruppe aus dem Tartarus" (D. 583) 35, 39, 119
"Gute Nacht" 60
"Heidenröslein" 209–10, 212
"Hektors Abschied" 35, 39
"Hippolits Lied" 35
"Im Frühling" 196–200, 205, 212, 233–34
"Im Walde" 211
"Iphigenia" 35, 39
"Kennst du das Land" 9, 18
"Klage der Ceres" 35
"Lied des Orpheus" 35, 182, 183, 187–90, 191, 192–93, 201, 205
"Lied eines Kindes" 145
"Lied eines Schiffers an die Dioskuren" 35, 39
"Memnon" 34, 35, 39–53, 54, 55, 59, 61, 71
"Nachtstück" 18
"Nähe des Geliebten" 210, 212
"Nur wer die Sehnsucht kennt" (D. 877, no. 4) 17
"Orest auf Tauris" 35, 36
"Pause" 191–96, 205, 211, 212
"Philoktet" 34, 35, 39
"Prometheus" 35, 39, 97
"Schlaflied" 118, 126–28
"Sehnsucht" (D. 52) 230
"Sehnsucht" (D. 123) 226, 228–29
"Sehnsucht" (D. 516) 231–33, 236
"Sehnsucht" (D. 636) 230–31, 233
"Sehnsucht" (D. 879) 119, 211
"Ständchen" 206
String Quartet in A Minor (D. 804) 40
"Szene aus Faust" 186–87, 201, 205
"Todtenkranz für ein Kind" 145
"Totengräbers Heimweh" 18
"Uraniens Flucht" 35
"Vedi quanto adoro" 35
"Verklärung" 18
"Vollendung" 18
"Vor meiner Wiege" 18, 118, 134–36, 138, 144, 147, 200–04, 205
"Wandrers Nachtlied I" 18
"Wandrers Nachtlied II" 18
"Widerspruch" 119
"Wiegenlied" (D. 304) 118, 132–33
"Wiegenlied" (D. 498) 118, 123–25, 126, 127, 134, 137, 138, 209, 212
"Wiegenlied" (D. 867) 118, 125–26, 128
Winterreise 18
Schulz, Johann Abraham Peter 142, 178, 208–09
Schulze, Ernst 196–200, 233–34
Schütze, Johann Stephan 113
Schumann, Clara 119
  "Liebst du um Schönheit" 17
Schumann, Felix 243
Schumann, Robert 15, 63, 180
  Album für die Jugend 140
  "Aus alten Märchen winkt es" 1–3, 4
  "Aus meine Tränen sprießen" 243
  "Die Stille" 223–25, 235
  "Flügel! Flügel!" 236–39
  Genoveva 221
  Kinderszenen 140, 148
  "Kinderwacht" 144
  Lieder-Album für die Jugend 142
  "Mondnacht" 214–16, 234
  "Schöne Wiege meiner Leiden" 18
  "Sehnsucht" (Op. 51, no. 1) 235–36
  "Warte, warte, wilde Schiffmann" 8
  "Wenn ich ein Vöglein wär" 217, 218, 225
  "Widmung" 17
Seidl, Johann Gabriel 41, 118, 125–26, 128
Sengle, Friedrich 111
Severus, Septimius, Emperor 42
Shakespeare, William 11, 14, 28, 29, 176
Sharpe, Lesley 58–59
Silcher, Friedrich 180, 217, 219
  "Jugendland" 147
Simonides 77, 78
Simrock, Karl 140, 177
Smeed, J. W. 179
Socrates 121–22

Sophocles 26
Spaun, Josef von 33, 36, 49–50
Spazier, Carl 141
Spinoza, Benedict de 29
Spohr, Louis
   "Der Rosenstrauch 147
   "Lied aus Aslauga's *Ritter*" 218
   "Wiegenlied (In drei Tönen)" 144
Starobinski, Georges 149, 168
Stolberg, Christian, Graf zu 177
Stolberg-Stolberg, Friedrich Leopold, Graf zu 36, 177
Storm, Theodor 180
Strauss, Richard 15, 67
   "Auf ein Kind" 146
   "Frühlingsfeier" 64, 66
   "Gesang der Apollopriesterin" 32, 64, 66
   "Meinem Kinde" 145
   "Rückleben" 147
   "Rückkehr in die Heimat" 147
   Vier letzte Lieder, no. 2: "Frühling" 17
   Vier letzte Lieder, no. 4: "Im Abendrot" 243
   "Wie sollten wir geheim sie halten" 17
   "Wiegenlied" (Op. 41, no. 1) 145
   "Wiegenliedchen" (Op. 49, no. 3) 145

Taubert, Wilhelm 142, 217
Temperly, Nicholas 60
Theocritus 75
Thibaut, Justus 149, 173–76
Tieck, Ludwig 14, 25, 148, 170
Tobler, Johann Christoph 76, 77
Traherne, Thomas 102
Treitschke, Friedrich von 218
Trevelyan, Humphrey 75, 76

Uhland, Johann Ludwig 25, 65, 105, 147, 177, 180
Uz, Johann Peter 75

Vaughan, Henry 102
Virgil 11
Vogl, Johann Michael 33–34, 36, 37, 48, 53
Voss, Johann Heinrich 28, 177, 209

Wackenroder, Wilhelm Heinrich 25
Wagner, Richard 9, 15, 25, 31, 63, 67–68, 69, 71, 72, 82–88

Walker, Frank 71, 72, 98
Weber, Carl Maria von 112, 180, 217
Weiße, Christian Felix 141
"Wenn ich ein Vöglein wär" (traditional) 214–45
Werner, Heinrich 209
Wieland, Christoph Martin 58, 76, 81, 170
Wigmore, Richard 131
Wilhelm, Carl 217
Williamson, George S. 27
Winckelmann, Johann Joachim 10, 26, 27, 30, 32, 63, 66, 121
Wolf, Friedrich August 28, 30
Wolf, Hugo 15, 19, 22, 32, 66–99
   "An eine Aolshärfe" 32, 64, 65
   "Anakreons Grab" 64, 65, 70–88
   Der Corregidor 67, 68
   "Der neue Amadis" 147
   "Die ihr schwebet" 144
   "Epiphanias" 142
   "Fußreise" 8
   "Ganymed" 32, 64, 97–99
   "Genialisch Treiben" 64
   "Grenzen der Menschheit" 64, 70–71, 88–99
   "Heimweh" 18
   "Im Frühling" 18
   "Nachtzauber" 18
   "Prometheus" 64, 97–99
   "Sehnsucht" 226
   "Sonne der Schlummerlosen" 18
   Spanisches Liederbuch: Geistliches Lieder 9
Wordsworth, William 106–07, 110

Xenophon 75

Youens, Susan 17, 47, 88, 99, 124, 133, 137, 139, 196, 198–99, 233

Zachariä, Justus Friedrich Wilhelm 75
Zarnack, August 177
Zelter, Carl Friedrich 178, 209, 226
   "An eine Mutter, deren Tochter als Kind starb" 145
   "Die Kindheit" 147
   "Erster Verlust" 17
Zimmermann, Wilhelm 147
Zuccalmaglio, Wilhelm von 148, 177
Zumsteeg, Johann Rudolph 36, 209